The Unveiled Christ of the Indian Gurus

Interfaith Treasures Uncovered

Under this Series, the Publishers endeavor to focus on Comparative Studies pertaining to Christian Faith & Living in the central matrix and Hinduism, Buddhism, Sikhism, Islam, Judaism, etc., on the peripheral. The Studies shall cover topics like Literature & Poetry, Indigenous Philosophizing, Ethical response towards Agriculture, Health & Healing, Science & Technology, Ecofeminist Theology, Sociological approach towards Human Rights, Law & Politics, Arts, History of Ideas, Ancient Civilizations, Cultural Contiguity, Religious Cosmologies & Mysticism, Footsteps of famous Theologians, World Peace & Harmony, Global Capitalism, Network Marketing, Cybertheology, Population & Demographics, Epigraphic Studies, Contextualized Education, and many others. We welcome a Mss. on any topic/s mentioned, whether they are original works, scholarly monographs, collections of conference papers, revised dissertations, or translations of historical documents. Through the Series, we are striving to put forward published works that may help Institutions, Academic Bodies, Researchers, Scholars and the World at large in furthering their respective knowledge and understanding on the concerned subject. We welcome your comments on our efforts and further suggestions on how we can foster the upcoming books on parallel interfaces between and among Christianity and other religions.

Interfaith Treasures Uncovered - 9

The Unveiled Christ of the Indian Gurus

A Study on the Contemporary Gurus' Interpretations of Jesus Christ

Rodinmawia Ralte

CWI

Christian World Imprints™

First Published in 2017 by

Christian World Imprints™
Christian Publishing & Books from India
H-12 Bali Nagar, **New Delhi-110015**
info@christianworldimprints.com
www.ChristianWorldImprints.com
Phone: +91 11 25465925

ISBN 13: 978-93-5148-201-7 ISBN 10: 93-5148-201-4

Cataloging in Publication Data--DK
Courtesy: D.K. Agencies (P) Ltd. <docinfo@dkagencies.com>

Ralte, Rodinmawia, author.
The unveiled Christ of the Indian Gurus : a study on the contemporary Gurus' interpretations of Jesus Christ / Rodinmawia Ralte.
pages cm. -- (Interfaith treasures uncovered ; 9)
Includes bibliographical references and index.
ISBN 9351482014 (hardback)
ISBN 9789351482017 (hardback)

1. Jesus Christ--Hindu interpretations. I. Title. II. Series: Interfaith treasures uncovered ; 9.

BT304.917.R35 2017 DDC 232.0882945 23

Printed in India.

Contents

Preface ix

Introduction xi

Chapter 1: Origin and Development of Guru Tradition in Hinduism: A Survey 1

1. Etymological Consideration 2
   1.1. The Word meaning 2
   1.2. Who is a Guru? 4
2. Guru in the Hindu *Śāstras*: A Textual-Historical Survey 5
   2.1. Guru in *Śṛuti* Literature 6
   2.2. Guru in *Smṛti* Literature 8
3. Factors Responsible for the Emergence of Contemporary Guruism 11
4. The Distinctive Features of Modern Guruism 16

Concluding Remarks 20

Chapter 2: Jesus Christ in the Thoughts of Modern Hindu Thinkers and Neo-Vedantins: A Brief Survey 23

1. Jesus Christ in Renascent Hinduism: Select Hindu Reformers 25
   1.1. Raja Rammohun Roy: *The Precepts of Jesus* 26
   1.2. Keshub Chunder Sen: *Jesus Christ, Divine Humanity* 29
   1.3. Mahatma Gandhi: *Jesus Christ, One of the Greatest Teachers* 35
2. Jesus in Neo-Vedānta: Select Neo-Vedāntins 42
   2.1. Swami Vivekananda: *Jesus Christ, A Growth from Human to Divine* 42
   2.2. Swami Akhilananda: *Jesus Christ, the Incarnation of God* 48
   2.3. S. Radhakrishnan: *Jesus Christ, More Human than Divine* 54

Concluding Remarks 58

Chapter 3: Some Modern Indian Gurus on Jesus Christ: A Brief Survey 61

1. Swami Sivananda 61

2. Swami Chindananda 63
3. Sri Swami Krishnananda 65
4. Mata Amritanandamayi 67
5. A. C. Bhaktivedānta Swami Prabhupāda 68
6. Maharishi Mahesh Yogi 70
Concluding Remarks 71

Chapter 4: Paramhansa Yogananda's Interpretation of Jesus Christ 73
1. A Brief Sketch of the Life of Yogananda 74
2. Philosophical and Religious Teachings of Yogananda: An Overview 78
2.1. God 78
2.2. Human Being 80
2.3. *Karma-Saṃsāra* 81
2.4. Creation 82
2.5. Heaven - the Astral World 83
2.6. Kriya Yoga 83
2.7. The Spiritual Eye – Christ or *Kutaṣtha* Center 87
2.8. Communion with God 87
2.9. Journey to Self-Realization 87
2.10. Emphasis on Intuition 89
2.11. Harmony of Religions 89
3. Yogananda's Interpretation of Jesus Christ: *Jesus, the Embodiment of Universal Consciousness* 92
3.1. The Influences 92
3.2. Yogananda's Approach to Jesus 94
3.3. The Person of Jesus Christ 96
3.4. Works of Jesus Christ 101
3.5. The Message of Jesus Christ 105
3.6. The Realization of Christ Consciousness 111
Concluding Remarks 114

Chapter 5: Sri Sathya Sai Baba's Interpretation of Jesus Christ 117
1. A Brief Account of the Life of Sathya Sai Baba 118
2. Sathya Sai Baba's Philosophical and Religious Teachings: An Overview 123
2.1. Unity of Religions and Brotherhood/Sisterhood of Men and Women 124
2.2. God, Human and Creation – One Whole 127
2.3. Paths of Liberation 129
2.4. The Five Primary Human Values 130
2.5. Emphasis on Love 131

2.6. Emphasis on Service (*Seva*) 132
2.7. Emphasis on Togetherness 133
3. Sathya Sai Baba and Jesus Christ 135
4. Sathya Sai Baba's Interpretation of Jesus Christ: *Jesus, the Kārana-Janma* 137
4.1. The Person of Jesus 138
4.2. The Work of Jesus Christ 143
4.3. The Teachings of Jesus Christ 146
4.4. Merging with Jesus Christ 150
4.5. Some Problems with Baba's Version of Jesus Christ 150
Concluding Remarks 153

Chapter 6: Osho Rajneesh's Interpretation of Jesus Christ 157
1. A Brief Life Sketch of Osho Rajneesh 158
2. Influences on Osho 164
3. Glimpse of Osho's Methodological Framework 165
4. Philosophical and Religious Teaching: An Overview 167
4.1. Religionless Religion 168
4.2. Godless Spirituality 168
4.3. Human Being 170
4.4. On Sex and Sexuality 171
4.5. Meditation and Enlightenment 172
4.6. A New Creation – Zorba the Buddha 175
4.7. Osho's Vision for Oneness of Human Beings 176
4.8. Key Terms in Osho's Teaching 177
5. Osho's Interpretation of Jesus Christ: *Jesus, the Christified* 180
5.1. Osho's Approach to Jesus Christ 181
5.2. Jesus' Methodology 182
5.3. The Real Jesus Lost in Christianity 184
5.4. Jesus a Real Human 185
5.5. Jesus a Rebel 186
5.6. Jesus a Man of Celebration 186
5.7. Jesus Christ – the Son of Man and the Son of God 188
5.8. Jesus Christ - Jesus and Christ 189
5.9. Jesus as Love 190
5.10. Cross and Resurrection 191
5.11. Jesus' Enlightenment 193
5.12. The Significance of Jesus' Baptism 194
5.13. The Real Miracle of Jesus 194
5.14. Jesus did a Zen-Act 195
5.15. Some of the Prominent Christian Doctrines on Jesus Rejected 196

5.16. Other Aspects of Jesus 197
5.17. A Negative Portrayal of Jesus 198
Concluding Remarks 199

Chapter 7: Sri Sri Ravishankar's Interpretation of Jesus Christ 203

1. A Brief Life Sketch of Ravishankar 204
2. Philosophical and Religious Teachings of Ravishankar: An Overview 207
   2.1. God, Human Being and Creation 207
   2.2. Love is God 211
   2.3. Ways of Spiritual Elevation 212
   2.4. Enlightenment 213
   2.5. The Place of Other Religions 214
   2.6. Belongingness to Others 215
   2.7. Sudarshan Kriya 215
3. Ravishankar's Interpretation of Jesus Christ: *Jesus, the Embodiment of Love* 217
   3.1. The Background of his Interpretation 217
   3.2. Jesus as One of the Prophets 218
   3.3. Jesus the Embodiment of Love 219
   3.4. The Kingdom of God is within You 219
   3.5. Jesus is *Not* the Only Way! 220
   3.6. The Cross of Jesus 222
   3.7. Transcending Mind 222
   3.8. Jesus at the Doorsteps 223
   3.9. Jesus Lived in India 223

Concluding Remarks 224

Chapter 8: The Unveiled Christ of the Indian Gurus: A Critical Consideration 227

1. Why Look to Jesus? 228
2. Their Perspectives 228
3. Methodological Error 229
4. Relations with other Indian Interpretations 230
5. Their Weaknesses 231

Appendix 237
Bibliography 243
Glossary of Sanskrit Terms 271
Index 277

Preface

It is satisfying to write a short '*Preface*' to this book which is part of my doctoral thesis. I want to use this space for expressing my gratitude to some people who have made great contributions towards the publication of this book. I am greatly indebted to the members and leaders of my Church - the Baptist Church of Mizoram (BCM) for allowing me to do doctoral studies and shouldering the entire financial burden for my studies. It is largely because of them that this book could be materialized.

I give thanks and salutation to my Guru, Prof. K. P. Aleaz under whom I studied Master of Theology and Doctor of Theology in the department of religion at North India Institute of Post Graduate Theological Studies (NIIPGTS), Kolkata. His constant encouragement, academic guidance and support are invaluable to me as I grow towards academic maturity.

I am deeply grateful to Sri Sri Ravishankar, who may be the greatest living guru in terms of worldwide followings and activities, for giving me time to sit with him in a personal interview for my research work. I also thank Swami Smarananda Giri, the General Secretary of Yogoda Satsanga Society of India, Ranchi, and Prof. Gangadhar Shastri of Sathya Sai Institute of Higher Learning, the Head of Prashanthi Nilyam Campus, Puttaparthi, AP, for sparing their valuable time in personal interviews and interactions which enriched the contents of this book. I deeply cherish the help I received from Rev. Dr. V. J. John, Professor of New Testament at Bishop's College and NIIPGTS, and a senior colleague of mine. He painstakingly read the whole manuscript, and gave me useful comments and suggestions for improvement. My thanks also go to Mr. Sudhanshu Kanda of Christian World Imprints for taking interest in publishing this book.

I want to record my gratitude to my devoted and supportive wife, C. Laltanpuii, who stood by me in all seasons, and whose presence around me alone is great encouragement and strength, and our three lovely-singing kids – Dindina, Felfeli and Puipuii for their love and support.

Some two thousand years ago, a profound theological and philosophical question was asked of Jesus, the Christ. Till today, people all over the world are struggling to give suitable answer to that question and this book is, with all its inadequacy and incompleteness, another attempt to response to the that question: **Who is this Man?**

Rodinmawia Ralte
Kolkata

Introduction

The universality of the person, work and message of Jesus Christ persuades the minds of men and women of all walks of life – both religious and irreligious, the so called 'believers' and 'skeptics', clerics and laypeople, philosophers and realists – to advance their understanding of Jesus Christ by interpreting him from biblical and non-biblical sources. Some of these interpretations may look heretical for many and thus a distortion of the authentic and original Jesus, but alternatively, they also serve as an indicator of the multidimensional, multifaceted veracity and inexhaustibility of Jesus Christ himself, and thus these attempts are to be welcomed. Hindu religious reformers and spiritual leaders were and are no exception in this regard. The renascent Hindus, right from the time of Raja Rammohan Roy and down to Mahatma Gandhi, had their way of understanding and interpreting Jesus which is not always congruent with the orthodox Christian Christology.[1] Likewise, a host of Neo-Vedāntins like S. Radhakrishnan, Swami Vivekananda and other leaders of Ramakrishna movement also developed an understanding of Jesus Christ which is substantially different from that of the Christian image of Jesus.[2] All these understandings and interpretations, though faced with opposition from the Christian missionaries, churches, and Christian theologians who identify them as heretical, add new dimensions to an overall understanding of Jesus in India.

One of the most striking features of the modern Hinduism is the emergence of modern gurus and the role they play in the overall religious arena of Hindus and to people of other faiths. Contemporary gurus, within Hinduism and other religions, are significantly different from the traditional gurus. I have discussed in this books, the distinctive characteristic features of the contemporary gurus

[1] For detail study cf. M.M. Thomas, *The Acknowledged Christ of the Indian Renaissance*, (Madras: CLS, 1970) and also S.J. Samartha, *The Unbound Christ of Hinduism*, (Madras: CLS), 1974.

[2] Cf. K.P. Aleaz, *Jesus in Neo-Vedanta: The Meeting of Hinduism and Christianity*, (Delhi: Kant Publications, 1999).

along with the reasons behind the blooming of guru movement in our time. However, the main purpose of this book is not to provide an in-depth study of the contemporary guru movement, but, to bring out their interpretations of Jesus Christ with critical observation.

The modern Indian gurus throw a new light, through their interpretations, to an overall understanding of Jesus in India, thereby enriching Indian understanding of Jesus as they add other dimensions to the already-rich-insights of Jesus from India. This study, therefore, is an attempt to investigate how the contemporary Indian gurus, with special reference to Yogananda, Sathya Sai Baba, Osho and Ravishankar, interpret Jesus Christ so as to expose the differences in their approach and interpretation and also their contributions to Indian understanding of Jesus.

Importance of the Study

The study of modern gurus' interpretation of Jesus Christ may be considered as important because of the following reasons –

1. A number of Indian gurus display certain degree of interest in Jesus Christ. For instance, every year since 1970[3] Christmas has been celebrated at Prasanthi Nilayam, the *āśram* of Sai Baba[4] where Sathya Sai Baba and some of his devotees gave Christmas messages. Moreover, Prasanthi Nilayam is decorated with Jesus' huge statue showing the positive attitude the guru of this *āśram* had developed towards Jesus Christ. A famous and controversial Indian guru, Osho, not only made numerous references to Jesus in a number of his talks, but also gave lectures exclusively on Jesus and those were published in seven volumes.[5] Likewise, Christmas is celebrated every year in the *āśrams* of Sivananda and Mata Amritananda Mayi. A highly respected Indian guru named Yogananda, who is well-known in America, seems to be most attached to Jesus Christ amongst these gurus. He claimed to have communion with Christ several times, where Jesus appeared before him in flesh and blood. He also testified that he has seen Jesus before his crucifixion and after resurrection in his glorious form.[6] Ravishankar, another important living guru, does not talk

---

[3] This conclusion is drawn from the fact that the earliest record of discourse on Jesus made by Sri Sathya Sai Baba was in 1970; earlier than that no record has been found.

[4] Christmas celebration at Prasanthi Nilayam usually include some carol singing by Western devotees, speeches by Sai devotees of Christian background, a special discourse on Christmas by Sathya Sai Baba. Cf. Howard Murphet, *Sai Baba: Invitation to Glory*, (Delhi: Macmillan India Limited, 1982), p. 134.

[5] Osho, *Come Follow to You: Reflections on Jesus of Nazareth, Vols. 1-4*, (Pune: Tao Publishing Pvt. Ltd., 2006); Osho, *The Mustard Seed: The Revolutionary Teachings of Jesus, Commentaries on the Gnostic Gospel of Thomas*, (Mumbai: Osho Media International, 2009); Osho, *I Say unto You, Vols. 1-2.* (Pune: Osho Media International, 2011).

[6] Paramhansa Yogananda, *The Second Coming of Christ,* p. xxvii.

about Jesus as much as other gurus under investigation do, but often mentions the name and teachings of Jesus in affirmative manner, sometimes even uses Jesus to support his teachings. In such a setting, it is felt that they deserve our attention and investigation to bring to light what exactly are their contributions for the deeper understanding of Jesus in the pluralistic context of India.

2. Substantial studies had been done on Hindu reformers' interpretations of Jesus Christ as well as on the Neo-Vedāntins' interpretations of Jesus. But, systematic study on the contemporary gurus' interpretations of Jesus had not been undertaken. Therefore, it is important to study this aspect so as to have a fuller picture of the Indian interpretations of Jesus Christ.

3. Jesus Christ is understood to be universal and not the monopoly of Christians, so people of other faiths have every right to interpret the person, work and message of Jesus Christ, and their interpretations is hoped to throw new light on an overall Indian understanding of Jesus Christ, thereby enriching our knowledge of him in India. At the same time, it is also necessary to verify, as far as possible, the validity of their interpretations – whether they distort the real Jesus due to their pre-conceived and biased attitude or are they genuinely trying to understand him - thus the importance of this study.

4. These gurus with one voice assert that Christians today do not understand the real meaning of Jesus' words and works, for they are distorted as they passed through the Church's dogmas and traditions. They claim that they know the real meaning of Jesus' teachings, for they acquired this knowledge directly from Christ himself as a result of their communion with him, and not gained from the interpretations of theologians. It is important to investigate this claim.

Area of Study

The main focus of this book is the select Indian gurus' interpretation of Jesus Christ where the four contemporary gurus, such as, Paramhansa Yogananda, Sri Sathya Sai Baba, Osho Rajneesh and Sri Sri Ravishankar are selected for studies. I also discuss in brief other modern gurus' interpretations of Jesus Christ. Apart from these, a brief discussion on Jesus Christ as interpreted by Hindu reformers and Neo-Vedantins, and a survey of the origin and development of gurism in Hindu religious tradition highlighting the distinctive features of modern gurusim are provided.

Selecting several gurus and trying to do justice in investigating them may appear a formidable task at a glance, but the scope of this study is to investigate their interpretations of Jesus Christ only. Most of these gurus do not put Jesus Christ at the center of their philosophical or theological teachings, nor do they consider him as indispensably important in their movement. However, due to some reasons they make references to Jesus in their discourses, sometimes making discourses exclusively on him - commenting on Jesus' message found in the Bible. However, literature available to us is comparatively less that it is not too formidable a task to investigate their interpretations of Jesus. The rationale behind selecting these gurus includes – (i) their popularity and significance in and outside of the country, and the huge followings they have, make us interested in these gurus in general and their interpretations of Jesus Christ in particular; (ii) unlike many other contemporary gurus, they constantly refer to Jesus in their discourses and writings as an ideal model to follow; they even produce certain amount of literature on Jesus Christ which makes it possible to study their interpretations.

Method of Study

The study employed '*Textual-philosophical*' method. The study needs to be '*textual*' because it investigates select Indian gurus' interpretations of Jesus - 'the method they employed', 'the influences', 'the seriousness in their approach to understand Jesus Christ', 'the actual interpretation' and the likes by examining books written by these gurus. In other words, their books served as text for investigation and with the help of the hermeneutical principle called '*Contextual Critiquing*' an attempt is made to interpret these texts.

The hermeneutical method of study employed is 'Contextual Critiquing'. It is a critical reading of the gurus' interpretations, critiquing them taking seriously their religio-philosophical and personal experiential context to see how far the context and the diverse experience they acquired have influenced them in the way they look at Jesus and interpret him. For example, Sathya Sai Baba's self-understanding as the Incarnation of God and God Himself may have deeply conditioned the way he looks at Jesus; similarly the Vedāntic worldview inherited by Yogananda and Ravishankar appears to have been instrumental in their readings of Jesus. Moreover, Yogananda's personal experience of communion with Christ Himself, with Babaji, 'the deathless guru' who is said to have constant communion with Christ, and his educational background in the Christian mission institute and his training in spirituality under a guru who had high regards for Jesus – all these seem to have lasting impression upon his life and works and of course, the way he interprets Jesus Christ. Likewise, the feeling of superiority complex and the philosophy of 'be yourself' and the complete negation of any tradition as valid under which Osho operates appear to have influenced the way he interprets Jesus. So, the context of their interpretation is taken seriously in the reading of these gurus. Using 'Contextual Critiquing' as the hermeneutical tool, in other words, using their context as a framework for critiquing them, I have ventured to read the select gurus' exposition of Jesus Christ.

Secondly, it is also a *philosophical study*. This is important because all these gurus are philosophical in their approach to religion, depending on or influenced deeply by one of the most prominent Indian philosophical schools, i.e., Advaita Vedānta. However, it is to be noted here that the Western notion of philosophy of religion which is primarily a philosophical defense of religious convictions or a philosophical thinking about religion,[7] is rejected by Indian scholars in religion on the ground that it draws a clear demarcating line between religion and philosophy. On the contrary, Indian scholars emphasize the essential unity of religion and philosophy, because in India, religion does not need philosophical defense as the philosophical speculation of the Ultimate Reality itself is the highest religious conviction.[8] In Indian religious understanding, the goal of philosophy and religion is the same, that is, the attainment of *mokṣa*, the liberation of the bonded soul from the cycle of birth and re-birth. T. M. P. Mahadevan notes: "Man's (*sic*) supreme end was generally regarded as *mokṣa*, spiritual freedom and this is the fulcrum on which both philosophy and religion turned."[9] According to him the integration of philosophy and religion is felt because the logical methods of enquiry adopted by philosophers were found to be wanting for realizing the goal of life. Likewise, a life lived in accordance with moral principles alone was not enough as we need to go beyond, to the higher region of transcendent experience.[10]

The three main branches of Indian philosophy, *viz*., Metaphysics, Epistemology and Ethics all indicate the weight lay upon human life. The Indian metaphysics deal with the theory of human person, the universe and the Ultimate Reality. The Epistemology which deals with the source of valid knowledge (*Pramāṇas*) points to the integral relationship between reason and revelation i.e. between philosophy and religion because Indian *pramāṇas* includes both reason and revelation. Again, Ethics is given a prominent place by all Indian systems. So, Indian philosophy is not a mere theoretical or contemplative one but rather it is an applied religious discipline.[11] Chatterjee and Datta notes that all the Indian philosophical systems,

> regard philosophy as a practical necessity and cultivate it in order to understand how life can be best led. The aim of philosophical wisdom is not merely the satisfaction of intellectual curiosity, but mainly an enlightened life led with far-sight, foresight and insight. It became a custom, therefore, with an Indian writer to explain,

---

[7] John Hick, *Philosophy of Religion*, Second Edition, (New Jersey: Prentice-Hall., INC., 1973), p. 1.

[8] K.P. Aleaz, *Dimensions of Indian Religion: Study, Experience and Interaction*, (Calcutta: Punthi Pustak, 1995), p. 17.

[9] T.M.P. Mahadevan, "The Religio-Philosophic Culture of India" in *The Cultural Heritage of India*, Suniti Kumar Chatterji, etc. (eds.), (Calcutta: Ramakrishna Mission Institute of Culture, 1982), p. 165.

[10] *Ibid.*

[11] K.P. Aleaz, *Dimensions of Indian Religion*, pp. 25-26.

at the beginning of his (*sic*) work, how it serves human ends (*puruṣārtha*).[12]

So, in India philosophy and religion cannot be separated, philosophy is the path way to religion and also the culmination of religion. This integral relationship between philosophy and religion prevents philosophy from becoming barren, and religion from becoming blind.[13] Therefore, philosophical approach to the study of religion, for India is neither a philosophical defense of religious convictions nor a philosophical thinking about religion, but it is an integration of philosophy and religion so as to arrive at the inner meaning of religion.

Thus, according to Indian discernment, the combination of philosophy and religion is found to be a necessity to attain the highest spiritual attainment. The same thing applies to the study of Indian gurus' interpretations of Jesus Christ. To understand any of these gurus, philosophical approach to the study of religion is needed because they are not only philosophical, but at the same time they maintain the essential oneness of religion and philosophy. By looking at their interpretations of Jesus Christ from the perspective of philosophy of religion, it is hoped that better and clearer picture will emerge.

Sources:- Each guru investigated produced literature in the form of books on their interpretations of Jesus. Mostly these are collections of lectures and discourses but some of these are also written by themselves. For examples, apart from the collections of his lectures where plentiful mentions are made on Jesus, Yogananda wrote two volumes on Jesus entitled '*The Second Coming of Christ: The Resurrection of Christ Within You, Vol. 1& 2*'[14] where he provides his understanding of Jesus and supplies commentary to his teachings found in the Bible. Sathya Sai Baba's Christmas messages delivered on every Christmas day at Prasanthi Nilayam, the *āśram* of Sai Baba, were to be found in a number of volumes under the title - *Sathya Sai Speaks: Discourse of Bhagavan Sri Sathya Sai Baba*. For the benefit of researcher like me, fortunately, these discourses were collected together and published in a book form under a title *"Be Like Jesus": The Good News of Jesus in the Words of Sri Sathya Sai Baba*.[15] Likewise, Osho's numerous lectures on Jesus were transcribed into books, making the total volume of books up to seven, viz., *Come Follow to You: Reflections on Jesus of Nazareth Vols. 1-4; I Say unto you Vols. 1-2;*

---

[12] Satischandra Chatterjee and Dhirendramohan Datta, *Introduction to Indian Philosophy*, (Kolkata: University of Calcutta, 2004), p. 12.

[13] K.P. Aleaz, *Dimensions of Indian Religion*, p. 27.

[14] Yagonanda Paramhansa, *The Second Coming of Christ: The Resurrection of the Christ Within You, Vol. I & II*, (Los Angles: Self Realization Fellowship, 2004).

[15] Sri Sathya Sai Baba, *"Be Like Jesus": The Good News of Jesus*, compiled by Debra and William Miller, (Prashanthi Nilayam: Sri Sathya Sai Sadhana Trust, Publication Division, 2009).

The Mustard Seed: The Revelatory Teachings of Jesus.[16] Apart from these a large number of his books contain his teachings on Jesus Christ. Ravishankar did not have much material on Jesus. Apart from some of his books where he makes references to Jesus here and there, he gives one whole chapter in his book *Wisdom for the New Millennium* for interpreting Jesus Christ.[17] There is an audio CD which contains his discourse on Jesus[18] which is also an important source.

Apart from these books, I have conducted personal interviews with Ravishankar at his Bangalore *āśram* on 27th October, 2012; and also with Prof. Gangadhar Shastri, Sathya Sai Institute of Higher Learning (Deemed to be University), Head of Prasanthi Nilyam Campus, Puttaparthi, on 29th October, 2012; and with Swami Smarananda, the General Secretary of Yogoda Satsanga Society of India, Yogoda Satsanga Skha Math, Ranchi, India on 20.07.2013. These personal interviews become useful sources for this work. It may also be mentioned here that Osho Commune International, Pune which is the headquarters of Osho movement, is not opened to visitors including researchers unless one is enrolled to do the course. So, I failed to secure access to this commune, in spite of a repeated plea.

Thus, books authored by these gurus are used as 'primary sources' and 'basic texts' along with personal interviews from which investigation is made. There are also a number of books written by scholars on these gurus, details of which are not provided here, but are consulted in the studies.

Chapter Division

The book is divided into eight Chapters where the first and second Chapters deal with an overview of the origin and development of guru tradition in Hinduism and Jesus Christ in Hindu religious thought respectively. A brief survey on some of the modern Indian gurus' interpretations of Jesus Christ is provided in Chapter three. Chapter four to Chapter seven contain select contemporary gurus' interpretations of Jesus Christ. Here, the interpretations of Jesus advanced by gurus such as, Yogananda, Sathya Sai Baba, Osho and Ravishankar are explained in detail. The last Chapter is a concluding Chapter that critically analysed the 'unveiled Christ of the Indian gurus' weighing its positive and negative aspects.

---

[16] Osho, *Come Follow to You: Reflections on Jesus of Nazareth, Vols. 1-4*, (Pune: Tao Publishing Pvt. Ltd., 2006); Osho, *The Mustard Seed: The Revolutionary Teachings of Jesus, Commentaries on the Gnostic Gospel of Thomas*, (Mumbai: Osho Media International, 2009); Osho, *I Say unto You, Vols. 1-2*. (Pune: Osho Media International, 2011).

[17] Ravishankar, Sri Sri, *Wisdom for the New Millennium*, (Mumbai: Jaico Publishing House, 2005).

[18] Sri Sri Ravishankar, "Jesus Embodiment of Love", a lecturer delivered at California, USA on 8th Aug. 1996, in Audio CD produced by Sri Sri Publication Trust, Bangalore, 2011.

Chapter 1

Origin and Development of Guru Tradition in Hinduism
A Survey

A great *ācārya-guru* by the name Ādi Śaṅkara in his Bhagavad Gītā *Bhasya* states that liberation (*mokṣa*) is not possible for a person without the help of a competent guru. He says, "It is unattainable to those who have not been properly initiated into the traditional knowledge by the guru."[1] In the same vein one of the principal Upaniṣads, *Mundaka Upaniṣad* advices the seeker to approach a guru for knowledge – "For the sake of the knowledge of that (which is not made), one should approach … a preceptor who is well-versed in scriptures and also established in Brahman" (*Mundaka Upaniṣad* 1.2.12). *Tantrika* scriptures lay great importance to guru even claiming for gurus a position higher than gods.[2] Such is a long tradition inherited by the Hindus of our time and thus, it is not surprising to see that modern Hinduism witnesses a mushrooming of gurus for which Khushwant Singh cynically observes, "There are many self-styled *Bhagawāns* (Gods), *Swamis* (Lords), *Ṛṣis* (Sages), *Maharṣis* (Great Sages), *Ācāryas* (Teachers) and *Sants* (Saints) and *gurus* with large followings."[3]

---

[1] *Bhagavad Gītā with the Commentary of Śri Śaṅkarācharya*, translated by A. Mahadeva Shastri, (Mysore: Government Oriental Library, 1901), XVIII:50, p. 442.

[2] For a detailed study of guru in Tantric literatures cf. *Kularnava Tantra*, Chapters XII and XIII.

[3] Khushwant Singh, "Gurus, Godmen and Good People", in *Gurus, Godmen and Good People*, edited by Khushwant Singh, (New Delhi: Orient Longman Ltd., 1975), p. vii.

Guruism is intrinsic to Indian culture. Clarence O. McMullen rightly observes, "The concept of guru is a product of Indian society and is typical to it. This is reflected in the fact that the term has not been translated in other languages but is taken as it is."[4] Though Buddhism and Jainism are considered as the offshoots of Hinduism or at least as old as Hindu Dharma itself, the term 'guru' is not widely used in these religions whereas Sikhism, another offshoot of Hinduism, is known as 'religion of the gurus'. Hindu religious tradition is certainly the richest of all in this aspect. Right from the time towards the end of Vedic period till the present time, there were a multitude of gurus who shape, guide and lead people in multiple ways. I will make an attempt to understand the term 'guru' and advance a historical survey of guruism among the Hindus with a view to presenting factors responsible for the emergence of modern guruism and its distinctive characteristics.

1. Etymological Consideration

1.1. The Word meaning

The Sanskrit word '*guru*' is very popular today and is being used in different ways having different connotations and meanings, covering both religious and secular field, even in business. Because of this it almost lost its original meaning. Again, as it is explained in a variety of ways due to the richness of this word, it is difficult to deduce and pinpoint the exact meaning of the word. According to Dictionary, '*guru*' has broadly two meanings – *Firstly*, it connotes heavy, weighty, great, large, long, important, momentous, best, excellent, etc. *Secondly*, it also means father, guide, teacher, preceptor, head, lord, ruler, elder, any venerable or respectable person, etc.[5] Prasannabhai maintains that the word 'guru' can be analyzed as follows:– *Gu – guptam, Ru – roopayati*, hence guru means one who shapes or represents the invisible. Again, *Gu – goodham, Ru – rauti*, hence guru means one who speaks or proclaims the hidden. Also, *Gu – andhakāra, Ru – prakāsha*, hence guru means one who expels darkness of ignorance by giving correct knowledge.[6] Sri Sri Ravishankar has interesting explanation of the term 'guru' – "Guru is nothing but wisdom and love. Guru is that principle which is wisdom and love… You also call that person a Guru in whom there is no gap between life and wisdom

[4] Charence O. McMullen, "The Nature of Guruship: A Sociological Perspective" in *The Nature of Guruship*, edited by Clarence O. McMullen, (Delhi: ISPCK, 1976), p. 113 and footnote no. 9 of this article.

[5] Vaman Shivram Apte, *The Student's Sanskrit-English Dictionary*, (Delhi: Motilal Banarsidass, 2000). See for the meaning of 'Guru', W. Owen Cole, *The Guru in Sikhism*, (London: Darton, Longman & Todd, 1982), p. 2.

[6] Prasannabhai, "Sadguru" in *Vidyajyoti: Journal of Theological Reflection*, (Vol. XL, No. 7, August, 1976), p. 316.

and love."[7] Referring to the meaning of 'guru' as heavy, Jan Gonda states that "it must primarily have described the man (*sic*) who on account of his (*sic*) special knowledge and function was held to be a bearer of power conspicuous by his prestige, 'weight', and influence."[8]

According to B.B. Chaubey, an expert in Sanskrit language, the term '*guru*' is derived from '*gur*' meaning 'to raise, to lift up, to hurt, to kill, to make effort, to eat, to go. A person is called guru because he tortures, kills or eats up his/her disciple's ignorance and elevates his/her character and ultimately leads him/her to the path of salvation. Also, guru is derived from '*gr*' 'to sink' or 'to swallow. So, a person is called guru because he/she swallows his/her ignorance.[9] Some people suggests still another meaning of guru saying that it is derived from the Sanskrit root '*giri*' meaning 'one who calls'. Proposing this Kirpal Singh states: "Thus, he (*sic*) who always hears this (divine) call within himself (*sic*), and is devotedly attached to the call and can make it manifest in others is described … as guru."[10] It is also said that the word 'guru' is a combination of two words – '*Gu*' meaning darkness or ignorance and '*Ru*' denoting the removal of that darkness. "Therefore, one who removes the darkness of ignorance is a guru."[11] One of the leading contemporary Hindu Gurus Sri Sathya Sai Baba, supporting this argument, also explains: *Gu* means darkness or ignorance; *Ru* means its removal. So, guru must know the process by which ignorance can be removed in another. How can he/she do it when he/she has not done it for himself/herself. The blind cannot lead the blind. *Guru* has another meaning too. *Gu* means *gunathitha* or beyond the three strands of which the cosmos is composed and 'ru' means *rupa-rahitha* or devoid of any particular form. Now, no mortal has transcended the *guna* and *rupa*. God alone can be described as unaffected by these. So, God is the Guru. A real guru (God) is all-knowing, all-powerful, all-pervading.[12]

Tantrika literature gives detailed explanation of the word 'guru' by splitting the word into syllables and letters. According to *Kularnava Tantra*

---

[7] Sri Sri Ravi Shankar, *An Intimate Note to the Seeker Volume 4: July 30, 1998 – July 28, 1999*, Compiled by Anne Elixhauser & Bill Hayden, (Bangalore: Vyakti Vikas Kendra, 1999), p. 120.

[8] Jan Gonda, *Change and Continuity in Indian Religion*, cited in Joel D. Mlecko, "The Guru in Hindu Tradition" in *Numen*, (Vol. 29, No. 1. J1, 1982), pp. 33-34.

[9] See B.B. Chaubey, "The nature of Guruship According to the Hindu Scriptures" in *The Nature of Guruship,* edited by Clarence O. McMullen, (Delhi: ISPCK, 1976), p. 9.

[10] Kirpal Singh, *Godmen*, (Delhi: Ruhani Satsang, 1967), p. 8, cited in Joel D. Mlecko, "The Guru in Hindu Tradition", p. 34.

[11] M.L.Ahuja, *Gurus: Ancient, Medieval and Modern*, (New Delhi: Rupa & Co, 2009), pp. xi-xii.

[12] *Sri Sathya Sai Speaks*, *Vol. 9*, compiled by N. Kasturi, (Delhi: Bhagavan Sri Sathya Sai Seva Samithi), n.d., p. 99.

(hereafter KT), the foremost *Tantra* of the Kaula School, '*gu*' refers to darkness whereas '*ru*' signifies what restrains it; consequently, '*guru*' is a person who restrains darkness of ignorance (KT. XVII.7). KT also explains in another way where '*gu*' signifies giver of fulfillment, '*r*' stands for destroyer of sin and '*u*' for Viṣṇu. So, anyone who possesses these three in himself/herself is the supreme guru (KT. XVII.8). Or, '*gu*' signifies the wealth of knowledge; '*r*' connotes illuminator whereas '*u*' refers to Śiva and he/she who contains these in himself/herself is the guru (KT. XVII.9).[13]

Thus, the word meaning of '*guru*' leads us to the understanding of who the guru is as we shall discuss below.

1.2. Who is a Guru?

There are some words used popularly in Hinduism which have more or less the same meaning, but also different in some aspects, viz. *Ācārya, Ṛṣi, Swami, Sant, Mahant, Purohita, Pundit, Guru, Avatāra, etc.* According to McMullen, unlike *Ācārya, Purohita, Mahant* or *Pundit* who derive their authority from their great learning, right to perform rituals or their position in the religious organization, the guru possesses authority because of his/her charisma.[14] Opposed to the *Avatāras* who claimed that they are the incarnations of God, a guru (in olden days) never claims that he/she is god, or sent by a particular god for a particular purpose. But this is not the case today as some of the contemporary Hindu gurus claim that they are incarnations of gods. Unlike other religious functionaries like *Ācārya, Ṛṣi, Purohita, Mahant*, etc. who are faithful to traditions and scriptures, a modern guru has been a nonconformist and a person who protested, explicitly or implicitly against the existing religious order.[15]

Then who is a guru? How can we identify him/her? A guru is a person "who is believed to possess divine or transcendental knowledge (enlightenment) and is capable of, and willing to pass this knowledge or its aspects to the disciples and whose authority is based on his (*sic*) own claim and also on the disciples' belief in these claims."[16] According to Mervyn C. D'Souza, "A true guru, therefore, is more than one who hands over the sacred thread (*upanayana*) and whispers the sacred formula (*mantra*); a true guru in the fullest form is one who, while reorienting the *Śiṣya*'s moral cords and teaching a doctrine,

---

[13] Cf. Ahuja, *Gurus: Ancient, Medieval and Modern*, pp. xi-xii.

[14] McMullen, "The Nature of Guruship: A Sociological Perspective" in *The Nature of Guruship*, p.164.

[15] *Ibid.*

[16] Quoted in *Ibid.*

also transposes the *Śiṣya*'s being to a higher level."[17] Vandana defines Guru as 'a man/woman, who has received the flash of vision, the chosen of Him ordained not by the hand of human but by the Hand of God. She/he is the one who gives form to the invisible God, and who reveals Him, who proclaims the Reality, the Mysterious Being. The Guru is the one who removes the darkness (*andhakar*) from the heart of the disciple. Removing this ignorance (*avidya*) she/he elevates her/him to *mokṣa* (liberation).[18]

Considering the diverse meanings given to 'guru' Joel D. Mlecko concludes,

> If the word "guru" means many things, it is because the guru is many things. He (*sic*) is an entity which in Western culture has no exact counterpart. For the guru is a teacher, counselor, father-image, mature ideal, hero, source of strength, even divinity integrated into one personality. Primarily, however, the guru is the personal teacher of spirituality, that is, of the basic, ultimate values perceived within the Hindu tradition. Further, the guru possesses experiential knowledge, not only intellectual knowledge, of these values. In a word, the guru is indispensable for spiritual development.[19]

Though there is a significant change in the understanding of guru from ancient to modern time, generally we can conclude that a guru is a person who is considered to have attained the highest spiritual attainment, who possesses an extra-ordinary charisma and charm, is well versed in scripture, having an ability to attract others and in possession of a kind of mystical knowledge or experiences, who is an enlightened person who can dispel ignorance of his/her disciple, who is more than willing to pass on his/her 'truth' to others and who very often rebels against the existing religious order and introduces new spiritual order.

2. Guru in the Hindu *Śāstras*: A Textual-Historical Survey

The Hindu scriptures provide us with ample of sources from which we can reconstruct the development of guruism in Hindu religious tradition. In this section a brief survey is made of the scriptural records concerning guru from Vedic literature down to the Tantras.

---

[17] Mervyn C. D' Souza, "Kṛṣṇa and Arjuna: A Model of Guru - *Śiṣya* Relationship", in *Journal of Dharma*, (Vol. XI, No. 1, Jan-March, 1986), p. 10.

[18] Vandana, "The Guru - *Śiṣya* Relationship in the Indian Tradition", in *Third Millennium*, (Vol. III, No. 2, 2000; April-June), pp. 61.

[19] Mlecko, "The Guru in Hindu Tradition", p. 34.

2.1. Guru in *Śṛuti* Literature

The concept and practice of guruism was not found explicitly in the highly ritualistic early Vedas; and the word '*guru*' is also missing in the early Vedic lore. But in Ṛg Veda there is a word '*Śākta*' which denotes 'teacher'. In Atharva Veda we see another word '*ācārya*', which is still popular even today, that also refers to 'teacher.'[20] However, towards the end of the Vedas, during the time of Upaniṣads, when Vedic rituals had lost their hold on the people as the people turned to a more sophisticated and inner-seeking contemplative spirituality than that of complex ritual practices, we see the concept of guruism fully developed. The prominence of *Jñāna* as the way for human salvation and the development of *Āśrama Dharma* increased the need for a competent guide and teacher, the guru. During this time religious understanding shifted from ritualistic approach to God to the emphasis on *Jñāna* (knowledge) as mean to reach and attain God. So, naturally, ones who were knowledgeable, who can lead people from darkness to light, from death to immortality and impart salvific knowledge are more in demand.

There are four *Āśramas* – *Brahmacharya*, *Gṛhasthya*, *Vanaprasthya* and *Sannyāsya*. The *ācārya* (guru) of the first *āśrama,* i.e. *Brahmacharya* is different from the rest; here the guru is responsible for teaching the student – *brahmachari*. In the case of the second *āśrama* – *Garhasthya*, the guru is called *Purohita-Guru* who is responsible for the welfare of a householder especially in the performance of his religious activities. In the third *āśrama,* the *ācārya* (or ascetic-guru) is a person who has realized oneness with Brahman and his/her responsibility is to help the one who has retired from his household responsibility for spiritual realization.[21]

In the Upaniṣads we see a number of verses that talk about the nature, status and responsibility of guru, and instructions to the seekers concerning how to approach such a guru. Here are a few instances:

2.1.1. The Necessity of a Guru

Upaniṣadic ideal is that a student must learn not by himself/herself but by sitting at the feet of a guru. As a matter of fact 'Upaniṣad' itself means 'sitting near (the guru)'. Thus it is declared: "For the sake of the knowledge of that, one should approach … a preceptor who is well-versed in scriptures and also established in Brahman". (*Mundaka Upaniṣad* 1.2.12). It is also said, "For I have heard from persons like you, Revered sir, that you teach me, that the knowledge which has been learned from a teacher best helps one to attain his end" *(Chāndogya Upaniṣad* IV. 9.3). So, with the view of acquiring higher knowledge, a pupil used to approach a guru – "Then he went to Gautama, the

[20] Cf. Chaubey, "The Nature of Guruship According to the Hindu Scriptures", p. 10.

[21] *Ibid.*, p. 11.

son of Haridrumat and said, 'I wish to become a student of sacred knowledge. May I become your pupil, Venerable Sir" (*Chāndokya Upaniṣad* IV.4.3).

2.1.2. Guru- *Śiṣya* Relationship

During the time of Upaniṣads, transmission of knowledge of any kind took place from guru to *śiṣya* (disciple).[22] Gurus are no ordinary persons as they have already realized Brahman, and due to this they are eligible to teach others about Brahman. "He (*sic*) who cannot even be heard of by many, whom many even hearing, do not know, wondrous is he (*sic*) who can teach (Him) and skilful is he (*sic*) who finds (Him) and wondrous is he (*sic*) who knows even when instructed by the wise" (*Kaṭha Upaniṣad* I.2.7). Also, "Taught by an inferior man (*sic*) He cannot be truly understood as He is thought of in many ways. Unless taught by one who knows Him as himself (*sic*), there is no going thither for it is inconceivable, being subtler than the subtle" (*Kaṭha Upaniṣad* I.2.8). As gurus are so important, *Śiṣyas* should show equal respect to God and his/her guru. Thus states *Śvetāśvatara Upaniṣad*, "These subjects which have been declared shine forth to the high-souled one who has the highest devotion for God and for his (*sic*) spiritual teacher *(guru)* as for God" (IV.23). The student on his/her part should develop the earnest zeal for knowledge, he/she should develop a general attitude of restraint of senses and fully submit to his/her teacher, only then he/she is eligible to learn the secret truth. Thus, states *Śvetāśvatara Upaniṣad*, "The highest mystery in the Vedānta which has been declared in a former age should not be given to one whose passions are not subdued, nor again to one who is not a pupil" (VI. 22).

2.1.3. Pattern of Learning

In the Upaniṣadic period, the prospective student would approach the guru and live with him/her for several years during his/her studentship. The first step for the student is to offer firewood and alms to his/her guru. In this act the *śiṣya* signified a desire to share in the guru's domestic sacrifice and to accept the duty of helping to maintain it over the several years of his/her living with the guru and his/her family. A function of the guru is to intellectually and verbally explain the scripture, its letters and spirit; but he/she also teaches by his/her life, daily acts, casual words, silence, overseeing the *śisya*'s health, sleep, diet, the company he/she keeps and the places he/she visits. To be near the guru, to humbly and reverently serve and obey him, is to find, to know, and to experience the 'Way'.[23] Moreover, the period of studentship was not only a time of learning and of vigorous discipline but also of humble service to the guru. The student had to attend to the guru's sacred fire *(Chāndogya Upaniṣad*

---

[22] See *Bṛhadāraṇyaka Upaniṣad* I.5.17; II.6.1-3; IV.1-3; VI.1-4.

[23] Mlecko, "The Guru in Hindu Tradition", p. 37.

IV, 10, 1), look after his cattle (*Chāndogya Upaniṣad* IV. 4. 5), collect alms for him/her (*Chāndogya Upaniṣad*, IV.3.5), and await his/her every command (*Bṛhadāranyaka Upaniṣad* III. 1. 2).[24] The formal method of teaching during this time was mainly a dialogical approach where the student asked questions and the teacher responded. Such a method is to be seen in a number of Upaniṣads; few examples include, conversation between Nachitekas and his guru Yama in the *Katha Upaniṣad*, Guru Yājnayavalkya responding questions raised by his wife Maitreyi in *Bṛhadāranyaka Upaniṣad,* dialogue between Guru Uddālaka and his son Śvetaketu in *Chāndogya Upaniṣad* and so on.

2.2. Guru in *Smṛti* Literature

The importance of guru seems to have increased as we enter the period of *Dharma Śāstras, Itihasas, Purāṇas* and *Tantras*. The status and function of guru had also undergone certain changes.

2.2.1. Guru in the *Dharma Śāstras*

According to *Manu Smṛti*, the most popular of all the *Dharma Śāstras*, there are two types of guru – firstly, *upādhyāya* who taught only a portion of the *Vedas* and who taught for his livelihood and secondly, the *ācārya* who invested the student with the sacred thread, taught the *Vedas* with its *Kalpasūtras* (concerning sacrifices) and the *Upaniṣads,* and who taught free (II, 140-141).[25] For Manu, *ācārya* is far more important than *upādhyāya* because he is a guru par excellence. Manu maintains that father and mother should also be regarded as gurus because they provide food, shelter to their children and also perform all the necessary rites for their children (Manu II.145).[26]

In *Viṣṇu purāṇas* (XXXII. 1-2) and *Manu Smṛti* (II. 227-37) the *ācārya,* the father, and the mother are described as the three highest gurus and as such deserve the utmost reverence. Another Dharma *Śāstra* literature - *Āpastamba* maintains that the pupil was to look upon the teacher as God: "Alms are declared to be sacrificial food. In regard to them the teacher holds the position which a deity holds in regard to food offered at a sacrifice" (*Āpastamba* I. 1. 3, 42). It also states: "He (the pupil) shall approach his teacher with the same reverence as a deity, without telling idle stories, attentive and listening eagerly to his words" (*Āpastamba* I. 2. 6, 13).[27] The Dharma *Śāstras* laid down the duty of the student similar to that which is found in Upaniṣads such as fetching water, collecting fuel, cleaning the area around the sacred fire, begging for food, etc. (*Āpastamba* I. 1. 1-7).

---

[24] *Ibid.*, p. 38.

[25] *Ibid.*

[26] Chaubey, "The nature of Guruship According to the Hindu Scriptures", p. 12.

[27] Mlecko, "The Guru in Hindu Tradition", pp. 39-40.

2.2.2. Guru in the Epics

According to the *Epics* both human and divine beings need guru. For example, the celestial beings have Bṛhaspati as their guru; he is their chief offerer of prayers and sacrifices and their counselor *(Rāmāyana* II, 1, 24; II, 4, 22; IV, 54, 4). Even Lord Rāmā and Lord Kṛṣṇa, the very incarnations of Viṣṇu, had to bow down before their gurus.[28] In the Mahābhārata we see that the greatest of all virtues is delineated as respect for father, mother, and guru. It is the instruction of the Mahābhārata that the disciple should always pay homage to the preceptor and free from negligence, should always desire sacred instruction.[29] Bhagavad Gītā, which is part of Mahābhārata clearly depicted *Guru-Śisya* relationship in the form of dialogue between Lord Kṛṣṇa, a guru and Arjuna, a disciple just like Upaniṣadic pattern wherein Arjuna asking questions and Kṛṣṇa imparting religious truths by way of responding him. Lord Kṛṣṇa advised Arjuna to approach a guru and submit to him in order to understand the truth: "Just try to learn the truth by approaching a spiritual master (guru). Inquire from him (*sic*) submissively and rendering service unto him (*sic*). The self-realized soul can impart knowledge unto you because he (*sic*) has seen the truth" (Bhagavad Gītā 4.34). Here, Kṛṣṇa underlines the responsibility of a disciple – to approach, to be submissive, and to render service to his/her guru; this unquestionably reflects the kind of guru-disciple relationship portrayed in the Upaniṣads and Dharma *Śāstras*.

It is noteworthy that the Epics, in contrast to Vedic-Upaniṣadic concept where god(s) always occupied the central place, emphasize the greatness of human rather than gods. For instance, Lord Kṛṣṇa and Lord Rāmā, being themselves the *avatāras*, were depicted more as human beings than gods. They were considered as gurus par excellence suggesting faintly that this may be the genesis of deifying human guru as god – the concept which became fully developed in the later time when the term '*Godman*' became popular as the synonym for guru. This trend continues and developed more in *Purāṇas* and *Tantras* as we shall see in the following discussion.

2.2.3. Guru in the *Purāṇic* and *Tantrika* Literatures

The importance of Guru increased in the time of *Purāṇas* and *Tantras*. R. C. Hazra, observes, "The *Bṛhannāradiya-purāṇa* says that there is no truth *(tathya)* higher than the preceptor (the guru). This high idea about the preceptor is perhaps one of the reasons why he is found to play an important part in the *Purāṇic* religious rites."[30] In the *Varāha Purāṇa* a devotee is to identify his

[28] *Ibid.*, pp. 40-41.

[29] *Ibid.*, p. 42.

[30] R. C. Hazra, *Studies in the Purānic Records on Hindu Rites and Customs* (Dacca: The University of Dacca, 1940), p. 262 cited in Mlecko, "The Guru in Hindu Tradition", p. 43.

guru with Viṣṇu and honour the spiritual preceptor accordingly. In the same vein, the *Bhāgavata Purāṇa* teaches that the guru is to be regarded as the deity (XI, 3) and worshipped (X, 86), for *mokṣa* (liberation) is attained only under the guidance of a guru.[31] It is mandatory for the disciple to accept the spiritual master as the representative of the Supreme Personality of Godhead for it is written, "The *ācārya* should never at any time enviously be disrespected with the notion of him being a mortal being, for the guru is the representative of all the gods" (*Bhāgavata Purana* XI.17.27), and also because the guru is not different from God (*Bhāgavata Purana* IV.29.51).

Due to the nature of *tantric* religion which is characterized by high secrecy of tantric rituals and practices, the need of a competent guru is all the more increased which in turn adds to the importance of the guru. One of the most popular *Tantras* states: "The form of the guru is the root of *dhyāna,* the lotus feet of the guru is the root of *pūjā,* the word of the guru is the root *of mantra,* and the grace of the guru is the root of *siddhi* (supernatural power).[32] Guru is highly esteemed and regarded as reaching the highest Reality and thus it is declared: "Guru is the father, guru is the mother, guru is God...himself" (*Kulārnava Tantra* XII, 49)[33]. Such is the importance of guru as portrayed in the *Tantrika* literature that John Woodroffe concludes, "The *Tantra Śāstras* are full of the greatness of the guru. He (*sic*) is not to be thought of as a mere man (*sic*)... Guru, it is said, can save one from the wrath of Śiva, but in no way can one be saved from the wrath of the guru."[34] The importance of guru for liberation is stated in *Kulārnava Tantra* XIV.93 saying that there can be no liberation without initiation, and there can be no initiation without a teacher.[35]

There is another important development of guruism with the advent of sectarian scriptures such as *Purāṇas* and *Tantras*, where the understanding of guru underwent radical change. By this time the guru was no longer *teacher-guru,* or *purohita-guru,* or *ascetic-guru* as in the time of Upaniṣads; but the founders of a certain sects or creeds are recognized by their followers as 'guru'. With the change in their identity, their role also has undergone radical change – from a teacher to a preacher. Another important development was the segregation of the group from the others – for example, a sect will keep itself aloof from the rest, the guru of that particular sect is for the members

---

[31] *Ibid.*, p. 44.

[32] *Kulārnava Tantra* (X. 13) cited in *Ibid.*, p. 45.

[33] *Ibid.*

[34] Sir John Woodroffe, *Shakti and Shakta* (Madras: Ganesh and Co, 1951), pp. 491-492, cited in *Ibid.*, p. 46.

[35] Cited in Monia Marchetto, "The Function of the Guru in Tantric Traditions", *Guru the Spiritual Master in Eastern and Western Traditions: Authority and Charisma*, edited by Antonio Rigopoulos (Venice: Venetion Academy of Indian Studies, & New Delhi: D.K. Printworld (P) Ltd., 2007), p. 231.

of the sect only as he/she would not give *mantra* to a person belonging to another sect. Unlike those gurus in the time of Upaniṣads, where the guru of a particular *āśrama* is respected by the other, here, the followers of one sect began to regard their guru as superior to all other gurus so they will not give respect to the gurus of a different sect.[36]

Our Scriptural survey of the development of guruism has revealed the fact that guruism is intrinsic to Hindu religious tradition right from the Vedic time and that gurus were indispensable as they were the source of the scripture itself, indispensable guidance and the required spiritual leaders for the attainment of the highest religious aspiration, and the visible gods. The status, role and importance of gurus grew with the progress of time. So, a teacher of a *Brahmacharin* in the Upaniṣadic period was put more or less in the same footing with gods during the time of Purānas and Tantras. This trend further developed with the emergence of the contemporary gurus where most of them, with the development of the non-dualistic concept of God, considered themselves as the very God – so the popular epithet 'God-man' emerged along with the surfacing of the popular practice of 'guru-worship'. Now, contemporary gurus are no longer considered as 'teachers of the Vedas' and 'guides to spiritual realization' alone, they were gods to be worshipped, to pray to and to be venerated as such.

3. Factors Responsible for the Emergence of Contemporary Guruism

A Number of sociological and psychological giants such as Max-Weber, Karl Marx, Emil Durkheim, Sigmund Freud, Friedrich Nietzsche, etc. had predicted more than a hundred years ago that modern scientific development will bury religion. Owing to scientific advancement people will become more and more critical of supernatural things and the time will come when religion will be pushed out of the mind of the people to die a natural death. In support of this assumption, a prominent sociologist of religion, Peter L. Berger wrote a famous book – *The Sacred Canopy: Elements of a Sociological Theory of Religion* in 1967, where he argued that the decline of religion is inevitable because of the industrial development. However, this proved to be wrong as Peter Berger himself admitted it in 1999 after more than thirty years when he says, "That idea is simple: Modernization necessarily leads to a decline of religion, both in society and in the minds of individuals. And it is precisely this idea that has turned out to be wrong."[37] Meera Nanda observes, "By the close of 20th century, theories of secularization lost steam. Predictions of the decline of

[36] Chaubey, "The Nature of Guruship According to the Hindu Scriptures", p.15.

[37] Peter L. Berger, "The Desecularization of the World: A Global Overview", in *The Desecularization of the World: Resurgent Religion and World Politics*, edited by Peter L. Berger, (Washington, D.C./Grand Rapids: Ethics and Public Policy Center/ William B. Eerdmans Publishing Company, 1999), pp. 2-3.

religion became impossible to sustain in the face of the resurgence of religion in public and private spheres all over the world."[38] Contemporary gurus play a significant role in the resurgence of religion in the minds of the people.

Guru movement is never absent from Indian soil as it is essential feature of Hinduism itself. However, guruism among the Hindus in India has been subsided temporarily after Guru Nanak in the fifteenth century till the time of the contemporary gurus who made an appearance in the 20th century C.E. where a number of gurus such as Swami Sivananda Saraswati, Yogananda Paramhansa, Sathya Sai Baba, Osho Rajneesh, Maharishi Mahesh Yogi, etc. emerged as a new religious force. According to Mangalwadi during these five centuries guruism was overshadowed by Islamic domination, Christian missionary enterprise and the Hindu Renaissance.[39] After the tapering down of these three forces, India once again, witnesses the blossoming of guruism and the resurgence of sectarianism in the form of guru movement. There are some reasons for the emergence of contemporary Guru Movement which is discussed in brief as follows:

3.1. Vishal Mangalwadi underlines in his book *The World of Gurus* certain reasons responsible for the emergence of Guruism. The Christian missions, Hindu reformers coupled with the industrialization of society weakened to a great extent the binding force of caste/class system with its sister institutions such as idol worship and the authority of scriptures. This has opened the doors for gurus to come in and play in the religious field of the Indian fertile soil. The result is - Brahmanism was overshadowed by Guruism. So, traditional Hinduism was weakened in need of a savior, the gurus provided the needed saviour resulting into the replacement of idol worship by guru worship.[40]

Interestingly guruism flourishes in the West as much as in India and in fact many modern gurus are known and followed in India because of the West where the fertile Western soil makes the infant guru of India grow into adulthood.[41] According to Mangalwadi guruism flourished in the West due to the "intellectual vacuum" created in the minds of the Westerners because of their rejection of Christianity on one hand and on the other hand, the failure of Humanism with its utter philosophical nakedness to which they are exposed to in bringing spiritual satisfaction. The Westerners were convinced that the

---

[38] Meera Nanda, *The God Market: How Globalization is Making India More Hindu*, (Noida: Random House Publishers India, 2009), pp. 187-188.

[39] Vishal Mangalwadi, *The World of Gurus*: *A Critical look at the Philosophies of India's Influential Gurus and Mystics,* Revised Edition, (Chicago: Cornerstone Press, 1992), p. 9.

[40] *Ibid.*, p. 12.

[41] It is to be noted here that a number of Indian gurus like Paramhansa Yogananda, Swami Prabhupada, Osho Rajneesh, etc. became popular only after they left the country and established themselves in the West, i.e. USA. So, the West is more responsible for making these people the full-fledged gurus.

intellect was incapable of knowing the truth and so they were drawn to a more mystical and miracle-accompanied teachings offered by the Indian gurus.[42] Again, due to the influence of scientific advancement, enlightenment, atheistic philosophies and materialism the Western countries which are predominantly Christian lost faith in their faith. The general masses no longer consider Christianity as having absolute authority and begin to look for alternatives which they find in the warm and sympathetic hands of the gurus. Another reason for the unprecedented popularity of the Hindu gurus in the West is the 'reaction to hollow materialism'. Christianity taught the negation of material benefits but at the same time the Western Christians are so materialistic. Mangalwadi observes:

> When people became dissatisfied with materialism, they look around for spiritual values and lifestyle. Turning to the Church, they found it engulfed by the same hollow materialism they hated. But the gurus – preaching essentially an otherworldly philosophy of life, spiritual peace, and bliss – captured their imagination.[43]

Rationalism which is the product of Enlightenment, though popular it may be in the West, 'failed to provide credible answers' to the questions of the people which made them to opt for a more practical and experiential philosophy – Existentialism. However, the experience taught by existentialists such as Kierkegaard, Sartre, Jaspers and Heidegger "lacked sufficient mystique and authority", notes Mangalwadi, "their popularity is being superseded by that of the Indian gurus, who have greater tradition, mystique and charisma."[44]

3.2. Guruism as it is found in Hinduism is the distinctive feature of this religion, the similar form of which is absent in other religious traditions. According to Charence O. McMullen this is due to "the absence of a specific or objectively given reference-point on which religious authority could be based and against which the validity of religious claims could be tested," and this opens a wide door "for charismatic personalities to establish their religious authority, essentially on their claimed enlightenment and personal charisma. This facilitated the origin and growth of the institution of guru."[45] Again, in close proximity with this is the absence of a unified system and concrete dogma in Hinduism that helps guruism to flourish among the Hindus. S. Radhakrishnan highlights a Hindu view of religion, "Belief and conduct, rites and ceremonies, authorities and dogma, are assigned a place subordinate to the art of conscious

---

[42] Mangalwadi, *The World of Gurus,* p. 14.

[43] *Ibid.*, pp. 15-16.

[44] *Ibid.*, p. 17.

[45] McMullen, "The Nature of Guruship: A Sociological Perspective", p. 165.

self discovery and contact with the divine."[46] He continues, "Faith for the Hindu does not mean dogmatism. He (*sic*) does not smell heresy in those who are not entirely of his (*sic*) mind."[47] A person may claim that he is god and gives himself/herself a *Bhagavan*-ship as Bhagavan Rajneesh did, or claims to be an *avatāra* as Sri Sathya Sai Baba did, and he/she will receive no criticism let alone rejection but will manage to gather large followings depending on his charisma and mystique power. So, the liberal nature of Hinduism and the anti-dogmatic character foster the growth of guru Movement.

3.3. The Hindu *varna* system and a strong Brahmanic dominance of the socio-religious affair may also account for the emergence of modern guruism. As for that matter, guru movement may be seen as a reaction or revolt against Brahmanism with its oppressive nature. The caste system, patronized by the Brahmins with its strong binding force denied religiosity and salvation to the non-twice born Hindus.[48] The institution of modern guruship is undoubtedly a movement against Brahmanism and caste system.

3.4. Meera Nanda argues that Globalization that paves the way for economic improvement of the Indian middle class, instead of eroding the religious interest, has increased the spirituality and religiosity of the middle class India. This in turn enhances the nurturing of guruism in India. In what ways? According to Nanda, "free markets are not only good for improving the choice of cars and toothbrushes and such, but also for improving the choice of religion and gods", because, "neo-liberal economic policies have worked to the advantage of the God market… rising wealth of the middle-classes have increased both the demand for, and supply of, religious services", as "the new economy has opened up more spaces in the public sphere for religion to penetrate."[49] According to recent survey Faith in religion is far from declining, but on the rise in the country as a whole. The data provided by a Hindustan Times-CNN-IBN State of the Nation Survey conducted by Centre for the Study of Developing Societies (CSDS) shows the following interesting results: 93 per cent believes in God; education makes no difference to this; 64 per cent visits worship places regularly; 53 per cent of the Indians offer prayer daily; the more educated prays more regularly; 46 per cent villagers believe in the existence of ghosts; 24 per cent consults a palmist at least occasionally, and

[46] S. Radhakrishnan, *Eastern Religions and Western Thought*, (London: Oxford University Press, 1940), p. 21 cf. S. Radhakrishnan, *The Hindu View of life*, (London: George Allen & Unwin Ltd.), 1931, pp. 11-33 where he discussed religious experience: its nature and conflict.

[47] *Ibid.*, p. 314.

[48] McMullen, "The Nature of Guruship: A Sociological Perspective", p. 167.

[49] Nanda, *The God Market,* p. 202. Cf. pp. 70-71 where the author explains some of the statistical data collected from various surveys that shows how globalization has increased the religious interest of Indian.

68 per cent participates or get involved or takes interest in religious functions of religions other than their own.[50]

The middle class who are benefitted from the free market economy become substantially rich and to their advantages the modern gurus give "a divine stamp of approval" – 'to be rich is divine' is the message coming from the modern gurus. "The Bhagavad Gītā and the Yoga Sūtras have been turned into self-help manuals for making money and achieving success" observes Meera Nanda. She continues, "They (modern gurus) offer a theology of prosperity which combines fashionable new age spirituality with discourses on the Bhagavad Gītā and Vedānta, all suitably reinterpreted as successful management tools."[51]

In the past spirituality is achieved through poverty – the most spiritual persons like *Sannyāsins* who lived by begging food were materially the poorest of the poor. But this concept of worldly poverty as the source of spiritual riches seems to have died down in our contemporary world with a paradigm shift in the whole conception of spirituality where 'prosperity religion' occupies the central place. So, "both the elites and the masses are turning to Gurus and *pūjāris* who are more than willing to find religious justification for getting rich.[52] Thus, the prosperity brought home by globalization to the houses of the middle class Indian, instead of weakening the spiritual appetite, only increases the longing for spiritual riches that makes them turn to the spiritual preceptors – visible gods, *saguṇa* gods or in other words Godmen.

3.5. According to Peter Brent there are two reasons that account for the flourishing of guruism in modern India, both of which are rooted deeply in the social system of India. The *first one* is repressive sexual puritarianism of Indian society where male and female have no freedom to mingle publicly to express their love. Indian young men and women "are the pathetic victims of that social stricture which prevents displays of tenderness between the sexes." They are not free to express their feeling like the Westerners. So, for a middle class Indian "there are often only two directions he can go to prove that he can love, that he can be loved. One is towards homosexuality, the other towards the Guru. (These are not, of course, mutually exclusive)."[53] In a way, the Indian youths are finding satisfaction in the warm company of their gurus where free expression of love, may not be necessarily homosexuality or heterosexuality, took place between gurus and disciples with societal approval.

Another reason Peter Brent gives is the absolute authority of fathers in general Indian homes that makes and molds other members psychologically

[50] *http://ibnlive.in.com/news/what-makes-indians-keep-the-faith/32015-3.html,* (21.07.2007).

[51] Nanda, *The God Market,* pp. 105, 107.

[52] *Ibid.*, p. 190.

[53] Peter Brent, *Godmen of India*, (Middlesex, England: Penguine Books, 1973), p. 285.

to be submissive and to bow down before a person whom they consider authoritarian. The average Indian is almost incapable of doing anything of which his/her father disapproves. "In this situation, the Guru can appear as a rescuer. For, with him, the whole conditioned mechanism of happy slavery can come into operation without conflict. He is the father who has been chosen… the disciple remains free in his bondage…Taught to be non-attached, he can cut himself off from his family without guilt."[54] So, on one hand Indians are accustomed to bow down before authority that helps gurus to climb the ladder of fame and on the other hand, for Indian youth guru provides freedom from their bondage in the family under the authoritarian rule of fathers but of course to be bound again, this time willingly, to their respective gurus.

These factors discussed above may have contributed to the emergence and development of the contemporary guruism to a great extent but are not the only factors or may not be the primary cause either. History of Hindu religious tradition is self-evident in providing the fact that this great religion revived itself from time to time due to its inherent vitality. The resurgence of guruism in the twentieth century appears to be primarily due to the instinctive potential of Hindu *Dharma* that revitalizes itself even when it was plunged into a deep religious depression. Therefore, factors such as, Muslim and Christian missionary works, oppressive nature of Brahmanism and caste system coupled with the inbuilt spiritual potency – the inherent vitality of Hinduism itself, work towards the resurgence of contemporary guruism. This in turn galvanizes revival of Hinduism within India, and also popularizes Hindu *Dharma* in the Western countries.

4. The Distinctive Features of Modern Guruism

Guruism as we have observed is not a new phenomenon; rather, it has a long history which can be traced back to the Vedas. The 'distinctive features' of modern guruism I am going to discuss here may not be altogether 'distinct' to the contemporary gurus as such, because, most of their beliefs and practices are the continuation of what has already been practiced which are adopted with or without modifications. However, there are characters that are distinctive to modern gurus as well.

4.1. Way back in 1940s J. Russell, who did a research on Hindu gurus, in his article "The guru in Hinduism" highlighted some of the important features of modern guruism. Though at that time some of the most important modern gurus were still yet to blossom, the characteristics of the modern gurus presented by him are highly relevant and are pertaining to even the contemporary gurus. According to Russell modern guruism has theistic emphasis, this is to appease people's desire and longing for personal God. But they preached that God is

[54] *Ibid.*, p. 287.

not to be found outside of oneself as God is there within us. Each guru has their emphasis –social application of religion for some, caste distinction is forbidden by all gurus. In some love and peace is emphasized, others yoga is emphasized. In all huge literatures are produced to proclaim their teachings. Though they are different in many areas, they have one thing in common – the understanding of God as '*Aham Brahmāsmi*' – 'I am the Brahman'. In general, worship or veneration of guru as god is common.[55]

4.2. Modern gurus can be put into three categories: In the first category is *miracle-working Gurus*, here, miracles of various types from healing the sick and materializing things from nowhere, etc. are used to attract people and to prove that they are true-guru (*sadguru*). Sri Satya Sai Baba may be the most famous in this category followed closely by Mata Amritanandamayi and Swami Sivananda. The second group is the philosophical gurus who are known for their expertise in the field of expounding Hindu and other philosophies. In this category include Bhagavān Rajneesh and Swami Daynanda Saraswati,[56] their main center of attraction is their philosophical teaching, and of course, meditational practice as well. The third category, may be the most popular one, is *yoga-gurus* where we have a number of gurus like Maharashi Mahesh Yogi of Transcendental Meditation, Paramhansa Yogananda who taught *Kriya Yoga*, Baba Ramdev who popularizes Yoga through TV shows and camps, Sri Sri Ravishankar with his *Sudarshan Kriya*, etc.

4.3. Most of the contemporary gurus are deeply influenced by Śaṅkara's Advaita Vedānta where some of them follow *in toto*, some others modify it to suit their purpose. Paramhansa Yogananda and Sri Sri Ravishankar are quite faithful to Śaṅkara's Advaita Vedānta whereas Sri Sathya Sai Baba makes an attempt to harmonize the three Vedāntic schools – Advaita, Viśiṣṭādvaita and Dvaita.[57] Swami Sivananda is again deeply influenced by Vedānta philosophy as interpreted by Śaṅkara and his main objective is the realization of 'Divine Life' in human being in a Vedāntic way.[58] Thus, most of the contemporary

---

[55] See J. Russell, "The Guru in Hinduism", in *The Pilgrim: The Quarterly Bulletin of the Christian Society for the Study of Hinduism,* Vol. V. No. 3, October, 1945, pp. 10-11.

[56] This Guru is not to be confused with Swami Daynanda Saraswati of Ārya Samāj. He is the founder of 'Hindu Mission' which is similar to the Chinmaya Mission or the Divine Life Society. He was previously a missionary of Chinmaya Mission. In his headquarters center in Pennsylvania, USA, he offered courses on Advaita Vedānta, Yoga, Sanskrit, Ayurveda, Astrology, etc.

[57] *Summer Showers in Brindavan 1974 Part –I: Discourses by Bhagavan Sri Sathya Sai Baba on Brahman*, (Prasnathi Nilayam: Sri Sathya Sai Books and Publications Trust, 2004), p. 247. Cf. *Sathya Sai Speaks Vol. 5: Discourses of Bhagavan Sri Sathya Sai Baba,* Downloaded in a *pdf* format from the official website of Sri Sathya Sai Sadhana Trust, Publications Division - *http://www.sssbpt.info/english/sss.htm*, (10.8.2012), pp. 64-65.

[58] Satish Chandran Gyan, *Sivananda and his Ashram*, (Madras: Christian Literature Society, 1980), p. 48.

gurus are non-dualists, but unlike Śaṅkara, many gurus adopted personal god and *Bhakti* way of life at the same time.

4.4. One of the most prominent distinctive features of the contemporary Guruism is the concern for the welfare of humanity. Many of the gurus run a number of social centers where they undertake a number of philanthropic activities such as education, medical services, upliftment of the poor, etc. Apart from this, our stressful generation is in need of psychological attention to cure many stress-related illnesses, and gurus come into ease the stress, reduce tension, hatred and bring joy, love and peace.

4.5. Most of the famous modern gurus are running a type of empire which involves huge amount of money and they become immensely rich. For example, gurus such as Maharashi Mahesh Yogi, Bhagavan Rajneesh, Sri Sathya Sai Baba, etc. died as billionaires. So, what Meera Nanda has said of these gurus – "The modern gurus… are practically CEOs of huge business empires"[59] is not without a weight.

4.6. The emergence of female gurus, who are as popular and prominent as male gurus, is another important feature of contemporary guruism. Marie -Therese Charpentier who did in depth studies on Indian female gurus identified seventy female gurus having their own *āśram* and large followings.[60] Considering the condition of women under Brahmanism, this new development is remarkable and is an indicative of protest, if not revolt, against Brahmanical religion.

4.7. Another significant development in the history of guruism is undoubtedly the emergence of *guru-worship*. In Upanishads, Dharma Śāstras, Epics, Purāṇas and Tantras gurus were venerated almost like gods but guru-worship as we find today was not common and the God-man concept, which is most probably the contribution of Sikhism, which is prevalence today was not widespread before. The God-man concept and guru-worship where some of our contemporary gurus have claimed themselves to be the very god or at least the incarnations of gods are something distinctive to the contemporary guruism the parallel of which is not seen in the traditional guruism.

4.8. Caste system, which once characterized *Hindu Dharma*, has broken down under the contemporary guruism. The devotees of these gurus do not only comprise of various castes but also of no-caste as many contemporary gurus have large followings in the foreign lands. A guru may believe in the

[59] Nanda, *The God Market,* p. 92.

[60] See Marie-Therese Charpentier, *Indian Female Gurus in Contemporary Hinduism: A Study of Central Aspects and Expressions of their Religious Leadership*, (Biskopsgatan, Abo, Finland: Abo Akademi University Press, 2010).

caste system, for example Sri Sri Ravishankar who expresses that he sees no wrong in caste system as such,[61] but the movement is definitely devoid of it.

4.9. In the contemporary guru movement Yoga becomes more prominent and many gurus develop their own yoga technique to lead people to a higher spiritual plane. Paramhansa Yogananda popularizes *Kriya Yoga*, an ancient spiritual exercise; Sri Si Ravishankar develops a certain form of yoga and spiritual technique called *Sudarshan Kriya*; Maharishi Mahesh Yogi uses *Transcendental Meditation* as his primary spiritual technique; Osho suggests more than a hundred meditation techniques in total, the most famous of these is what is *called Dynamic Meditation*; Swami Sivananda develops his yoga by synthesizing *karma yoga*, *jñāna yoga*, *bhakti yoga* and *raja yoga* and he calls it as '*Yoga of Synthesis*'. Another guru who is famous for his yoga practice is Baba Ramdev who establishes one of the largest yoga institute known as *Patanjali Yogpeeth* for treatment of patient, research & development in Yoga and *Ayurveda*, as well as the manufacturing of *ayurvedic* medicines.

4.10. Another important distinctive feature of contemporary guru movement is the role of women in the functioning of the movement. In many of the guru movements, we see women as the guru or at least occupying a high position in the movement. For instance, Paramhansa Yogananda was replaced by Sri Daya Mata after his death as the head of the organization, women always occupied a high and powerful position in Osho's movement, with the exception of ISKCON where women occupy the peripheral position especially in the beginning of this movement.

4.11. Many of the Contemporary gurus are associated with miracles which act as an attracting force to magnetize people towards them and also establish the authenticity of their guruship in the mind of the devotees. To mention few - Sri Sathya Sai Baba is popular as miracle-working guru;[62] a female guru Mata Amritanandamayi is also well known for her miracles; Sri Sri Ravishankar also performs a number of miracles. Miracles like changing stone into diamond or silver or gold, healing of sick from cancer, heart problem, mental illness, etc. are reported to have taken place in his ministry.[63] A number

---

[61] *Reader Digest*, February 2007, p. 98.

[62] Nagamani Purnaiya has written a book in Telugu which was translated into English, entitled, *Divine Leelas of Bhagwan Sathya Sai Baba*. This book describes more than 140 miracles, of which she says "more than 115 were witnessed by me with abundant joy", cf. In *http://www.saibaba.ws/miracles2/abookonhim.htm,* (27.07.2011). For details, see Nagamani Purnaiya, *Divine Leelas of Bhagwan Sathya Sai Baba*, (Puttaparthi: Sri Sathya Sai Towers Pvt. Ltd. 1998). Lists of numerous miracles performed by Sri Sathya Sai Baba can be seen in the website: *http://www.saibaba.ws/miracles.htm.* Cf. also Howard Murphet, *Sai Baba: Man of Miracles*, (Delhi: Macmillan, 1975).

[63] For further study on miracles of Sri Sri Ravishankar, see Francois Gautier, *The Guru of Joy*, where chapter ten of this book talks about miracles associated with Sri Sri Ravishankar. See for miracles, Sri Sri Ravi Shankar, *An Intimate Note to the Seeker Volume 4,* p. 80; Sri Sri

of miracles have been associated with Swami Sivananda as well though he taught that 'miracles' are not primary in human's life.[64]

4.12. One of the most significant features of the contemporary guruism is the emphasis on peace and harmony among the various religious groups of the world. Cordial inter-faith relations seem to be one of the main concerns of these gurus. It is a well-known fact that Hindus, through the ages, by and large are religiously tolerant and accommodative, so it is no surprise that these gurus are positive towards other faiths. However, the inclusion of people of other faiths among their devotees on one hand and their dependence on the Western people, who are predominantly Christians or are deeply influenced by Christian values, for financial support on the other hand, may be another reason that makes contemporary gurus accommodative of other religions. In any case, there can be no contention that most, if not all, of the contemporary gurus are in possession of reverence and appreciation of other religious traditions that make them attach importance to religious masters including Jesus Christ. Therefore, one of the most significant features of the modern guruism which makes it different from the traditional guru institution is the importance given to Jesus Christ as we shall see in the following discussion.

Concluding Remarks

Guruism is intrinsic to Hinduism. It was there right from the Vedas. More importance is given to Guru in Upaniṣadic era, and *Smṛti* literature shows a growth in the importance and prominence of guru which culminates in *Tantras* where guru is treated more or less like god. In the time of Tantras an important development took place in gurusim where guru is not only a religious teacher, but also the founder of a religious sect. This trend continues in the contemporary guru movement. The contemporary guruism has retained the nature of guruship of the olden days to a great extent but also exhibited distinctiveness in many areas. Poverty and spirituality have no more connection in the vision of contemporary gurus. With the emergence of *Advaitic* spirituality as the leading theological and philosophical force, the concept of guru as a teacher of Vedic corpus, who uplifts the devotees' spiritual status to the realization of God is not

---

Ravi Shankar, *An Intimate Note to the Sincere Seeker, Volume 5*, compiled by Anne Elixhauser & Bill Hayden, (Bangalore: Vyakti Vikas Kendra, 2002), pp. 31, 68, 77, 84, 97; also Sri Sri Ravi Shankar, *An Intimate Note to the Seeker Volume 6*, compiled by Bill Hayden and Anne Elixhauser, (Bangalore: Vyakti Vikas Kendra, 2002), pp. 25, 27, 65; Sri Sri Ravi Shankar, *An Intimate Note to the Seeker Volume 1*, compiled by David L. Burge, (Santa Barbara: Art of Living Foundation, 2002; first published in 1997), p. 61. Also Sri Sri Ravi Shankar, *An Intimate Note to the Seeker Volume 2*, compiled by David L. Burge, (Santa Barbara: Art of Living Foundation, 2000), p. 66.

[64] For details of Swami Sivananda's miracle, see *Miracles of Sivananda*, Third Edition (Shivanandanagar: A Divine Life Society Publication, 1992).

occupying a central place in modern guruism as many gurus claim themselves to be the very God and demand worship from their devotees. Each guru runs a sort of a sectarian group away from the masses and is no longer trying to be faithful to the Vedic or traditional practices, in fact some gurus show rebellious attitude towards both of these. They run a kind of small empire where the gurus are emperors commanding loyalty, devotion and wealth of their multitude of devotees, in turn the devotees are contented with the joy, peace and miraculous healing they experience with their gurus.

Hindu religious tradition with its un-orthodox and liberal characters foster the growth of guruism in our contemporary time where any charismatic person with a mystic gift can start a movement, teaching a new doctrine, developing a new spiritual technique without being criticized. The decline of Brahmanism and caste system gives more opportunity for the modern gurus to exercise their power which is to a great extent fueled by globalization and economic liberalization that paved the way for the middle class Indians who received economic blessing from this to become more religious and promotes tremendously the growth of guruism. Many Westerners who have given up hope in Christianity as well as in secular ideologies have less choice as they see the futility of materialistic pursuit for the fulfillment of their life. So, the new message and technique propagated by the Indian spiritual giants seems to be most appealing to them. They embrace it with full devotion. In this way the contemporary world in general and India in particular witnesses the burgeoning of guruism where a number of gurus, authentic and fake ones, plant their religious and spiritual seed in the fertile soil of India and the West.

Chapter 2

Jesus Christ in the Thoughts of Modern Hindu Thinkers and Neo-Vedantins

A Brief Survey

The Gospel of Jesus Christ is believed to have reached the Indian soil in the first century of the Christian era itself with one of the twelve apostles Thomas landed in India in the middle of the first century C.E.[1] There is a long tradition in India, the authenticity of which is not possible to ascertain though, that Jesus came to India as a youth, spent 14-18 years, travelled widely, preaching to people and learning from the Indian spiritual masters both belonging to Buddhism and Hinduism and returned to Palestine at the age of around thirty to minister to the people there, an assumption endorsed by most of the modern Indian gurus.[2] So, it is no wonder that Jesus is familiar in India and may be

---

[1] See A.M. Mundadan, *History of Christianity in India, Vol. 1*, (Bangalore: Theological Publications in India, 1984); Stephen Neill, *A History of Christianity in India: The Beginnings to A.D. 1707*, (London: Cambridge University Press, 1984); C.V. Cheriyan, *History of Christianity in Kerala*, (Kottayam: Kerala Historical Society, 1973); P.V. Mathew, *Acta Indica: (The Acts of St. Thomas in India)*, (Ernakulam: P.V. Mathew, 1986).

[2] A number of works have been published on the issue that Jesus had lived in India and most of the Hindu leaders, except Swami Vivekananda who vehemently opposed to this theory, including most of the contemporary gurus believed in this theory. Cf. Paramhansa Yogananda, *The Second Coming of Christ: The Resurrection of the Christ Within You – A Revelatory Commentary on the Original Teachings of Jesus, Vol. 1,* (Los Angeles: Self-Realization Fellowship, 2004), pp. 80f; Sri Sathya Sai Baba, *"Be Like Jesus": The Good News of Jesus*, compiled by Debra and William Miller, (Prashanthi Nilayam: Sri Sathya Sai Sadhana Trust, Publication Division, 2009), p. 19; Sri Sri Ravishankar, *Wisdom for the New Millennium,* (Mumbai: Jaico Publishing House, 2005), pp. 124-127. For detail study ref. Nicholas Notovitch, *The Unknown Life of Jesus Christ*, translated from French by Alexina Loranger, Fourth Edition, (Chicago: Indo-American Book Agency, 1916); Holger Kersten, *Jesus Lived in India: His Unknown Life Before and After*

because of such a familiarity or may be because of his worldwide popularity or may be because of the influence of Western missionaries or still may be because of the influence of the Western colonizers such as the English, French, Danish and Portuguese who were all predominantly Christians and rulers of India for some two hundred years,[3] many spiritual leaders, mostly Hindus were somehow drawn to Jesus Christ that made them interpret in their own way the person, works and message of Jesus Christ. This chapter gives an overview of these interpretations.

There are a number of Hindu spiritual leaders and philosophers who have positive attitude towards Jesus Christ and make attempts to interpret his life, works and message in relation to Hindu religious thought, deviating from the traditional and orthodox Christian interpretations. Hindu reformers like Raj Rammohun Roy, Keshub Chunder Sen, Pratap Chander Mozoomdar and Mahatma Gandhi are well known in their attempts to present Christ to Indian populace as they feel that the Western interpretation of Christ is not only unsuitable for India, but also misses the real Jesus who is Asiatic, that needs a contextual interpretation, in relation to Asian context. Likewise, the hosts of Neo-Vedāntins who are mostly the leaders of Ramakrishna Order also make genuine attempts to understand Jesus and present him in relation to Neo-Vedānta school of Philosophy. Swami Vivekananda, the founder of Ramakrishna Order, Swami Abhedananda who is the contemporary of Swami Vivekananda, S. Radhakrishnan, a well known philosopher and religious thinker, who is not of Ramakrishna movement, and other leaders of Ramakrishna movement like Swami Akhilananda, Swami Prabhavananda, Swami Satprakashnanda, Swami Ranganathananda are prominent Neo-Vedāntins who interpret Jesus Christ.

For our survey I select three Hindu reformers such as, Raja Rammohun Roy, Keshub Chunder Sen and Mahatma Gandhi, and three Neo-Vedāntins namely, Swami Vivekananda, Swami Akhilananda and S. Radhakrishnan to discuss their interpretations of Jesus Christ comprehensively, leaving the rest of the names mentioned above including P.C. Mozoomdar, Swami Abhedananda, Swami Prabhavananda, Swami Satprakashnanda, and Swami Ranganathananda.[4]

---

the Crucifixion, (New Delhi: Penguin Books India Pvt. Ltd., 2001); Swami Abhedananda, *Journey to Kashmir and Tibet*, (Calcutta: Ramakrishna Vedānta Math, 1987); Elizabeth Clare Prophet, *The Lost Years Of Jesus: Documentary Evidence Of Jesus' 17-Year Journey to the East*, (Gardiner: Summit University Press, 1984); Alan Jacobs, *When Jesus Lived in India: The Quest for the Aquarian Gospel: The Mystery of the Missing Year*, (Mumbai: Yogi Impression, 2010).

[3] For factors responsible for the Indian awareness of Jesus Christ, cf. P. Fallon, S.J, "A Critical Evaluation of Hindu Interpretation of Christ" in *Indian Journal of Theology*, (Vol. 18, No.1 January-March, 1969), p. 81.

[4] For a detailed study of Mozoomdar's interpretation of Christ, see P.C. Mozoomdar, *The Oriental Christ*, (Boston: Geo. H. Ellis, 1883). For a detailed study of Swami Abhedananda's understanding of Jesus Christ, see Swami Abhedananda, *Why a Hindu Accepts Christ and Rejects Christianity*, (Calcutta: Ramakrishna Vedānta Society, n.d.); Swami Abhedananda, *Who*

The writer is quite aware that it is not really possible to differentiate between Hindu reformers and Neo-Vedāntins as both of these are Hindu reformers and also to some extent the Neo-Vedāntins. However, this differentiation is made just for clarity sake where the first category represents those leaders who made great contribution in the Hindu reformation and the emergence of the so-called 'Neo-Hinduism', and the second category represents those people who used Vedānta philosophy more in their philosophical and theological endeavours and may not be regarded strictly as 'Hindu reformer' like Sri Radhakrishnan and Swami Akhilananda; Swami Vivekananda, of course, is definitely regarded as a Hindu reformer.

1. Jesus Christ in Renascent Hinduism: Select Hindu Reformers

There are various factors responsible for the renaissance of Hinduism in the nineteenth century C.E. that includes among others, the advancement of Western scientific education, the Christian missionary enterprise, the oppressive nature of British administration and the inherent vitality of the long spiritual tradition of Hinduism.[5] Consequently there arose in this period a number of reformers, teachers, saints and scholars who purified Hinduism by denouncing some of its non-essentials and confirming its ancient truths. In this reform movement, the contribution of Jesus Christ is considered as vital as many of the reformers make use of his precepts and examples which are adopted as a model for righteous living. Unlike the Neo-Vedāntins who emphasize mystic experience of oneness with Jesus, the reformers, especially Raja Rammohun Roy and Mahatma Gandhi concentrate on the ethical and moral value of Jesus' teaching as M.M. Thomas puts it: "Brahmo approaches to Jesus Christ were attempts to understand him within the framework of Hindu theism and its struggle ontologically to comprehend the absolute the divine personality and

---

is the Saviour of Souls?, (Calcutta: Ramakrishna Vedānta Society, n.d.); Swami Abhedananda, *The Great Saviours of the World*, (Calcutta: Ramakrishna Vedānta Math, 1977); Swami Abhedananda, *The Word and the Cross in Ancient India*, (Calcutta: Ramakrishna Vedānta Society, 1938). For a detailed study of Swami Prabhavananda's interpretation of Jesus, see Swami Prabhavananda, *The Sermon on the Mount according to Vedānta,* (Madras: Sri Ramakrishna Math, 1979). For a detailed study of Swami Satprakashananda's presentation of Jesus Christ, see Swami Satprakashananda, *Hinduism and Christianity: Jesus Christ and his Teachings in the Light of Vedānta*, (St. Louis: Vedānta Society of St. Louis, 1975). For a detailed study of Swami Ranganathananda's interpretation of Christ, see Swami Ranganathananda, *The Christ We Adore*, (Calcutta: Ramakrishna Mission Institute of Culture, 1969).

[5] Cf. D.S. Sarma, *Studies in the Renaissance of Hinduism in the Nineteenth and Twentieth Centuries*, (Benares: Benares Hindu University, 1944), p. 68-69; Lajpat Rai, *Young India: An Interpretation and a History of the Nationalist Movement from Within*, (London: Home Rule for India League, British Auxiliary, 1917), pp. 8-33. Cf. for more on India under the British rule, R.C. Vermani, *Colonialism and Nationalism in India*, (New Delhi: Gitanjali Publishing Home, 2000), and also V.D. Mahajan, *The Nationalist Movement in India,* (New Delhi: Sterling Publishers Pvt. Ltd., 1979).

the relative human persons."[6] In this section I select three Hindu reformers such as, Raja Rammohun Roy, Keshub Churder Sen and Mahatma Gandhi to see their interpretations of Jesus Christ.

1.1. Raja Rammohun Roy: *The Precepts of Jesus*

Raja Rammohun Roy (1772–1833)[7] was a zealous Hindu, proud of the India's past and of his race, eager to conserve all that is good and great in his ancestral religion, greatly influenced by Islamic Unitarianism and deeply affected by Upaniṣadic Vedānta thought and highly appreciative of Jesus' ethical teachings. He was the founder of the Brāhmo Samāj, a socio-religious, and educational reformer, the pioneer of the modern Indian renaissance, whose "opposition to the Christian missionaries attacking Hinduism was as great as his opposition to Hindu orthodoxy which defended the evil and corrupt practices of that religion."[8] So, he devoted his entire life to address this dual target – defending Hinduism from the attack of missionaries and attacking Hindu orthodoxy that defended evil practices.

Roy may be the first Hindu who had shown deep appreciation to Jesus Christ and interpreted his life and message in a systematic way. His understanding of Jesus comes to us through the publication of his controversial booklet - *The Precepts of Jesus, the Guide to Peace and Happiness*[9] in 1820 and the subsequent debates between him and the Baptist Missionaries at Serampore. Roy collected ethical teachings of Jesus found in the four gospels and published it because he found the ethical teachings of Christ better tools for social reformation than any other doctrines he had come across.[10] This publication evoked stern response from the Baptist missionaries at Serampore, who thought that Roy has perverted Christ's teaching in separating the moral teachings from the historical and miraculous account. They felt that Roy did

---

[6] M.M. Thomas, *The Acknowledged Christ of the Indian Renaissance*, (Madras: CLS, 1970), p. 115.

[7] For details about his life and work see B.N. Dasgupta, *The Life & Times of Rajah Rammohan Roy,* (New Delhi: Ambika Publication, 1980); S.R. Bakshi, *Raja Rammohan Roy: Pathmaker of India*, (New Delhi: Om Publications, 2001); Sarma, *Studies in the Renaissance of Hinduism in the Nineteenth and Twentieth Centuries*; J.N. Farquhar, *The Modern Religious Movement in India*, (New York: Mackmillan Co., 1915).

[8] Sarma, *Studies in the Renaissance of Hinduism in the Nineteenth and Twentieth Centuries,* p. 72.

[9] The full title the book is *Precepts of Jesus, the Guide to Peace and Happiness, Extracted from the Book of the New Testament Ascribed to the Four Evangelists (with translations into Sanskrit and Bengalese)*, cf. Raja Rammohun Roy "The Precepts of Jesus: The Guide to peace and Happiness; Extracted from the Books of the New Testament, Ascribed to the Four Evangelists", in *The English Works of Raja Rammohun Roy*, edited by Kalidas Nag and Debajyoti Burman, (Calcutta: Sadharan Brahmo Samaj, 1995).

[10] Farquhar, *The Modern Religious Movement in India*, p. 32.

not understand the full meaning of Christ and His message.[11] In response to the missionary criticisms published in a Journal *Friend of India*, Roy brought out three booklets between 1920-1923, under the title *An Appeal to Christian Public in Defense of the Precept of Jesus;* the first *Appeal* is 18 pages long, the second 112 and the third, the *Final Appeal* is nearly 200 pages.[12] These '*Appeals…*' become our important source for understanding Roy's interpretation of Jesus Christ.

Rammohun Roy has three ideas that shape and control his religious thought: *Firstly*, a monotheistic faith in the oneness of God influenced most probably by Islamic monotheism; *secondly*, the conviction that morality is the essence of true religion, and *thirdly*, a belief in rationalism which demands that religion should hold only to beliefs which are reasonable. This makes Roy reject superstition, mysteries and the significance of miracles.[13] When he considers Jesus and his works, these three religious ideas evidently play a significant role.

1.1.1. Precepts of Jesus: For Salvation of Humanity

For Rammohun Roy, the significance of Jesus Christ lies neither in his death and resurrection as the orthodox Christians project it nor in his miracles, nor himself being the Son of God nor the incarnation of God, nor being himself God, but in his moral and ethical teachings – in the precepts. He dares to maintain that the precepts of Christ are superior to all other religious teachings – "No other religion can produce anything that may stand in competition with the precepts of Jesus, much less that can be pretended to be superior to them."[14] The precepts of Jesus are not only a guide for peace and happiness, but are, for those who obey, absolutely commanded as indispensable and all-sufficient to inherit eternal life. So, Roy argues that the teachings of Jesus, like moral doctrines taught in the Sermon on the Mount, are all necessary for salvation.[15] He maintains that Jesus' precepts should not be considered similar with other

[11] For details on the controversy and debate between Roy and the Serampore Baptist missionaries represented by Joshua Marshman, see B.N. Dasgupta, *The Life & Times of Raja Rammohun Roy*, pp. 235-291, and also Thomas, *The Acknowledged Christ of the Indian Renaissance*, pp. 1-38; Cromwell Crawford, "Raja Ram Mohan Roy's Attitude toward Christians and Christianity", in *Neo-Hindu Views of Christianity*, edited by Arvind Sharma, (Leiden: Brill Academic Publishers, 1988), pp. 16-65.

[12] Thomas, *The Acknowledged Christ of the Indian Renaissance*, p. 2.

[13] Cf. *Ibid.*, pp. 2-3.

[14] Raja Rammohun Roy, "Second Appeal to the Christian Public in Defence of 'The Precepts of Jesus'", in *The English Works of Raja Rammohun Roy*, edited by Kalidas Nag and Debajyoti Burman, (Calcutta: Sadharan Brahmo Samaj, 1995), p. 44.

[15] Raja Rammohun Roy , "An Appeal to the Christian Public in Defence of 'The Precepts of Jesus'", in *The English Works of Raja Rammohun Roy*, edited by Kalidas Nag and Debajyoti Burman, (Calcutta: Sadharan Brahmo Samaj, 1995), p. 64.

codes of moral law given by the ancient philosophers of Greece, Egypt and India, but the precepts preached by Jesus are sufficient to lead humans to eternal peace and happiness.[16]

1.1.2. Orthodox Christian Doctrines Rejected

Rammohun Roy rejects most of the fundamental Christian doctrines including Jesus as the Son of God, the Incarnation of God, and the doctrine of trinity[17] on the ground that accepting it will create problem with his strict Unitarian belief. He uses for Jesus Christ phrases like 'our gracious Saviour', 'the Saviour', 'the Redeemer', 'the Divine Teacher', 'the greatest of all prophets', etc., without elaborating their meaning and significance in his religious thought.[18] He consistently maintains, by citing numerous verses mainly from the Gospel of John, that Jesus was inferior to God,[19] and concludes that "Jesus spoke himself throughout all the scriptures only as the promised Messiah,"[20] who is "produced by the Supreme Deity among created Beings."[21] He rejects rightly the doctrine of trinity as it is contrary to his firm monotheistic belief. The only oneness they have as a Son and a Father is the union of will and design.[22]

Another significant point in Roy's interpretation of Jesus is his rejection of the death of Jesus on the cross as a vicarious sacrifice for the atonement of the sins of human beings. He states that there is not "even a single passage pronounced by Jesus, enjoining a refuge in such a doctrine of the cross, as all-sufficient or indispensable for salvation."[23] He argues that statements like, "I am the living bread…if any man eats of this bread, he shall live forever," "The Son of Man is come to give his life a ransom for many" etc. are more than a mere statements of facts requiring figurative interpretation.[24] According to him, the idea that Jesus was crucified on the cross as a sacrifice for the atonement of humans' sin is inconsistent with the God of Old Testament who forbids

---

[16] Raja Rammohun Roy, "Final Appeal to the Christian Public in Defence of 'The Precepts of Jesus'", in *The English Works of Raja Rammohun Roy*, edited by Kalidas Nag and Debajyoti Burman, (Calcutta: Sadharan Brahmo Samaj, 1995), p. 8.

[17] Roy, *Second Appeal to Christian Public in Defence of 'The Precepts of Jesus'*", pp. 8-11.

[18] Cf. Philip J. Santram, "Christ of the Brahmo Samaj Movement", in *Religion and Society*, (Vol. 11, No. 3, 1964, p. 9; also Roy, "An Appeal to the Christian Public in Defence of 'The Precepts of Jesus'", pp. 35, 38.

[19] Cf. Roy, "Second Appeal to the Christian Public in Defence of 'The Precepts of Jesus'", pp. 8-16.

[20] *Ibid.*, p. 9.

[21] *Ibid.*, p. 16.

[22] *Ibid.*

[23] *Ibid.*, p. 5.

[24] *Ibid.*, p. 31.

human sacrifice.[25] So, Jesus' death on the cross cannot be for the atonement of human sin.

Rammohun Roy, again, does not assign importance to miracles performed by Jesus Christ and omits in the Booklet – *Precepts of Jesus* on the ground that "Jesus even speaks in terms of reproach of those that seek for miracles for their conviction as to his divine mission."[26] He feels that Hindus will not be drawn to Jesus because of such miracles as "miracles infinitely more wonderful are related of their gods and saints" than Jesus and his Apostles.[27] However, he states that he has no doubt of the authenticity of Jesus' miracles or has no intention to slight them down by omitting them form *The Percepts of Jesus*.[28]

Rammohun Roy is not only pioneer in Hindu interpretations of Jesus but also paves the way for others to foster a non-orthodox understanding of Jesus Christ. So, he is important in establishing "a trend that was to become one of the hallmarks of the neo-Hindu interpretation of Christianity: that of drawing a sharp distinction between Jesus the moral teacher and later Christian tradition concerning Jesus the savious."[29] However, his interpretation of Jesus Christ with the selection of his moral teaching alone as guide to peace and happiness, and his negligence of other aspects of Jesus' life and work like his death and resurrection which are undoubtedly the focal point of Christianity, seem to be inadequate. Here, Samartha's comments is meaningful, "The scriptures of any particular religion have a basic unity and integrity which have to be respected by anyone studying them. To ignore them and to give importance to only those sections in which one is personally interested is to do violence to the integrity of the Scriptures."[30] Nevertheless, the significance and importance of Roy's exposition of Jesus Christ still stand as a pioneer and a path finder in understanding Jesus Christ in the context of multi-religious setting like India.

1.2. Keshub Chunder Sen: *Jesus Christ, Divine Humanity*

Keshub Chunder Sen (1838–1883),[31] one of the prominent Brahmo leaders, has gone far ahead of Raja Rammohun Roy and other Brahmo leaders, and even

---

[25] Roy, "Final Appeal to the Christian Public in Defence of 'The Precepts of Jesus'", p. 19.

[26] Raja Rammohun Roy, "Second Appeal to the Christian Public in Defence of 'The Precepts of Jesus'", p. 43.

[27] Raja Rammohun Roy, "An Appeal to the Christian Public in Defence of 'The Precepts of Jesus'", p. 64.

[28] Raja Rammohun Roy, "Second Appeal to the Christian Public in Defence of 'The Precepts of Jesus'", p. 43.

[29] Eric J. Sharpe, "Neo-Hindu Images of Christianity" in *Neo-Hindu Views of Christianity*, edited by Arvind Sharma, (Leiden: Brill Academic Publishers, 1988), p. 7.

[30] S.J. Samartha, *The Hindu Response to the Unbound Christ*, (Madras: CLS, 1974), p. 39.

[31] For details of his life and teaching cf. P.C. Mozoomdar, *The Life and Teachings of Keshub Chunder Sen*, (Calcutta: J.W. Thomas, Baptist Mission Press, 1887).

most of the Hindu interpreters of Jesus Christ, in appreciating Jesus and having personal attachment to him. David C. Scott may be right when he observes, "Indeed it is abundantly clear in the selections from his speeches and writings ... that Keshub found a vision of Christ himself, beyond the pale of historical Christianity, and that this vision became the determinative force in his own life as well as the source of the 'New Dispensation', a universal religion of the Spirit."[32] Philip J. Santram also notes: "In his expression of personal attachment and devotion to Jesus Christ he puts many a devout Christian to shame."[33] In 1879 Sen poured out his attachment to Jesus in one of his lectures as follows: "I am not a Christian...I have not been nursed on the laps of Christian parents, or have I been brought up under Christian teachers. The country in which I dwell is not a Christian country, or is my home a Christian home. I am not well versed in Christian scriptures, nor am I skilled in exegesis. Yet, must I speak of Christ. My love for Christ constraints me to speak of him. My loyalty to Christ is my apology." He continued, "My Christ my sweet Christ, the brightest jewel of my heart, the necklace of my soul – for twenty years have I cherished him in this my miserable heart. Though often defiled and persecuted by the word, I have found sweetness and joy unutterable in my master Jesus."[34]

Many people brand him as an eclectic which is not astounding considering Sen's attempts to harmonise various religious teachings and practices, especially Christian and Hindu religions in the running of his 'Church of New Dispensation'. Scott says that K.C. Sen "came to realize the validity of both the Hindu and Christian, the Indian and English components in his heritage and spent his life trying to synthesize and integrate the two" and "his spiritual life was nourished by the twin streams of Vaiṣṇava *bhakti* with its logic mysticism and incarnational theology, and a devotion to Jesus Christ, disassociated from the Western trappings of organized Christianity."[35] Here is a brief survey of Sen's understanding of Jesus Christ.

1.2.1. Jesus Christ: God-man

Regardless of all his love for and personal attachment to Jesus Christ, K.C. Sen refuses to admit Jesus as God. He empathetically states, "Christ is not, never was, never will be, God the Father. He is humanity pure and simple, in which Divinity dwells. In him we see human nature perfected by true affiliation to

---

[32] *Keshub Chander Sen*, edited and compiled by David C. Scott, (Madras: CLS Press, 1978), p. xii.

[33] Philip J. Santram, "Christ of the Brahmo Samaj Movement", p. 9.

[34] K.C. Sen, "India asks: Who is Christ", a lecture delivered on 9th April, 1879, in *Keshub Chander Sen,* pp. 198, 217.

[35] *Ibid.*, pp. xi-xii.

the Divine nature."[36] Emphasizing the humanity of Jesus, he says that Jesus Christ, even after his resurrection, went up to heaven as a human being. "He rose exactly as he was, and though now in the high heavens, he retains his humanity in the fullest measure."[37] He gives to Jesus the Christological title – '*Divine Humanity*'[38] which is equivalent to another term he uses 'God-man' or 'Divinity in Humanity'. Jesus Christ is not a *Man-God*, but a *God-man*. A man-God is not intelligible, it is untrue and absurd, a lie and a fiction, whereas a God-man is quite intelligible, a possibility in the nature of thing. In a God-man, "man remains man and God is only super added to his nature. Humanity continues to be humanity, but Divinity is engrafted upon humanity."[39] So, for Sen Jesus is truly human. He says in one of his lectures, "Christ never said I am God. He never proclaimed himself the Infinite Father, the Unbegotten Eternal Spirit. He was simply the Logos, an emanation from the Creator… Yet, there is divinity in Christ."[40] Sen declares, "Let the misguided and the heretical then fling away the fiction 'Christ is God' and proclaim Jesus as the son of God in whom the Father lives and is glorified."[41]

1.2.2. Jesus Christ: An Incarnation

Sen accepts Jesus as an incarnation of God, but unlike other Indian interpreters who go along with Hindu concept of incarnation in understanding God's incarnation as Jesus, he maintains that Christ incarnation is in Christian sense – "As the Father dwells in the Son, not as God Himself transformed into humanity."[42] One of the most striking features of Sen's incarnational Christology that makes him deviate from other Indian interpreters is that for him Christ is the incarnation not of *deity* by of *sonship*. "It is the son we see in history. Not the Creator, the Unborn, Eternal but the First-Begotten Son."[43] As the Son, Christ manifests the Father. So, "Christ may be regarded as a *filial* incarnation of the Father". In other words, the son is the father reproduced, made of the image of the father, in the body and in mind of the son, we see the father reproduced in miniature; so, "The Lord God lives in Himself."[44] So,

---

[36] K.C. Sen, "That Marvelous Mystery – The Trinity", a lecture delivered on 21st January, 1882, in *Ibid.*, p. 230.

[37] *Ibid.*

[38] Sen, "India ask: Who is Christ", p. 203.

[39] *Ibid.*, p. 229.

[40] Sen, "Incarnation", Excerpt from *The New Dispensation*, in *Keshub Chander Sen*, pp. 312-313.

[41] *Ibid.*, p. 314.

[42] *Ibid.*, p. 313.

[43] *Ibid.*, p. 312. Cf. W. Roy Pape, "Keshup Chunder Sen's Doctrine of Christ and the Trinity: A Rehabilitation" in *Indian Journal of Theology*, (Vol. 25, No. 2, April-June 1976), p. 60.

[44] K.C. Sen, "Incarnation", p. 313.

Christ, according to Sen, is a created being.[45] This process of Christification does not stop with Jesus, but continues in order to make all people Christ. "And all who are in Christ are also sons and co-heirs of the Father's kingdom."[46]

Sen's incarnational theology is a clear departure from the Hindu understanding of *avatāra* where the very God becomes incarnated into human or animal forms, and also a divergence from other Indian interpreters of Jesus who always take the Hindu framework of *avatāra* and apply upon Jesus Christ.

1.2.3. Jesus Christ: The Second Person in the Trinity

K.C. Sen confesses that he is too little to explain this 'so sublime, so marvelous' doctrine as Trinity. "These mortal lips, black as sin, dare not touch a theme so scared," notes Sen,[47] but, at the same time claims that he has acquired the knowledge of 'the Father and His threefold nature' in his sanctuary after much prayer where he receives light.[48] He explains Trinity in the form of a triangle as follows:

> Here you have the complete triangle figure of the Trinity, three profound truths – the Father, the Son, and the Holy Ghost – making up the harmonious whole of the economy of creation… The apex is the very God Jehovah, the Supreme Brahman of the Vedas, Alone in his own eternal glory, He dwells. From him comes down the Son in a direct line, an emanation from Divinity. Thus God descends and touches one end of the base of humanity, then running all along the base permeates the world, and then by the power of the Holy Ghost drags up regenerated humanity to Himself. Divinity coming down to humanity is the Son; Divinity carrying humanity to heaven is the Holy Ghost.[49]

A just glimpse of Sen's Trinity reveals the superiority of the Father and it has deviated from popular Christian explanation of Trinity and that is why Manilal Parekh brands Sen's Trinity as '*Uni-Trinitarianism*', saying that he is still under the influence of Unitarianism of his early youth.[50]

---

[45] Pape, "Keshup Chunder Sen's Doctrine of Christ and the Trinity: A Rehabilitation", p. 60.

[46] *Ibid.*

[47] Sen, "That Marvelous Mystery – The Trinity", p. 219.

[48] *Ibid.*, p. 220.

[49] Sen, "That Marvelous Mystery – The Trinity", pp. 227-228.

[50] Manilal C. Parekh, *Brahmarshi Keshub Chunder Sen*, (Rajkot: Oriental Christ House, 1926), p. 148, cf. p. 170.

Sen relates for the first time, though peripherally, the Trinity with the Upaniṣadic concept of Brahman as *Saccidānanda*:

> The Father, the Son, and the Holy Ghost; the Creator, the Exemplar, and the Sanctifier... the Still God, the Journeying God, the Returning God... *Sat, Chit, Ānanda*; 'Truth, Intelligence and Joy... Thus the Trinity of Christian theology corresponds strikingly with the Sachchitdānanda of Hinduism. You have three conditions, three manifestations of Divinity. Yet there is one God, One Substance, amid three phenomena. Not three gods, but one God.[51]

This way of relating Christian doctrine of Trinity with Hindu concept of Brahman as *Saccidānanda* is definitely a stepping stone for other interpreters who develop a more comprehensive Indian expression of Trinity in relation to *Saccidānanda*.

1.2.4. Cross and Resurrection

K.C. Sen points out how the members of the New Dispensation used to spend days at the foot of the cross, pondering the mystery of the Cross with an earnest prayer, wondering at the miracle it has wrought in the world. For eighteen centuries the Cross has deluged the world with faith, love, and righteousness. It has strengthened many weak hearts, sanctifying and saving many sinners, giving light and peace to many nations.[52] For Sen there is only one meaning of the Cross, that is – "the crucifixion of the flesh, the destruction of animal propensities, the annihilation of the old man (*sic*)."[53] The crucifixion shows that our hands are nailed and cannot hold the things of the world; our feet are nailed and are incapable of moving in the paths of sin and carnality. "It means *Yoga* posture, humanity dead yet alive. The old man (*sic*) in us must die upon the cross, nailed by communion and Yoga."[54] Sen opines that the Cross of Christ is vital for the regeneration of India whose sufferings are brimful. He declares, "Nothing short of total self-abnegation will save our country. I assure you, brethren, nothing sort of self-sacrifice, of which Christ has furnished so bright an example will regenerate India."[55]

Sen accepts bodily resurrection of Jesus Christ but gives a different meaning. He says, "The doctrine of bodily resurrection, which seems to be the corner-stone of popular Christianity, however, untenable on scientific ground, suggests a very important idea. It suggests the continuity of Christ's

[51] Sen, "That Marvelous Mystery – The Trinity", p. 228.

[52] Sen, "The Cross", Excerpt from *The New Dispensation,* in *Keshub Chander Sen*, pp. 294-295.

[53] *Ibid.*, p. 295.

[54] Sen, "The Cross", Excerpt from *The New Dispensation,* in *Keshub Chander Sen*, p. 295.

[55] Sen, "Jesus Christ: Europe and Asia" in *Keshub Chander Sen*, p. 71.

humanity."[56] Resurrection means that though Christ was immeasurably exalted on earth as the Son of God, and though he represented and manifested Divinity in his own character, yet when he went back to his Father, he returned with all his humanity, and still he is with his God as His human son."[57]

1.2.5. The Universal Christ

One interesting part of K.C. Sen's Christology is his consideration of Christ as a universal principle which is not confined to Jesus of Nazareth. This seeming exclusive statement of Sen – "If you go (to God) not through the son you have no access to the father… Through sonship alone are we accepted by the Father"[58] is understood only in the light of the universalism of Christ, which is equivalent, for Sen, to 'the Son of God'. For him, the sleeping *logos*, the Christ lives potentially in the Father long before the incarnation. This Christ is present in Greece, Rome, Egypt and in India. This Christ was the theme of Ṛg Vedic poets. The Christ of the universal humanity, the Son of God is everywhere, in all human beings, in every true Brahmin, in every loyal votary of the Veda on the banks of the sacred Ganges. India is not, never was an enemy of this *Logos*, rather, unto the eternal *Logos* every true Hindu has sworn fealty.[59]

Amid controversies and criticisms, Sen's interpretation of Jesus Christ stands as a pioneering works in many aspects and no wonder that he is considered as the pioneer in the development of Indian Christian Theology. M.M. Thomas highlighted three significant contributions of Sen – He is the one who introduced systematically Christ to the Indian people especially to Hindus, secondly, through him a number of individuals came to a fuller vision of and commitment to Jesus Christ. Thirdly, Sen was the origin of a number of seminal ideas like his exposition of the doctrine of Trinity in terms of Brahman as *Saccidānanda*, or the idea of 'Divine humanity' as that which best describes the nature of Christ.[60] Unlike other Hindu reformers who emphasize the moral and ethical teachings of Jesus, Sen stresses the mystical aspect of Jesus' person and work as the Son of God. 'Love for God', 'prayer', 'sitting at the foot of the Cross', 'learning at the feet of Christ', 'crucifying oneself', 'becoming Christ', and the likes are emphasized in order to get everlasting life. Sen has left a foundation for the Indian theologians to build on a theology suitable for Indian masses and has opened up the door widely for better inter-religious relations in a multi-religious setting like India. Here, Roy Pape's remark stands acceptable,

---

[56] Sen, "That Marvelous Mystery – The Trinity", p. 229.

[57] *Ibid.*

[58] *Ibid.*, p. 240.

[59] *Ibid.*, pp. 237-239.

[60] Thomas, *The Acknowledge Christ of the Indian Renaissance*, p. 58.

"...he provides a very open (yet not uncommitted) basis for Christians engaged in inter-religious dialogue."[61]

However, K.C. Sen sounds ambiguous and contentious in a number of issues. His rejection of the Son as God while accepting the Father and the Holy Ghost as God; his proposal of the Holy Ghost as a Saviour and not the Son; his explanation of Trinity where the Father has always received a lion share which makes it looks like an Uni-Trinitarianism than a true Trinity – all invite severe criticism from theologians. Nevertheless, Sen's personal life is deeply affected by Jesus Christ which makes him says, "You cannot resist his influence; you may deny his doctrines, you may even hate and repudiate his name, but he goes straight into your hearts and leavens your lives."[62]

1.3. Mahatma Gandhi: *Jesus Christ, One of the Greatest Teachers*

Mohandas Karamchand Gandhi (1869-1948), better known as Mahatma Gandhi is as much a religious leader and a reformer as he is a political leader and social activist. His political and social philosophy is evidently shaped by his religious conviction and not *vice versa* which indicates that his religious conviction is the nucleus of all his activities. Gandhi was neither a systematic philosopher nor a religious thinker that makes it difficult to put in a systematic way his Christology as we need to gather and systematize pieces from his numerous talks and writings where he deliberately tries to understand the person, work and message of Jesus Christ. Our attempt here is to collect these fragmentary pieces and put together to make Mahatma Gandhi's interpretation of Christ looks more systematic.

1.3.1. Mahatma Gandhi's Philosophical and Theological Framework

Mahatma Gandhi's interpretation of Jesus Christ is apparently shaped by his philosophy of life and religion. He is guided by his belief in *satya* (Truth), *ahiṃsā* (Non-Violence) and the essential similarity of all religions. In the concluding remarks of his autobiography he states the essential unity of Truth and Non-Violence: "My uniform experiment has convinced me that there is no other God than Truth... the only means for the realization of Truth is *Ahiṃsā*."[63] He even proposes Truth and Non-Violence to be the only method of fighting for India Independence. He says in one of his speeches, "I prescribe only one condition, viz., let our pledge of truth and non-violence as the only means for the attainment of *swaraj* be faithfully kept."[64] In a number of occasions, he

[61] Pape, "Keshup Chunder Sen's Doctrine of Christ and the Trinity: A Rehabilitation", p. 70.

[62] Sen, "India Asks: Who is Christ", p. 213.

[63] M.K. Gandhi, *My Experiments with Truth: An Autobiography*, (Ahmadabad: Jaico Publishing House, 2010), pp. 489-490.

[64] *The Collected Works of Mahatma Gandhi, Vol. 48*, (New Delhi: Publications Division, Ministry of Information & Broadcasting, Government of India, 1999, Revised and CD-

suggests and insists that Truth and Non-violence to be made not only as the policy but the Creed of the Congress.[65]

His philosophy of religion does not allow him to exalt one religion by denouncing the other. The various religions of the world should be treated as "complementary to one another, in no case exclusive. Their true meaning, their interdependence and interrelation, have still to be revealed to us."[66] So, the world can no more do without the teaching of Jesus than we can without that of Muhammad or the Upaniṣads. For Gandhi differences in the creedal aspect of religion is to be there as long as there are different brains. He maintains, "For me the different religions are beautiful flowers from the same garden, or they are branches of the same majestic tree. Therefore they are equally true, though being received and interpreted through human instruments equally imperfect."[67] He admits that there was no such thing as only one true religion, every other being false. There is no religion that is absolutely perfect. All are equally imperfect or more or less perfect.

With this conviction of plurality and authenticity of all religions on one hand and his commitment to *non-violence* and *truth* as the highest ideals human being can achieve, Mahatma Gandhi looks at Jesus Christ.

1.3.2. Bible as the Sole '*Pramāna*'

He maintains that he studied intensely the life, message and work of Jesus Christ.[68] In his *Jail Diary* he writes on September 2, 1923, "Finished reading the Bible yesterday, started reading an illustrated account of Jesus today". After one week, on September 9, the same year he writes, "Finished reading the illustrated account of Jesus."[69] So, it is evident that Gandhi was a devote student of the Bible, especially the account of Jesus found in the four gospels. Unlike some of the Indian spiritual teachers who claim to have direct communion with Christ in a mystical union and learn from such a communion about Jesus Christ, Mahatma Gandhi's source of knowledge of Jesus Christ is the Bible which he handles rationally. No claim he makes of a mystical experience of Jesus. He looks at Jesus rationally and intellectually, but of course, with appreciative mind set and learns from the written word of God.

ROM Version), p. 404. Hereafter referred to as - *CWMG* with volume number. Elsewhere he also says, "I have no other means but truth and non-violence for fighting India's battle for freedom", because only "those whose means are truth and non-violence, have as their guide God who is known as Truth". Cf. *CWMG, Vol. 31,* p. 191 and *CWMG, Vol. 50,* p. 71.

[65] Cf. *CWMG, Vol. 52*, p. 121; *CWMG, Vol. 81*, p. 453; *CWMG, Vol. 63,* p. 509.

[66] *CWMG, Vol. 33*, p. 313.

[67] *CWMG, Vol. 70*, p. 367.

[68] *CWMG, Vol. 36*, p. 321.

[69] *CWMG, Vol. 26*, p. 448.

1.3.3. A Distorted Picture of Jesus

Mahatma Gandhi mentions several times that the Church and Western Christians have missed the real Jesus and that the message of Jesus of Nazareth, the Son of Peace, has been little understood in Europe.[70] He says that the nations of Europe have forgotten the teachings of Christ; they may read the Bible or study the Hebrew language, but they do not act according to the teachings of the former. He boldly goes on to the extent of saying that they have forgotten Jesus himself.[71] Although Gandhi deeply appreciates Jesus Christ, he vehemently opposes orthodox Christianity or the Christianity represented by the then missionaries. He says, "I rebel against orthodox Christianity, as I am convinced that it has distorted the message of Jesus. He was an Asiatic whose message was delivered through many media and when it had the backing of a Roman emperor it became an imperialist faith as it remains to this day."[72] Gandhi maintains that Jesus' message was misunderstood even during his own time, and even today who call themselves Christian do not know the true message of Jesus, "today's Christianity is a denial of his central teaching- 'Love your enemy.'"[73]

1.3.4. Jesus Christ: One of the Greatest Teachers of the World

Mahatma Gandhi's understanding of Jesus can be summarized in one line by using his own declaration – "I consider Christ as one of the great teachers of the world. Beyond that I have not gone."[74] He denies most of the traditional Christian doctrine of Jesus such as "Jesus as God", "Jesus as Son of God", "Jesus as the only Saviour", etc. Then, what does Jesus mean to Gandhi? He answers this question, "To me He was one of the greatest teachers humanity has ever had."[75] Elsewhere, he says,

> I believe that Jesus Christ was one of the greatest teachers of the world. I consider him as an incarnation in the Hindu sense of the term. I do not believe him to be the World Saviour in the sense in which orthodox Christianity understands the expression but he was a saviour in the same sense as Buddha, Zoroaster, Mohammed, and

---

[70] *CWMG, Vol. 15*, p. 160.

[71] *CWMG, Vol. 23*, p. 76.

[72] *CWMG, Vol. 68*, p. 425.

[73] *CWMG, Vol. 74*, pp. 131, 388.

[74] *CWMG Vol. 45*, p. 419; Cf. *CWMG, Vol. 40,* p. 466; *CWMG, Vol. 34*, p. 289; *CWMG, Vol. 39*, p. 65; *CWMG, Vol. 52*, p. 23; *CWMG, Vol. 61*, p. 224; *CWMG, Vol. 64*, p. 368; *CWMG, Vol. 71*, p. 132.

[75] *CWMG, Vol. 81*, p. 261.

> many other teachers were. In other words, I do not believe in the exclusive divinity of Jesus.[76]

Gandhi confesses in one of his letters that while he has the highest regard for the teachings of Jesus, he has never considered Jesus as 'the Son of God'. He puts it bluntly, "My regard for the life of Jesus is indeed very great. His ethical teaching, his common sense, his sacrifice commands my reverence. But I do not accept the orthodox teaching that Jesus was or is God incarnate in the accepted sense or that he was or is the only son of God."[77] Jesus was to the devotees of his generation no doubt 'the only begotten son of God', but that cannot be applied to all. The adjective 'begotten' has, for Gandhi, a deeper and possibly a grander meaning than its literal meaning. For him it implies spiritual birth.[78] According to him the epithet 'only begotten Son' in its material interpretation is quite unacceptable. Metaphorically we are all begotten sons of God, but for each of us there may be different begotten son of God in a special sense. Thus for some *Chaitanya* may be the only begotten son of God.[79]

Again, Gandhi rejects the idea that Jesus was sinless throughout his life but accepts that he is one of those who attained sinlessness.[80] Moreover, Jesus was neither the best teacher nor the perfect one. Gandhi maintains,

> Jesus came as near to perfection as possible. To say that he was perfect is to deny God's superiority to man. And then in this mater I have a theory of my own. Being necessarily limited by the bonds of flesh, we can attain perfection only after dissolution of the body. Therefore God alone is absolutely perfect.[81]

Elsewhere, he also says, "I regard Jesus as a human being like the rest of the teachers of the world. As such He was undoubtedly great. But I do not by any means regard him to have been the very best."[82] So, for Gandhi Jesus was at the most a divine teacher, one of the greatest teachers but not the most perfect man ever born.

1.3.5. Jesus' Death on the Cross: An Embodiment of Sacrifice

Mahatma Gandhi does not ascribe mystical salvific power to the death of Christ on the cross but it has ever been a unique episode in the world's history

---

[76] *CWMG, Vol. 18*, pp. 42-43. Cf. *CWMG, Vol. 41*, p. 19; *CWMG, Vol. 61*, p. 224.

[77] *CWMG, Vol. 29*, p. 90.

[78] *CWMG, Vol. 64*, p. 368.

[79] *CWMG, Vol. 71*, p. 132.

[80] *CWMG, Vol. 45*, p. 419.

[81] *CWMG, Vol. 71*, p. 2.

[82] *CWMG*, Vol. 39, p. 65.

- a magnificent example of what disobedience to the law really meant.[83] Jesus wore a crown of thorns to win salvation for his people, allowed his hands and feet to be nailed and suffered agonies before he gave up the ghost. This has been the law of *yajña* from times immemorial. Without *yajña* this earth cannot exist even for a moment.[84] The magnificent thing is that though Jesus had the power to consume his enemies to ashes, he refrained and permitted himself to be killed for he so loved.[85]

Having rejected the traditional Christian view of the crucifixion as possessing redemptive property, Mahatma Gandhi says,

> My reason was not ready to believe literally that Jesus by his death and by his blood redeemed the sins of the world. Metaphorically there might be some truth in it. ...I could accept Jesus as a martyr, an embodiment of sacrifice... His death on the Cross was a great example to the world, but that there was anything like a mysterious or miraculous virtue in it my heart could not accept.[86]

He does not believe in the doctrine of appropriation of another's merit. Jesus' sacrifice is a type and an example for us. Every one of us has to be "crucified" for salvation.[87] Gandhi plainly states:

> The argument utterly failed to convince me. I humbly replied: 'If this be the Christianity acknowledged by all Christians, I cannot accept it. I do not seek redemption from the consequences of my sin. I seek to be redeemed from sin itself, or rather from the very thought of sin. Until I have attained that end, I shall be content to be restless.'[88]

Jesus atoned for the sins of those who accepted his teachings by being an infallible example to them. But the example was worth nothing to those who never troubled to change their lives. A regenerate outgrows the original taint even as purified gold outgrows the original alloy.[89] For Gandhi not what had happened on the cross that saves, but following the teachings, especially 'Sermon on the Mount' that redeems the sinners.

---

[83] *CWMG, Vol. 8*, p. 483.

[84] *CWMG, Vol. 20*, p. 404.

[85] *CWMG, Vol. 17*, p. 159.

[86] *CWMG, Vol. 44*, p. 192.

[87] *CWMG, Vol. 29*, p. 90.

[88] *CWMG, Vol. 44*, p. 183.

[89] *CWMG, Vol. 64*, p. 368.

1.3.6. The Message of Jesus Christ

For Gandhi the message of Jesus is summarized in the 'Sermon on the Mount', but it is adulterated in the West where it lost the original intention. He says,

> The message of Jesus, as I understand it, is contained in his Sermon on the Mount unadulterated and taken as a whole, and even in connection with the Sermon on the Mount, my own humble interpretation of the message is in many respects different from the orthodox. The message, to my mind, has suffered distortion in the West. It may be presumptuous for me to say so, but as a devotee of truth, I should not hesitate to say what I feel. [90]

This 'sermon' has great impact upon the life of Gandhi as he finds his basic principle – *Ahiṃsā* being confirmed by it. He says, "The teaching of the Sermon on the Mount echoed something I had learnt in childhood and something which seemed to be part of my being and which I felt was being acted up to in the daily life around me."[91] For this he is indebted to Leo Tolstoy's interpretation of Sermon on the Mount which seems to have great influence upon Gandhi's understanding of this Sermon.[92] He confesses that Jesus' Sermon on the Mount fills him with bliss and its sweet verses have the power to quench his agony of soul.[93] He has derived much comfort and happiness from the contemplation of Jesus' life and teachings as summarized in the Sermon on the Mount.[94]

He has the impression that Christians do not follow 'Sermon on the Mount' and expresses his desire to see it followed by Christians as it is the 'whole of Christianity.'[95] Gandhi states, "If Indian Christians will simply cling to the *Sermon on the Mount,* which was delivered not merely to the peaceful disciples but a groaning world, they would not go wrong, and they would find that no religion is false, and that if they act according to their lights and in the fear of God, they would not need to worry about organizations, forms of worship and ministry."[96] His attachment to Sermon on the Mount is so

---

[90] *CWMG, Vol. 40,* p. 372.

[91] *CWMG, Vol. 54,* p. 308.

[92] For details of how Gandhi had been influenced by Leo Tolstoy see K.P. Aleaz, *Dialogical Theologies: Hartford Papers and Other Essays*, (Kolkata: Punti Pustak, 2004), chapter III, pp. 55-82. This book gives us Leo Tolstoy's interpretation of the Sermon on the Mount and its impact upon Mahatma Gandhi. For more see Kalidas Nag, *Tolstoy and Gandhi*, (Patna: Pustak Bhandar, 1950).

[93] *CWMG, Vol. 22,* p. 158.

[94] *CWMG, Vol. 34,* p. 289.

[95] *Ibid.*, pp. 287, 308.

[96] *CWMG, Vol. 24,* p. 291.

great that makes him say, "I may say that I have never been interested in a historical Jesus. I should not care if it was proved by someone that the man called Jesus never lived, and that what was narrated in the Gospels was a figment of the writer's imagination. For the Sermon on the Mount would still be true for me."[97]

It may not be wrong to conclude that the life and message of Christ exerts an indelible influence upon Mahatma Gandhi, though the extent of the influence is not easy to ascertain. His loyalty to Hindu religious tradition, faithfulness to its religious text – Bhagavad Gītā, his preferential option for the Hindu *Dharma* remains unshaken. It is apparent that he takes from Jesus and the Bible whatever goes together with his religious conviction. He appreciates the message of Christ, summarized in the Sermon on the Mount, and exalts it as having redemptive power but rejects most of the works of Jesus Christ like the miracles, death and resurrection as significant for the salvation of human being or the regeneration of a degenerated person. Moreover, he denounces Jesus as God, the messiah, the son of God, having equal divinity with the Father – the doctrines central to Christianity. What Stanley Jones had said to Gandhi appears to be the position we have here - "You have grasped the principles but have missed the person."[98]

One of the most important contributions of Gandhi towards a fuller understanding of Jesus Christ is his insistence upon reaching the unadulterated Christ who is free from the Western colonial clothing. He feels that the Western Christianity has distorted the real meaning of the message of Christ. But, India can give it. As Jesus was Asiatic, Indian contribution towards unraveling the real meaning of Jesus is significant, because "the real meaning of the teachings of Jesus will be delivered from India."[99] Another significant contribution of Gandhi is his positive attitude towards other faiths and readiness to absorb, accumulate and follow the teachings of other religions. He perceives other religious traditions as equally true along with his own, worthy of consideration and absorption for his spiritual growth. He suggests considering religious traditions of the world as a common property. Gandhi writers in *Modern Review*, October 1941: "I believe that He (Jesus) belongs not solely to Christianity, but to the entire world; to all races and people, it matters little under what flag, name or doctrine they may work, profess a faith, or worship a god inherited from their ancestors."[100] The slogan which he coined: *sarva dharma samabhav* (equal respect to all religions) is the outcome of his philosophy of religion and

---

[97] *CWMG, Vol. 54*, p. 308.

[98] Quoted in Daniel Thomas, "What Jesus Meant to Gandhi", in *Religion and Society*, (Vol. ii, No. 3, 1964), p. 35.

[99] *CWMG, Vol. 18*, p. 43.

[100] *CWMG, Vol. 81*, p. 262.

also the life he led. Therefore, Gandhi demonstrates in his interpretation of Christ a model for Inter-religious relations.

2. Jesus in Neo-Vedānta: Select Neo-Vedāntins

Neo-Vedānta school of philosophy is a re-conception of the classical Śaṅkara's Advaita Vedānta to make it more relevant in the modern context. It is similar with Śaṅkara's Advaita Vedānta in holding that reality is one but differs from Śaṅkara "since it tries to synthesise Advaita, Viśiṣṭādvaita and Dvaita, and is also practical Vedānta applicable to social life."[101] Swami Vivekananda and S. Radhakrishnan are highly responsible for the emergence of this system, though there are a number of persons associated with it. It is noteworthy that with the emergence of Neo-Vedānta school as the leading system of religious thought in India, the way Jesus is interpreted also became largely different from the interpretations of the Hindu reformers. M.M. Thomas observes, "Jesus Christ, the Christian religion, and the relation between religions began to be interpreted in the context of the experience of mystic oneness with the ultimate and the supporting *advaitic* metaphysics."[102] Thus, a new way of interpreting Jesus and his message has sprouted in the Indian soil that has added diversity and richness in Indian understanding of Jesus Christ. In this section I select three Neo-Vedāntins namely, Swami Vivekananda, Swami Akhilananda and S. Radhakrishnan to discuss their interpretations of Jesus Christ.

2.1. Swami Vivekananda: *Jesus Christ, A Growth from Human to Divine*

There is no doubt that Swami Vivekananda (1863–1902) had high regards for Jesus. He says, "Some years ago one of your Christian teachers, a friend of mine, said, 'You believe in Christ?' 'Yes,' I answered, 'but perhaps with a little more reverence.'"[103] This is basically because he sees no essential difference between his religion – *Vedānta* and the pure religion of Jesus Christ. He states, "There is very little difference between the pure religion of Christ and that of the Vedānta. You find there the idea of oneness; but Christ also preached dualistic ideas to the people in order to give them something tangible to take hold of, to lead them up to the highest ideal."[104]

However, he also maintains that the real message of Jesus was not properly understood by the Western Christians. "Christ's teachings are now

---

[101] K.P. Aleaz, *Jesus in Neo-Vedānta: A Meeting of Hinduism and Christianity*, (Delhi: Kant Publications, 1995), p. 8.

[102] Thomas, *The Acknowledged Christ of the Indian Renaissance*, p. 115.

[103] *The Complete Works of Swami Vivekananda*, Vol. 8, Mayavati Memorial Edition, (Calcutta: Advaita Ashrama, 1994), p. 114. Hereafter these volumes are referred to as *CWSV* with volume number.

[104] *CWSV, Vol. 2*, p. 353.

very little understood in this country. If you will excuse me, I will say that they have never been very well understood."[105] He perceives Jesus Christ in Hindu terms and tries to explain him in relation to Advaita Vedānta stand point. His religious conviction – 'that principle and not personality is the essence of religion' – is constantly visible in his interpretation of Jesus. M.M. Thomas comments, "What Vivekananda does is to take out Jesus Christ from the religious framework which exaggerates historicity and personality and convert him into a manifestation of the eternal spiritual principle of the Vedānta."[106] This may be the reason why Vivekananda has dealt with much of Jesus teachings but discussion on the works of Christ like Cross and resurrection is minimal. With such a religious frameworks Swami Vivekananda looks at Jesus Christ and tries to give a new interpretation.

2.1.1. Jesus: The *Avātara*

Vivekananda has no reservation in accepting Jesus as an *avatāra,* but with a proviso that there are also a number of such *avatāras*. India is rich in such incarnations of God where Kṛṣṇa, Rāmā, Buddha, etc. are considered as *avatāras*. He states, "It can almost be demonstrated that after each 500 years the world sinks, and a tremendous spiritual wave comes, and on the top of the wave is a Christ."[107] Jesus of Nazareth took human form, not by the compulsion of his past actions, but just to do good to humankind.[108] As Christ is the manifestation of God, so we see God in and through Jesus Christ – "It is in Christ that God will be manifest. God was everywhere, in all beings, before Christ; but in Christ we became conscious of Him. This is God."[109] This is an indication of the fact that Jesus Christ is God as Vivekananda also admits it – "Jesus Christ was God - the Personal God becomes man." If so, the worship of Jesus as God is legitimate. He continues, "God in His absolute nature is not to be worshipped. Worshipping such God would be nonsense. We have to worship Jesus Christ, the human manifestation, as God."[110] He makes an interesting confession: "If I, as an Oriental, have to worship Jesus of Nazareth, there is only one way left to me, that is, to worship him as God and nothing else."[111] He reiterates the importance of worshipping the 'manifestations of God' in the following lines - "These great Incarnations of God are to be worshipped. Not only so, they alone can be worshipped; and on the days of their birth, and on

[105] *CWSV, Vol. 1*, p. 323.

[106] Thomas, *The Acknowledged Christ of the Indian Renaissance*, p. 124.

[107] *CWSV, Vol. 8*, p. 179.

[108] Cf. *CWSV, Vol. 5*, p. 286.

[109] *Ibid.*, p. 191.

[110] *Ibid.*, p. 190.

[111] *CWSV, Vol. 4*, p. 147.

the days when they went out of this world, we ought to pay more particular reverence to them. In worshipping Christ I would rather worship Him just as He desires; on the day of His birth I would rather worship Him by fasting than by feasting - by praying."[112]

But at the same time he maintains, "The worship of Buddha and of Christ constitutes a *Pratika*, a drawing near to the worship of God. But this worship of Buddha and of Christ will not save a man (*sic*), he (*sic*) must go beyond them to Him who manifested Himself as Jesus Christ, for God alone can give us freedom,"[113] which indicates that worshippers should always go beyond the images or manifestations to the Ultimate or God which is the source of all these images and manifestations.

Vivekananda constantly maintains that Jesus is not the greatest of all *avatāras* but inferior to some *avatāras* such as Sri Ramakrishna, Kṛṣṇa and Buddha. He says, "As a character Buddha was the greatest the world has ever seen; next to him Christ. But the teachings of Kṛṣṇa as taught by the Gītā are the grandest the world has ever known."[114] A disciple asks, "Do you, may I ask, believe him (Ramakrishna) to be an *Avatāra* (Incarnation of God)? Vevekananda responses, "Tell me first — what do you mean by an *Avatāra*?" A Disciple answers, "Why, I mean one like Shri Ramachandra, Shri Krishna, Shri Gauranga, Buddha, Jesus, and others." Then Vivekananda states, "I know Bhagavan Shri Ramakrishna to be even greater than those you have just named. What to speak of believing, which is a petty thing - I know!"[115] Expounding the Gospel of John 1:1 - "In the beginning was the Word, and the Word was with God, and the Word was God," Vivekananda comments,

> The Hindu calls this *Māyā*, the manifestation of God, because it is the power of God. The Absolute reflecting through the universe is what we call nature. The Word has two manifestations - the general one of nature, and the special one of the great Incarnations of God - Kṛṣṇa, Buddha, Jesus, and Ramakrishna. Christ, the special manifestation of the Absolute, is known and knowable. The absolute cannot be known: we cannot know the Father, only the Son. We can only see the Absolute through the "tint of humanity", through Christ.[116]

[112] *Ibid.*, p. 32.

[113] *Ibid.*, pp. 46-47.

[114] *The Complete Works of Swami Vivekananda, Vol. 7*, Mayavati Memorial Edition, (Calcutta: Advaita Ashrama, 1994), p. 22.

[115] *CWSV, Vol. 5*, p. 389.

[116] *CWSV*, Vol. 7, p. 3.

He also states that Jesus as incarnation of God can help the devotees. "The Christ who is the Incarnation of God, who has not forgotten His divinity, that Christ can help us."[117]

2.1.2. Jesus - A Growth from Human to Divine

Vivekananda wisely differentiates between Jesus of Nazareth, a normal human being and Christ, the Cosmic Intelligence which is no less than God. Christhood was attained by Jesus at some point of his life. He says, "Jesus attained to that and became the Christ. All of you will attain to that state."[118] Stating when Jesus attained Christhood, he says, "Jesus of Nazareth goes into his transfiguration, and when he comes out, he has become Jesus the Christ."[119] Elsewhere he also states that Christ is not to be confused with Jesus of Nazareth as Christ is the Cosmic Intelligence whereas Jesus is a historical person. "This cosmic intelligence is what people call Lord, or God, or Christ, or Buddha, or Brahman, what the materialists perceive as force, and the agnostics as that infinite, inexpressible beyond; and we are all parts of that."[120] So, what you call 'Buddhas' and 'Christs' are only the names of certain states of realization.[121]

The attainment of Christhood makes Jesus an object of worship. He states, "The Absolute cannot be worshipped, so we must worship a manifestation such a one as has our nature. Jesus had our nature; he became the Christ; so can we, and so must we. Christ and Buddha were the names of a state to be attained; Jesus and Gautama were the persons to manifest it."[122] Referring to the first five verses of the first chapter of the Gospel of John as containing "the whole essence of Christianity", he expounds this chapter and says, "In the twenty-ninth verse, 'taketh away the sin of the world' means that Christ would show us the way to become perfect. God became Christ to show man his true nature, that we too are God. We are human coverings over the Divine; but as the divine Man, Christ and we are one."[123] With his conviction that 'human beings are potentially divine' Vivekananda maintains that we are not essentially different from Jesus Christ in the sense that we can also attain that perfection, the Christhood. He says, "Be not an imitation of Jesus, but be Jesus, you are quite as great as Jesus, Buddha, or anybody else."[124]

---

[117] *Ibid.*, p. 4.

[118] *CWSV*, *Vol. 1*, p. 303.

[119] *CWSV*, *Vol. 4*, p. 213.

[120] *CWSV*, *Vol. 2*, p. 231.

[121] *CWSV*, *Vol. 8*, p. 105.

[122] *CWSV*, *Vol. 7*, p. 29.

[123] *Ibid.*, p. 4.

[124] *CWSV*, *Vol. 1*, p. 483.

2.1.3. Working Out One's Own Salvation

Vivekananda does not accept the idea that Jesus' death on the cross is sufficient for those who believe in it as their salvation. He rather maintains that one should work out his or her own salvation. "What Jesus, or Buddha, or Moses did is nothing to us, unless we too do it for ourselves. It would not satisfy our hunger to shut ourselves up in a room and think of what Moses ate, nor would what Moses thought save us."[125] According to him religion is not sets of doctrine but realization of spirit. "The Christian believes that Jesus Christ died to save him. With you it is belief in a doctrine, and this belief constitutes your salvation. With us, doctrine has nothing whatever to do with salvation. Each one may believe in whatever doctrine he likes or in no doctrine."[126] This is because, "Religion is a growth. Each one must experience it himself (*sic*)... Records of great spiritual men (*sic*) of the past do us no good whatever except that they urge us onward to do the same, to experience religion ourselves. Whatever Christ or Moses or anybody else did does not help us in the least, except to urge us on."[127]

So, Vivekananda explains salvation in *advaitic* term as contained in one self, to search within and realize it. He asks,

> 'Blessed are the pure in heart, for they shall see God.' 'The Kingdom of Heaven is within you.' Where goest thou to seek for the Kingdom of God, asks Jesus of Nazareth, when it is there, within you? Cleanse the spirit, and it is there. It is already yours. How can you get what is not yours? It is yours by right. You are the heirs of immortality, sons of the Eternal Father."[128]

Salvation lies not in 'believing' on the cross of Christ, but 'experiencing' Christ himself. He says, "But if you go to the fountain-head of Christianity, you will find that it is based upon experience. Christ said he saw God; the disciples said they felt God; and so forth."[129] So, personal experience of a mystical union with God, becoming Christ, etc. consist one's own salvation.

2.1.4. Jesus' Crucifixion

To a question, "Do you believe in Christ's crucifixion?" he gives this answer – "Christ was God incarnate; they could not kill him. That which was crucified

---

[125] *CWSV*, *Vol. 4*, p. 45.

[126] *CWSV*, *Vol. 6*, p. 98.

[127] *Ibid.*, p. 99.

[128] *CWSV*, *Vol. 4*, p. 149.

[129] *CWSV*, *Vol. 1*, p. 126.

was only a semblance, a mirage."[130] The meaning is somewhat ambiguous. It is unlikely that Vivekananda denies the crucifixion of Jesus. He rather affirms Jesus' crucifixion. He has no problem in maintaining that a man Jesus, the body was crucified on the cross and died, but not the Christ, who is immortal. This seems to be the result of his differentiation of Jesus, the man and Christ, the divine which the man Jesus attained in some point of his life. He says, "Philosophically speaking, there was no such human being living as Christ or Buddha; we saw God through them. In the Koran, Mohammed again and again repeats that Christ was never crucified, it was a semblance; no one could crucify Christ."[131]

Vivekananda's interpretation of Christ is important not only because he exerted great influence upon a well known person in Indian religion and philosophy by the name Radhakriahnan, and also the younger leaders of Ramakrishna movement but also due to the fact that most of his interpretations were delivered before the Western audiences, who are assumed to have been influenced one way or the other by his message and thus enrich their knowledge of Christ and resulting into some of them shifting their Christological stand. He presents Jesus in Hindu terms with *advaitic* framework that makes him put Jesus as a '*Bhakta,*'[132] a '*Sannyāsin,*'[133] a '*Jivanmukta,*'[134] and a *tirthamkara* (a ford-maker).[135] His acceptance of Jesus Christ as one of the *avatāras*, his insistence that Jesus, with his own experience, shows humans their true reality, that is divine, and his rejection of Jesus being trained by Indian spiritual Masters,[136] a theory which received well-acceptance among the Indian spiritual leaders including the contemporary gurus are monumental.

---

[130] *Ibid.*, p. 328.

[131] *CWSV*, *Vol. 8*, p. 190.

[132] *CWSV*, *Vol. 1*, p, 55.

[133] *CWSV*, *Vol. 6*, p. 109.

[134] Thomas, *The Acknowledged Christ of the Indian Renaissance*, p. 115.

[135] Nalini Devdas, "The Christ of the Ramakrishna Movement," in *Religion and Society*, (Vol. 11, No. 3, 1964), p. 23.

[136] Swami Vivekananda rejected a well-known theory that Jesus came to India, spent a number of years with Hindu and Buddhist spiritual masters, learning from them and preaching to them, proposed by a Russian Traveler, Nicholas Notovitch who visited India in 1887. Vivekananda says, "There was a book written a year or two ago by a Russian gentleman, who claimed to have found out a very curious life of Jesus Christ, and in one part of the book he says that Christ went to the temple of Jagannath to study with the Brahmins, but became disgusted with their exclusiveness and their idols, and so he went to the Lamas of Tibet instead, became perfect, and went home. To any man who knows anything about Indian history, that very statement proves that the whole thing was a fraud, because the temple of Jagannath is an old Buddhistic temple...That is Jagannath, and there was not one Brahmin there then, and yet we are told that Jesus Christ came to study with the Brahmins there. So says our great Russian archaeologist." *CWSV*, *Vol. 3*, p. 220.

However, his inadequate discussion of the Cross and his silence on Jesus' resurrection on one hand, and the negligence of the moral and ethical teachings of Jesus in his interpretation on the other hand make it fallen short of a full flagged presentation of Jesus Christ. However, Vivekananda's contribution in expounding Jesus Christ, though lacks a proper systematic arrangement, is the foundation upon which his younger followers such as Swami Akhilananda and other leaders of Ramakrishna movement as well as a well known Indian philosopher – Radhakrishnan build their interpretations of Jesus Christ, of course, with more systematic arrangement and clarity.

2.2. Swami Akhilananda: *Jesus Christ, the Incarnation of God*

Swami Akhilananda, a monk of Ramakrishna Mission, a missionary to the United State of America is known to be the first Neo-Vedāntin to write a book on Jesus Christ and his message.[137] His book – *Hindu View of Christ*[138] published in 1949 from America contains his interpretation of Christ. Though this book is entitled "*Hindu View...*" the content seems to be the author's comprehension of Jesus and may not necessarily reflect the view of majority Hindus or even the Neo-Hinduism. This book stems from the conviction that Christian theologians have missed some of the basic teachings and person of Jesus Christ, so it is an attempt to present it to the West, basically, the real meaning and significance of Jesus. Akhilananda's main purpose is to establish harmony and understanding between religions and to show the common background of the various religious ideas imparted by the founders of the different religions.[139] Having this end in mind, he interprets the person, work and message of Jesus Christ.

2.2.1. Christ, the Incarnation of God

Walking in the footsteps of his teachers and leaders of Ramakrishna Order, such as Ramakrishna Paramhansa, Swami Vivekananda, Swami Brahmananda, Swami Saradananda, Swami Ramakrishnananda, etc. who had considered Jesus as the incarnation of God, Akhilananda, without a slightest hesitation, states that Jesus was the incarnation of God and suggests that a Hindu may worship Jesus as an incarnation of God.[140] According to him, Jesus, like other incarnations of God, came to this world with a definite purpose and was "fully conscious of His mission as an incarnation and clearly understood the objective of His life."[141]

---

[137] Aleaz, *Jesus in Neo-Vedānta*, p. 90.

[138] Swami Akhilananda, *Hindu View of Christ*, (Boston: Branden Press Publishers, 1949).

[139] Swami Akhilananda, *Hindu View of Christ*, (Boston: Branden Press Publishers, 1949). p. 13.

[140] *Ibid.*

[141] *Ibid.*, p. 17.

An incarnation is called '*trikalajana*' – one who knows everything, the knower of time in three periods – past, present and future. Jesus as an incarnation must have understood what was going to happen and with this understanding he gave his message.[142] Another characteristic feature of Divine incarnations including Jesus is that they possess intense love for the people which is their main tool for transforming their followers. It is the love that even forgives their enemies, which is a distinctive mark of the *avatāras* from all others.[143] Yet again, Divine incarnations, being the manifestations of God, have the power of grace.[144] One of the most significant points which Akhilananda has made of Jesus is when he says, "God is manifested to the fullest extend in Him, nay, He is God." He even quotes Swami Vivekananda to support his point, who says, "If I, as an Oriental, have to worship Jesus of Nazareth, there is only one way left to me, that is, to worship Him as God and nothing else."[145]

Akhilananda claims that a Hindu view of Christ is closer to an orthodox Christian's view than the position taken by the liberal Christians; however, with a reservation that Jesus is not the only incarnation of God. "The Hindu will agree with orthodox in regarding Christ as unique in comparison with ordinary men; yet he will defer in holding that there have been and will be numerous incarnations of God."[146]

2.2.2. Christ, an Oriental

Preaching to the Western audiences who are considered as the custodian of Christianity for many centuries, that Christ is an Oriental seems a daring task; but it is what Akhilananda did. According to him Jesus' oriental identity is demonstrated by the place he was born and brought up and his message. "In considering the teachings as a whole, we find that He was Oriental of Orientals; He was the ideal of typical Oriental life. In other words, He was the embodiment of the ideals of the Oriental people cherished and manifested in their thoughts and actions."[147] Just like other Oriental religious leaders Jesus was otherworldly, emphasizing 'spirituality' unlike the contemporary Greco-Roman emphasis on pleasures and treasures of the world. The Hindu view of life, Hindu evaluations and objectives are completely in harmony with those of Jesus' teachings and other Orientals.[148] The Oriental spirituality is different in the sense that it emphasizes realization of God as the most important thing just

---

[142] *Ibid.*, p. 36.

[143] *Ibid.*, pp. 37-38.

[144] *Ibid.*, p. 40.

[145] *Ibid.*, p. 43.

[146] Swami Akhilananda, *Hindu View of Christ*, (Boston: Branden Press Publishers, 1949). p. 43.

[147] *Ibid.*, p.46.

[148] *Ibid.*, pp. 55-56.

as Jesus emphasizes Kingdom of God or knowledge of God.[149] Akhilananda projects Jesus, like Buddha as a realist who understands religion as actuality, who is positive about the world – an optimist. This is seen in his statement: "Be perfect as your Father who is in heaven is perfect". Jesus believed that there is a possibility in every human to become perfect as the "Father in heaven". There is an opportunity, a way to enter into perfection and Jesus' main mission is to show the way to perfection.[150]

According to Akhilananda, Jesus' Oriental identity is also seen in the way he practiced religion. Jesus practiced religion in two ways. Firstly, he practiced what is known as prayer by Christians, meditation or yoga by Hindus. The second way by which Jesus practiced religion was in his application of spiritual ideals in everyday life. "He was an oriental in religious matters in that one must first have realization of God and then apply that knowledge practically in everyday life…Jesus as an Oriental applied religion in a practical manner."[151] Like other Oriental religious teachings, Jesus emphasized 'renunciation', but renunciation does not mean negation of the world, but it is only negation of false values, a change of emphasis from worldly pursuits to Godly pursuits.[152] In this sense, Akhilananda sees Jesus as exactly demonstrating oriental spirituality.

2.2.3. Christ, a Yogi of the Highest Type

Taking the meaning of 'yoga' and 'yogi' as union with God and the one who attains such a glorious union respectively and considering the power of a yogi to transform the lives of others, Akhilananda concludes that Jesus is 'a yogi', not an ordinary yogi, but yogi of the highest type. An ordinary yogi can change the lives of few persons and help them to realize God, whereas a yogi of the highest type, the incarnation of God like Jesus, can pick anyone from anywhere and lift him/her to a higher plane, a yogi of the highest type can also lift a group of people simultaneously to the higher plane.[153] For Akhilananda, transfiguration and resurrection are examples of Jesus' yogic power – a transformation from human to the divine plane, a manifestation of His power.[154] As a yogi of the highest type, he was full of compassion and love. He did the so called 'miracles' for the benefit of the ignorant people, even raising the dead (Lazarus), this is his ways of expressing his love for them.

[149] *Ibid.*, p. 58.

[150] *Ibid.*, p. 62.

[151] *Ibid.*, pp. 65-66.

[152] Swami Akhilananda, *Hindu View of Christ*, (Boston: Branden Press Publishers, 1949). p. 69.

[153] *Ibid.*, pp. 80-81.

[154] *Ibid.*, p. 79.

However, it is not Jesus alone who performed miracles, a yogi of the highest type like Sri Kṛṣṇa, etc. also performed the same kinds of miracles.[155]

Jesus was the follower of the path of love. He was nothing but love. Unlike ordinary persons who are always seeking blessing from God, Jesus expressed love for God without expecting anything in return. He had love for love's sake.[156] So, Jesus was a natural *Bhakta*, an exponent of the path of love. His teaching was primarily directed to the path of love or *Bhakti Yoga*. Jesus was also a *Karma Yogi*, a follower of the path of action. The acts performed at the Last Supper prove that Jesus also taught *Karma Yoga*. He himself washed the feet of his disciples. He was serving humanity by providing their needs, healing them, feeding them, etc.[157] Jesus was a *Raja Yogi* who was established in meditation and mental control. His whole personality showed the effect of *Raja Yoga* which is the royal method of God-realization.[158] Again, Jesus was a *Jñāna Yogi* whose aim is to remove the basic ignorance of cosmic illusion which creates multiplicity. Akhilananda maintains, "In the statements of Jesus that 'I and my Father are one' and '… I am in my Father, and ye in me, and I in you', He makes oneness clear. He was indeed a *Jñāna Yogi* in the state of superconscious union."[159]

One interesting thing about Akhilananda's interpretation of Jesus is that while some Indian interpreters make as that Jesus learnt some spiritual secrets from Indian spiritual masters, including most probably yoga, he opines that as Jesus was an incarnation of God and he did not need to learn yoga from anyone, He "was a born teacher, He was intimately aware of all ways of spiritual life and development."[160]

2.2.4. Christ's Death and Resurrection

Akhilananda looks at the death of Jesus on the cross with an understanding of the fact that an incarnated God "does not do anything that is not deeply significant"[161] and concludes that Jesus' death on the cross has a great significance. Jesus died on the cross willingly and voluntarily without any resistance though that is possible for him. So, the cross is a symbol of God's love and forgiveness.[162] By voluntarily dying on the cross, Jesus taught the world that aggression is not the method for solving the problems of life or

---

[155] *Ibid.*, pp. 86-87.

[156] *Ibid.*, pp. 88-89.

[157] *Ibid.*, pp. 91-92.

[158] *Ibid.*, p. 94.

[159] Swami Akhilananda, *Hindu View of Christ*, (Boston: Branden Press Publishers, 1949). p. 95.

[160] *Ibid.*, p. 96.

[161] *Ibid.*, p. 180.

[162] *Ibid.*, p. 179.

conquering the obstacles, but used spiritual method to overcome aggression and obstacles, that is, overcoming by the use of a soul force – a manifestation of spiritual power to conquer evil, i.e. by praying for the enemy as he did on the cross, by means of non-violence, by giving blessings for blows rather than blow for blow, by remaining pure, loving, and sympathetic to evil doers - this spiritual force will effectively influence the people at large.[163]

Akhilananda understands Jesus' resurrection as a victory against corruptible life. In the resurrection of Jesus "we learn that until this corruptible life is changed, there is no possibility of eternal, immortal, incorruptible life. Jesus demonstrated that we must overcome the obstacles, difficulties, and limitations of corruptible life on this plane."[164] Jesus demonstrated that the flesh must be crucified in order to ascend in spirit.[165] Jesus established with his death that we must allow our empirical selves to be crucified in order to conquer the flesh and its carvings which alone is the way for changeless immortal life. St. Paul, a great exponent of Jesus also affirms this when he says that "flesh and blood cannot inherit the kingdom of God." The spirit of Easter proves that in spite of the mortality of physical nature, there remains something in human which is abiding – the celestial and spiritual body.[166] So, it is necessary to conquer the flesh in order to attain immortality. But Akhilananda maintains that it is not possible to gain immortality or eternal life by "the mere acknowledgement of this historical fact or even by mere acceptance of this personality, for 'the devils also believe and tremble.'"[167] It is necessary to comprehend the light or the divinity of Jesus which can be attained only when we have the direct or immediate experience of Godhead through the incarnation. When the light comes, ignorance or darkness vanishes and then immortal life dawns. However, it takes considerable time to achieve the dawn of light in us. "Until we become extremely alert and vigilant and tenaciously fight the cravings of the flesh with its natural tendencies, we cannot overcome them so easily."[168]

The moment our inner nature is thoroughly purified, the moment we transform our mind and its attitudes, that very moment the Kingdom of God reveals itself and when this takes place, we will attain immortality. Easter shows us the fact that human can overcome and defy death and reach a stage where there will be no further cause for birth and death. The one who has

---

[163] *Ibid.*, pp. 183, 189, 191.

[164] *Ibid.*, p. 198.

[165] *Ibid.*, p. 200.

[166] Swami Akhilananda, *Hindu View of Christ*, (Boston: Branden Press Publishers, 1949). pp. 209-210.

[167] *Ibid.*, p. 213.

[168] *Ibid.*, p. 114.

reached this state of consciousness is the one who can say like St. Paul "O death, where is thy sting? O grave, where is thy victory?" Death can be defied only when we have that realization of the abiding presence of God in us. So, this is what we learn from the resurrection of Christ that we can defy death only by realizing the truth.[169]

Akhilananda is exemplar in his exposition of Jesus in the sense that he is not only faithful to the written word of God but also demonstrating his acquaintance with Christian theology and some of the most prominent theologians. He is not only the first Neo-Vedāntin who wrote a book on Jesus Christ that shows his seriousness in his approach to Jesus, but also, according to S.J. Samartha, he "represents the world mission of modern Hinduism" carrying her message to lands "which were so far used to send missionaries, not to receive them."[170] He uses both the four Gospels as well as Pauline writings in his interpretation. At the same time he never moves away from the *Advaitic* world view and his spiritual gurus – Ramakrishna and Vivekananda and other leaders of the Ramakrishna Order whose quotations become the cornerstones of his writings. He accepts some of the most fundamental Christian doctrines like Jesus as the incarnation of God, his miracles, his death on the cross and subsequent resurrection from the death – but in all these, he interprets in relation to Advaita Vedānta. Though he claims that his interpretation of Christ is closer to an orthodox Christian theology than the stand taken by Christian liberals but he is still far away from it.

For Akhilananda, Jesus Christ is one of the incarnations of God, an Oriental Christ, who is not only Oriental by birth but also his teachings are basically akin to the Oriental spiritual ideals. Jesus is a yogi of the highest type, one who has attained oneness with God. The cross of Christ is significant as "a moral example for the conquest of self, egoistic and egoistic passions,"[171] resurrection of Jesus is a clear demonstration of the fact that human can overcome and defy death and attain immortality. Balwant Paradkar may be right when he says that in Akhilananda's work we find the attempt to work out in more orderly way, and in a strictly Vedānta setting, the numerous scattered suggestions of Swami Vivekananda,[172] but definitely he goes further towards Christian orthodoxy than Swami Vivekananda.

---

[169] *Ibid.*, pp. 216-217.

[170] Samartha, *The Hindu Response to the Unbound Christ*, p. 61.

[171] Balwant A.M. Paradkar, "Hindu Interpretation of Christ from Vivekananda to Radhakrishnan" in *Indian Journal of Theology*, (Vol. 18, No. 1, Jan-Mar, 1969), p. 70.

[172] *Ibid.*, p. 68.

2.3. S. Radhakrishnan: *Jesus Christ, More Human than Divine*

Sarvepalli Radhakrishnan (1888-1975) is a well known personality in the field of religion and philosophy in the world that makes his interpretation of Christ important. His interpretation of Jesus is said to have been conditioned by various factors that include among others the inclusive characters of Vedāntic exclusivism, a massive national reaction against the West, his thirteen years of study in Christian missionary schools and colleges, the theologically liberal reductionist interpretation of Christ, and most probably by Vivekananda's method of accounting for Jesus.[173] Apart from this, his philosophy of religion, that is, the truth of the religion behind the religion – not a particular faith with doctrines and dogmas, structures and organizations, but 'religion of the spirit' also has a significant place in his exposition of Jesus. He maintains that religions are different in their outward appearance but in a deep down spiritual level all religions are the same. It can also be assumed with fairly high degree of accuracy that his conviction on the influence of Eastern religious thought and practices in the growth and development of Christianity might have conditioned his interpretation of Jesus Christ. With these conditionings he turns to Jesus and interprets his life, work and message.

2.3.1. The Western Christianity had Missed the True Jesus

Like most Indian interpreters of Jesus Christ, Radhakrishnan also maintains that the Western Christianity has distorted the meaning of the person, works and message of Jesus. He says, "The distinction between the pure and simple teaching of Jesus and the developments Christianity assumed in the West is a striking illustration of the difference between the Eastern and the Western attitudes to religion."[174] It is not possible to confine Jesus with Church's tradition and dogmas because Jesus is "the expression of timeless spirit which transcends the confines of churches and creeds."[175] He writes in *East and West in Religion* that the religion of Jesus and Western Christianity are comparatively different. The hallmarks of Jesus' life and teaching as recorded in the Gospels are intuitive realization, non-dogmatic toleration, insistence on the non-aggressive virtues, etc. over against the emphasis on definite creeds and absolutist dogmatism, with its consequences of intolerance, exclusiveness and confusion of piety patriotism in Western Christianity. Again, Jesus'

---

[173] *Ibid.*, p. 77.

[174] S. Radhakrishnan, *East and West in Religion*, (London: George Allen & Unwin Ltd., 1933), p. 47.

[175] Sarvepalli Radhakrishnan, "Reply to Critics" in *The Philosophy of Sarvepalli Radhakrishnan*, edited by Paul Arthur Schilpp, (Delhi: Motilal Banarsidass Publishers, 1992), p. 808.

religion is one of love and sympathy, tolerance and inwardness. He was utterly indifferent to labels and creeds.[176]

2.3.2. Jesus: One of the *Avatāras* – a Growth from Human to Divine

One of the most striking features of Radhakrishnan's understanding of Jesus Christ is his acceptance of Jesus as a historical person, "a supreme illustration of the growth from human origins to divine destiny."[177] He considers Jesus as a great hero who exemplified the noblest characteristics of human-hood, one who brings home to us the ideal of human perfection by embodying it visibly in himself.[178] Radhakrishnan distinguishes between *historical Jesus* and *universal Christ* in his own ways. He writes,

> The saving knowledge of God is not the knowledge of and faith in Jesus as a historic person portrayed in the Gospels. Christ is not to be equated with the historic Jesus. Christ is the spirit of the Supreme, the Eternal Word. The manifestation of this Word in history is not limited to Jesus. Salvation is mediated through the Eternal Christ, the Word of God, which is not to be confused with the historic Jesus.[179]

He accepts Jesus as an *avatāra*, but not the *only* one. In fact his concepts of *avatāra* and the orthodox Christian view of Jesus as the Incarnation of God is quite different. For him, "the *avatāra* is the demonstration of human's spiritual resources and latent divinity. It is not so much the contraction of Divine majesty into the limits of the human frame as the exaltation of human nature to the level of Godhead by its union with the Divine."[180] So, the *avatāras* are the most intense manifestation of the Infinite in us. These *avatāras* differ from general ones in degree only.[181] Jesus, like Rāmā, Kṛṣṇa, Buddha, is an *avatāra* since His love for the sinful in forgiving them at the cross, is of a piece of God's love for His Children.[182] For him, Jesus is a *human becoming God* rather than *God becoming human* and maintains that anyone can become Christ-like, the perfection Christ had attained is attainable by all humans.[183]

---

[176] Radhakrishnan, *East and West in Religion,* p. 58.

[177] Radhakrishnan, "Reply to Critics", p. 807.

[178] *Ibid.*, p. 807.

[179] Radhakrishnan, *Recovery of Faith*, (Delhi: Orient Paperbacks, 1967), p. 147.

[180] S. Radhakrishnan, *The Bhagavad Gita*, (New Delhi: HarperCollins Publishers, 2010), p. 28.

[181] Joshua Kalapati, *Dr. Radhakrishnan and Christianity: An Introduction to Hindu-Christian Apologetics*, (Delhi: ISPCK, 2002), p. 69.

[182] Sarvepalli Radhakrishnan, *The Heart of Hindusthan*, (Madras: G.A. Natesan & Co., 1936), p. 104 cited in *Ibid.*

[183] Joshua Kalapati, *Dr. Radhakrishnan and Christianity,* pp. 70-71.

The liberating aspects of Radhakrishnan's interpretation of Christ lies here, which is emphatically put in a *advaitic* framework as everyone has in him/her the possibility of spiritual freedom, the essence of enlightenment. Therefore, "The divine sonship of Christ is at the same time the divine sonship of every man (*sic*)."[184]

According to Radhakrishnan, Jesus was more human than Divine. This is evident in his remarks:

> He was not exempt from feelings incidental to humanity – hunger, thirst, weariness, pain, temptation. It is not derogatory to His nature to think that he felt genuine pain, shed tears at the grave of friend, or was insulted, beaten, and crucified, and felt the shame and pain of it all, it cannot be derogatory to think that He shared the political passions of His contemporaries and gradually shook them off. It would be to give full weight to 'Luke's statement that 'Jesus advanced in wisdom and stature.'[185]

2.3.3. The Cross of Jesus

The greatest work of Jesus according to orthodox Christianity would definitely be the death of Jesus on the cross which is believed to be done for the redemption of sinful humanity. It is this that Radhakrishnan vehemently opposes. He cannot admit the death of Jesus as the atonement for the sin of humans. "The past guilt cannot be wiped away by the atoning suffering of an outward substitute", so, "the sacrifice of Christ has no significance for a man (*sic*) as a propitiation for sin."[186]

He accepts the death of Jesus on the cross as a real happening with reservation that Jesus himself may not be aware of what is going to happen in the beginning – the death on the cross, "Possibly this knowledge came to him later."[187] Nevertheless, for Radhakrishnan the significance of the cross lies in its power to destroy the 'ego', he says, "The secret of the cross is the crucifixion of the ego and the yielding to the will of God. 'Thy will be done'. Every man (*sic*) by merging his (*sic*) will in the will of God, by losing his (*sic*) self in submission to God, finds the truth of his (*sic*) own self."[188] The individual must experience a sense of crucifixion, a sense of the agonizing annihilation,

---

[184] Sarvepalli Radhakrishnan, "The Religion of the Spirit and the World's Need: Fragments of a Confession" in *The Philosophy of Sarvepalli Radhakrishnan*, edited by Paul Arthur Schilpp, (Delhi: Motilal Banarsidass Publishers, 1992), p. 68.

[185] S. Radhakrishnan, *Eastern Religions and Western Thought*, (London: Oxford University Press, 1940), p. 169.

[186] Quoted in Joshua Kalapati, *Dr. Radhakrishnan and Christianity,* p. 95.

[187] Radhakrishnan, *Eastern Religions and Western Thought*, p. 168.

[188] *Ibid.*, p. 97.

a sense of utter nothingness of all this empirical existence in order to achieve immortality. Only through loneliness can nearness to reality be achieved. We must endure terrible awakening as Jesus: "My God, my God, why has thou forsaken me?" When the individual withdraws from the empirical, he affirms the reality of spirit and can say like Jesus or Buddha, "I have overcome the world". "Faith in such a non-object principle is the defeat of death, and the renewal of life. When spirit is affirmed, dread is annulled."[189]

According to Radhakrishnan, to a Hindu the Cross is the great symbol of the redemptive activity of God; it shows how love is rooted in self-sacrifice. The cross of Christ brought about a transvaluation of all values. The principle of the Cross, suffering without retaliation was repugnant to classical antiquity but was quite familiar to Indian thought.[190]

2.3.4. The Resurrection of Jesus

As in the case of the cross, so also with other events in the life of Jesus Christ, Radhakrishnan uses *Advaitic framework* as hermeneutical tool to interpret the resurrection of Jesus Christ. He attaches no importance to the historical bodily and physical resurrection of Jesus but stresses its spiritual significance. So, resurrection of Jesus is taken as a symbolic act:

> Resurrection is the resurrection of the Christ in us from the tomb of our carnal nature… our present, earthly, mortal nature. The higher spiritual self in each of us is buried in the tomb of the mortal self, but the grave has no power to hold the divine in it, which must inevitably rise. The life, death and resurrection of Christ are an illustration of universal principle.[191]

In the same vein he says elsewhere,

> The resurrection is not the rise of the death from their tombs but the passage from the death of self-absorption to the life of unselfish love, the transition from darkness of selfish individualism to the light of universal spirit, from falsehood to truth, from the slavery of the world to the liberty of the eternal.[192]

For him, the upliftment of embodied human consciousness into the unborn eternal is the meaning of the Christian doctrine of resurrection. He states,

---

189 *Ibid.*, p. 56.

190 Cf. Aleaz, *Jesus in Neo-Vedānta*, pp. 81-82.

191 Radhakrishnan, *Eastern Religions and Western Thought*, pp. 222-223.

192 *Ibid.*, p. 47.

> The physical resurrection of Jesus is not the important thing but the resurrection of the Divine. The rebirth of man as an event that happens within his soul, resulting in a deeper understanding of reality and greater for God and man, is the true resurrection which lifts human life to an awareness of its own Divine content and purpose (*Exclusive language in the text*).[193]

Radhakrishnan may surpass all Indian interpreters of Jesus in the knowledge of the Bible and Christian theology. However, his interpretation appears to be the replicate of what has done before him by Hindu interpreters especially Vivekananda but in a more systematic and organized manner. He criticizes Western Christianity as distorting the real Jesus of the Gospel with its creeds and dogmas, subscribes the historicity of Jesus with the emphasis on Jesus as more human than Divine, an example of a true human attaining divinity which is, of course, possible for all of us. Using *Vedāntic frameworks* as his hermeneutical method, he interprets the Bible, respecting what has been written in it. Though Radhakrishnan does not accept the significance of Jesus death and resurrection as the atonement for the sin of humans, and even declines to discuss these subjects in his later writings, he attaches some significance to both in his earlier works.[194] However, both are taken as symbolic acts where the death of Christ on the cross is taken as the destruction of ego, the resurrection of Christ is understood as a symbol of new life, realization of self and union with God.

Concluding Remarks

Jesus Christ is not unknown in India. Due to various factors like Christian missionary works, Christian schools and colleges, newspapers, radio talks during Christmas and Good Friday, etc. many Hindus are aware of Jesus Christ and his story, and millions of them show deep respect and veneration to him. The Hindu religious view - the broadmindedness and tolerance, the accommodative attitude and acceptance of the theology of religious pluralism that pave the way for accepting other 'saviours' as valid way to God – all help the Hindus to appreciate Jesus Christ. A number of Hindu spiritual leaders, thus, make an attempt to understand Christ in relation to Indian context. From our study, the following conclusion emerged:

1. The Hindu interpreters are analogous in asserting that the Western Christian description of Jesus is distorted due to the cultural and political influences of the West that debar the interpreters to present

[193] Radhakrishnan, *The Bhagavad Gītā,* footnote no. 75, in p. 33.

[194] S.J. Samartha, "S. Radhakrishnan: Jesus Christ – One among the Many" in *Religion and Society*, (Vol. 11, No. 3, 1964), p. 48.

the real Jesus, and that as Jesus is Asiatic, Indian interpretation is nearer to the truth as it take Asian context into consideration.

2. The Hindu interpreters of Christ try to put Jesus within the framework of Hindu religious and philosophical thought. The Hindu reformers read Jesus in the light of the Hindu theism on one hand, and on the other hand the zeal for purifying Hinduism which is polluted with so many anti-social practices, and try to draw the relevance of Jesus for reforming the Hindu social and religious life. They are more inclined towards the moral and ethical teachings of Jesus, though we should not fail to recognize K.C. Sen's emphasis on mystical experience of Jesus. But, the Neo-Vedāntins fix Jesus within the framework of oneness of reality, and stress the mystic experience of oneness with Jesus in the true spirit of Advaita Vedānta; by employing Neo-Vedāntic world view as their hermeneutical principle, they interpret Jesus as a true *advaitin* whose principle is oneness with the Father. By taking the India spiritual heritage as a tool in reading an Asiatic Jesus, the Hindu interpreters are confident that they do a better job in unearthing the real Jesus than the Western interpreters who are farther away from Jesus in terms of religio-cultural and physical measurement.
3. The Hindu interpreters unanimously reject some of the most important and popular doctrines of orthodox Christianity such as – the death of Jesus on the cross as vicarious suffering, equality of the Son with the Father, Jesus as God in ontological sense and Jesus Christ as the only way for human salvation.
4. The extent of commitment they have to Jesus differ, so also the extent they move towards the orthodox Christian understanding of Jesus. While Rammohun Roy and Mahatma Gandhi are rational in their approach to Jesus, K.C. Sen, Vivekananda, Radhakrishnan are more on the mystical experience of Jesus. While most of them accept Jesus as an *avatāra*, Rammohun Roy rejects it; while Vivekananda, Radhakrishnan, Akhilananda take the Hindu concept of incarnation for Jesus, K.C. Sen utterly rejects it, saying that it is not God that becomes human, but it is the 'sonship' which is incarnated. The Hindu reformers are less sympathetic in giving to Jesus 'divinity' – For Gandhi Jesus is 'a great teacher', for Raja Rammohun Roy Jesus is 'a great moral and ethical code giver', for K.C. Sen Jesus is a perfect human being in whom divinity dwells – divinity in humanity. On the other hand, the Neo-Vedāntins, with their *advaita* worldview that reality is one, that is Brahman, are more liberal in ascribing divinity to Jesus. They recognize Jesus as 'divine' but always maintain that 'we are also divine' in our truest being, capable of growing from humanity to divinity just like Jesus.

5. There is no doubt that the Hindu interpreters select parts of Jesus life which appear to be suitable for their purpose leaving aside others that are less appealing to their spiritual aspiration and philosophical interest. For instance, most of them hardly consider the significance of the Cross and resurrection and subsequent ascension to heaven which are apparently central in Jesus' life and ministry. This way of looking at Jesus may invite danger of misinterpretation for religious phenomena should be interpreted in relation to the whole context of the religious tradition to which they belong.
6. The remarkable thing emerged from their interpretations is the recognition of Jesus as one of the saviours that can satisfy spiritual hunger and thirst, that can lead the devotee back to God or give eternal salvation. They do not consider Jesus as someone 'foreign' to them, someone beyond the horizon of their religious experience, but count him as part and parcel of their spirituality. Even though the Hindu interpreters do not give superiority to Jesus, they consider him as worthy of adherence, worthy of making alliance to and clinging on to for spiritual growth and progress. This way of understanding Jesus would definitely add to mutual enrichment, peace and harmony, promoting inter-religious relations in a pluralistic country like India. So, their interpretation, though may not be acceptable for many contemporary Christians, calls for harmony of religions and promotes inter-religious dialogue and therefore, deeply significant for securing inter-religious relations.

Chapter 3

Some Modern Indian Gurus on Jesus Christ
A Brief Survey

Many of the modern Indian gurus, especially those who have large followings in the Western countries, have displayed their attachment to Jesus Christ in one way or the other through their teachings and practices. Though the main focus of this book is to unearth select gurus' interpretations of Jesus where I select four modern gurus viz. Yogananda, Sathya Sai Baba, Osho and Ravishankar, this chapter will provide a brief discussion on the interpretations of Jesus Christ by some of the modern gurus, other than the above four.

1. Swami Sivananda (1887–1963), the founder of Divine Life Society, is one of the earliest Indian gurus who had a certain degree of attachment to Jesus Christ. There is a book entitled - *Life and Teachings of Jesus Christ*[1] which contains Swami Shivananda's teaching on Jesus and along with some of his disciples' interpretations of Christ. From this book one comes to know that Sivananda accepts Jesus as an *avatāra* in the same manner as he accepts Lord Kṛṣṇa.[2] The Cross for him is the "Holiest Symbol of sacrifice and Love."[3] It appears that he simply accepts the life of Jesus as written in the Gospels uncritically. According to him Jesus was God. He says, "Jesus was God Himself. The Holy Scripture reminds us of this fact again and again... Yet... he behaved like any other human being; and while so doing, fully demonstrated in His own brief but eventful life the Great Sermon that He gave on the Mount."[4]

---

[1] Swami Shivananda, *Life and Message of Jesus Christ*, (Shivanandanagar: The Divine Life Trust Society, 2012, first published in 1959).

[2] *Ibid.*, p. 19.

[3] *Ibid.*, p. 34.

[4] *Ibid.*, pp. 43-44.

His Christmas message delivered in 1945 shows his genuine admiration for Jesus Christ: "The great Jesus embodied in Himself the triple quality of *Satya*, *Ahiṃsā* and absolute *Brahmacharya*. During the entire duration of His sublime life, Christ lived as the visible expression of the highest Truth. He was a living witness to the Supreme Reality essentially indwelling in Man (*sic*)."[5] In the true spirit of *Advaitic* spirituality, Sivananda urges his listeners to awaken Jesus within them – "Awaken Him within you. Awaken the Christ-consciousness within you."[6] He lavishly uses for Jesus terms like 'the Son of God', 'a great *Ṛṣi*', 'God-man', 'the Divine Messenger', 'my Saviour' without elaborating them, suggestive of his approval of the Christian usage of these terms. He explains Jesus Christ in the light of Lord Kṛṣṇa's teaching in the Bhagavad Gītā:

> The great *Ṛṣi* that He was, the Man of Galilee exemplified in Himself the *"Sthitadheeh Muni"* Lord Kṛṣṇa describes in the sacred Gītā. Jesus was forever the Self-absorbed Sage, perfectly balanced in the midst of opposites. He never lost His calm even for a single moment of His intensely-lived life. He neither rejoiced in pleasure nor grieved in pain. Looking with perfect equal vision upon friend and foe…the compassionate voice of this God-Man called aloud to all mankind (*sic*) "Come unto me, all ye that are weary and heavy-laden" and promised to "relieve their burden" and grant them rest.[7]

According to Sivananda, Jesus Christ was first to advocate in that part of the world the necessity to shed racial and class bigotry and to identify oneself as a common member of the vast family of humankind where everyone was a child of God with equal rights and opportunities to live in peace. Jesus was agitated against Jewish superiority complex as a chosen nation, having special privileges before God and taught that God had nothing to do with one nation's comfort and another's suffering, and that He was a loving Father to all humankind, claiming no favourites absolutely: impartial, kind and merciful. Jesus sought to break up all differentiation through the gospel of universal brotherhood/sisterhood and all-inclusive love.[8] The message of Jesus is a key to world peace. Sivananda says, "He laid with his own life and blood, a path for mankind (*sic*) to tread. It is essential that mankind (*sic*) should…reflect on

---

[5] Swami Shivananda, *Life and Message of Jesus Christ*, (Shivanandanagar: The Divine Life Trust Society, 2012, first published in 1959). pp. 56-57.

[6] *Ibid.*, p. 72.

[7] *Ibid.*, p. 58.

[8] *Ibid.*, pp. 62-63.

the glorious life of the Lord over His Message. For, in it lies the key to world peace and brotherhood (*sic*)."[9]

Sivananda is exemplar in his approach to Jesus in a positive way. His interpretation is so close to the traditional understanding of Jesus that even conservative Christians may have little opposition. However, he does not betray the Hindu core doctrine – the transmigration of soul from one body to another; he rather holds Jesus as accepting this very doctrine, saying that in the New Testament there is sufficient evidence for reincarnation. Jesus does not deny the law of re-incarnation. Lord Jesus also accepts that Elijah reincarnated as John.[10] In any case, his influence is seen in his disciples who also show genuine appreciation to Jesus and his teaching as we shall see below.

2. Swami Chindananda (1916-2008), the president of Divine Life Society who succeeded Swami Sivananda, the founder of Divine Life Society after his death in 1963, is another Indian spiritual leader and *yogi* who developed most probably genuinely positive attitude towards Jesus and his message. He pours out his adoration for Jesus in the following lines:

> My heart's love and adoration, my countless crores of humble and devout prostrations again and again at the blessed feet of Lord Jesus, Divinity incarnate upon earth, for the redemption of man (*sic*) and for showing man (*sic*) the path to supreme blessedness, bliss and Highest Atomic Illumination. Worshipful salutations to Jesus the Christ, the Son of God, the radiant exemplar of a Divine Life in this world. Blessed indeed am I, a humble servant of His sacred feet to have this privilege of dwelling upon His sublime Personality and life.[11]

For Chindananda, Jesus is Divine Incarnation, the Son of God to whom he prostrates in humble worship as a servant. He is God's Love embodied in human form, which came to teach us the way to attain the joy and perfection of the Divine Kingdom. He lived and taught us to find out the Kingdom of Heaven that is within ourselves. Jesus taught that the realization of the *Ātman* is much more important than the entire wealth of all the world put together, for the *Ātman* is the Supreme Treasure more precious than all earthly treasure. Jesus by His life has taught us that to die in the lower life of the flesh is verily to be reborn into the glorious life in the spirit. We have His significant saying, "He who loses his life for my sake shall find it." The life of *Tapasyā* and

[9] *Ibid.*, Preface of this book, p. 7.

[10] Sri Swami Sivananda, *Practice of Karma Yoga*, (Shivanandanagar: A Divine Life Society Publication, 1995), p. 68.

[11] Sri Swami Chidananda, "Thy Kingdom Come" in Swami Shivananda, *Life and Message of Jesus Christ*, pp. 100-101.

Titikṣa, of self-denial, sacrifice, hardship and penance is the taking up of the Cross in order to follow Him unto glory. Humility, righteousness, compassion, purity are the portals to the Blissful Kingdom of Heaven.[12]

Speaking about the Beatitudes, Chindananda says that in it we have the essence of all scriptures and all the religions. Herein you have the heart of the Vedas and the Upaniṣads, expounding the royal path to Godhead, by dying to the lower self to live the Divine Life of utter egolessness, humility, purity, righteousness, compassion, devotion and surrender. To live in the spirit of the Sermon on the Mount is to imitate and to follow Christ in the truest manner. The one who follows Jesus faithfully shall ascend from the unreal to the Real, from darkness into Eternal Light, from mortality to Immortality.[13] Chindananda benedicts his article on 'Kingdom of God' with a beautiful exaltation to Jesus Christ,

> Glory be to Lord Jesus, the Prince of purity and peace, the Messenger of mercy, the Lord of Love, Divine Deliverer of mankind (*sic*), God incarnate, Who dwelt in flesh and showed by His life the path to perennial Bliss and Spiritual Glory! Hail Jesus, hail Mary, Mother of God! Hail Almighty, Thy Kingdom come![14]

According to Chindananda Jesus is an ever-present Presence, that He is an eternal witness, a companion who walks by us, who lives with us and who notes every movement, every thought, within and without us. Jesus the Christ is not dead; great ones who have merged in Brahman do not die. They step out of the body and continue to prevail, pervading all space as a Presence that is relevant to everyone who recognizes kinship with them. The relevance of Jesus and the Christianity that He taught is His divine presence here and now, and always unto worlds without end.[15] He says, "Lord Jesus the Christ IS; here and now! Christ is Eternal. He has proclaimed this truth to the world not so much by words but by His glorious Resurrection. … O beloved Brethren! be ye also like Jesus and you shall find Christ within yourself now."[16] Chindananda does not attach much importance to the personality of Jesus but the Christ Consciousness which is in the person and what is important for us is to rise

[12] Sri Swami Chidananda, "Thy Kingdom Come" in Swami Shivananda, *Life and Message of Jesus Christ*, pp. 101-102.

[13] *Ibid.*, p. 104.

[14] *Ibid.*, p. 105.

[15] Sri Swami Chidananda, "Essence of Christianity", in the Facebook account created by Divine Life Society Mumbai Circle at *http://www.facebook.com/note.php?note_id=171079982929051* (23.07.2012).

[16] Chidananda, "Christ's Divine Life" in Swami Shivananda, *Life and Message of Jesus Christ*, p. 110.

from the little human personality and ascend into the Christ Consciousness, which is the way to ascend from the unreal to the Real, from darkness to Light Everlasting and from death to joyous Immortality.[17]

Chindananda is not so much philosophical in his approach to Jesus. He loves Jesus and adores him and asks his listeners to have the same attachment to Jesus. We see no deep theological or philosophical discussion on Jesus in his interpretation, but he is a lover pouring out his endless love for Jesus.

3. Sri Swami Krishnananda (1922–2001), another disciple of Sivananda who served as the General Secretary of the Divine Life Society in Rishikesh, from 1958 until 2001, has few works on Jesus Christ. In his Book - *Spiritual Import of Religious Festivals,* there is a chapter - "Christ Consciousness" where he presents his view on Jesus Christ. He admits Christological titles – *Son of God* and *Son of man* for Jesus and says that the speciality of referring to Jesus as 'the Son of man' is that Jesus was 'the son of the *total humankind*' and 'the expression of the total feeling of humanity.'[18] Christ was a great *Yogin*, a Master *Yogin*, one of the greatest *Yogins* the world has produced, a *Yogin* in the true sense of the term. He was perpetually in unison with the Spirit, drew sustenance from the Spirit and operated upon the Law of the Spirit in the world or the realm of matter.[19] Differentiating Christ Consciousness from Christ the person, he states that when Jesus says, "Empty thyself and I shall fill thee," it is not that the Christ as Jesus, the personality, but it is the consciousness that was meant as being capable of filling the emptied vessel of human personality.[20] In order to have Christ Consciousness filled us, we have to contemplate daily the mystery of creation, the majesty of God, the greatness of spiritual life, the stupendousness of *yoga* and the glorious consummation that is ahead of us which is supreme Liberation, Christ consciousness or God-realization.[21]

Like his guru Sivananda, Krishnananda has no hesitation in admitting Jesus as the *avatāra* and considers Jesus' incarnation as "the descent of Divine Power for the overcoming of error on earth and the establishment of the law of Truth."[22] He emphasizes Jesus' teaching over against his person and work, in fact, there is no discussion on the significance of Cross and resurrection. He observes, "The teachings of Jesus offer solutions to all problems of

[17] Chidananda, "Christ's Divine Life" in Swami Shivananda, *Life and Message of Jesus Christ*, p. 111.

[18] Swami Krishnananda, *Spiritual Import of Religious Festivals*, (Shivanandanagar: The Divine Life Society, 2006, Third Edition), p. 192.

[19] *Ibid.*, p. 193.

[20] *Ibid.*, pp. 195-195.

[21] *Ibid.*, p. 203.

[22] Krishnananda, "Characteristics of the Teachings of Jesus" a Chapter from a book - *World Parliament of Religions Commemoration Volume*, published in 1956, in *http://www.swami-krishnananda.org/disc/disc_31.html* (23.07.2012).

life. Metaphysical, ethical, social and individual relations, commonwealth, national good, and all the values of life, are finally centred in the nature of God-consciousness."[23] For him, salvation lies in following the teaching of Jesus, because Christ's mission is to reveal the greatness of God, the glory of Truth, the worthlessness of things mundane, the importance of renunciation and fortitude. "Those who have these virtues are truly Christians, sons of God, the beloved of the Son of Man. They shall enter the Kingdom of Heaven and united with Him in spirit", for Jesus says, "Not everyone that saith unto me, Lord, Lord, shall enter into the Kingdom of Heaven; but he that doeth the will of my Father which is in heaven."[24]

The life of Christ is a veritable sacrament, an outward and visible sign of inward and spiritual grace that descends from the Sovereign of the universe. It is the unbounded love of God that came in flesh and suffered for the sins of humanity to raise the latter to the source of this love. The miracles which Christ performed are indicative of the Omnipotence of Him for whose sake Christ came here.[25] Christ was a great realist when he stressed the importance of kindness, love, service and worship of God as the Father in heaven. He was a great idealist when he asserted that the kingdom of heaven is within. The oneness and the organic nature of the universe is what is made explicit by his synthesis of the real and the ideal nature of human experiences in the universe. God is within and also without.[26]

Krishnananda creatively differentiates the three titles of Jesus Christ such as 'the Son of man', 'the Son of God' and 'the Mystic Christ'. He says, "Christ, the Son of Man, representing the life and voice of humanity and forming as it were the sum, and substance of the essence of man (*sic*), is the Son of God, the incarnate effulgence of the Sovereign of the Universe. It is the crystallisation of spirit that we call the Mystic Christ, the Light that is born to save the world of darkness."[27] Swami Krishnananda projects Jesus as embodying an Indian concept of *Jīvanmukta* who experiences cold and heat, bliss and trouble simultaneously, whose head and heart are in heaven and feet on earth.[28] The whole life of Jesus, from birth to crucifixion, is one tale of the march of the soul to its destination which is the complete unfolding of consciousness. He says

---

[23] Krishnananda, "Characteristics of the Teachings of Jesus" a Chapter from a book - *World Parliament of Religions Commemoration Volume*, published in 1956, In *http://www.swami-krishnananda.org/disc/disc_31.html* (23.07.2012).

[24] *Ibid.*

[25] Krishnananda, "A Sacramental Life" in Swami Shivananda, *Life and Message of Jesus Christ*, pp. 108-109.

[26] *Ibid.*, p. 109.

[27] Krishnananda, "The Christ to the Spiritual Aspirant", in Swami Shivananda, *Life and Message of Jesus Christ*, pp. 113-114.

[28] *Ibid.*, p. 115.

that the central message of Christ's teaching is Oneness of reality. "Christ was the matchless spiritual teacher who pointed out that the Kingdom of Heaven is within. All his other teachings are a commentary on this text. His teaching is summed up by his statement: 'I and my Father are one.' The individual soul is one with the Supreme Being."[29]

4. Mata Amritanandamayi (b. 1953), a prominent female contemporary guru is no less positive towards Jesus and his message. Her positive attitude towards Jesus Christ is revealed from the fact that the birth of Christ has been celebrated every year at her *āśram* in Amritapuri. Thousands of foreign and Indian devotees used to gather at Amritapuri *āśram* to celebrate Christmas with Mata, 'a hugging saint' as she is known due to her practice of hugging her devotees. The celebration is a blend of Eastern and Western elements – bhajan singing, carol singing, dramas and Santa Claus with Christmas message from Amma (Mata).[30] It is from these Christmas messages that we know Amma's understanding of Jesus Christ.

For her, Jesus is an *avatāra*. He is the Son of man and the Son of God. These two titles have no different meaning, but indicate the same thing. Jesus as the Son of man has body, but as he is also the Son of God, he is not limited by the body because he is firmly rooted in the supreme consciousness and beyond time and space.[31] By referring himself to as the Son of man and the Son of God, Christ meant he was both the body, which exists in time, and the *Ātma*, which is beyond time. He meant that he was both a human being, as well as God. "He meant 'I am this (the world) and I am that' (consciousness)."[32] She speaks of the Christ who is living in us today, "Christ is born along with each and every human being. Christ is still alive and will always continue to be. He lives as our very essence. We need to realize this: The real Christ is our inner 'I,' our consciousness. Only when this understanding dawns, will we become true 'Christians.'[33] So, the best way to celebrate Christmas is "to remember the teachings of Jesus Christ and to try to put them into practice in one's life."[34]

Amritanandamayi is firm in her commitment that Jesus is the incarnation of God, but there are other incarnations as well who are as valid paths to God as Jesus Christ. She maintains, "Jesus was God manifest in human form. Amma

---

[29] Krishnananda, "The Christ to the Spiritual Aspirant", in Swami Shivananda, *Life and Message of Jesus Christ*, p. 117.

[30] Christmas celebrations at Amritapuri 2009, in *http://www.amritapuri.org/7414/09 christmas.aum* (14.07.2012).

[31] *Ibid.*

[32] "May the Christ take birth in your heart" Christmas Celebrtation at Amritapuri, 2008, in *http://www.amritapuri.org /2472/christbirth.aum* (14.07.2012).

[33] Christmas celebrations at Amritapuri 2009, in *http://www.amritapuri.org/7414/09 christmas.aum.*

[34] Christmas celebrations in Amritapuri 2006, in *http://archives.amritapuri.org/news/2006/612xmas.php* (14.07.2012).

has absolutely no problem accepting that. However, this doesn't mean that all the great incarnations before and after Him are not *Avatārs* (God descended in human form) or are incapable of saving those who have faith in them." The implication of this according to Amma is that "it is completely wrong and illogical to say that all others who don't believe in Christ will go to hell. When Christ said, "Love your neighbor as you love yourself,' he didn't mean, 'Love only Christians,' did he? To say, 'All others, except Christians will go to hell,' is not considering others due to a total lack of love."[35] According to Amma, Christ's word 'the kingdom of heaven is within you' means that God dwells within us. If heaven is within, hell is also within. It is in our mind. The mind is a very effective tool. We can use it to create both hell and heaven.[36] Amma is one of the most popular contemporary gurus and her positive attitude towards Jesus Christ is believed to have great weight among the Hindus. Though, she does not take the whole Christological concept in her interpretation, her message of Christ must be a great path toward securing inter-religious relations among the various religious groups.

5. A. C. Bhaktivedānta Swami Prabhupāda (1896–1977)[37] later known as Śrīla Prabhupāda, the founder of *International Society for Kṛṣṇa Consciousness* (ISKCON) is another significant guru for our survey on the modern gurus' interpretations of Jesus Christ not only because he had a large number of references to Jesus in his works,[38] but also his attachment to and regard for Jesus were great. More importantly, Swami Prabhupāda is unique in the sense that while most of the Hindu interpreters of Christ depend on Vedāntic world view, he "articulated his view of Jesus while remaining firmly committed to the theology and ecclesiastical authority of a specific *Vaiṣṇava sampradāya.* This both set boundaries and opened up new possibilities for Prabhupāda's understanding of Jesus."[39]

Swami Prabhupāda considers Jesus Christ as his guru. He says, "Once, in Melbourne, a group of Christian ministers came to visit me. They asked, 'What

---

[35] "Christ & Christianity" in *http://www.myspace.com/ammachi/blog/458874693* (14.07.2012).

[36] *Ibid.*

[37] For Śrila Prabhupāda's life and work, see Satsvarupa Dasa Goswami, *Śrīla Prabhupāda Līlāmṛta: A Biography of His Divine Grace A.C. Bhaktivedānta Swami Prabhupāda,* (Los Angeles: Bhaktivedanta Book Trust, 1980); Satsvarupa Dasa Goswami, *Prabhupāda: He Built a House in which the Whole World Can Live*, (Los Angeles: Bhaktivedanta Book Trust, 1983).

[38] According to Ravi M. Gupta, there are nearly 1500 references to Jesus in Swami Prabhupāda's written and spoken teachings. Cf. Ravi M. Gupta, "'He is our master': Jesus in the Thought of Swami Prabhupada", in *Journal of Hindu-Christian Studies*, (Vol. 23, Art. 7, 2010), p. 16. For detailed study of Swami Prabhupada's understanding of Christ and Christianity cf. Peter Schmidt, *Krishna Meets Jesus: A.C. Bhaktivedanta Swami Srila Prabhupiida's Interpretations and Conclusions about Christianity,* (Germany: Books on Demand GmbH, 2002).

[39] Gupta, "'He is our master': Jesus in the Thought of Swami Prabhupāda", p. 16.

is your idea of Jesus Christ?' I told them, 'He is our *guru*. He is preaching God consciousness, so he is our spiritual master.'"[40] Ravi M. Gupta notes: "Thus the possibility of redemption through Jesus Christ is never called into question by Prabhupāda, for he repeatedly affirms Christ's role as guru."[41] For Prabhupāda, there is no difference between Kṛṣna and Christ. He says,

> When an Indian person calls on Kṛṣṇa, he often says, 'Kṛṣṭa.' '*Kṛṣṭa*' is a Sanskrit word meaning 'attraction'. So when we address God as 'Christ', 'Kṛṣṭa', or 'Kṛṣṇa', we indicate the same all-attractive Supreme Personality of Godhead. When Jesus said, 'Our Father, who art in heaven, sanctified be Thy name,' that name of God was 'Kṛṣṭa' or 'Kṛṣṇa'... 'Christ' is another way of saying 'Kṛṣṭa', and 'Kṛṣṭa' is another way of pronouncing 'Kṛṣṇa', the name of God.[42]

Prabhupāda frequently presents Jesus as an exemplary model of an ideal Vaiṣṇava. He cites Jesus as a perfect model. There are 54 places in his entire works where he cites Jesus as a perfect model to follow.[43] Jesus was equipped with strong sense of compassion for the suffering people and tried to liberate them though his own death on the cross. He was a perfect, all-knowing, God-conscious son of the Supreme.[44] For Prabhupāda, Jesus' life itself is more important for his mission on earth than his crucifixion and resurrection.[45] Jesus felt no pain during his crucifixion. Like all pure devotees, he was free from the laws of nature controlling ordinary people as he lived only for serving God.[46] He maintains,

> Jesus, like God, was not controlled by the law of material nature, so at the time of his crucifixion, Jesus did not really undergo biological death at all indicating that the whole event was staged in order to deliver divine benefit to the spoilt humanity. Thus the resurrection story, though accepted by him as truth, appears in a new light.[47]

Thus for Prabhupāda, redemption through Christ is primarily a result of discipleship, and Jesus' suffering is evidence of that redemption. His

---

[40] A.C. Bhaktivedanta Swami Prabhupāda, *The Science of Self Realization*, (Los Angeles: Bhaktivedanta Book Trust International, 1972-2004: Internet Version), p. 141.

[41] Ravi M. Gupta, "'He is our master': Jesus in the Thought of Swami Prabhupāda", p. 17.

[42] Prabhupāda, *The Science of Self Realization*, p. 131.

[43] Schmidt, *Krishna Meets Jesus*, p. 52.

[44] *Ibid.*, p. 44.

[45] *Ibid.*, p. 51.

[46] *Ibid.*, p. 46.

[47] *Ibid.*, p. 51.

unbounded compassion led him to be extraordinarily liberal in inviting disciples, which resulted in his suffering on the cross. Prabhupāda holds that Jesus' death was only apparent, what we call death is merely a separation of the self from the body, but the very fact that Jesus reappeared in the same body is evidence that he did not die.[48] He does not attach much significance to cross and resurrection, but primary message of Christ's life is his suffering, and the kindness, forbearance, and courage that, such a sacrifice requires.[49]

Ravi Gupta may be right when he says, "There is little doubt that Prabhupāda's Jesus is a Vaiṣṇavized Jesus, understood in terms of Caitanya Vaiṣṇava metaphysical assumptions and theological categories such as *ātma, sādhu, avatāra,* and guru."[50] His adoration for Jesus is magnificent. He considers Jesus as his own guru, a perfect model, equivalent to Lord Kṛṣṇa of Hinduism. Though he believes in the crucifixion and resurrection of Jesus Christ, he denies the real death of Jesus on the cross and the subsequent resurrection from the death. The vicarious suffering aspect of Jesus' death is also rightly rejected. He asserts, "Christ can take the sufferings for the previous sins of his devotees. But first they have to be sane: 'Why should I put Jesus Christ into suffering for my sins? Let me stop my sinful activities.' 'No. You have committed the murder; you must be hanged.' Similarly, when you commit sinful activities, you must suffer - not Jesus Christ. This is God's law."[51]

6. Maharishi Mahesh Yogi (1917-2008), the master of *Transcendental Meditation* (TM), does not speak much about Jesus but expresses his adoration for him. He accepts that religions of the world are sailing towards the same goal, so also the teachings of great Masters. He says, "So my message is that of Infinity; Christianity and Infinity both meet towards the end. So there is a meeting point in the goal towards the end - Christianity and Infinity and therefore if they are two parts they meet in the end. All is well that ends well.[52] He states that he has no opposition to Christianity or Jesus, "I love Christ very much and he must be enjoying with all this growth of infinity in the individual life because 'find the kingdom that lies within you' I think has been the main teaching of Christ. And therefore, *Transcendental Meditation* which takes the awareness to that level which Christ wanted every Christian to have, is only a friend of Christianity."[53]

---

[48] Gupta, "'He is our master': Jesus in the Thought of Swami Prabhupāda", pp. 17-18.

[49] *Ibid.*, p. 18.

[50] *Ibid.*

[51] "Understanding Kṛṣṇa and Christ" in *http://theharekrishnamovement.wordpress.com /2012/04/08/ understanding -krsna-and-christ-2/#more-3139*, (24.07.2012).

[52] In a Video record of Interview with him, in *http://www.youtube.com/watch?v=AIWqJ8tJ8JU*, (27.07.2012).

[53] In a Video record of Interview with him, in *http://www.youtube.com/watch?v=AIWqJ8tJ8JU*, (27.07.2012).

According to him, every religion teaches basically the same thing – purification of life and communication with the higher state of evolution. Any great Master of any religion never dies; he/she is ever alive. "Kingdom of heaven is within you" is a truth which will always have the same meaning – within you is the kingdom of heaven. Something which is within you can easily be gained by you. This is the truth of TM which is the automatic procedure to get Kingdom of God within you. TM meditators experience Kingdom of God within which Jesus teaches. Maharishi states that Christ was a great Master. He negates the power of suffering. "All this is good. But what is not good is suffering. No Christian should suffer because Christ has saved – Kingdom of God is within you. Every Christian should enjoy this consciousness. Freedom is the essential message of Christ. No follower of Christ should suffer."[54]

Mahesh Yogi sees no difference between TM and the teaching of Jesus summarized in 'the Kingdom of God is within you'. With his emphasis on happiness he negates the value and necessity of suffering; his concept of human as possessing inner an unlimited reservoir of energy, intelligence, and happiness makes him reconcile his teachings and Jesus' slogan – the Kingdom of God is within you.' The realization of this 'Kingdom within' is the goal of his religious aspiration.

Concluding Remarks

One of the most significant developments in modern guruism, which probably paves the way for inter-religious relations, is the positive attitude the gurus have adopted towards Jesus Christ. They not only accept him as one of the *avatāras* in equal term with those of the Hindu *avatāras*, but also consider him as contributing to their own life and ministry as they use Jesus' teaching to disseminate their Hindu doctrine among the Western audiences in particular who are predominantly Christians or deeply influenced by Christian worldview.

There is no doubt that the modern gurus, especially those who have large followings in the Western countries, have a positive and adoring attitude toward Jesus and his teachings. The methods they adopt in interpreting Jesus Christ are in accordance with their religious stand so also the Jesus they produce. For instance, Prabhupāda sees Jesus as a vaiṇavized Christ, who is not different from Kṛṣṇa; Mahesh Yogi pictures Jesus as teaching *Transcendental Meditation*; likewise the gurus of Divine Life Society univocally declares that Jesus had realized the Divine Life in him and can help us to realize the same. A loving mother-like figure, a 'hugging saint' Amritanandamayi emphasizes the Christ-*ness* of each individual in his/her inner most being and says that a true Christian is one who has realized that the 'I' in us, our innermost consciousness is nothing but Christ. Unfortunately these gurus do not pay enough attention

---

[54] *Ibid.*

to the significance of Jesus' death on the Cross and his resurrection, which is considered as essential for a full-fledged Christological discussion, instead, they are arrested by the life and teachings of Jesus Christ which make them pour out, in relation to each of their theological and philosophical conviction, their love for and adoration to Jesus Christ. The way and extent of their interpretations is open to debate, but their positive attitude towards Christ definitely helps them to relate with the Western people who are predominantly Christian in securing better relationship on the one hand, and on the other hand, such attitude is healthy not only for interfaith relations in a pluralistic country like India but it is also a challenge for Indian Christians who are called by His name.

Chapter 4

Paramhansa Yogananda's Interpretation of Jesus Christ

Paramhansa Yogananda (1893-1952) was the first Indian Yogi to preach the spiritual science of Indian yoga in the West. He went to America with a specific mission – to spread the ancient spiritual science, *Kriya Yoga* and to establish the essential unity of the Gospel of Christ and the teaching of Lord Kṛṣṇa by re-interpreting the Bible and Bhagavad Gītā. Over thirty years long ministerial life was spent in America initially in giving lectures and sermons in various cities of the USA and then building up the organization he founded – Self-Realization Fellowship. He wrote a number of books including Self-Realization lessons and commentaries on scriptures. He was known to the world by his *Autobiography* where he brought out a number of innovative and fascinating stories of both himself and other yogis. He was responsible for the establishment and the spread of *Kriya yoga* in the world. His contribution towards inter-religious harmony with special reference to Christian-Hindu relations is commendable. His unconditional love for and commitment to God is well recognized, together with his love for Hindu religious tradition and his mother land, India. He was dying chanting a poem he composed '*My India*'.

Yogananda is not as popular in India as other gurus studied in this research, may be because he spent all of his ministerial activities in America. But he is not less-significant in our investigation of contemporary gurus' interpretations of Jesus Christ. He seems to be more systemic and authentic in his approach to Jesus, more faithful to the written Word of God, more serious in his interpretation and more attached to Jesus Christ than all other gurus investigated in the present study. His commitment to the traditional Hindu philosophy and religious practices is as strong as his adaptation to the Western world with its religio-social practices. In him we see a beautiful blend of Western and Eastern spirituality.

This chapter starts with a brief biographical sketch of Yogananda followed by highlights on his philosophical and religious teachings. His interpretation of Jesus Christ is then provided, with concluding remarks at the end. We depend mainly on his writings to deduce his teachings and interpretations, of course, without neglecting other sources. Looking at him from the perspective of philosophy of religion, we read him critically from these sources having in mind his religious and philosophical context to arrive at his interpretations of Jesus Christ.

1. A Brief Sketch of the Life of Yogananda

"Little mother, thy son will be a yogi. As a spiritual engine, he will carry many souls to God's kingdom," thus foretold Lahiri Mahasaya, the renowned Master, looking at an infant Yogananda in the arms of his mother.[1] What had been foretold has precisely come to pass as the child Mukunda Lal Ghosh became a great yogi by the name Yogananda. Born on January 5, 1893, in Gorakhpur, Utter Pradesh, into a devout and well-to-do Bengali family, Yogananda from his earliest years was deeply religious with miracles and visions of god associated with him that corroborates his divine call to be a Yogi.[2] He himself testifies – "My first experience in hearing the Divine Voice came when I was a little child." Then he explains how God in the form of the Himalayan Yogi appeared before him and talked with him.[3] In his spiritual journey, in pursuit of spiritual riches, he is reported to have met several renounced yogis of that time including Swami Pranabananda who can appear in two different locations at the same time, Sohong Swami, who was known as 'Tiger Swami' because of his ability to defeat tigers, Ram Gopal Muzumdar who is known as 'a sleepless saint' as he spent many years without sleeping - awake in an ecstatic consciousness, then his guru's guru Lahiri Mahasaya who also has power to appear in body simultaneously at two different places and Mahāvatar Babaji 'a deathless Yogi' who is said to retain his

---

[1] "Life of Paramhansa Yoganandan", in *http://www.yogananda-srf.org/tmp/py_notitle.aspx?id=44#.UZc7gUpPXi4*, an official website of Self-Realization Fellowship (29.05.2013); cf. Sri Sananda Lal Ghosh, *"Mejda": The Family and the Early Life of Sri Paramhansa Yogananda*, (Dakshineswar: Yogoda Satsanga Society of India, 2012, first published in 1980), p. 17.

[2] Yogananda's brother Sri Sananda Lal Ghosh reports a numbers miracles associated with his birth and childhood. Cf. Sri Sananda Lal Ghosh, *"Mejda": The Family and the Early Life of Sri Paramhansa Yogananda,* pp. 24-45, 91.

[3] Paramhansa Yogananda, *Autobiography of a Yogi*, (New Delhi: Ananda Sangha Publications, 2010; first published in 1946), pp. 11-12. Cf. Paramhansa Yogananda, *How You Can Talk with God*, (Dakshineswar, Kolkata, Yogada Satsanga Society of India, 2005, first published in 1957), pp. 4-5; Sri Sailendra Bejoy Dasgupta, *Paramhansa Swami Yogananda: Life-portrait and Reminiscences*, translated into English by Yoga Niketan Team, (Michigan: Yoga Niketan, 2006), p. 21-22.

body for hundreds or may be thousands of years, the guru of Lahiri Mahasaya. The encounter with these great saints prepared Yogananda to be a Yogi.[4]

At the age of seventeen, in 1910, he became the disciple of the revered Swami Sri Yukteswar Giri, and after his graduation from Serampore College under Calcutta University in 1915, he was formerly initiated into the age-old monastic Swami Order and was given a new name – 'Yogananda'.[5] In the later part of his life, in the year 1935, his guru Sri Yukteswar Giri conferred on him a title '*Paramhansa*' – *sannyāsin* of the fourth or highest order.[6] After founding *Yogoda Satsanga Brahmacharya Vidyalaya*, known as 'How to live school' for boys at Ranchi in 1917, where modern educational methods and yoga training and instruction in spiritual ideals were combined,[7] he moved to USA and spent most part of his life there till he breathed his last at the age of 59 in 1952.[8]

It was Babaji who appeared before Yogananda and urged him to go to USA and teach people there the message of *Kriya Yoga*. He writes in his *Autobiography*:

> He spoke melodiously in Hindi. 'Our Heavenly Father has heard your prayer. He commands me to tell you: Follow the behests of

[4] The account of his meeting with several famous yogis is to be seen in the various chapters of his *Autobiography*. cf. Paramhansa Yogananda, *Autobiography of a Yogi*.

[5] "Life of Paramhansa Yogananda" in *http://www.yogananda-srf.org/tmp/py_notitle.aspx?id=44#.UZc7gUpPXi4*

[6] Paramhansa Yogananda, *Autobiography of a Yogi*, p. 383.

[7] See *Paramhansa Yogananda In Memoriam: Personal Accounts of the Master's Final Days*, (Dakshineswar: Yogoda Satsanga Society of India, 2012, first published in 1958), pp. 78-79. Cf. "Life of Paramhansa Yogananda", p. 3.

[8] There are some books that narrate Yogananda's life. Paramhansa Yogananda, *Autobiography of a Yogi, op.cit.* is the most popular and exhaustive one. The first publication was made in 1946 six years before he died. A biography of Yogananda by his close disciple Swami Kriyananda is another important work on Yogananda. This book - Swami Kriyananda, *Paramhansa Yogananda: A Biography with Personal Reflections and Reminiscences,* (Gurgaon: Ananda Sangha Publications, 2011) contains stories of him which are not to be found in *Autobiography of a Yogi*. Another significant book on Yogananda is authored by his own brother Sri Sananda Lal Ghosh, *"Mejda": The Family and the Early Life of Sri Paramhansa Yogananda, op.cit.* There is still another book that gives an account of Yogananda's final days – *Paramhansa Yogananda In Memoriam, op.cit.* Another book on Yogananda written in Bengali during 1983-1984 by Sri Sailendra Bejoy Dasgupta, the founder of Yoga Niketan, was translated into English - Sri Sailendra Bejoy Dasgupta, *Paramhansa Swami Yogananda: Life-portrait and Reminiscences, op.cit.* A part from these, a brief biography of Yogananda is put in a book entitled *Undreamed-of Possibilities: An Introduction to Yogoda Satsanga Society of India* (Dakshineswar: Yogoda Satsanga Society of India, n.d.), and in almost all the books published by Yogoda Satsanga Society of India/ Self-Realization Fellowship, and also in the official website of Self-Realization Fellowship, an organization founded by Yogananda in 1920 – "Life of Paramhansa Yogananda" in *http://www.yogananda-srf.org/tmp/py_notitle.aspx?id=44#. UZc7gUpPXi4.*

> your guru and go to America. Fear not; you will be protected. You are the one I have chosen to spread the message of *Kriya Yoga* in the West. Long ago I met your guru Yukteswar at a Khumbh Mela; I told him then I would send you to him for training.'[9]

According to Yogananda, Mahāvatār Babaji is a mysterious Himalayan yogi who used to roam about the Himalayan region along with his few disciples, showing themselves to a few select people. He is said to have retained his earthly body hundreds or may be thousands of years. It is believed that it was Babaji who "gave yoga initiation to Śaṅkara, ancient founder of Swami Order". Yogananda in his *Autobiography* for the first time disclosed to the world the existence of this 'deathless guru' and said that Babaji and Jesus Christ have constant communion, working together for the betterment of humanity: "The Mahāvatār (Babaji) is in constant communion with Christ; together they send out vibrations of redemption, and have planned the spiritual technique of salvation for this age. The work of these two fully-illumined masters – one with the body and one without it – is to inspire the nations to forsake suicidal wars, race hatred, religious sectarianism, and the boomerang evils of materialism."[10]

In one of his lectures, Yogananda reveals another purpose of his American visit: "Mahāvatar Babaji ordained that I come to America to interpret the teachings of Christ for the purpose of showing their parallelism with the yoga teachings of India's Lord Kṛṣṇa … That is why Babaji, who is in divine communion with Christ, gave me the special dispensation of carrying this message to the West."[11] The year he landed in Boston, USA in 1920 as an Indian delegate to the International Congress of Religious Liberals in America, he founded 'The Self-Realization Fellowship', a non-sectarian and non-profit organization, solely for the dissemination of his teaching with emphasis on *Kriya Yoga*. For three decades, Yogananda worked tirelessly for the promotion of the same.[12] His message has been disseminated to the public through lectures and numerous books written by him.[13]

---

[9] Paramhansa Yogananda, *Autobiography of a Yogi*, pp. 336-337.

[10] *Ibid.*, pp. 291-293.

[11] Paramhansa Yogananda, *Man's Eternal Quest: Collected Talks and Essays on Realizing God in Daily Life*, *Volume I*, (Dakshineswar: Yogoda Satsanga Society of India, 2008, First published in 1975), pp. 291-292.

[12] Cf. Susunaga Weeraperuma, *Divine Messengers of Our Time*, (Delhi: Sri Satguru Publications, 1998), pp. 118-119.

[13] Yogananda was a great writer, apart from his most celebrated book – *Autobiography of a Yogi*, *op.cit.* which is ranked among the top books of the world, sold more than one million copies and translated into 19 languages, his works include – the three-volumed books containing his Talks and Essays - *Man's Eternal Quest, Vol. I, op.cit.; Divine Romance: Collected Talks*

Swami Kriyananda reports several miracles performed by and connected with his Master before and after he became a *sannyāsin*. Miracles like stopping of a heavy downpour; helping the helpless fishermen, who could not catch any fish, catch a boat-full of fish; saving a drowning ship with all the people on board; ceasing the storm and rain; resurrecting the dead; multiplying food for the guests, and several more. Kriyananda even says that Yogananda appeared in body to a number of peoples after his death.[14] It is reported by Harry T. Rowe, Mortuary Director that even after 20 days from his death, Yogananda's body has no sign of decomposition – "The absence of any visual sign of decay in the dead body of Yogananda offers the most extraordinary case in our experience," says the report.[15]

Yogananda is known for his love for God and fellow human beings. His guru Sri Yukteswar had referred to him as an incarnation of divine love; his disciple and the first spiritual successor, Rajarsi Janakananda, bestowed on him the title of *Premāvatār* or "Incarnation of Divine Love."[16] In a Tribute to Yogananda, Swami Sivananda of the Divine Life Society writes: "A rare gem of inestimable value, the like of whom the world is yet to witness. H.H. Sri Paramhansa Yogananda has been an ideal representative of the ancient sages and seers, the glory of India."[17] His followers regard him as an *avatāra*, descent

and Essays on Realizing God in Daily Life, Volume II, (Dakshineswar, Kolkata: Yogada Satsanga Society of India, 2008); *Journey to Self-Realization: Collected Talks and Essays on Realizing God in Daily Life, Volume III,* (Dakshineswar, Kolkata: Yogada Satsanga Society of India, 2004). Others include, *The Second Coming of Christ: The Resurrection of the Christ Within You – A Revelatory Commentary on the Original Teachings of Jesus, Vol. I & II,* (Los Angeles: Self-Realization Fellowship, 2004); *God Talks With Arjuna: The Bhagavad Gītā — A New Translation and Commentary*, (Los Angeles: Self-Realization Fellowship, 2002); *Wine of the Mystic: The Rubaiyat of Omar Khayyam — A Spiritual Interpretation,* (Los Angeles: Self-Realization Fellowship, 1996); *Songs of the Soul*, (Dakshineswar, Kolkata: Yogada Satsanga Society of India, 2010, first published in 1983); *Whispers from Eternity,* (Dakshineswar, Kolkata: Yogada Satsanga Society of India, 2008, first published in 1959); *Scientific Healing Affirmation,* (Dakshineswar, Kolkata: Yogada Satsanga Society of India, 2008); *The Science of Religion,* (Dakshineswar, Kolkata: Yogada Satsanga Society of India, 2008; first published in USA, 1953); *Metaphysical Meditations,* (Dakshineswar, Kolkata: Yogada Satsanga Society of India, 2007; first published in 1964); *Where There is Light: Insights and Inspiration for Meeting Life's Challenges*, (Dakshineswar, Kolkata: Yogada Satsanga Society of India, 2008); *The Law of Success*, (Dakshineswar, Kolkata: Yogada Satsanga Society of India, 2010, first published in 1961); *How can you talk with God, op.cit.; Cosmic Chants*, (Los Angeles: Self-Realization Fellowship, 1974). Apart from these, a number of booklets are published by Yogoda Satsanga Society of India and Self-Realization Fellowship which are mainly extracts of *Man's Eternal Quest.*

[14] See Swami Kriyananda, *Paramhansa Yogananda: A Biography,* pp. 28, 168-177.

[15] *Paramhansa Yogananda In Memoriam*, p. 18, cf. pp. 121-123 for the full text of report sent to Self-Realization Fellowship by the Director.

[16] "Life of Paramhanśa Yogananda".

[17] *Paramhansa Yogananda In Memoriam,* p. 51.

of Divinity into flesh.[18] Such was a Yogi, Yogananda, a highly respected guru, quite popular even among some section of American Christians.

2. Philosophical and Religious Teachings of Yogananda: An Overview

There are three gurus who were instrumental in shaping the life of Yogananda. Not only they exerted great influence upon his life, but also unanimously directed his life and gave him a mission to fulfill. They are Swami Sri Yukteswar Giri, his guru; Sri Lahiri Mahasaya the guru of Yukteswar Giri and Mahāvatar Babaji, the guru of Lahiri Mahasaya. Another influence was from the life and teachings of Jesus Christ and Lord Kṛṣṇa found in the Bible, especially the Gospels and Bhagavad Gītā respectively.[19] He quoted frequently and even wrote a commentary on the select passages of the four Gospels. In addition, he was deeply affected by his childhood experiences of miracles and visions.[20] All these three factors – his guru and other gurus in the line, Jesus and Kṛṣṇa, and his childhood experiences - had lasting impression on his life and teachings. However, one of the main guiding forces of his life and philosophical formulation is 'his direct intuitive experience of truth.' He says that his main source of knowledge is not what he had read or studied, but his "own direct experience of Truth."[21] A brief discussion on his religious and philosophical teaching is given below.

2.1. God

Yogananda's religious teaching, shaped by his unconditional commitment to God, is centered on God. "References to God are plentiful in his books."[22] When Yogananda prepared to leave his father and the whole family in search of his prospective guru who will train him in spiritual matter, his father who lost his wife already was not ready to part his beloved son even after repeated plea. At last Yogananda told him: "Revered Father, how can I tell you my love for you! But even greater is my love for the Heavenly Father."[23] This

[18] A personal interview with Swami Smaranananda, General Secretary of Yogoda Satsanga Society of India at Yogoda Satsanga Math, Ranchi on 20.07.2013, and also an informal chat with Swami Amarananda at Yogada Satsanga Math, Dhaksineswar on 22.06.2013.

[19] He says, "There are three Bibles from which I draw my inspiration: the Christian Bible, the Hindu Bhagavad Gītā, and my *Whispers from Eternity*, which were given to me by God." Paramhansa Yogananda, *How to be Happy All the Time*, (Gurgaon: Ananda Sangha Publications, 2010), p. 66.

[20] He reported in his celebrated book *Autobiography of a Yogi* how he was miraculously healed from cholera at the age of eight, his vision of Himalayan yogis, his prediction of having a boil which came true, miracle of obtaining two kites for his sister. Paramhansa Yogananda, *Autobiography of a Yogi*, pp. 10-14.

[21] Yogananda, *Divine Romance,* p. 284.

[22] Weeraperuma, *Divine Messengers of Our Time,* p. 111.

[23] Paramhansa Yogananda, *Autobiography of a Yogi*, p. 85.

clarifies his uncompromising commitment to God. He confesses, "There is no other desire, no other ambition left for me, but God."[24] His passion for God is evidently expressed in his famous poem "*God, God, God*" which appeared in a number of his books. The Poem basically is an expression of his yearning for God; the last stanza explains it all –

> *In waking, eating, working, dreaming, sleeping,*
> *Serving, meditating, chanting, divinely loving,*
> *My soul constantly hums, unheard by any:*
> *God! God! God!*[25]

Like majority Hindus, Yogananda believes in the oneness of God who manifests in various forms like Brahma the creator, Viṣnu the preserver and Śiva the destroyer. He is the Supreme Cause, the Cause of matter and intelligence. He confesses that he belonged to the ancient Swami Order of India recognized centuries ago into its present form by Ādi Śaṅkarācharya.[26]

As a true follower of Śaṅkara, he acknowledges that God in Its true reality is impersonal, but at the same time, strongly emphasizes personal aspect of God who can be worshipped, with whom personal relationship is possible, to whom fervent prayers should be offered and who alone is to be loved. Brahman being a non-dual Absolute, He became dual by his magical measuring power of *māyā*. "But even though He has created the universe out of delusion, He Himself is not deluded by it. He knows that everything is but a diversification of His one Cosmic Consciousness. Experiences of senses and emotions, the dramas of war and peace, sickness and health, life and death – all are happening in God."[27] Therefore, God is both personal and impersonal. The impersonal aspect of God is explained by Yogananda as "Full of bliss, bestowing joy transcendent, Essence of wisdom, untouched by duality… the utterer of Thou art That, the one eternal, pure, immovable, the omnipresent, Witness, free from Nature's three qualities, beyond the reach of thought…"[28] . At the same time, the wonderful universe suggested to us the immanence of God.

---

[24] Paramhansa Yogananda, *To be Victorious in Life*, (Dakshineswar, Kolkata: Yogada Satsanga Society of India, 2011, first published in 2002), p. 81.

[25] See Yogananda, *Autobiography of a Yogi*, p. 342; Paramhansa Yogananda, *Man's Eternal Quest*, p. 463; Paramhansa Yogananda, *Songs of the Soul,* pp. 172-173. It is said that Yogananda saw a vision of St. Francis of Assisi whom he loved so much, coming to him and he was so moved and composed this beautiful poem. See Paramhansa Yogananda, *Man's Eternal Quest*, p. xii.

[26] Yogananda, *Journey to Self-Realization,* p.178.

[27] *Ibid.*, p. 32.

[28] Yogananda, *Whispers from Eternity*, p. 3.

He is visible everywhere and in everything.[29] So, God is both personal as well as impersonal because God is everything: personal and impersonal. He created persons, human beings. Their Originator could not be wholly impersonal.[30]

Thus, the God of Yogananda is the Absolute, beyond form, but He also makes Himself manifests in many ways. "God is Eternal Bliss. His being is love, wisdom and joy… and manifests Himself in whatever He pleases. He appears to His saints in the form each of them holds dear: a Christian sees Christ, a Hindu beholds Kṛṣṇa or the Divine Mother and so on."[31] The impersonal Spirit became personal Lord the moment he created the physical world and assumed the role of Creator.[32] The impersonal God cannot be described or even understood with the intellect, the only way to know the Absolute is to be one with the Spirit. Deviating from Śaṅkara's thought, Yogananda said that in order to make Himself known to the people God incarnates into human forms – like Jesus, Kṛṣṇa, etc. As a matter of fact, we are all gods, but some people are called the *avatāras* of God because they reflect His light more than others.[33]

2.2. Human Being

Yogananda's conception of human is not different from Śaṅkara's view point. He says, "God is spirit; and man (*sic*), in his (*sic*) essential nature, is also Spirit."[34] The whole human body, the consciousness and motion in it are the representation of God. In consciousness human is omniscience and omnipresence. So, all the attributes that God has like consciousness, reason, will, feeling, love, human has too.[35] He states, "I know that I am not the body, not the blood, not the energy, not the thoughts, not the mind, not the ego, not the astral self. I am the Immortal soul that illumines them all, remaining unchangeable in spite of their changes."[36] He often uses Christian term 'image of God' to denote the inherent divinity of human. According to Yogananda, the Biblical passage that says, "For in his own image God made humankind" (Genesis 9:6) has not been fully explained – in what ways human is the image of God. He exhorts saying - God is Spirit, human being, in his or her essential

---

[29] Paramhansa Yogananda, *The Divine Romance,* p. 377.

[30] For details See Yogananda, *How You Can Talk with God*, pp. 8-10.

[31] *Sayings of Paramhansa Yogananda*, (Dakshineswar, Kolkata: Yogada Satsanga Society of India, 2008, first published in 1980), p. 17. Cf. Paramhansa Yogananda, *The Divine Romance*, p. 377.

[32] Yogananda, *How You Can Talk with God*, p. 17.

[33] Yogananda, *The Divine Romance,* pp. 379-380.

[34] Yogananda, *How You Can Talk with God*, p. 11.

[35] *Ibid.*, pp. 12-13.

[36] Yogananda, *Metaphysical Meditations*, p. 75.

nature is also Spirit. This is the primary meaning of the Biblical passage.[37] Having denied the concept of human being as sinner,[38] he emphasizes the greatness of human – "I am fearless; I am made of the substance of God. I am a spark of Spirit. I am an atom of the Cosmic Flame. I am a cell of the vast universal body of the Father. 'I and my Father are one.'"[39] He asks his people to affirm, "No birth, no death, no caste have I; father, mother, have I none. Blessed Spirit, I am He. I am the infinite Happiness."[40] Like a true Advaitin, Yogananda stresses the oneness of human with God. There are two poems composed by him: '*Thou and I are One*' and '*I am He*' that explicate essential oneness of human with God.[41]

2.3. *Karma-Saṃsāra*

Yogananda, as a typical Hindu, believes in the *Karma-Saṃsāra* doctrine and uses the term 'reincarnation' for this which, he says, can be proved scientifically.[42] He argues that if we believe in the existence of a *just* God, we should also believe in reincarnation because these two are dependent on one another,[43] otherwise it is impossible to reconcile humans' inequalities while some are rich, healthy, beautiful, etc. others poor, unhealthy, deformed, etc. with divine justice.[44] So, all the so-called 'hereditary advantages' and 'lucky' opportunities in life are not the whims of chance but the lawful result of *karma-saṃsāra* set in motion by one's own karmas in the past.[45] Yogananda sees the positive aspects of 'reincarnation' as the progress of a soul through many lives on the earth to attain the immortal perfection of oneness with God;[46] thus, 'incarnation' is the soul's journey to perfection. Again, reincarnation of soul gives an individual a chance to purge his/her evil inclinations until he/she becomes pure and reaches

---

[37] Yogananda, *How You Can Talk with God*, pp. 11-12.

[38] He says, "Don't think of yourself as a sinner. You are a child of the Heavenly Father. No matter if you are the greatest sinner, forget it. If you have made up your mind to be good, then you are no longer a sinner." Yogananda, *Man Eternal Quest*, p. 196.

[39] Paramhansa Yogananda, *Living Fearlessly: Bringing Out Your Inner Soul Strength*, (Dakshineswar, Kolkata: Yogada Satsanga Society of India, 2011; first published in 1903), p. 76.

[40] Paramhansa Yogananda, *Spiritual Diary: An Inspirational Thought for Each Day of the Year*, (Dakshineswar, Kolkata: Yogada Satsanga Society of India, 2010; first published in 1982), no page number.

[41] Yogananda, *Songs of the Soul,* pp. 46, 89.

[42] Yogananda, *Man's Eternal Quest*, pp. 211ff.

[43] *Ibid.*, p. 211.

[44] *Ibid.*, p. 230. Cf. Yogananda, *The Divine Romance,* p. 269.

[45] Yogananda, *To be Victorious in Life*, p. 11.

[46] Yogananda, *Man's Eternal Quest*, p. 216.

his/her true nature as a child of God.[47] Thus, Yogananda brings out the positive side of *Karma-Saṃsāra* which is otherwise seen as the great cause of suffering where a soul is imprisoned in the prison of cycle of birth and rebirth.

2.4. Creation

Yogananda affirms that creation is unnecessary for God in the sense that as He is perfect and in need of no other thing to make Him perfect. But the reason why God created the worlds is solely for His own enjoyment. So, the world is God's *lila*, divine play. "God was infinite omniscient Bliss, but being alone, there was no one but Him to enjoy that Bliss. So He says, 'Let Me create a universe and divide Myself into many souls that they may play with Me in My unfolding drama.'"[48] So, in reality the whole creation is nothing but God Himself.

According to Yogananda, matter exists as a cosmic delusion. In creation the unmanifest Spirit projects, as its vibratory expression, two natures – consciousness and matter. Consciousness is the subjective aspect of Spirit's vibration whereas matter is its objective aspect. The Cosmic Consciousness or Spirit is potentially immanent in matter and manifests itself subjectively as the consciousness in all creation. The only difference between matter and consciousness lies in the rate of vibration and not in the essence. In other words, it is the difference in the rate of vibration not in the difference of essence that distinguishes matter and consciousness. So, there is no essential difference between matter and consciousness – the difference is in degree not in kind. The power of *māyā*, the cosmic illusion makes matter to appear so distinct and unrelated from the Spirit to the mind of human.[49] Thus, the phenomenal world operates under *māyā*, the law of duality. It is an unreal world that veils the Divine Oneness and Unchangeableness.[50] As everything in the universe, seen and unseen, like mind, energy, matter of all kinds, are created by God, evil is also created by Him. God has a purpose in creating evil. "Evil provides the contrast that enables us to recognise and experience goodness…without the blackboard of evil, the good things in the world could not be magnified."[51]

---

[47] Yogananda, *The Divine Romance,* p. 273.

[48] Yogananda, *Journey to Self-Realization*, pp. 31-32; Paramhansa Yogananda, *Why God Permits Evil and How to Rise Above It*, (Dakshineswar, Kolkata: Yogada Satsanga Society of India, 2010, first published in 2002), pp. 31-32; also p. 15 where he argues that the world is God's hobby.

[49] Yogananda, *Scientific Healing Affirmations*, pp. 27-29. Cf. Yogananda, *Man's Eternal Quest*, p. 360.

[50] Yogananda, *Scientific Healing Affirmations,* p. 31.

[51] Yogananda, *Why God Permits Evil and How to Rise Above It*, p. 3.

2.5. Heaven - the Astral World

Yogananda believes in the existence of an astral world which he calls 'heaven', where "those who love God and put their trust in Him go there when they die."[52] Though he calls this 'heaven' using Christian term, but the astral world he talks about and Christian heaven seems to be quite different, because this is not a permanent or eternal home. This astral world is perfect where souls live in complete peace and harmony with joy and happiness without any terrestrial blemish.[53] The various spheres of different standard are occupied by the souls in accordance with their spiritual life on the earth. Some enjoy more than the others, having more freedom and experience of beauty. After the karmically predestined time is over, the ordinary souls reincarnate on earth while highly advanced souls can remain in the astral world as long as they wish before they are finally united with God.[54]

2.6. Kriya Yoga

One of the main missions of Yogananda is to spread *Kriya Yoga* to the Western worlds. The lost *Kriya Yoga*, an ancient spiritual exercise, instituted by Lord Kṛṣṇa, was rediscovered by Babaji and passed it on to Shri Lahiri Mahasaya his disciple who popularized it and proclaimed it to his disciples. Sujan Singh Uban notes, "*Kriya Yoga*, the technique of spiritual advancement…is a highly sophisticated yoga technique, consisting of breathing exercises and concentration on the psychic centres."[55] Yogananda confessed that he could not give a full explanation of *Kriya Yoga* in the form of a book because of certain ancient yogic injunctions as the actual technique is destined to be learnt under the instruction of a *Kriya Yogi*. But, he explained the detailed step by step techniques in *Self-Realization Fellowship (SRF) Lesson* which is not published as it is intended only for those who enrolled themselves to do the course and initiated into *Kriya Yoga*.[56]

The following are the detailed technique to be followed in the *Kriya Yoga* meditation:

---

[52] Yogananda, *Where There is Light,* p. 158.

[53] Cf. *Ibid.*, pp. 158-159.

[54] Yogananda, *The Divine Romance,* pp. 289, 294. Detail explanation of astral world was given to Yogananda by his guru Sri Yukteswar when the latter, after his death, appeared to the former in flesh and blood on the 19 July 1936 in Bombay. For detailed explanation of the astral world, see Yogananda, *Autobiography of a Yogi,* Chapter 43: "The Resurrection of Sri Yukteswar", pp. 398-417.

[55] Sujan Singh Uban, *The Gurus of India*, (New Delhi: Sterling Publishers Pvt. Ltd., 1978), p. 9.

[56] *Self-Realization Fellowship Lesson* is not published for public use. The present researcher happened to access this rare book – a cyclostyle copy in the Yogoda Satsanga Sakha Math, Ranchi when he visited this *āśram* on 20.07.2013.

2.6.1. Preparatory Steps Prescribed Before Doing the Real Kriya:[57]

- Correct posture – the spine should be erect, sitting on the cushioned floor cross-legged or on the armless chair with spine erect, abdomen in, chest out, shoulders back, chin parallel to the ground, hands with palms upturned rest on the legs.
- Inhale slowly deeply through the nostrils holding the breath to a count of 20 and exhale slowly to the count of 20. To repeat this six to twelve times.
- Inhale, tensing the whole body, then relax all the body parts at once, expelling the breath through the mouth in a double exhalation, "huh, huh". Repeat this six times.
- With the eyelids half closed or completely closed, focus the attention on a point between the eyebrows, the Christ-Consciousness center which is the site of the single eye spoken of by Christ, "The light of the body is the eye; if therefore thine eye be single, thy whole body shall be full of light" (Matt. 6:22). With full concentration try to realize that you are not the body, but the eternal sphere of light and joy, one with the Father.

With this preliminary and preparatory practice of meditation, the devotee will get himself/herself ready for the practice of *Kriya Yoga* proper.

2.6.2. Technique of Kriya Yoga

After an appropriate initiation into *Kriya Yoga*, a devotee is eligible to practice *Kriya Yoga* proper. There are nine lessons in SRF Lesson that deal with the practice of *Kriya Yoga*. In Lesson *Kriya 1 & 2* Yogananda explains the eightfold steps of Patanjali yoga; Lesson *Kriya 3* contains the historical basis and purpose of *Kriya Yoga*. In Lesson *Kriya 4* he explicates how Kriya quickens soul evolution; and the actual technique of *Kriya Yoga* is given in the next Lesson – *Kriya 5*. *Kriya* proper ends with Lesson 5; however, *Maha Mudra* Technique and *Yoyti Mudra* Technique, which are also part of *Kriya Yoga*, are given in Lesson *Kriya 6*. Lesson *Kriya 7* contains aids to *Kriya* practice and in Lesson *Kriya 7A* a step-by step outline of *Kriya* is provided. Lesson *Kriya 8* explains control of Cosmic energy by *Kriya* and the teaching concludes with the benefits of *Kriya* practice given in Lesson *Kriya 9*. There

[57] See Paramhansa Yogananda, *Self-Realization Fellowship (SRF) Lesson, S-1, P-3, A*, (Los Angeles: Self-Realization Fellowship, 1984, first published in 1956), pp. 1-4.

is a prescribed preliminary exercise to be done before the actual meditation,[58] only after this, the following *Kriya* techniques are to be followed:[59]

- Body posture for the practice of *Kriya* proper is as given in the preparatory steps.
- With eyelids half closed or completely closed, turn the eyeballs upward and fix the gaze, without strain, at the point between the eyebrows.
- Expand the inner opening of the throat by rolling the tongue back toward the palate as far as possible. Let the tongue return to normal position but retain the expansion of the throat.
- Inhale calmly and slowly, through the mouth and nose simultaneously, making the barely audible sound "AW" deep in the expanded throat. The "AW" sound should be continuous, like "AAAWWW" not "AW, AW, AW". The duration of inhalation should be ten or fifteen counts.
- Imagine that the breath is ascending quietly and smoothly through the hollow cerebrospinal canal, rather than going in the lungs. (In the preparatory exercise, one should imagine the spine as a hollow tube starting from the coccyx at the base and ending in the brain at the Christ center, the point between the eyebrows).
- Concentrate on the sound of "AW" and feel that the cool breath is rising from the coccyx, moving upward through the imagined hollow spine till it reaches the 'Christ center.'[60]
- Slowly exhale through mouth and nose to a the count of ten or fifteen with the sound "EEEE", imaging the warm breath going out from the Christ center through the hollow tube, flowing downward to the coccyx.
- Practice this fourteen times in the morning and fourteen times in the evening. This is for the beginner; the more advanced devotee may practice more than this.

---

[58] See Paramhansa Yogananda, *Self-Realization Fellowship Lesson, Kriya 5,* (Los Angeles: Self-Realization Fellowship, 1984, first published in 1956), pp. 2-3 where some preliminary exercises to be done are explained.

[59] *Ibid.*, pp. 3-5. A Step-by-Step outline of Kriya proper as well as Maha *Mudra* and *Joyti Mudra* techniques are given in Lesson 7A – *Kriya 7A* for the benefit of devotees which are the summarized form of Lesson 5 - *Kriya 5.* Cf. Paramhansa Yogananda, *Self-Realization Fellowship Lesson, Kriya 7A,* (Los Angeles: Self-Realization Fellowship, 1984, first published in 1956), pp. 1-7. The summary of the whole *Kriya Yoga Lesson* is also supplied in *Kriya 9A.* Cf. Paramhansa Yogananda, *Self-Realization Fellowship Lesson, Kriya 9A,* (Los Angeles: Self-Realization Fellowship, 1984, first published in 1956), pp. 1-7.

[60] 'Christ Center' is explained in the next point.

- *Kriya Yoga* should not be practiced on a full stomach. Morning before breakfast and evening before dinner or before going to bed is the most preferable time for practicing *Kriya.*
- After practicing the Kriya technique, remain in meditation posture for at least ten to fifteen minutes, the longer the period, the better the result.

Kriya proper ends with this, however, Yogananda prescribes the practice of *Maha Mudra Technique* and *Joyti Mudra Technique* which are considered as part of *Kriya Yoga.*[61]

Interestingly, Yogananda maintains that *Kriya Yoga* is not the monopoly of those who call themselves Hindus, rather, it was known by other spiritual leaders including that of Christian saints. Babaji re-established the forgotten *Kriya Yoga* and initiated in to it his disciple Shri Lahiri Mahasaya telling, "The *Kriya Yoga* I am giving to the world through you in this nineteenth century is a revival of the same science which Kṛṣṇa gave, millenniums ago, to Arjuna and which was later known to Patanjali and to Christ, St. John, St. Paul and other disciples."[62] It is claimed that *Kriya Yoga* has powerful effect on the person who practiced and mastered it where the body of a practitioner becomes transformed day by day and "is finally fitted to express the infinite potentials of cosmic energy."[63] Yogananda, himself, and his followers praise *Kriya Yoga* as the greatest of all yogas.[64] Talking about *Kriya Yoga* Swami Smarananananda, the General Secretary of Yogada Satsanga Society of India says that it is "the greatest or most supreme of all the yoga meditation techniques ever given to humankind, Yoganandaji spoke of it as 'aeroplane route' to God… It is not any breathing exercise but deals directly with *pranic* current in the human body raising it to higher centres. Peace, love and joy are definitely experienced by practitioners."[65]

---

[61] *Maha Mudra* and *Joyti Mudra* are nothing but the practice of Kriya proper with different body postures. For detailed information of Maha *Mudra* and *Joyti Mudra* techniques cf. Paramhansa Yogananda, *Self-Realization Fellowship Lesson, Kriya 5,* (Los Angeles: Self-Realization Fellowship, 1984, first published in 1956).

[62] Yogananda, *Autobiography of a Yogi*, p. 231.

[63] *Ibid.*, p. 235. For fuller discussion on *Kriya Yoga* cf. *Ibid.*, pp. 231-239.

[64] See Yogananda, *To be Victorious in Life,* p. 64.

[65] Swami Smarananananda, the General Secretary of Yogada Satsanga Society of India, in a personal interview with him at Yogoda Satsanga Math, Ranchi on 20.07.2013. Swami Amarananda one of the leaders whom the researcher met at Yogada Satsang Math in Dakshineswar, Kolkata on 22.06.2013 also claims *Kriya Yoga* as greater than all other yogas.

2.7. The Spiritual Eye – Christ or *Kutaṣtha* Center

The so called 'the third eye' which lies between the two eyebrows is of great importance in the teaching of Yogananda. He calls this as 'Spiritual eye' or 'Christ Center' or '*Kutashtha* Center'. This particular point is the 'door to the kingdom of heaven', 'the entryway into the divine consciousness'. By awakening and penetrating the Spiritual eye, the devotee experiences what Yogananda calls 'Christ Consciousness' or '*Kutaṣtha Chaitanya*' or 'Kṛṣṇa Consciousness' which leads to absolute consciousness, that is, Cosmic Consciousness. He differentiates between 'Christ Consciousness' or 'Kṛṣṇa Consciousness' which is the projected consciousness of God immanent in all creation, the cosmic intelligence of Spirit present in creation and Cosmic Consciousness which is the Absolute, Spirit beyond creation. It also refers to the absolute meditation state of oneness with God both within and beyond vibratory creation.[66] It can be said that 'Christ Consciousness' signifies a personal aspect of God, God in relation to creation whereas 'Cosmic Consciousness' refers to God in Its absolute state, impersonal or rather '*suprapersonal*' aspect of God, God beyond Its vibratory activities.

2.8. Communion with God

Yogananda, time and again, reiterates the importance of communion with God. 'Experiencing God', 'direct intuitive knowledge of God' are his watchwords. He always maintains that academic knowledge gained from the reading and hearing of books and lectures alone is not sufficient, one needs to have intuitive-experiential knowledge. His emphasis on direct communion with God is such that religion for him is basically communion with God. The real purpose of a church or temple is to encourage the devotee to have communion with God. He goes on to the extent of saying that, "If religion loses sight of communion with God, it has failed in its duty."[67]

2.9. Journey to Self-Realization

The primary goal of Yogananda's ministry and of the Self-Realization Fellowship and Yogoda Satsanga Society of India he had founded is to drive people into Self-realization by attaining Christ Consciousness or Kṛṣṇa Consciousness. He defines Self-realization as follows: "Self-realization is the knowing – in body, mind, and soul – that we are one with the omnipresent God; that we do not have to pray that it come to us, that we are not merely near it all times, but

---

[66] See Yogananda, *Journey to Self-Realization*, pp. 175, 355, 425-426; Yogananda, *The Divine Romance,* pp. 258, 467; Paramhansa Yogananda, *Man's Eternal Quest*, pp. 329, 334, 475; Paramhansa Yogananda, *Where there is Light,* p. 163; Paramhansa Yogananda, *To be Victorious in Life*, pp. 1-2.

[67] Yogananda, *The Divine Romance,* p. 357.

God's omnipresence is our omnipresence; that we are just as much a part of Him now as we ever will be. All we have to do is improve our knowing." In other words Self-realization "means knowledge of one's own soul and of its oneness with the Father."[68] He prescribes the following steps for knowing God or Self-realization: *Firstly*, one has to shun evil practices such as stealing, telling lies, killing, adultery and the likes. *Secondly*, to practice the positive rules like love, kindness, sincerity, truthfulness and the likes. *Thirdly*, to learn to quite the body and mind with a correct body posture. *Fourthly*, to switch off the life force from the body by practicing *prāṇāyāma* which will lead to interiorization of consciousness, which is the *fifth* step. When the consciousness becomes interiorized, deep concentration and meditation, the *sixth* and *seventh* steps, are possible. The moment one can shut out restless thoughts at will, and put the attention wholly on God, the real beginning of divine communion happens. The *last* steps, *Samādhi* or oneness with God occurred to a person who has constant divine communion with God.[69]

Yogananda also gives three paths to Cosmic Consciousness: The *first* one is the social way – to live for others, to show unconditional love to everyone, to serve all humans as ourselves, to expand our consciousness to include others' interest and well-being. The *second* one is self-control: to be alike in heat and cold, pleasure and pain, health and sickness. Meditation is the *third* path, the metaphysical path for which one should take *Kriya Yoga* as laid down by Self-Realization Fellowship/Yogoda Satsanga Society of India.[70] Meditation is given utmost importance because it is only through meditation and unceasing effort that God consciousness is achieved.[71] Though he accepts traditional paths of liberation such as loving devotion (*Bhakti*) followed by action or activity (*Karma*), he maintains that "greater than activity, devotion or reason is meditation."[72] For attaining God, he prescribes:

> God-contact can be achieved through regular, intense, long-continued meditation. During deep meditation, when the breath becomes calm, one experiences an enjoyable state of peace... By deeper meditation, learn to calm the breath and the senses… Seek Him by meditating deeply with utmost devotion. Steadily use your

[68] Paramhansa Yogananda, *Self-Realization Fellowship Lesson, S-1, P-5*, (Los Angeles: Self-Realization Fellowship, n.d.), p. 5.

[69] See Yogananda, *The Divine Romance,* pp. 368-371.

[70] Yogananda, *Man's Eternal Quest*, pp. 169-170, 329.

[71] *Ibid.*, pp. 333-334.

[72] *Ibid.*, pp. 6-7. The actual meditation technique of *Kriya Yoga* is given to those who enrolled for the course of Yogada Satsanga Lesson only. However, there are two books written by Yogananda that deals with meditations – *Scientific Healing Affirmation,* and *Metaphysical Meditation.*

will power day after day, week after week, year after year, until the cosmic silence of ages is broken and you receive His answer.[73]

2.10. Emphasis on Intuition

According to Yogananda, God is beyond the grasp of mind and intellect; His true nature can be felt through the power of intuition. "We must find His consciousness through the superconscious mind and intelligence. His infinite nature is revealed to man (*sic*) through the intuitive superconsciousness of the soul."[74] It is fascinating to note that apart from the six ways of knowing (*pramānas*) recognized by Indian philosophical systems,[75] Yogananda admits the seventh one – *Intuition* as the most valid source of knowledge insofar as knowledge of God is concerned. Other sources of knowledge cannot bring us to God as it is necessary to go beyond senses and thought.[76] He says, "It is through intuition that humanity reaches Divinity, that the sensuous is brought into connection with the super-sensuous, and that the latter is *felt* to express itself in and through the sensuous. The influence of senses vanishes, intruding thoughts disappear; Bliss-God is realized; the consciousness of 'all in One and One in all' dawns upon us."[77]

2.11. Harmony of Religions

One of the missions of Yogananda for which he was sent to the West, as stated before, was to demonstrate the harmony between the teachings of Lord Kṛṣṇa and Jesus Christ, to show to the Western Christians the parallel between these two, to encourage people to have mutual sharing and mutual learning as it was his conviction and the conviction the three gurus – Babaji, Lahiri Mahasaya and Sri Yukteswar that Jesus and Kṛṣṇa lead to the same goal. Babaji once said to Sri Yukteswar, the Yogananda's guru, "East and West must established a golden middle path of activity and spirituality combined… You, Swamiji, have the part to play in the coming harmonious exchange between Oriental and

[73] Paramhansa Yogananda, "Contacting God in Meditation" in *http://www.anandaclaritymagazine.com/2003/09/ yogananda-meditation-god-peace/*, (24.07.2011).

[74] *Ibid.*, p. 23.

[75] The Cārvākas recognize only one source of valid knowledge, i.e. Perception (*Pratyakṣa*). The Bauddhas and Vaiśeṣikas admit two – Perception and Inference (*Anumāna*). Sānkhyas, apart from Perception and Inference, admit Authority or Testimony (*Śabda*). Naiyāyikas add the fourth one Comparison (*Upamāna*), Prābhākaras recognize, in addition to the above four pramānas, Postulation or Assumption (*Arthāpatti*). Mimāmsa and Vedānta schools recognize the five *pramānas* stated above and add the sixth one, Non-cognition (*anupalabdhi*) as source of knowing. For a detailed study of six valid source of knowledge as found in Indian philosophical schools, cf. D.M. Datta, *The Six Ways of Knowing*, (Calcutta: University of Calcutta, 1997, first published in 1932).

[76] See Yogananda, *The Science of Religion*, pp. 78-79.

[77] *Ibid.*, p. 78.

Occidental."[78] This resulted in sending Yogananda to USA for this mission and on his part Yogananda did not forget to present the harmonious relationship between Jesus' teachings and Lord Kṛṣṇa's teaching in his numerous lectures across America. It is no wonder that the funeral service of Yogananda was conducted by Rajarsi Janakananda, who succeeded him and a Christian Priest Rev. M.W. Lewis with the reading of texts from Bhagavad Gītā and the Bible,[79] indicative of Yogananda's contribution towards harmony of religions.

In his last speech, delivered at the Biltmore Hotel on 7th March 1952 in a banquet in honour of an Indian Ambassador to USA, he stressed the need for unity among the various nations and religions of the world, to work hand in hand to make the world a better place. He says, "I hope and pray … that you will always emphasize the airplanes of mercy from one country to another instead of airplanes that carry bombs to destroy. Let us work for peace on earth as never before… to make this world a better home, a spiritual home with God as our Guide." After saying this Paramhansa Yogananda chanted one verse from his poem "*My India*" and slid to the floor and breathed his last.[80]

He acknowledges true religion of the world as authentic paths to Self-realization, as branches of God's one immeasurable tree of truth. He fervently prays with earnestness, "Teach us to chant in harmony the countless expressions of our supreme devotion…Break Thy vow of silence and sing to us the heart-melting melody of human brotherhood (*sic*)."[81] For him, the diverse religions are branches of God's immeasurable tree of truth.[82] He built a temple in Hollywood called 'Church of All Religion' in which people of all religions are welcomed. He says, "We should begin to build unity with the idea that has been initiated by Self-Realization Fellowship a 'Church of All Religions', not eclecticism, but for all religions as constituting various paths to God."[83] The '*Aims and Ideals*' of Yogada Satsanga Society and Self-Realization Fellowship, which is put at the end of most the books published by the organization, states – "To reveal the complete harmony and basic oneness of original Yoga as taught by Bhagavan Kṛṣṇa and original Christianity as taught by Jesus Christ." When asked about his special emphasis on Christianity while talking about inter-religious relations as a whole, Paramhansa replies, "It is the wish of Babaji that I do so. He asked me to interpret the Christian Bible and the Hindu Bible to point out the basic unity of Christianity and Vedic scriptures. He sent me to the West to fulfill that

[78] Yogananda, *Autobiography of a Yogi,* p. 326.

[79] *Paramhansa Yogananda In Memoriam*, p. 58.

[80] *Ibid.*, p. 69.

[81] Yogananda, *Whispers from Eternity,* p. 3.

[82] *Ibid.*

[83] Yogananda, *Man's Eternal Quest*, p. 14. Cf. Paramhansa Yogananda, *Journey to Self-Realization*, pp. 239-240.

mission."[84] So, while stressing unity of religions of the world, he put special emphasis on Hindu-Christian unity in his ministry and writings.

Stressing the importance of feeling of oneness, he says that we should think in terms of universality, loving all nations for "every Church is a church of God, every place of worship is a temple of God, every human being is a child of God."[85] Those who achieve oneness with God can no longer think exclusively for them. Yogananda testifies, "I feel that I am present in all bodies. I have no awareness of race and other distinctions at all… I feel you all to be a part of me."[86] Such feeling of belongingness to all is possible only when one is submerged in Christ Consciousness or Kṛṣṇa Consciousness.

The striking feature of Yogananda's method of teaching is his usage of Christian concepts and terms to explain Hindu doctrines. Phrases and terms such as 'Kingdom of God', 'heaven', 'Father', 'Father in heaven', 'Spirit', 'Satan', 'faith in God', 'image of God', etc. which are not commonly used in Hindu religious tradition and its scriptures or by other Hindu gurus and philosophers, are frequently used by him. He also heavily employs Biblical stories, personalities, concepts and verses to explicate his message. This is done presumably in order to communicate meaningfully to his Western audience, with whom he spent thirty years of his ministerial life, who were Christians or were deeply influenced by Christendom. So, in this sense it is just a communication *modus operandi*. But, more likely, it can also be the result of his genuine love for the Bible and its massage for it is said: "The Bible was one of Yogananda's favourite books. He used apt quotations from it to illustrate his views on various subjects."[87] Yogananda himself testifies that Bible, Bhagavad Gītā and *Whispers from Eternity*, his own composition are the three books that inspire him.[88] In any sense it is certain that his theological and philosophical method to disseminate his message to the Western audience is inculturation or to use a more appropriate term – interculturation or enreligionization[89] - presenting his Hindu religious truths by using the religious resources, terms

---

[84] Paramhansa Yogananda, *Sayings of Paramhansa Yogananda*, p. 19.

[85] Yogananda, *Journey to Self-Realization*, p. 173.

[86] *Ibid.* 171.

[87] Weeraperuma, *Divine Messengers of Our Time,* p. 112.

[88] Paramhansa Yogananda, *How to be Happy All the Time*, p. 66.

[89] A number of scholars are eager to go beyond the concept and practice of 'inculturation' or 'indigenization' and suggested the alternate terms – enreligionization or interculturation. Cf. K.P. Aleaz, *The Gospel of Indian Culture*, (Calcutta: Punthi Pustak, 1994), pp. 165-168; Arvind P. Nirmal, "Theological Implications of the Term 'Indigenous'" in *Dialogue in Community: Essays in Honour of S.J. Samartha*, edited by C.D. Jathanna, (Mangalore: The Karnataka Theological Research Institute, 1982), p. 169; Aloysius Pieris, *An Asian Theology of Liberation*, (Maryknoll: Orbis Books, 1988), p. 52.

and concepts of the recipients so as to make his message meaningful and understandable.

Yogananda, like other gurus investigated, teaches with authority and confidence. He is sure of what he says and that makes him declare, "Each word that is coming to you through me is coming from God. And what I tell you, I have experienced. If you practice these truths you will see for yourself that what I am saying is real."[90] Be it God, Jesus, Kṛṣṇa, fact of *Karma* doctrine or astral world – everything he teaches, comes from a personal intuitive experience which makes him bold and confident.

3. Yogananda's Interpretation of Jesus Christ: *Jesus, the Embodiment of Universal Consciousness*

Inter-religious relations is quite prominent in the whole movement of Yogananda. Though he has a concern for harmony of all authentic religions of the world, his primary purpose was to establish relationship between Hinduism and Christianity. Jesus Christ acquires, therefore, reasonably high degree of standing in the whole movement. This is visible from the aims and objectives of his organizations, viz. Yogoda Satsanga Society of India and Self-Realization Fellowship, where it states that Hindu-Christian unity is given priority. They have a line of gurus where Jesus was included along with Lord Kṛṣṇa, Babaji, Lahiri Mahasaya Sri Yukteswar and Yogananda himself. Such a background stands high in the way he looks at Jesus Christ. Again, Yogananda has an assumption that the message of Jesus "can be understood only by developing the inner consciousness, spiritualizing the inner self."[91] So, intuitive experiential knowledge is always emphasized in Yogananda's over all interpretation of Jesus. With this background in mind we will turn to his interpretation of Jesus Christ.

3.1. The Influences

In formulating any theology or philosophy, or interpreting a person or texts, the context, the cultural and religious background of a person who interprets or formulates and the influences on him or her always play a pivotal role. Raimundo Panikkar maintains that "every interpretation depends on the context and the cultural approach of the person who elaborates it."[92] K.P. Aleaz also attaches great importance to the context and goes to the extent of saying, "the Indian religio-cultural context will decide the content of the Gospel of

---

[90] Yogananda, *To Be Victorious in Life*, p. 4.

[91] Yogananda, *Divine Romance,* p. 339.

[92] Raimon Panikkar, *The Fullness of Man: A Christophany*, (New York/New Delhi: Orbis/ ISPCK, 2006), p. 3.

God in Jesus for India."[93] The same thing echoes in the writing of Christopher Duraisingh who says that we comprehend whatever is given to us "only in terms of concepts and categories given in our context. There is no conceptual experience apart from our immediately given linguistic structure that shapes our ordinary human experience."[94] Yogananda is no exception. His religious upbringing, his college education in a Christian college, his guru Sri Yukteswar Giri who seems to be genuinely influenced by Christian teachings with whom he spent a number of years, the Christian Western context where he lived, his strong commitment to the Yoga of Bhagavad Gītā - all played a far-fetched role in the formation of what we may call his 'Christology'.

Yogananda and his guru Sri Yukteswar (1855-1936), who hailed from Serampore, did their college education in the Serampore College, a Christian Institution founded by the Baptist missionaries William Carey, Joshua Marshman and William Ward. When Sri Yukteswar did his studies, the missionary influence might have been at its peak. Therefore, it is almost safe to conclude that Yogananda's guru was deeply influenced by Christianity. The lone book ever written by Sri Yukteswar at the request of Babaji, entitled *The Holy Science*, the purpose of which is to discern the underlying unity between the scriptures of Christianity and *Sanātana Dharma*, only confirms our proposition that he, the guru of Paramhansa Yogananda, himself was deeply affected by the Christian teachings. In this book, the author tries to underline the similarities between Christian faith and Hinduism by comparing basically the *Book of Revelation* of the Bible and the Saṃkhya Philosophy of Hinduism with a view to show that there is no real discrepancy, much less any real conflict between the teachings of Christianity and Hinduism.[95]

Another influential personality in the life of Yogananda, though he met only once, is the so-called 'the deathless yogi' - Mahāvatar Babaji who is said to have constant communion with Christ, working together with him.[96] So,

---

[93] K.P. Aleaz, *Theology of Religions: Birmingham Papers and other Essays*, (Calcutta: Moumita Publishers & Distributors, 1998), p. 180.

[94] Christopher Duraisingh, "Indian Hyphenated Christians and Theological Reflection Part II: An Alternate Modes of Theologizing now Prevalent in India" in *Religion and Society*, (Vol. XXVII, No. 2, June 1980), pp. 85-86.

[95] Cf. for a detailed study Swami Sri Yukteswar Giri, *The Holy Science*, (Dakshineswar, Kolkata: Yogoda Satanga Society of India, 2007, first published in 1949).

[96] Paramhansa Yogananda maintains that it was this Babaji, of course, in consonance with the wish of Christ, who had sent him to the West with dual purpose – to proclaim the ancient Hindu spiritual science – *Kriya Yoga* and to interpret properly for the world the profound meaning of the words of Christ. His close disciple Swami Kriyananda also attests: "Paramhansa Yogananda... was sent by God to the West with the commission of restoring the teachings of Jesus Christ to their full and original glory." See Yogananda, *The Second Coming of Christ Vol. 1,* p. xxviii, and also Swami Kriyananda, *Revelations of Christ Proclaimed by Paramhansa Yogananda*, (Gurgaon: Ananda Sangha Publications, 2007), p. 15.

definitely Babaji's cosmic friendship with Christ also contributed immensely to the interest and love Yogananda had developed for Christ.

Yogananda's guru Swami Sri Yukteswar seemed to be well versed in the Bible. Much of Yogananda's knowledge of the Bible is derived from his learning of the Bible at the feet of his guru and not from the reading of it. He confesses, "It was from my guru, Swami Sri Yukteswar, in his *āśram* in India, that I learned about Christ and the real meaning of his teaching. And I never forget it."[97] He writes in his *Autobiography*, "Master expounded the Christian Bible with a beautiful clarity. It was from my Hindu guru, unknown to the roll call of Christian membership, that I learned to perceive the deathless essence of the Bible."[98] Thus, it can be said that Yogananda is greatly indebted to his guru for his knowledge of Jesus Christ and the Bible. Another significant influence which shaped Yogananda's understanding of Jesus Christ is his personal intuitive and corporeal experience of Jesus Christ. Many times he said that Jesus appeared before him 'in flesh and blood', talking and meditating with him, sometime the whole night. Yogananda narrates: "I know that Christ is real, for I have seen him many many times. Jesus was not as fair complexioned as most of you in the West. He had dark skin. And his eyes were not pale blue, as many artists paint them; they were dark. Nor was his hair blond, it also was dark."[99] Such a living experience of the living Christ makes him bold and precise in his interpretation.

3.2. Yogananda's Approach to Jesus

Yogananda's approach to Jesus and his teaching is basically a combination of phenomenological and philosophical methods. He is phenomenological in the sense that he emphasizes experiencing the essence of religious phenomena with a direct intuitive communion rather than critical-analytical reading of the written scripture to deduce the meanings. He is also philosophical in the sense that his approach to religion delineates the oneness of philosophical speculation and religious experience, the rational logical deduction of truth and intuitive knowledge of truth – a combination suggested in Indian philosophy of religion. He says that the three components of philosophy such as ethics, psychology and metaphysics "taken together and put into practice, constitute religion."[100] Besides, he is not free from his advaitic philosophical stand as he interprets

---

[97] Yogananda, *The Divine Romance*, p. 260.

[98] Yogananda, *Autobiography of a Yogi,* p. 169.

[99] Yogananda, *Man's Eternal Quest,* pp. 290-291. He mentions in a number of places, a number of encounters he had with Christ. See Yogananda, *Whispers from Eternity,* pp.114, 127; Yogananda, *The Second Coming of Christ, Vol. 1*, pp. xxvii, xxx, xxxii; Yogananda, *Man's Eternal Quest,* pp. 233, 291. Cf. Paramhansa Yogananda, *Journey to Self-Realization,* p. 351; Paramhansa Yogananda, *The Divine Romance*, p. 264.

[100] Yogananda, *The Second Coming of Christ, Vol. 1*, p. xxv.

Jesus and his message. It is quite clear that he looks at the whole issue from these standpoints. He claims to be more *intuitive* than *rational* in his approach, which does not, however, nullify his rationality and speculative nature.

He rejects rational-intellectual and academic pursuit as primary method to understand the life and teaching of Jesus. Intellectual analysis from the perspective of a specific dogma will always miss the real message of Jesus Christ, because the factual understanding of Jesus' message comes through communion with Christ Consciousness.[101] He maintains,

> The only reliable standard of scriptural interpretation is the testimony of actual perception… The words of Jesus fully unfold their wisdom only to those who meditate deeply on the Christ Consciousness that Jesus possessed. Then one understands Jesus in the light of his (*sic*) spiritual experience of the Cosmic Consciousness of the Heavenly Father."[102]

He states that his knowledge of the Bible comes from God himself through direct perception rather than from books which he seldom read.[103] It is the product of his communion with Christ himself. He says, "From personal experience I know the reality of his life and miracles, for I have seen him many many times, and commune with him and receive his direct confirmation about these matters."[104] He reveals that Jesus has come to him often as baby Jesus and as young Christ. He also said that he has seen Jesus before his crucifixion, his face very sad; he has also seen him in the glorious form in which he appeared in his resurrection.[105] He claims that what he had written on Jesus is given by Jesus himself where he acts as one who took down carefully what Jesus has said. He writes in the Introduction to his *Commentary*:

> Identifying myself with the consciousness of Jesus, I have felt what he felt when he spoke to his disciples and to the crowds as recorded in the Gospels. What I have tried to convey are the thoughts and consciousness of Jesus that were behind his words. I commune with Christ and ask him: 'I don't want to interpret the Bible from my own views. Will you interpret it?' Then he comes to me. In attunement with Christ in ecstasy and in spirit, I have taken down his explanation to the best of my ability as they came through me; those revelations are written in these treaties. I do not explain, I

[101] Yogananda, *The Second Coming of Christ, Vol. 1*, p. xxii.

[102] *Ibid.*

[103] Yogananda, *How You Can Talk With God*, p. 11.

[104] Yogananda, *The Second Coming of Christ, Vol. 1,* p. xxvii.

[105] *Ibid.*

> see. I do not tell you what I think, but what I am led to say by inner realization.[106]

However, we should also remember, without skeptical in the validity of his personal communion with Christ, that the many years stayed with his guru itself apart from whatever studies he had on the Bible and extra-biblical material[107] gave him substantial knowledge of the Christian scripture so as to expound the life and teaching of Jesus. His ability to quote numerous Bible verses exactly as written in the Bible shows that he also did an in-depth academic study of the Bible.

We will look at Yogananda's interpretation of Jesus Christ under four main headings – The person of Jesus Christ, The work of Jesus Christ, The Message of Jesus Christ and The Realization of Christ Consciousness.

3.3. The Person of Jesus Christ

The 'person of Jesus Christ' here refers to 'who Jesus is'. Who is Jesus Christ according to Yogananda is the focus of this section.

3.3.1. Unveiling the Real Jesus

Like other Indian interpreters, who are unanimous in their claim that Christianity represented by the West distorts the real Jesus, Yogananda, with his emphasis on the direct experiential knowledge of Jesus, maintains that the West has forgotten the true meaning of Jesus Christ. He says, "Christ has been much misinterpreted by the world. Even the most elementary principles of his teachings have been desecrated, and their esoteric depths have been forgotten. They have been crucified at the hands of dogma, prejudice, and cramped understanding."[108] As the real Jesus is unknown today, Yogananda had undertaken, as he claims, the meticulous task of unveiling the real Jesus by re-interpreting the Gospels from Indian perspective, especially in relation to the ancient science of Yoga taught by Lord Kṛṣṇa in Bhagavad Gītā. Indian perspectival commentary is necessary basically because Jesus was an Oriental in birth, blood and training,[109] and it needs oriental mind and methods to unveil the real Jesus.

---

[106] Yogananda, *The Second Coming of Christ, Vol. 1,* p. xxx.

[107] Paramhansa Yogananda shows his acquaintance with William Hone's *The Apocryphal New Testament.* Cf. *Ibid.*, p. 70. See for detailed studies of this book William Hone, *Apocryphal New Testament*, (London: Ludgate Hill, 1820). The full title is *Apocryphal New Testament, Being all the Gospel, Epistles and Other Pieces Now Extant, Attributed in the First Four Centuries to Jesus Christ, His Apostles and Their Companions and not Included in the New Testament by Its Compilers.*

[108] Yogananda, *The Second Coming of Christ, Vol. 1,* pp. 89-90.

[109] *Ibid.*, p. 90.

3.3.2. Jesus as the Bridge between the West and the East

There are a number of Hindu interpreters who emphasize the Orient-ness of Jesus. Swami Akhilananda projects Jesus as an Oriental whereas for K.C. Sen Jesus is Asiatic. In the same manner Yogananda deems Jesus Christ to be an Oriental through and through – in birth, upbringing and training. But, unlike Akhilananda, he emphasizes Jesus' role as a bridge, a liaison between the East and the West. "Jesus is a divine colossus standing between Orient and Occident telling East and West to exchange their better qualities."[110] In fact the very reason why Jesus became incarnated is "to give to the world a new expression of *Sanātana Dharma.*"[111] Like the sun, Jesus rises in the east and goes to the west where the people regard him as their guru and saviour. He radiates the spiritual strength and power of the Orient to the West and becomes a divine liaison to unite God's peoples of the East and the West.[112]

3.3.3. Jesus Christ as an *Avatāra*

Yogananda asserts: "Without the guiding hand of God's *avatāras* it would scarce be possible for humanity to find the path unto God's kingdom."[113] Jesus is one of such incarnations (*avatāras*) amongst Gautama Buddha and Bhagavan Kṛṣṇa. The purpose of God's incarnation in the form of Jesus is "to demonstrate the forgiveness and compassion of God, whose love is a shelter even from exacting law."[114] While a number of Hindu interpreters of Jesus consider him as an *avatāra*, but maintain Jesus as attaining the avatārship at some point of his life,[115] Yogananda seems to have gone closer to Christian consideration of Jesus as incarnation of God by accepting that Jesus was born as *avatāra*. Moreover he puts Jesus in the same footing with Lord Kṛṣṇa and maintains that even though all the *avatāras* are the same as they are one with God, Jesus and Kṛṣṇa stand supreme, they are free from the karmic compulsion of rebirth and are created perfect by God.[116] Jesus was not born according to the natural process of reproduction; rather he was born in the immaculate way through the Virgin Mary when the Christ Consciousness came to her.[117]

---

110 Yogananda, *Man's Eternal Quest*, p. 284.

111 *Ibid.*, p. 285.

112 Yogananda, *The Yoga of Jesus: Understanding the Hidden Teaching of the Gospel*, (Los Angeles: Self-Realization Fellowship, 2009), pp. 14-15. [This book is an extract of *Second Coming of Christ, Vol. I & II*].

113 *Ibid.*, p. 3.

114 *Ibid.*, p. 4.

115 Cf. Chapter 1.

116 Yogananda, *Man's Eternal Quest*, pp. 294-296. Cf. Yogananda, *Whispers from Eternity*, p. 114, where he writes about his vision of Christ and Kṛṣṇa walking hand in hand.

117 Paramhansa Yogananda, *The Second Coming of Christ, Vol. I*, p. 49.

3.3.4. Jesus, the Man and Christ, the Consciousness

The main Christological contribution of Yogananda would be his understanding of Jesus Christ as comprises of Jesus, the human body who is like any other human being, and Christ, the universal consciousness. For him, in Jesus a human body the vast Christ Consciousness was born.[118] The universal Christ, Christ Consciousness or Kṛṣṇa Consciousness, the second person in the Trinity, is a cosmic intelligence present in the body of Jesus.[119] Jesus the man fully reflected the Christ-Consciousness that is in all creation and for that reason he was called 'Jesus the Christ.'[120] Yogananda explains the relationship between Jesus the man and Jesus the Christ as follows:

> The ordinary consciousness of Jesus the man was bound by his body occupying a little speck of vibratory region on the earth. But... in oneness with the Cosmic Vibration of *Om*, the consciousness of Jesus expanded from the small territory of the body to all vibratory regions of creation. By meditation and by feeling cosmic vibration in every particle of vibratory space, Jesus the man became Jesus the Christ.[121]

Christ-Consciousness is manifested in the body of Jesus, but it cannot be limited to one human form only. "It would be a metaphysical error to say that the omnipresent Christ-Consciousness is circumscribed by the body of any one human being."[122] He connects this dichotomy with the concept of 'the son of man' and the 'son of God' where Jesus is the 'son of man' and Christ 'the son of God' – the only begotten son.[123] He further explicates: "When Christ called himself the 'Son of God' he means the Universal Spirit dwelling in him...But, at other times, when Christ used another phrase – the 'Son of man' – he meant the physical body, the offspring of man, the flesh that is born out of another human body."[124] However, Jesus Christ is not 'the only son of God', there are a number of 'sons of God' like Buddha, Lord Kṛṣṇa, Sage Vyasa and many more.[125] Yogananda writes, "Jesus, Javadva (the birth name of Kṛṣṇa), Buddha,

---

[118] Yogananda, *Man's Eternal Quest*, p. 297; Yogananda, *The Second Coming of Christ, Vol. I*, p. 89; Yogananda, *Journey to Self-Realization,* p. 355.

[119] Paramhansa Yogananda, *Metaphysical Meditation*, p. 107. Cf. Yogananda, *The Second Coming of Christ, Vol. I*, p. xxxiii.

[120] Paramhansa Yogananda, *Self-Realization Fellowship Lesson S-6, P-157,* (Los Angeles: Self-Realization Fellowship, 1984, first published in 1956), p. 2.

[121] *Ibid.*

[122] Yogananda, *Man's Eternal Quest,* p. 297.

[123] Yogananda, *The Second Coming of Christ, Vol. I*, p. 17.

[124] Yogananda, *The Science of Religion*, p. 48.

[125] Yogananda, *The Second Coming of Christ, Vol. I*, p. 18.

Babaji – all are Christ, that is, they expanded their consciousness to receive the universal Christ Consciousness."[126] The union of two natures – God and human in one body formula of Chalcedonian Creed which is accepted by many of the churches is systematically rejected by Yogananda's Christology.

The first Hindu interpreter of Jesus who separated Jesus, the man and Christ, the universal consciousness was K.C. Sen. He explained the universal Christ or the Son of God in terms of *logos* and said that Christ is present everywhere, in all human being, and it was the theme of Ṛg Vedic Poet. India was or is never an enemy of Christ, the *logos*.[127] Swami Vivekananda followed K.C. Sen in this regard and said that Christ is not to be confused with Jesus of Nazareth as Christ is the Cosmic Intelligent whereas Jesus is a historical person. "This cosmic intelligence is what people call Lord, or God, or Christ, or Buddha, or Brahman, what the materialists perceive as force, and the agnostics as that infinite, inexpressible beyond; and we are all parts of that."[128] So, what you call 'Buddhas' and 'Christs' are only the names of certain states of realization.[129]

This type of separating Christ from the human person Jesus is also not uncommon in the history of Christian theology. The attempt to separate historical Jesus and Christ of faith is traced back to Martin Kahler (1835-1912), but it can be said that Gotthold Lessing (1729-1781) already laid the foundation for the separation of Christ of faith from Jesus of history. Way back in 1781, Immanuel Kant already wrote, in his *Critique of Pure Reason*, of a gulf between the *contingent truths* of our experience and the *necessary truths* of reason and the need to separate knowledgeable realm of facts and the unknowable realm of value. This dichotomy seems to have influenced the later disjunction between the Christ of faith and the Jesus of history. The Danish existentialist Soren Kierkegaard developed further the separation and it was Rudolf Bultmann who finally put a stamp to it by making a definitive and radical separation.[130] However,

---

[126] Paramhansa Yogananda, *Yogoda Lessons in Self-Realization, S.5-L-129*, (Dhaksineswar: Yogoda Satsanga Society of India, n.d.), p. 2.

[127] See K.C. Sen, "That Marvelous Mystery – The Trinity", a lecture delivered on 21st January, 1882, in *Keshub Chander Sen* edited and compiled by David C. Scott, (Madras: CLS Press, 1978), pp. 237-239.

[128] *The Complete Works of Swami Vivekananda*, (CWSV) *Vol. 2*, Mayavati Memorial Edition, (Calcutta: Advaita āśrama, 1994), p. 231.

[129] *CWSV, Vol. 8*, p. 105.

[130] See Norman Geisler, *Baker Encyclopedia of Christian Apologetics*, (Grand Rapids: Baker Books, 1999), pp. 53-55. For a detailed study, ref. Martin Kahler, *The So-Called Historical Jesus and the Historic Biblical Christ*, trans. by Carl E. Braaten (Philadelphia: Fortress Press, 1964); Hans Werner Bartsch (ed,), *Kerygma and Myth* by Rudolph Bultmann and Five Critics, (New York: Harper & Row, 1948); Rudolph Bultmann, *New Testament & Mythology and Other Basic Writings*, (Philadelphia: Fortress Press, 1984); J. Estlin Carpenter, *The Historical Jesus and the Theological Christ*, (Boston: American Unitarian Association, 1912); Soren Kierkegaard, *Concluding Unscientific Postscript to Philosophical*, edited and translated by Howard V. Hong

Yogananda comes out with a different proposal to separate Jesus, the human body and Christ, the universal Consciousness which is present in everyone and everywhere in the universe. Unlike K.C. Sen, he explains the universal Christ Consciousness in relation to Indian thought and identifies Christ Consciousness with *Kutaṣtha Chaitanya* or Kṛṣṇa Consciousness, not using Greek concept of *logos* as Sen did, but like Sen, he says that Christ is known in India.[131]

3.3.5. Jesus in India

For Yogananda, Jesus Christ was an Oriental and a Yogi.[132] He believes in the popular theory that Jesus spent 14-18 years in India before he started his public ministry. His stay in India among the masters helped him to reawaken and reinforce his own God-realization. The 'wise men from the East' who paid a visit to a new born Jesus were great sages of India. So, Jesus' visit to India is a reciprocal act to their visit.[133] He writes in the *Yogoda Lessons* that Jesus' teachings were influenced by Hindu Yoga.[134] So, Jesus' teachings were born internally from his God-realization and nurtured externally by his studies from the Masters in India.[135] But he cautions not to conclude that Jesus learned everything he taught from his spiritual mentors and associates in India both

---

and Edna H. Hong, (Princeton: Princeton University Press, 1992), Immanuel Kant, *Critique of Pure Reason*, translated by Paul Guyer and Allen W. Wood, (Cambridge: Cambridge University Press, 1998).

[131] Yogananda, *Journey to Self-Realization,* p. 169, 355.

[132] Paramhansa Yogananda, Christian Yoga: Super Advanced Course Number One Lesson 1 to 12, (Los Angeles: Yogoda Satsanga Society, 2007), p. 2.

[133] Yogananda, The Yoga of Jesus, p. 11; Yogananda, Divine Romance, p. 259. There is a popular story about Jesus' visit and stay in India for some 18 years. The first person who declared this was a Russian Traveler, Nicholas Notovitch who visited India in 1887. He claimed that he discovered in the Buddhist Monastery in Tibet a scroll which contains the account of the Saint Issa (Jesus) who came from Palestine and stayed in India till the age of thirty and left for Palestine to finish his ministry. Basing on what was discovered he published a book entitled: The Unknown Life of Jesus Christ in 1894. Two others, Swami Abhedananda, the President of Ramakrishna Math in 1922 and Nicholas Roerich from Russia in the mid 1920s also visited the same monastery in Tibet to prove the authenticity of what Notovitch had said. They also confirmed the testimony of Notovitch. See Yogananda, The Second Coming of Christ, Vol. I, Discourse 5, pp. 80-89. For a detailed study ref. Nicholas Notovitch, The Unknown Life of Jesus Christ, translated from French by Alexina Loranger, Fourth Edition, (Chicago: Indo-American Book Agency, 1916); Holger Kersten, Jesus Lived in India: His Unknown Life Before and After the Crucifixion, (New Delhi: Penguin Books India Pvt. Ltd., 2001); Swami Abhedananda, Journey to Kashmir and Tibet, (Calcutta: Ramakrishna Vedanta Math, 1987); Elizabeth Clare Prophet, The Lost Years Of Jesus: Documentary Evidence Of Jesus' 17-Year Journey To The East, (Gardiner: Summit University Press, 1984); Alan Jacobs, When Jesus Lived in India: The Quest for the Aquarian Gospel: The Mystery of the Missing Year, (Mumbai: Yogi Impression, 2010).

[134] Yogananda, Christian Yoga, p. 5.

[135] Cf. Yogananda, The Yoga of Jesus, p. 14.

belonging to Hinduism and Buddhism. As he is an *avatāra*, he came into this world with his own endowment of wisdom.[136] Even though Yogananda and most of the Indian gurus talk about this 'theory' as a historical fact, it is not without contention. A number of scholars including Max Muller put forth their opposition to it and among the Hindu leaders, Swami Vivekananda rejects this theory.[137]

3.4. Works of Jesus Christ

In Yogananda's scheme of thought, the person of Jesus Christ and message he preached are more significant and important than what he did during his earthly incarnation though these are not really possible to separate from one another owing to their interconnectedness. He appears to have accepted Jesus' activities recorded in the Bible, but his interpretation, done in a different context from a different perspective, seems to be quite different from Christian interpretation.

3.4.1. Miracles

Yogananda believes in the miracle-working-power of Jesus, because, being in tune with Christ Intelligence, he is capable of sending 'cosmic energy' to do super-natural things. He can make use of 'Christ Will' which governs the astral forces and entities to cast out demons.[138] For Yogananda miracle is not the most important thing in Jesus. He says that he had seen the same type of miracles performed by Indian masters, but these are not the criterion of their greatness. "A master's most important spiritual accomplishment is the conquering of *māyā*, delusion."[139] The greatest miracle which Christ performed, according to Yogananda, is what he did on the cross - allowing himself to suffer; his power

---

[136] Yogananda, The Second Coming of Christ, Vol. I, p. 87. Cf Yogananda, The Second Coming of Christ, Vol. II, p. 966 where he says in much more stronger tune – "Jesus did not acquire his knowledge from Vedāntic tradition of ordinary or religious schooling. His wisdom was from the infinite scroll of God-consciousness, holy writ enshrined in his soul in previous incarnations.

[137] *The Complete Works of Swami Vivekananda*, Vol. 3, Mayavati Memorial Edition, (Calcutta: Advaita āśrama, 1994), p. 220. Scholars like Max Muller, Robert Van Voorst, Marcus J. Borg, Paula Fredriksen, etc. disowned this theory. See Friedrich M. Mueller, *Last Essays*, (New York: AMS Press, Inc., 1973, first published in 1901); Simon J. Joseph, "Jesus in India?" *Journal of the American Academy of Religion,* (Volume 80, Issue 1), pp. 161-199. Robert E. Van Voorst, *Jesus Outside the New Testament: An Introduction to the Ancient Evidence,* (Grand Rapids: William B. Eerdmans Publishing Company, 2000); Marcus J. Borg, "The Spirit-Filled Experience of Jesus", in *The Historical Jesus in Recent Research: Sources for Biblical and Theological Study*, edited by James D. G. Dunn and Scot MacKnight, (Winona Lake: Eisenbrauns, 2005), pp. 302-314; Paula Fredriksen, *From Jesus to Christ*, (Yale: Yale University Press, 2000); Bradley Malkovsky, "Some Recent Developments in Hindu Understandings of Jesus" in *Journal of Hindu-Christian Studies*, (Vol. 23, Article 5, 2010), pp. 3-8.

[138] Yogananda, *The Second Coming of Christ, Vol. I,* pp. 420-421.

[139] Yogananda, *Man's Eternal Quest,* p. 295.

to withstand suffering and ability to say prayer of forgiveness, his refusal to save himself – this is the greatest miracle Jesus Christ performed.[140]

3.4.2. Cross

Yogananda, while believing in the importance of crucifixion, does not ascribe salvific power to it. Jesus' crucifixion is a demonstration that "the earth is not his kingdom" and also "that for all souls the material world is not their kingdom." It is a demonstration for all humans that they are immortal.[141] For him Jesus' crucifixion was purely a voluntary act. By wearing a crown of thorns Jesus "became a real emperor, ruling the hearts of millions through the ages."[142] Yogananda vividly explains away that it is the Jesus who is called 'son of man' – the human body that was dead, was crucified, *not* the Christ – not the 'son of God' who is residing in the human body of Jesus.[143]

3.4.3. Resurrection

Yogananda uncritically accepts the bodily resurrection of Jesus Christ. His resurrection is a demonstration that there is a way to conquer every delusion (*māyā*) imposed on human being. It testifies the supremacy of human's spirit over matter.[144] Jesus' resurrection was "the resurrection of the soul into oneness with Spirit" that "lifted his consciousness beyond all relatives of vibratory creation and merged his Self with the transcendental Father, Absolute Spirit."[145] But, resurrection is not the monopoly of Jesus Christ, because "in the resurrection of Jesus we have the assurance of our Creator that God-realized devotees, if they wish, can find not only immortality of the soul but also of the body."[146] Though he did not mention by name, Yogananda would surely have in mind people like Babaji and his own guru Sri Yukteswar when he says 'immortality of body' can be achieved as these two yogis are known to have resurrected. Yogananda reports in his *Autobiography* that some weeks after he passed away, his guru Sri Yukteswar appeared before him in flesh and blood. He embraced him for some two hours. They discussed about the nature of Astral world (heaven) for two long hours, after which he vanished in a thin air.

---

140 *Ibid.*, also Yogananda, *Divine Romance*, p. 259.

141 Yogananda, *The Second Coming of Christ, Vol. II*, pp. 1468-1469.

142 Yogananda, *Journey to Self-Realization*, p. 212.

143 Yogananda, *The Science of Religion*, p. 48.

144 Yogananda, *The Second Coming of Christ, Vol. II*, p. 1499.

145 *Ibid.*, p. 1500

146 *Ibid.*, p. 1499.

This confirms, for him, that bodily resurrection is possible and happened not only to Jesus Christ but to other advanced Masters.[147]

Yogananda often mentions the possibility of meeting the resurrected Christ in 'flesh and blood' just like the doubting Thomas and other hundreds of people. Not only he met Jesus several times as already mentioned, he says that St. Francis also met Jesus in flesh and blood 'every night'; we can also behold him if we are in tune with him.[148] He points to a specific spot where one can meet Christ: "Christ is right here, he can be seen if you look within your forehead at the point between the eyebrows; the center of Christ Consciousness (*Kutaṣtha Chaitanya*); the seat of single spiritual eye. If you want to see Christ, concentrate at this point of spiritual vision; look through the spiritual eye."[149]

3.4.4. The Work of the Resurrected Jesus Christ Today

Jesus Christ does not cease working even after resurrection. In spirit and in 'flesh and blood', he is still active in the world, working together with other enlightened Masters, especially with Babaji of the Himalaya, trying to uplift human spirituality and bring peace and harmony among the nations.[150] Yogananda testifies,

> Jesus Christ is very much alive and active today. In Spirit and occasionally taking on a flesh-and-blood form, he is working unseen by the masses for the regeneration of the world. With his all-embracing love, Jesus is not content merely to enjoy his blissful consciousness in Heaven. He is deeply concerned for mankind (*sic*) and wishes to give his followers the means to attain the divine freedom of entry into God's Infinite Kingdom. He is disappointed because many are the churches and temples founded in his name, often prosperous and powerful, but where is the communion that he stressed — actual contact with God?[151]

Yogananda maintains that metaphysically Jesus is already omnipresent now, smiling at us through every flower, feeling us through every matter,

---

[147] See Yogananda, Autobiography of a Yogi, chapter 43, "Resurrection of Sri Yukteswar", pp. 398-417, also Yogananda, *The Second Coming of Christ, Vol. II*, pp. 1510-1511.

[148] Yogananda, *Divine Romance*, pp. 258, 266.

[149] *Ibid.*, p. 258.

[150] See Yogananda, *Autobiography of a Yogi*, pp. 291-293; Yogananda, *Divine Romance*, pp. 256, 257.

[151] Yogananda, *The Second Coming of Christ, Vol. I*, pp. xxvii-xxviii.

breathing to us through the breath of wind. Jesus can appear to any one in flesh-and-blood form right now if we have complete devotion.[152]

3.4.5. The Second Coming of Christ

One of the main differences between Christianity and Hinduism is the way they look at time. For Christianity, time is linear having beginning and end whereas Hinduism like most of the ancient Greek philosophers believes in cyclical or circular time where there is no beginning or end. From a Hindu eye Yogananda looks at Jesus' promise of his second coming and life thereafter. He rejected Christian teaching of Jesus' second coming, day of judgment and concept of heaven, an eternal place for those who believe in Jesus Christ. Interpreting Jesus' words, "And if I go and prepare a place for you, I will come again and will tak you to myself, so that where I am, there you may be also" (Jn. 14:3-4), Yogananda denounces the reliability of a literal rendering of this verse - Jesus is preparing a dwelling place up in heaven for his people. He says that this refers to the fact that a guru like Jesus, even after his passing, would continue to help his disciples toward their attainment of Cosmic Consciousness.[153] When Jesus said, "I will come again", it is not that he would have to come again in person to his disciples in order to help them toward liberation, "but that through their communion with Christ Consciousness in spiritual ecstasy, his consciousness would appear a second time in their consciousness. Thereby their consciousness would expand into the omnipresence of Christ Consciousness."[154] So, second coming of Christ for Yogananda is the upliftment of a devotee's consciousness to receive and be one with the universal Christ Consciousness; once such union happened, the second coming of Christ would occur in the life of a devotee.

This way of interpreting Christ's return would mean the shedding of one of the core Christian doctrines, and the basic foundation of Christian hope which run through the length and breadth of the New Testament – the second coming of Christ and the genesis of a new life with a new resurrected body in heaven. Yogananda's interpretation of this passage not only betrays one of the foundations of Christianity but also militates against a number of other passages both in the Gospels and Epistles which talk about Jesus' second coming and the provision of everlasting life in heaven. Yogananda replaces the central Christian doctrine with his peculiar philosophical stuff derived from Hindu philosophical worldview. Such interpretation would invite strong criticism from Christians who would require a more respectful treatment of

---

[152] Yogananda, *Man's Eternal Quest*, pp. 232, 287. Cf. Yogananda, *Journey to Self-Realization*, p. 361.

[153] Yogananda, *The Second Coming of Christ, Vol. II,* p. 1372.

[154] *Ibid.*, p. 1373.

their fundamental belief. Therefore, Yogananda's interpretation of this passage could damage interfaith relations rather than fostering it.

3.5. The Message of Jesus Christ

Yogananda alleges that Christian version of Jesus' teaching does not represent the true meaning of Jesus' teaching. So, his intention is to unveil the actual teaching of Jesus Christ which was so much distorted. He asserts that he received the meanings of Jesus' teaching directly from him. With his new interpretation he believes that the actual meaning of Jesus' message that had been veiled for twenty centuries is now unveiled for people for the first time.[155] He insists that the teachings of Christ can be best understood in relation to his own background, that is, an oriental background especially that of Indian spiritual heritage. "Gospel can be rightly understood in the light of the teachings of India – not the caste-ridden, stone-worshipping, distorted interpretations of Hinduism, but the philosophical, soil-saving wisdom of her *riṣis*."[156] At the back drop of this Yogananda delivers his interpretation of Jesus' teachings basing on the four Gospels, and I shall discuss here some of the prominent aspects of this.

3.5.1. Oneness with the Father

Like any advaitic guru, some of the Yogananda's favorite passages on Jesus are: "I and my father are one" (Jn. 10:30) and "You are gods" (Jn. 10:34). By declaring "I and my father are one", Jesus means to say, "As the Christ Consciousness present in my body and omnipresent in vibratory creation is one with transcendent Cosmic Consciousness, I have truly told you, I and my Father are one."[157] These *oneness* statements of Jesus Christ that are in tune with Advaita Vedānta worldview indicate that it is the Christ Consciousness within the body of Jesus, that is referred to. So, when Jesus quotes the scripture that "You are gods", he means that all souls are made in the pure image of God, so, in their true essential nature, human beings are gods – but the degree of realization of it is different.[158] Yogananda concludes, "Jesus never said: 'I am God', but by his divine works he manifested the realization that his consciousness, having emanated from God was one with Him."[159]

---

[155] Yogananda, *The Second Coming of Christ, Vol. I*, p. xxxi.

[156] Yogananda, *The Yoga of Jesus*, p. 17.

[157] Yogananda, *The Second Coming of Christ, Vol. II*, p. 1020.

[158] *Ibid.*, p. 1021.

[159] *Ibid.*

3.5.2. On Trinity

Yogananda explains the Holy Trinity in relation to Advaita Vedānta but modifies when and where he wishes to serve his purpose. Before creation there is only undifferentiated Spirit which becomes, after manifesting creation, God the Father, God the Son and God the Holy Ghost. When Spirit evolves through the action of the cosmic magic measuring power of *māyā*, the Unmanifested Spirit became God the Father. In Hindu Scriptures He is called *Īśwara*, the Cosmic Ruler or *Sat* – the Transcendental Intelligence. The Vibratory force emanating from Spirit, endowed with the illusory creative power of *māyā*, is the Holy Ghost which is the Cosmic Vibration, the Word (*logos*), *Aum* (*Om*) or Amen. This Holy Ghost in Hindu scriptures is called *Aum* or *Maha-Prakṛti* (Cosmic Mother that gives birth to all creation). The transcendent consciousness of God the Father became manifests within the Holy Ghost vibration as the Son – the Christ Consciousness, the only begotten Son – the Cosmic Intelligence. In Hinduism this is called *Tat* – cosmic consciousness. Yogananda maintains that God the Father is always transcendent and beyond creation. Therefore, God the Father, God the Son and God the Holy Ghost is the representation of Hindu concept of *Sat*, *Tat* and *Aum*.[160] This concept is *not* congruent with the popular rendering of trinity as *sat-cit-ananda* – being, consciousness and bliss. Moreover, Śaṅkara used the term *Īśwar*a to indicate the manifested God (*saguṇa* Brahman),[161] not the unmanifested or transcendent God the Father as stated by Yogananda. Again, Yogananda, time and again prays to the 'Father in haven', giving praise and adoration to Him, and at the same time maintains that God the Father is always transcendent, unqualified, unmanifested and beyond creation. How will it be possible to offer praise and prayer in worship to the unmanifested and unqualified God? There seems to be inconsistency in his metaphysics and ethics.

3.5.3. The Only Begotten Son as the Only Saviour

Yogananda consistently maintains that "Jesus never referred to his Son-of-man consciousness, or his body, as the only saviour throughout all time… It is a metaphysical error to speak of the historical person of Jesus as the only saviour. It is the Christ Intelligence that is the universal redeemer."[162] When Jesus asked people to believe in the only begotten Son in order to have

---

[160] Yogananda, *The Second Coming of Christ, Vol. I*, pp. 10-12, 108-109. Cf. Yogananda, *The Second Coming of Christ, Vol. II*, pp. 1007-1008. Yogananda, *Metaphysical Meditations*, p. 48; *Sayings of Paramhansa Yogananda*, p. 11; Yogananda, *Journey to Self Realization*, pp. 118, 175; Yogananda, *Man's Eternal Quest*, pp. 299-300.

[161] Satischandra Chatterjee and Dhirendramohan Datta, *An Introduction of Indian Philosophy*, (Calcutta: University of Calcutta, 2004, first published in 1939), p. 387.

[162] Yogananda, *The Second Coming of Christ, Vol. I*, p. 274. Cf. *Sayings of Paramhansa Yogananda*, p. 48.

everlasting life, he was referring to the Christ Consciousness, which was fully manifest within himself and all God-realized masters throughout the ages, and latent within every soul.[163] Referring to the *exclusive* statement of Jesus – "No one comes to the Father except through me", Yogananda says,

> Explaining these verses, my revered guru Sri Yukteswasji said: 'Jesus meant, never that he was the sole Son of God, but that no man (*sic*) can attain the unqualified Absolute, the transcendent Father *beyond* creation, until he (*sic*) has first manifested the 'Son' or activating Christ Consciousness *within* creation. Jesus, who had achieved entire oneness with that Christ Consciousness, identified himself with it inasmuch as his own ego had long since been dissolved.'[164]

Here, Jesus means to say, "In truth, I declare unto you that the Christ Consciousness in me and in all other liberated souls, is the only door through which devotees can enter into Cosmic Consciousness."[165] Thus, Jesus as a person in history is not *the only way* to the Father, but the only way to the Father's kingdom is an attunement with Christ Consciousness, which is present in the historical body of Jesus as much as in other Masters (like Kṛṣṇa, for example). Thus, the only begotten Son – the Christ Consciousness is the only saviour.

3.5.4. Jesus on *Māyā*

Māyā is a Cosmic delusion, the magical power in creation by which limitations and divisions are apparently present in the Immeasurable and Inseparable. *Māyā* is not understood by Hindu *Ṛṣis* alone. The Old Testament prophets called *māyā* by the name of Satan. Satan or *Māyā* is the Cosmic Magician who produces multiplicity of forms to hide the One Formless Verity. The sole purpose of Satan is to divert human from Spirit to matter. Christ described *māyā* picturesquely as a devil, a murderer, and a liar in John 8:44.[166]

3.5.5. Bodily Resurrection, Heaven and Hell

Keeping his Hindu essential doctrine of *Karma-Saṃsāra* intact, Yogananda tries to explain Jesus' perspective on bodily resurrection, heaven and hell. Resurrection of the body so as "to be sent to Hades or Heaven is baseless, revolting, injurious and unreasonable"; for a just and loving heavenly Father

---

[163] Yogananda, *The Second Coming of Christ, Vol. I*, p. 274. Cf. *Sayings of Paramhansa Yogananda*, 273.

[164] Yogananda, *The Second Coming of Christ, Vol. II*, p. 1373.

[165] *Ibid.*, p. 1015.

[166] *Sayings of Paramhansa Yogananda*, p.105.

cannot do that; because it "is an untenable conception to ascribe to a just and loving God."[167] But this concept is clear when it is understood in the light of the law of *karma* and reincarnation. Bodily resurrection mentioned by Jesus in John 5:28-29 is nothing but a reincarnated life after the dead of a person. Likewise, a soul going to Hades or heaven after death corresponds to a soul putting on another earthly body or waking up into a spiritual kingdom not to return to the earthly world respectively.[168]

3.5.6. The Kingdom of God

When Jesus says, "The kingdom of God is within you", he means to say that kingdom of God is not something beyond us, but it is within us, it is not a visible kingdom or heaven, rather it is of eternal, immutable, ever-newly blissful Cosmic Consciousness.[169] Yogananda maintains that God's kingdom is to be found not by 'observation' using our matter-tuned five senses, but by interiorization of the consciousness to perceive the Divine Reality 'within us'.[170] To find the kingdom of God, one should concentrate within and find the sphere of God-consciousness hidden behind his/her material consciousness.[171] According to him there is a beautiful accord between Jesus' teaching: "The kingdom of God is within you" and the Raja yoga given by Kṛṣṇa in Bhagavad Gītā. Both teach that a devotee will enter the kingdom by concentrating on the spiritual eye, the Christ Consciousness center (*Kutaṣtha Chaitanya*) at the point between the eyebrows. When entering this door, one leaves behind all material attachments and experiences the interior infinitudes of God's kingdom.[172]

3.5.7. The Beatitudes Explained

Yogananda gives alternative explanation to the beatitudes, giving in general allegorical interpretation from Hindu standpoint. "Blessed are the poor in spirit…" The poor here signifies wanting in any outer superficial elegance of spiritual wealth. To be poor in spirit is to have divested one's inner being – his/her spirit of desire for and attachment to material objects. By renunciation a person achieves inner purity and possesses the Eternal Kingdom.[173] "Blessed are ye that weep now" – indicates utmost longing for God-realization. According to Yogananda, Jesus was speaking of the state of divine melancholy resulting from the awakening consciousness of separation from God, which

---

[167] Yogananda, *The Second Coming of Christ, Vol. I*, pp. 358-359.

[168] *Ibid.*, pp. 361, 364.

[169] Yogananda, *The Second Coming of Christ, Vol. II*, p. 1177.

[170] *Ibid.*, p. 1178.

[171] *Ibid.*, p. 1179.

[172] *Ibid.*, pp. 1181, 1183.

[173] Yogananda, *The Yoga of Jesus,* p. 75.

creates in the soul an insatiable yearning to be united with God. A person who really mourns in desirous of God, having deep longing for Self-realization will be satisfied.[174]_

"Blessed are they which do hunger and thirst..." – hunger and thirst are a metaphor for human's spiritual quest. One should thirst and hunger for both theoretical knowledge and realization of inner Truth which can be satisfied not by sense pleasure but only by righteousness – the actions, attitudes, and attributes that are right for the soul.[175] "Blessed are the merciful..." – Unlike the God of Moses who is depicted as a God of wrath, the God of Jesus was so gentle. Jesus expressed God's gentleness and mercy when he prayed for those who crucify him. To receive divine mercy, one needs to be spiritually qualified so that he/she may be a blessing to other deluded children of God.[176] "Blessed are the pure in heart..." – The final religious experience is direct perception of God for which purification of heart is mandatory. From the state in which consciousness is completely deluded by *māyā*, a person progresses through the successive states of the propelled heart, the steady heart, the devoted heart, and ultimately attains the clean heart. Having reached this stage of purity, the devotee gains the true perception of God as present in one's soul and omnipresent in all beings.[177]

"Blessed are the peacemakers, for they shall be called children of God" – 'Son of God' consciousness makes one feel love for all beings, because true God's children cannot feel the difference between nationality or race. Human beings have been given potentially limitless power, to prove that they are indeed the children of God. The true Christ-method of living, i.e. feelings of oneness with all beings, can do way with conflict and bring about peace and understanding on earth.[178]

Looking at the way Yogananda interprets the beatitudes, it is apparent that he does not explain these verses from their context, nor does he try to bring out their actual meanings, but rather uses them as a tool to communicate his own message. In other words, he seems to have too much presupposition in reading the beatitudes. His allegorical interpretation and too much spiritualization may miss the real message of the beatitudes. For instance, he takes 'those who weep' as an indicator of deep longing for God, but the literal meaning of this phrase – those who are mourning because of various problems right now shall be comforted – is likely to be nearer to the intended message of Jesus than what has been projected by Yogananda.

---

[174] Yogananda, *The Yoga of Jesus,* pp. 76-77.

[175] *Ibid.*, p. 78.

[176] *Ibid.*, pp. 79-80.

[177] *Ibid.*, pp. 80-82.

[178] *Ibid.*

3.5.8. Jesus on *Karma-Saṃsāra*

The most apparent fundamental difference between Indian religions, i.e., Hinduism and its offshoots and Semitic religions such as Judaism, Zoroastrianism, Christianity and Islam lies in the doctrine of transmigration of soul (*karma-saṃsāra*) which is commonly known as 'reincarnation'. The former accepts whereas the later is known to reject the doctrine. But, Yogananda propagates that Jesus believed and taught this doctrine. Some Christian scholars also argue infavour of this doctrine saying that both Jesus and early Christians endorsed it but Church fathers removed reincarnation from Christian theology.[179] Rev. 3:12 - "If you conquer, I will make you a pillar in the temple of my God, you will never go out of it (you will never take another birth?"); Matt. 11:14 - Talking about John the Baptist Jesus says, "... and if you are willing to accept it, he is Elijah who is to come"; Matt. 17:11-13 - "Elijah is indeed coming and will restore all things, but I tell you that Elijah has already come...Then the disciples understood that he was speaking to them about John the Baptist"; Jn. 3:3 - "No one can see the kingdom of God unless they are born again." are some of the biblical basis put forward as indicating Jesus' acceptance of reincarnation.

Yogananda maintains that Jesus himself reincarnated many times before he became perfect to be *avatāra*. In his last previous life, Jesus was Eliseus (Elisha). "I know for certain that he was Eliseus in a past life," whereas "John the Baptist was Elijah (Elias) in his former life."[180] Not only that Jesus revealed his knowledge of the truth of soul's reincarnation, the early Christianity also taught this doctrine.[181] "Jesus' perfect life on earth was the result of several previous life in which he had developed self-mastery."[182] Jesus is, thus, a normal human being who, by virtue of his spiritual attainment during many incarnations, became perfect and one with God eligible to be *avatāra*.

---

[179] For a detailed discussion on the alleged early Christians endorsement of the doctrine of Reincarnation, see, Geddes MacGregor, *Reincarnation in Christianity: A New Vision of the Role of Rebirth in Christian Thought*, (Wheaton, Illinios: The Theosophical Publishing House, 1978); Elizabeth Clare Prophet, *Reincarnation: The Missing Link in Christianity*, (Montana: Summit University Press, 1997); Marvin Vining, *Jesus the Wicket Priest: How Christianity was born of An Essene Schism*, (Vermount: Bear & Company, 2008); James M. Pryse, *Reincarnation in The New Testament*, (New York: Theolophical Society Publishing Department, 1904); Ethan Walker III, *The Mystic Christ: The Light of Non-Duality and the Path of Love According to the Life and Teachings of Jesus*, (Redmond, Oregon: Devi Press, 2003). Some of the Gnostic literature like *Pistis Sophia,* also contains Jesus' endorsement of Reincarnation doctrine. Cf. Pistis Sophia trans. into English by G.R.S. Mead, (Leeds: Celephais Press, 2007, first published in 1896).

[180] Yogananda, *Man's Eternal Quest*, p. 231. Cf. pp. 139, 305, and also Yogananda, *The Second Coming of Jesus*, Vol. I, p. 243.

[181] Yogananda, *Man's Eternal Quest,* p. 306.

[182] *Ibid.*, p. 230.

To take Jesus as accepting the doctrine of *Karma-Saṃsāra* is a contentious issue which is highly objectionable in the light of the Biblical witnesses where a number of verses, (to mention few - 2 Sam. 12:23; 14:14; Job 7:9-10; Ps. 78:39, Matt. 24:35, 25:31-46; Lk. 23:39-43, 16:20-25; Acts 17:31; 1Cor. 7:31; 2 Cor. 5:1, 4, 8; 4:18; Heb. 9:27-28; Rev. 20:11-15.) even John the Baptist's own words point otherwise. When John the Baptist himself was asked: "Are you Elijah?", he answered, "I am Not" (Joh. 1:21). One of the Church fathers, Origen whom some people like Geddes MacGregor considered as accepting reincarnation of soul, said in his commentary to Matthew thus – "In this place it does not appear to me that by Elijah the soul is spoken of, lest I should fall into the dogma of transmigration, which is foreign to the church of God, and not handed down by the Apostles, nor anywhere set forth in the Scriptures."[183] Origen continued to argue that as the scripture said that John would come "in the spirit and power", not "in the soul", it cannot refer to reincarnation doctrine. It should be taken in the form of - "the spirit of Elijah rested on Elisha" (2 Kings 2:15). John the Baptist came in the spirit and power of Elijah, not as the reincarnation of the soul of Elijah.[184] Moreover, according to the Hindu tradition, for reincarnation of soul to happen one must die physically and born again; but in the case of Elijah, the biblical witness clearly said that he did not experience physical death (2 Kings 2:11), thereby ruling out the possibility of reincarnation. Therefore, Yogananda's theory on Jesus' acceptance of reincarnation doctrine could not stand when we consider the whole biblical message.

Apart from what had been discussed, Yogananda interprets a numbers of select passages from the four Gospels of the New Testament. In all the interpretations, be it 'Jesus' baptism' or 'Sermon on the Mount' or 'I Am' sayings, or the Lord's Prayer or other ethical and moral teachings of Jesus Christ, he uses Hindu religious worldview, especially his understanding of universal Christ or Kṛṣṇa Consciousness and his advaitic stand of reality as the methodological device with which he measures, weights and deduces Jesus life, work and message.

3.6. The Realization of Christ Consciousness

The end of the whole religious and philosophical teaching of Yogananda and of his interpretation of Jesus Christ can be summed up as 'the realization of Christ Consciousness'. His mission is to help people to have direct communion with God which is possible only when one is in attunement with universal Christ Consciousness or '*Kutaṣtha Chaitanya*' or 'Kṛṣṇa Consciousness'. According to Swami Smaranananda, the primary work of Yogoda Satsanga Society

[183] John Patrick, *Origen's Commentary on the Gospel of Mathew, Book XIII*, in *Ante-Nicene Father*, Vol. 9, edited by Philip Schaff, (Edinburgh T&T Clark, 1897), p. 474.

[184] *Ibid.*, p. 475.

of India, an organization founded by Yogananda, "is the dissemination of spiritual teachings and scientific technique of meditation given by Pramhansa Yoganandaji... for direct personal experience of God."[185] Having denied the sufficiency of knowledge of Jesus Christ gained from the reading of the written scripture, Yogananda stresses the importance and obligatoriness of having a direct personal experience of Jesus Christ. He says, "Worshipping Jesus is not truly meaningful until one can expand his (*sic*) consciousness to receive within himself (*sic*) the Christ Consciousness. That is the second coming of Christ."[186] As Christ Consciousness is the door, if any one enters it through meditation, realizing the Christ Consciousness present in his/her soul, he or she will be saved.[187]

The Christ which is present within each individual at the divine center of consciousness should be realized. One should strive to be united with the Christ Consciousness within. This is "to rise from the tomb of ignorance and realize in the ascension of the resurrection of the Christ within."[188] All liberated masters achieved oneness with God through their perfect attunement with Christ Consciousness.[189] When this realization dawns in a person, he/she looses his/her ego, the "I" disappeared, he/she feels all things pervaded by One Life. Yogananda testifies this feeling of oneness in a true advaitic sense, "I feel that I am present in all body."[190] He tirelessly works throughout his life to help people get direct communion with Christ Consciousness which is possible in deep meditation with *Kriya Yoga* techniques. He concludes that realization of Christ within us in ecstatic communion will give us the real resurrection, the second coming of Christ into our life.[191]

There is hardly any doubt that Yogananda left a deep impact upon the life of his followers to revere Jesus Christ as the liberated master, guru and the *avatāra*. Some of his close disciples are reported to have testified that Jesus appeared before them in flesh and blood.[192] Swami Smaranananda narrates the

---

[185] Personal interview with Swami Smaranananda, the General Secretary of Yogoda Satsanga Society of India, at Yogoda Satsanga Math, Ranchi on 20.07.2013.

[186] Yogananda, *Man's Eternal Quest*, p. 292. Cf. Yogananda, *Journey to Self-Realization*, p. 119.

[187] Yogananda, *The Second Coming of Jesus, Vol. II*, p. 1016.

[188] *Ibid.*, p. 1524.

[189] Yogananda, *Journey to Self-Realization,* p. 355.

[190] *Ibid.*, p. 171.

[191] Yogananda, *The Second Coming of Christ, Vol. I,* p. xxxiii. Cf. Paramhansa, *Divine Romance*, p. 255; Paramhansa Yogananda, *Journey to Self Realization*, p.175.

[192] Swami Smaranananda, the General Secretary of Yogoda Satsanga Society of India, says that they know of devotees who have direct communion with Jesus Christ. Personal interview with him, op.cit. Swami Amarananda told the researcher during an informal conversation at Yogoda Satsanga Math, Dakshineswar, Kolkata on 22.06.2013 that Jesus Christ appeared in flesh and blood before some of the close companions of Paramhansa Yogananda. Also Sri

impact of Yogananda's teaching on Jesus to the members of Yogoda Satsanga Society of India (YSS) and Self-Realization Fellowship as follows –

> Jesus is one of the six gurus that we accept, revere and follow. We consider them to be an *avatāra*...We have a common altar in our *āśrams* and Centres all over the world in which Jesus Christ and Bhagavan Kṛṣṇa are included...Lord Jesus inspires me to first seek the inner communion of God...We understand and accept all that our Master said about Jesus...The core principles of Jesus' Ten Commandments is part of the introspection chart that are recommended to our devotees and monastics. Jesus' two commandments to 'Love the Lord their God....' and 'Love thy neighbor as thyself' are principles that YSS strives to inculcate among all devotees...[193]

Christmas celebration inaugurated by Yogananda in 1950, where a day long prayer and meditation is observed on Christmas Eve,[194] is continued by the Self-Realization Fellowship and Yogoda Satsanga Society of India wherein all the *āśrams* and centres organize spiritual programme all over the world. In short, Yogananda's teaching on Jesus Christ does not die with him, but is still followed by his followers as their guiding principle.

In his attempt to unveil the real Jesus, Yogananda definitely made a serious attempt, may be the most solemn and elaborate interpretation ever attempted by any Hindu religious leader down the ages. His attachment to Jesus Christ is beyond contestation. His emphasis on the importance of personal direct experience of Christ in intuitive communion is laudable. His faithfulness to the written scripture – the Bible and the highest degree of status he assigns to Jesus Christ alongside Lord Kṛṣṇa would be encouraging for many Christians. May be that is the reason why many Christians involve in his movement. He accepts almost all the important orthodox Christian doctrines on Christ but renders a new interpretation.

However, in his interpretation, he does not care to analyse the Greek vocabularies and sentences with which the New Testament was written, in order

---

Gyanamata who is one of the most trusted disciples of Paramhansa also testifies that Jesus used to appear before her, touching her with his hand and talking with her. Cf. *God Alone: The Life and Letters of a Saint Sri Gyanamata,* (Dakshineswar: Yogoda Satsanga Society of India, 2007, first published in 1984), pp. 33-34.

[193] Personal interview with Swami Smaranananda, *op.cit*. Jesus is counted as one of the gurus in their 'Line of gurus' which also includes Lord Kṛṣṇa, Babaji, Lahiri Mahasaya, Sri Yukteswar Giri and Yogananda. Cf. "The Self-Realization Fellowship/Yogoda Satsanga Society of India Line of Gurus" in *http://www.yogananda-srf.org/lineageandleadership/The_SRF_Line_of_Gurus.aspx#.UgE42ayLvEQ* (5.8.2013).

[194] Yogananda, *The Second Coming of Christ, Vol. I*, p. 55.

to arrive at the exact meaning of the original language nor does he employ any of the modern biblical criticism. Is it possible to unveil the real Jesus without a proper analysis of the original language with all its vocabularies and sentence construction? Or, will we get an accurate result without taking into consideration the historical and social settings of the first century Jewish and Roman world where Jesus lived? For Yogananda, intellectual, academic and rational analysis to understand Jesus is futile, so, he resorts to intuitive experiential knowledge – a direct knowledge gained not from the reading of the scripture but from communion with Christ Consciousness as a method of knowing the real Jesus Christ. There are a number of Christian mystics all over the world who claimed to have such a direct experience of the risen Christ. But the Jesus they knew is not a Hinduised Jesus as projected by Yogananda but the Jesus of the Bible and of the Christian theology and of the Christian Church which is substantially different from the Jesus of *Kriya Yoga*. Can Yogananda be correct while others are wrong? Again, interpreting Jesus' teachings and biblical witnesses to Jesus intuitively by depending on vision and subjective experience of Jesus Christ alone is precarious, because such interpretation can be easily misguided due to its highly subjective nature and objective truth may not be reached. Thus, the primary hermeneutical tool employed by Yogananda - a direct knowledge gained from communion with Christ Consciousness is highly questionable as to how far it produces the truth.

Concluding Remarks

Yogananda and his whole movement are deeply influenced by a line of gurus – his own guru Sri Yukteswar Giri, Lahiri Mahasaya who is the guru of Sri Yukteswar and Babaji the guru of Lahiri. These three gurus collectively are responsible for the making of Yogananda as a renowned Yogi and giving him a mission to fulfill – to spread the ancient science of *Kriya Yoga* to the West and to show the unity of Jesus' teaching in the Bible and Lord Kṛṣṇa's teaching in the Bhagavad Gītā. Yogananda belongs to the ancient Swami Order which was considered as regenerated by Śaṅkara, but he does not follow Śaṅkara in toto; he rather modifies to suit the contextual needs of the people. Unlike original Śaṅkarites, he believes in the doctrine of *avatāra*, Bhakti way of salvation, emphasizes on the worship of personal God (the incarnations of God) with prayer and devotion rather than contemplating on the supra-personal Brahman. His primary task is to lead people to have personal communion with God and for this *Kriya Yoga* is prescribed as the supreme way, an 'aeroplane route to God'. Two organizations he founded – Yogoda Satsanga Society of India and Self-Realization Fellowship, USA continue this work till today.

Yogananda's commitment and attachment to Jesus is just amazing. He inherited such a respectful attitude towards Jesus from his guru and other gurus in the 'Line of guru' which is augmented by a frequent experience of vision of Jesus in 'flesh and blood'. Among the gurus investigated in this research, he can be considered as having the highest degree of attachment to Jesus, and is presumably the most serious interpreter. He interpreted Jesus life, work and message with sublime respect and love for him, using his philosophical and religious commitment as the basis, in relation to which he read Jesus Christ.

However, his total rejection of Christian Christological formulations as missing the real Jesus and that his interpretation alone represents the reality of Jesus' life and works is a one sided position. No Christological formulation is perfect including that of Yogananda's. Strengths and weaknesses should be weighed and conclusion drawn instead of elevating one as the only true interpretation while bashing aside the others. European or American contextual interpretations of Jesus represented by a number of Christian scholars as well as Indian contextual interpretations of Jesus represented here by Yogananda had been done in particular socio-religious and political contexts. One cannot be fully right while other is fully wrong. Thus, Yogananda's conviction that his interpretation alone is correct cannot be justifiable.

Every aspect of Jesus is looked into from the perspective of ancient science of yoga without taking into consideration his Palestinian and Jewish religious and cultural context. In his interpretation, we see a Hinduised Jesus who is substantially different from the Jewish religious tradition, quite detached from Abrahamic covenant and disconnected from Mosaic Law. Yogananda, stressing the need of contextual interpretation, advocates taking the Oriental context into consideration in interpreting Jesus; however, his 'oriental context' is nothing but Hindu religious and cultural context, and does not pay attention to the huge difference between Indian religio-cultural context and that of Palestinian Jewish one. Can we expect the unveiling of the *real* Jesus from such a 'contextual interpretation' where some aspects of the context are taken into consideration, leaving others which seem to be equally important?

His emphasis on direct intuitive communion with Christ, which precisely is an impressive attempt, is the result of his own experience of communion with Christ. He teaches others to do so as this communion or intuitive experience is possible. He maintains that Christ is omnipresent, so he is present in us as our inner most being. The realization of this in an intuitive ecstasy is the religious goal of everyone, the salvation, the destiny of religious journey. He suggests *Kriya Yoga*, the scientific technique of meditation, as the best way for achieving such a communion. Again, he puts Jesus in a higher position than most of the Indian interpreters of Jesus do. Unlike Swami Vivekananda and S. Radhakrishnan for whom Jesus is a growth from human to divine, Yogananda perceives Jesus Christ as achieving union with God right from the beginning of his life as he came into this world as a true *avatāra*.

The main Christological contribution of Yogananda is his differentiation of Jesus Christ in to 'Jesus' the human person and 'Christ' the universal consciousness. This type of separating Jesus Christ into Jesus and Christ is already seen in the Christological formulations of Hindu religious reformers like K.C. Sen and Swami Vivekananda. It also reflects the age-old discussion of 'Jesus of history' and 'Christ of faith' by Christian theologians. Though it is difficult to ascertain whether Yogananda is influenced by these or not, the possibility of him being inspired by these Christological discussions cannot be ruled out either. Nevertheless, Yogananda further clarifies what had been dimly presented before in the works of Sen and Vivekananda. In his Christology, Jesus the human body is considered as hosting Christ, the universal consciousness, which is the real 'Son of God', the only saviour. This gives him room for fulfilling his mission to establish the essential unity between Hinduism and Christianity by using Christ Consciousness as a meeting point, because for him, 'Christ' is not the monopoly of Jesus, the son of Mary. However, this concept militates against the age-old Christological formula – the inseparable union of the two natures – human and divine in the person of Jesus Christ. It also betrays the biblical witness that Jesus of Nazareth, son of Mary is the eternal *logos*, the Word which was with God and which was God which became flesh (human) (Joh. 1:1, 14). Yogananda has to go much further in dealing with a number of Biblical texts that stand in opposition to his Jesus and Christ theory.

Yogananda, like many Indian interpreters, selects some portions from the Gospels and works on them. He does not consider the whole message of the Bible – both Old Testament and New Testament and their connections, the thought that runs through them, the salvation history portraits throughout the whole Bible. Unless one takes into consideration the unity of the whole Bible and its message, interpreting Jesus Christ from some selected passages from the four Gospels could possibly produce a wrong picture of Jesus. Yogananda, if at all he is a *śrutivādin*, one who depends on the written scripture, should take into account the larger context of the Bible while interpreting Jesus.

Chapter 5

Sri Sathya Sai Baba's Interpretation of Jesus Christ

Sri Sathya Sai Baba may be the greatest religious phenomenon in India in the twenty first century. His greatness lies not only in his teaching or the multi-million followers he gathered around himself from the nook and corner of the world, but primarily in the way millions of people regarded him as the very God who is clothed with human flesh and bones. His social works that extend in various fields of human existence – education, village development, medical services, drinking water supplies, sport developments, etc. may have no parallel in the world. He practically transformed, in hardly fifty years, a remote village, Puttaparthi which had no motorable road communication, or school, a remote village of a little over hundred inhabitants into a world-class town with railway station, airport, multi-storied buildings, market place, numerous hotels and restaurants, super speciality hospitals, sport complex, education institutions from Nursery to University offering doctorate level studies in various departments, planetarium, music institute and the like. When they look at his achievement, his devotees come to the conclusion that 'no human being could accomplish the work he had done in just fifty years, so he is no less than God'.

In so far as his theological and philosophical teaching is concerned Sathya Sai Baba has more or less nothing new to add to the general Hindu religious understanding. His positive attitude towards other religions, his emphasis on 'unity of religion' and the fact that religious festivals of major religious traditions of India are celebrated in his *āśram* – *Prasanthi Nilayam*, Puttaparthi, create an atmosphere of religious harmony. Among his devotees and admirers are people belonging to various faith traditions and they, and Baba himself, do not feel necessary to leave their religion in order to be the follower of Sathya Sai Baba. His daring claim of himself being the *Avatāra* or God in human flesh with multitudes of miracles attracted so many people. They come from every part of the world to a small village in Andhra Pradesh to witness the God who talks, walks, touches and sees people face to face. It can be said that overwhelming majority of the seekers who had personal or group interview with Baba went back home with satisfaction in their hearts and the good news of Swami (as Baba was known among his followers) in their mouths. Some 70 years of active public life makes him one of the most famous personalities in the world. When he died in 2011 at the age of 84, (much earlier than the predicted age of 96) he left a huge amount of wealth, enormous establishments, millions of followers and a large number of books that contain his public discourses and his own writings.

Like many Indian gurus and spiritual leaders, Sathya Sai Baba also speaks of Jesus in highly affirmative manner. His discourses on Jesus were mainly delivered on the Christmas Day when the devotees of Baba celebrated this great occasion at Prasanthi Nilayam with him to grace the festival. His interpretation of the person and works of Jesus Christ is not only interesting to learn but it is also assumed to have a far reaching impact upon the way millions of his admirers perceive and receive Jesus Christ. This Chapter unearths Sathya Sai Baba's interpretation of Jesus Christ based primarily on his discourses and other secondary sources. The Chapter has three main sections – In the first section I present a brief account of the life of Sathya Sai Baba, the second section contains an overview of his philosophical and religious teachings. The third and final section deals with Swami's interpretation of Jesus Christ with concluding reflection at the end.

1. A Brief Account of the Life of Sathya Sai Baba

Sathyanarayana Raju, who became the famous Sathya Sai Baba (1926 -2011)[1] was born on 23rd November, 1926 in a village called Puttaparthi in Andhra

[1] For a detailed study of the life of Sri Sathya Sai Baba ref. N. Kasturi, *Sathyam Sivam Sudaram, Vol - 1* (*Life Story of Bhagavan Sri Sathya Sai Baba 1926-1961*), Prasanthi Nilayam: Sri Sathya Sai Sadhana Trust, 2009, first published in 1990; N. Kasturi, *Sathyam Sivam Sudaram, Vol - 2 (Life Story of Bhagavan Sri Sathya Sai Baba 1962-1968*), Prasanthi Nilayam: Sri Sathya Sai Sadhana Trust, 2009, Third Edition; N. Kasturi, *Sathyam Sivam Sudaram, Vol - 3 (Life Story of Bhagavan Sri Sathya Sai Baba 1969-1972)*, Prasanthi Nilayam: Sri Sathya Sai Sadhana Trust, 2008, Revised and enlarged; N. Kasturi, *Sathyam Sivam Sudaram, Vol - 4 (Life Story of Bhagavan Sri Sathya Sai Baba 1973-1979)*, Prasanthi Nilayam: Sathya Sai Books and Publication Trust, 2003; B.N. Narasimha Murthy, *Sathyam Sivam Sudaram, Vol - 5 (Life Story of Bhagavan Sri Sathya Sai Baba 1980-1985)*, Prasanthi Nilayam: Sathya Sai Books and Publication Trust, 2005; B.N. Narasimha Murthy, *Sathyam Sivam Sudaram, Vol - 6 (Life Story of Bhagavan Sri Sathya Sai Baba 1986-1993)*, Prasanthi Nilayam: Sathya Sai Books and Publication Trust, 2007; B.N. Narasimha Murthy, *Sathyam Sivam Sudaram, Vol - 7 (Life Story of Bhagavan Sri Sathya Sai Baba 1980-1985)*, Prasanthi Nilayam: Sri Sathya Sai Sadgana Trust, Publication Division, 2010.

Pradesh to a *Kshtriya* family, eight year after the death of the famous Godman, Sai Baba of Shirdi who prophesized before his death that he would reincarnate again to continue his task. His father was Pedda Venkama Raju and mother was Easwaramma. Baba himself testifies that his birth was not through human conception (*prasavā*) but through a direct descent (*praveśa*).[2] From the day he was born till his death in 2011, Swami's name was associated with a variety of miracles. When he was born, unlike other new born babies, he did not cry, but gave an enchanting smile that surprised people around.[3] It is said that at the time of his birth the musical instruments kept in their house had started making music by themselves, a huge cobra snake was seen to slight out from under his bed.[4]

Right from his childhood, he had a strange behaviour – talked very less, shunned non-vegetarian food, never visited the houses of non-vegetarians, paid no interest in eatables and ate very less.[5] However, he was highly intelligent, interested in music, poetry, drama and a skillful organizer with high leadership capability. Several children of his age used to gather around him, singing and dancing, happily spending their time with him. He used to teach them religious truths such as to love and obey parents, "Never deviate from the path of truth", "Never speak untruth to cover up your faults", "The power of truth is far superior to even that of atom bomb", "Truth alone will protect you", "Evil qualities like anger, hatred, and jealousy must be given up", "You should not covet others' property."[6] In regards to Hindu boys participating in Muslim festivals, Baba narrated, "I used to teach the children, 'It is not the religion that is important. Morality is important…Hence, cast off all your differences of religion and caste and be friendly with everyone…Your religion is love and your caste is the caste of humanity. Therefore, you always keep that principle of unity as your goal.'"[7]

Raju (as he was known during his childhood) used to instruct his friends in the principles of spiritual *sādhanā*. He asked them not to eat meat and fish. He was agitated against Bullock-cart races and cockfighting competitions which were very common in his village, he used to campaign against these practices. His father, Venkama Raju came to know this and confronted him

---

[2] Don Mario Mazzoleni, *A Catholic Priest Meets Sai Baba*, translated by Christian Moevs, (Prasanthi Nilyam: Sri Sathya Sai Books & Publications Trust, 2008), p. 110.

[3] *His Story as Told by Himself: A Compilation from the Divine Discourses of Bhagawan Sri Sathya Sai Baba*, (Prasanthi Nilayam: Sri Sathya Sai Sadhana Trust, Publications Division, 2011, first published in 2005), p. 4.

[4] Kailash Kumar & Jorgen Hovgaard, *Sai Baba: The Source of Light, Love and Bliss*, (New Delhi: Sterling Paperbacks, 1995), p. 19.

[5] *Ibid.*, pp. 5-6.

[6] *Ibid.*, pp. 7-8.

[7] *Ibid.*, pp. 8-9.

saying that a small kid should not interfere in the affairs of the elders in the village. But Raju was firm in his commitment, saying, "I am not interfering in the affairs of the elders in the village. They are torturing mute animals and birds, just for the sake of fun. I do not at all agree to this."[8]

His childhood days were spent with miracles one after another, slowly and slowly revealing his unnatural or super-natural quality, in the company of his friends who considered him as their 'teacher', attending primary school in the neighbouring village called Bukkapatnam and middle school in a small town called Kamalapuram and high school in Uravakonda.[9] As he grew in age his teaching also grew in depth – from a simple 'obey your parent, do not eat meat' during his school days in Bukkapatnam to higher religious principles in the latter part of his school days, that one should not search God outside as God is the indwelling presence, our true identity. That which is seen is perishable, whatever you see is only an illusion, you are the *draṣta* (the seer), that is your true identity.[10] The ever increasing pressure from within and an increasing new spiritual development to be seen from outside finally made a young Raju threw away his books on the ground and declared:

> *Know that I am Sai in reality;*
> *Cast off your worldly relationship;*
> *Give up your efforts to restraint Me;*
> *The worldly attachment can no longer bind me;*
> *None, however great he may be, can hold Me.* (Telegu Poem)[11]

Masoud Kheirabadi, in his book *Sri Satya Sai Baba* reports:

> On October 20, 1940, Sathya returned home from school, threw away his books, and proclaimed, "I am no longer your Sathya. I am Sai." According to a later interview with his sister-in-law, who was present on that day, a bright halo surrounded Sathya's head and almost blinded her with its splendor. Sathya addressed her, "I am going, I don't belong to you, *māyā* (illusion) has gone, My devotees are calling Me, I have My work, I cannot stay any longer.[12]

---

[8] Kailash Kumar & Jorgen Hovgaard, *Sai Baba: The Source of Light, Love and Bliss*, (New Delhi: Sterling Paperbacks, 1995), pp. 10-11.

[9] See *Ibid.* Chapters. 6, 7 and 9.

[10] See *Ibid.*, p. 115-117.

[11] *Sathya Sai Speaks, Vol. 36: Discourses of Bhagavan Sri Sathya Sai Baba*, Downloaded in a *pdf* format from the official website of Sri Sathya Sai Sadhana Trust, Publications Division - *http://www.sssbpt.info/english/sss.htm,* (10.8.2012), p. 130.

[12] Masoud Kheirabadi, *Sri Satya Sai Baba*, (Philladelphia: Chelsea House Publishers, 2005), p. 34.

On that day, that is the 20th Oct. 1940, when a young boy Raju decided to leave his school education, family and friends to start his mission, he chose the name 'Sai Baba', the name unknown to the people either in Uravakonda where he declared his true identity for the first time or Puttaparthi, his native village. They thought that it is a Muslim name.[13] According to him 'sa' means 'Divine', 'ai' or 'ayi' means 'mother' and 'Baba' means 'Father'; so, 'Sai Baba' means '*Divine Mother and Father.*'[14] The name given to him at birth 'Sathya' and the new name he assumed 'Sai Baba' were taken together and he was thus known as 'Sathya Sai Baba.'[15] From that day onwards, he preached a subject dear to his heart throughout his life - the unity of religion. From Uravakonda he went back to his village Puttaparthi where his tensed and anxious parents were eagerly awaiting his return as they learnt his unnatural behaviour. His parents believed that he was possessed by a demon as he exhibited abnormal behaviour that made them call the exorcist to deal with the problem. It is said that the exorcist happened to be a cruel man and tortured Sathya without any positive result. His parents decided to stop putting him in the hands of the exorcist. His father, who was deeply worried and strained for his 'para-normal' child, angrily asked, "This is too much! It must stop! What are you? Tell me – a ghost, or a god or a madcap? To this Sathya calmly replied reveling himself, "I am Sai Baba… I have come to ward off your troubles, keep your houses clean and pure."[16]

Initially, he claimed that he was the *avatāra* of Sai Baba of Shirdi, later on he claimed that he was the incarnation of Shiva and Śakti. Apart from claiming *avatārship* for himself, Satya Sai Baba acknowledges all the mythic avatars including Buddha, Balarama, and the twenty-two *avatāras* named in the *Bhagavata Purāṇa*; and recognizes Śaṅkara, Ramakrishna, Aurobindo, and Jesus Christ as *amsavatāras* or fractional *avatāras*. However, Satya Sai Baba claims to be a full and integral *avatār* like Kṛṣṇa a *purnavatāra*.[17] For Sathya Sai Baba 'names' are not important. He declares:

> You are calling Me 'Sathya'. Hence, I am Sathya. If you call Me 'brother', I am 'brother'. Whoever calls Me by whatever name, I

---

[13] *His Story as Told by Himself*, pp. 122-123.

[14] *Sathya Sai Speaks,* Vol. 9*: Discourse of Bhagavan Sri Sathya Sai Baba,* compiled by N. Kasturi, (Delhi: Bhagavan Sri Sathya Seva Samithi, n.d.), p. 84.

[15] Cf. *His Story as Told by Himself*, p. 119.

[16] Vishal Mangalwadi, *The World of Gurus: Critical Look at the Philosophies of India's Influential Gurus and Mystics*, Revised Edition, (Chicago: Conerstone Press, 1992), p. 109.

[17] Daniel E. Bassuk, "Six Modern Indian Avatars and the Ways they Understand their Divinity" in *Dialogue & Alliance*, Vol. 1 no 2, summer 1987, pp. 88-89; cf. V.K. Gokak, *Bhagavan Sri Sathya Sai Baba: The Man and the Avatar – An Interpretation*, (New Delhi: Abhinav Publications, 1989), p. 15.

> assume that form. To tell you the truth, I have no worldly relationship with anyone. I answer by whichever name you call me; all these names are ascribed to Me; they are not the names with which I have taken birth in this world. I have come into this world only to make you realize this truth.[18]

He understood himself not only as the *avatāra* but God Himself. He says, "Before the beginning of things only Cosmic Consciousness existed and I am that Cosmic Consciousness. In the beginning there was nothing just an endless void, but I was always there, the Origin, the true Beginning."[19] In 1970 Discourse he also states, "I AM neither man nor God nor an aerial spirit; I am neither a *Brahmin*, nor a *Kshathriya*, nor a *Vaishya*, nor a *Suudhra*; I cannot be described as *Brahmachaari* or a house-holder, or a recluse or a monk; describe me as a Teacher of Truth, as *Sathyam* (Truth), *Shivam* (Goodness) and *Sundharam* (Beauty)."[20] In 1998 he declared: "*Love is My form, Truth is My breath, Bliss is My food, My life is My message, expansion is My life, No reason for Love, no season for Love, No birth, no death.* If anyone asks you to tell about Sai Baba, sing this song. It will convey the whole message. Tell him, Love is His form and His life is His message."[21] This shows that Sri Sathya Sai Baba claims himself to be none but God.

As so many miracles accompanied his teachings,[22] within no time he gathered a multitude of followers around him. However, in the midst of a huge followings and tremendous popularity, Sathya Sai Baba also bears a number of allegations that he practices fraud, deceits, lies, homosexual abuse and murder cover-up. Several Western devotees came out with allegations of Baba that he was forcing them to have homosexual relationship. Some came out in the form of books, whereas others in the News papers and Internet.[23]

---

[18] *His Story as Told by Himself*, p. 124.

[19] Kailash Kumar & Jorgen Hovgaard, *Sai Baba: The Source of Light, Love and Bliss*, p. 39.

[20] *Sathya Sai Speaks, Vol. 10: Discourses of Bhagavan Sri Sathya Sai Baba*, Downloaded in a *pdf* format from the official website of Sri Sathya Sai Sadhana Trust, Publications Division - *http://www.sssbpt.info/english/sss.htm*, (10.8.2012), p. 20.

[21] *Sathya Sai Speaks, Vol. 31: Discourse of Bhagavan Sri Sathya Sai Baba, Delivered during 1998,* (Prasanthi Nilayam: Sathya Sai Books and Publications Trust, n.d.), p. 477.

[22] Nagamani Purnaiya has written a book in Telugu which was translated into English, entitled, *Divine Leelas of Bhagwan Sathya Sai Baba*. The book describes more than 140 miracles, of which she says "more than 115 were witnessed by me with abundant joy". in *http://www.saibaba.ws/ miracles2/abookonhim.htm*, (27.07.2011). Lists of numerous miracles performed by Sri Sathya Sai Baba can be seen in the website: *http://www.saibaba.ws/ miracles.htm*. Cf. also *Miracles of Divine Love, Vol. 1*, (Prasanthi Nilayam: Sri Sathya Sai Sadhana Trust, Publication Division, 2011); Howard Murphet, *Sai Baba: Man of Miracles*, (Delhi: Macmillan, 1975).

[23] Some of the internet materials that contain allegations against Baba could be seen here - *http://www.saibaba-x.org.uk/6/saisex1.htm* (30.12.2012); *http://www.saibaba-x.*

One of the most popular allegations of sexual mis-conducts against Baba came out in the form of a book by one of his former disciple, Tal Brook. His book *Avatār of Night*[24] explained in detail how Sathya Sai Baba was guilty of sexual abuse. After this, two of the disciples Faye Bailey and David Bailey published various allegations against Baba in the Magazine '*The Quarterly*' under the title "The Findings"[25] in the year 2000. Faye Bailey happened to be the editor of this Magazine.

Sathya Sai Baba responded his to critics in his discourse in 2000 saying, "Some people out of their mean-mindedness are trying to tarnish the image of Sai Baba. I am not after name and fame. So, I do not lose anything by their false allegations. My glory will go on increasing day by day. It will never diminish even a bit if they were to publicise their false allegations in the whole world in bold letters" and continued with a tone of warning them, "People who indulge in false allegations are bound to come to woe. Those who investigate such false publicity too will meet their doom."[26] As claimed by him these allegations seem to have neither reduced Swami's popularity nor the faith of his multitude of followers.

2. Sathya Sai Baba's Philosophical and Religious Teachings: An Overview

Sathya Sai Baba's philosophical and religious teaching covers all dimensions of God, human and creation, encompassing every aspects of human life in relation to God and creation. He is unshakably God-centered and human oriented. He touches most of the Hindu *Śastras* and philosophical schools, Hindu sages, great men and women of the world, other religious traditions, about himself, education, service to the society, environmental protection, war and peace, ethical and moral aspects of life, development, riches and poverty,

---

org.uk/30/Haraldsson.html (4.01.2013) *http://www.saiguru.net/english/* (30.12.2012); *http://77.170.120.22/ex-baba/engels/articles/ allegations.html* (30.12.2012); *http://saibaba-invigilator.blogspot.in/2007/06/my-story-by-diana-scott-later-mrs.html* (30.12.2012); *http:// barrypittard.wordpress.com/2010/04/11/ typical-testimony-of-sathya-sai-babas-sex-abuse-of-young-males/* (30.12.2012); *http://www.saibabacontroversy.com/abs.html* (30.12.2012); *http://exposedsaibaba.blogspot.in/2009 /05/murder-deception-debauchery-and-deciet.html* (2.01.2013);.

[24] Tal Broke, *Avatar of Night: The Hidden Side of Sai Baba*, (New Delhi: Tarang Paperbacks, 1982).

[25] The whole script of 'The Findings' is available in *http://www.npi-news.dk/page152. htm (2.01.2013)*, and the Summary in *http://www.saibabacontroversy.com/Summary.html* (2.01.2013).

[26] *Sathya Sai Speaks, Vol. 33, Discourses of Bhagawan Sri Sathya Sai Baba, Delivered during 2000*, (Prasanthi Nilyam: Sri Sathya Sai Books and Publications Trust, n.d.), pp. 388-390.

etc.[27] In view of the scope and limitation of this study, I do not intend to present a detailed analysis of his teaching, but put forward, highlights of the important facets of his teaching.

The uniqueness of Sathya Sai Baba, which makes him different from many other gurus, is his assertion of himself as *avatāra* or God Himself who needs no education on physical and metaphysical things either from the scriptures or through meditation. From this standpoint he gives philosophical and religious teachings and his teaching is also different to some extent from other God-men/women of India. A number of times he asked his devotees to worship him as God, meditate on Him and pray to Him. The poem composed by him elucidates his claim:

I am all forms ascribed to the Almighty;
I am the Embodiment of Perfect Peace
I am known by all Names through which
The Almighty is addressed and adored
I am the Embodiment of Goodness
I am Being-Awareness-Bliss-Ātman, the One
Without a Second, Truth, Goodness, Beauty.[28]

As this is the perspective from which he delivered his message, he always sounds authoritative in all of his teaching.

2.1. Unity of Religions and Brotherhood/Sisterhood of Men and Women

Sathya Sai Baba's religious commitment can be summed up as 'unity of religions'. "Bhagavan stood for unity of religions", says Gangadhar Shastri, in a personal interview, "One of the fundamental aspects on which Bhagavan Baba went on working all the periods of his incarnation on this planet is unity of religion."[29] He never questions the validity of other religions, nor does he ask anyone to leave his/her religion to follow him, but says, "When the essence of all religions is one and the same, when all the scriptures proclaim the same

[27] His numerous discourses during more than fifty years were collected together and published as *Sathya Sai Speaks* in Forty Two (42) volumes by Sri Sathya Sadhana Trust, Publications Division formerly known as 'Sri Sathya Sai Books & Publications Trust'.

[28] Quoted in Kailash Kumar & Jorgen Hovgaard, *Sai Baba: The Source of Light, Love and Bliss*, p. 32.

[29] Gangadhar Sastri in a personal interview at Prasanthi Nilayam, Puttaparthi on 29th October, 2012. Prof. Gangadhar Shastri is one of the top leaders in Prasanthi Nilyam, Sathya Sai Baba's *āśram.* He works there in the company of Baba for thirty long years. Presently, he is the Head of Sri Sathya Sai Institute of Higher Learning (Deemed University), Prasanthi Nilayam Campus and the Head of Political Science Department. I met him and had extensive personal interview during my visit to the *āśram* where I stayed at Prasanthi Nilayam for three days.

truth, when the goal of all human efforts is one, where is the basis for any differences? The paths are varied, but the destination is one and the same."[30]

In his *āśram* – Prasanthi Nilayam – festivals of major religions are celebrated every year where Baba himself used to give discourses in accordance with the festival celebrated. Prof. Shastri proudly says, "What I would like to tell you is we celebrate Christmas as appreciably as any other Hindu festival."[31] The Emblem of Sathya Sai Organization known as '*sarva dharma symbol*' which was designed by Baba himself depicts a clear focus on the unity of religions.

Fig. Showing the Emblem of Sri Sathya Sai Baba known as Sarva Dharma Symbol'.[32]

On the five discs of the Emblem, Swami drew the symbols of major religions of humankind such as: *OM* for Hindu faith, Wheel for Buddhist faith, a *sheaf of flames* for Zoroastrianism, the *crescent and the star* for Islam and the Cross for Christianity. Baba said as he instituted this emblem, "All faiths are facets of the same Truth, which can be spelt as Love, as Purity, as Charity, as Sacrifice or as Surrender of the will."[33] The message of this '*symbol*' is unity of all religions and of all being.

Again, Swami's emphasis on unity of religions is displayed at Prasanthi Nilayam in a variety of ways. Inside the *āśram* campus, there are statues of Hindu deities along with Shirdi Sai Baba, Buddha, Zoroaster and Jesus Christ.

---

[30] *Sathya Sai Speaks, Vol. 23: Discourses of Bhagavan Sri Sathya Sai Baba*, Downloaded in a pdf format from the official website of Sri Sathya Sai Sadhana Trust, Publications Division - *http://www.sssbpt.info/english/sss.htm*, (10.8.2012), p. 154; cf. *Sathya Sai Speaks, Vol. 39: Discourses of Bhagavan Sri Sathya Sai Baba, during 2006,* (Prasanthi Nilayam: Sri Sathya Sai Books and Publications Trust, n.d.), p. 198.

[31] Gangadhar Sastri, in a personal interview.

[32] Picture taken from *http://www.sathyasaitoronto.org/ssefeat.shtml* (19.02.2013).

[33] *Prasanthi Nilayam Information Booklet*, compiled by Public Relations Office, (Prasanthi Nilayam: Sri Sathya Sadhana Trust, Publications Division, 2003), p. 16.

Some of these statues, especially those which are on the hillock near the Hill View Stadium, are very huge, measuring 15 meters and more including the statue of Jesus Christ. Bhagavan Baba constructed a Mosque and a Hall in 1978 for the use of the local Muslims.[34] He advises his devotees not to worship one name and revile another as it is not a true devotion, but rather to recognise that Divine dwells in all beings and to realize that the essence of Divine names is the same.[35] V.K. Gotak, who is considered as one of the most authoritative interpreters of Baba's teaching says, "He (Baba) always warned us again and again that we should not be limited by the form and name of Sai. All other names and forms are equally divine and we should have the same respect and affections for them."[36] In the 1988 Christmas celebration at Prasanthi Nilayam, Sri Sai Baba exhorts, "God belongs to all. He is Universal. All of you have to give up differences of every kind and give no room for narrow parochial and national loyalties. Consider yourselves as the children of one God. You may worship God in any form of your choice, but recognise the truth that God is only one."[37] Thus, oneness of God, religions and of humans is always the key tenant of Baba's thought, "Fatherhood of God and brotherhood/hood of human beings" his catchphrase.

In spite of his positive attitude towards other religions and his emphasis on unity of religions, Sathya Sai Baba does not move an inch away from his Hindu identity and commitment. He even asserts that he preaches no new message but the message of the Vedas. "… let me tell you, it is nothing strange to me. Nor is the message I bring anything new! It is the message of the *Vedhas*, (*sic*) tested by time and guaranteed by the experience of many who put it into practice."[38] His teaching thoroughly reflects the Hindu *śastras*; endorsing the six philosophical schools (*sad darśanā*), he primarily follows Advaita Vedānta of Śaṅkara. He maintains, "The pinnacle of Indian thought is *Adhwaitha*, (advaita) the experience of the One, of the negation of duality."[39]

---

[34] *Prasanthi Nilayam Information Booklet*, p. 36.

[35] *Sathya Sai Speak, Vol. 24: Discourses of Bhagavan Sri Sathya Sai Baba*, Downloaded in a *pdf* format from the official website of Sri Sathya Sai Sadhana Trust, Publications Division - *http://www.sssbpt.info/english/sss.htm*, (10.8.2012), p. 18.

[36] V.K. Gokak, *Bhagavan Sri Sathya Sai Baba*, pp. 24-25.

[37] *Sathya Sai Speaks, Vol. 21: Discourses of Bhagavan Sri Sathya Sai Baba*, (Downloaded in a *pdf* format from the official website of Sri Sathya Sai Sadhana Trust, Publications Division - *http://www.sssbpt.info/english/sss.htm*, (10.8.2012), p. 132.

[38] *Sathya Sai Speaks, Vol. 5: Discourses of Bhagavan Sri Sathya Sai Baba*, Downloaded in a *pdf* format from the official website of Sri Sathya Sai Sadhana Trust, Publications Division - *http://www.sssbpt.info/english/sss.htm*, (10.8.2012), p. 53.

[39] *Sathya Sai Speaks, Vol. 9: Discourses of Bhagavan Sri Sathya Sai Baba*, Downloaded in a *pdf* format from the official website of Sri Sathya Sai Sadhana Trust, Publications Division - *http://www.sssbpt.info/english/sss.htm*, (10.8.2012), p. 56.

He also says that Śaṅkara's Advaita Vedānta "is the ultimate Truth" which is "only confirmed, not shaken, by the discoveries of science or the flights of intellect."[40] However, Bhagavan Baba does not denounce the importance of other Vedāntic schools like Viśiṣṭādvaita and Dvaita.

2.2. God, Human and Creation – One Whole

According to Sathya Sai Baba, God is Eternal Power, Omnipotent and Omniscient, the Cause and the Consequence - the potter, the clay and the pot.[41] You may call God by the name of Allah or Jesus or Kṛṣṇa, it is all the same. In fact, there is only oneness in this world,[42] because "God is immanent in the entire cosmos. The Universe does not exist apart from God."[43] He willed and the Universe happened. It is His play, the manifestation of His power. Humans embody His Will, His power, His Wisdom. But, they are unaware of this glory.[44] Though God in Its reality is *nirguṇa* (characterless), the worship of *saguṇa* God is helpful for those who are spiritually immature. "Temples, images and pictures are the slates and boards for the children in spiritual progress," but "the Formless can be conceived only when you have transcended Form."[45] Swami consistently proclaims that there is only one God but with many names and forms, moreover, God is present in all beings, be it a small insect like an ant or a big animal like an elephant or a lion. He is present in a particle of sand and also in a particle of sugar.[46]

Human being, according to Baba is the combination of body, mind and *Ātman*. Actions are done by the body and cognition by the mind. The *Ātma* is that which abides and is the Divine spirit present in the human heart.[47] Explicating God in relation to Human being and creation, he says, "All that you see in the external world is nothing but the manifestation of God. All of

---

[40] *Sathya Sai Speaks, Vol. 3: Discourses of Bhagavan Sri Sathya Sai Baba*, Downloaded in a *pdf* format from the official website of Sri Sathya Sai Sadhana Trust, Publications Division - *http://www.sssbpt.info/english/sss.htm*, (10.8.2012), p. 39.

[41] *Sathya Sai Speaks, Vol. 14: Discourses of Bhagavan Sri Sathya Sai Baba*, Downloaded in a *pdf* format from the official website of Sri Sathya Sai Sadhana Trust, Publications Division - *http://www.sssbpt.info/english/sss.htm*, (10.8.2012), p. 205.

[42] *Sathya Sai Speaks Vol. 42: Discourses of Bhagavan Sri Sathya Sai Baba, Delivered during 2009*, (Prasanthi Nilayam: Sri Sathya Sai Sadhana Trust, Publications Division, 2010), p. 198.

[43] *Sathya Sai Speaks, Vol. 24*, p. 62.

[44] *Sathya Sai Speaks, Vol. 14,* p. 205.

[45] *Sathya Sai Speaks, Vol. 3,* p. 38.

[46] *Sathya Sai Speaks, Vol. 31,* p. 86; *Sathya Sai Speaks, Vol. 39: Discourses of Bhagavan Sri Sathya Sai Baba, Delivered during 2006*, (Prasanthi Nilayam: Sri Sathya Sai Books & Publications Trust, n.d.), pp. 67, 198.

[47] *Sathya Sai Speaks, Vol. 20: Discourses of Bhagavan Sri Sathya Sai Baba*, Downloaded in a *pdf* format from the official website of Sri Sathya Sai Sadhana Trust, Publications Division - *http://www.sssbpt.info/english/sss.htm*, (10.8.2012), p. 79.

you… are the embodiment of God. Even this hall is a manifestation of God. In fact, you are yourself God."[48] The whole universe is a phenomenon of cause and effect. It is foolish to look only at the external world considering it as mere *jada* (matter). There is reality behind the entire creation. If we see with divine vision, everything will be divine.[49] So, there is an integral relationship between God, human and creation as Swami explains: "Ātman takes the form of Brahman and adopts the human body as his chariot and move about the world. Therefore, the world is Brahman; the market is Brahman; the body is Brahman; Brahman is Brahman and everything is Brahman."[50] His conception of human being is a clear reflection of Śaṅkara's Advaita Vedānta. "He (sic) is Divinity, encased in human frame…Man (sic) is a unit of the Unity, he is a child of Immortality, set in the background of this mortal world."[51] That human in his/her true reality is God has been emphatically stated by Bhagavan Baba in many of his discourses. Few examples may be given:

> Your nature is *Sath, Chith* and *Aanandha* (Existence, Consciousness, Bliss Absolute),… *Sath, Chith, Aanandha are* the attributes of the *Aathma* (Self) and you are the Self not the body.[52]
>
> On deep enquiry, you will know that you are in God, God is in you and you are God… You should be able to say with conviction that you are a spark of the Divine.[53]

Delineating the indwelling presence of God, Swami says, "God is not external; God is not outside you; God is inside you. You are not a man (sic), you are God himself… Don't be under the delusion that God is somewhere and you have to search for Him. God is in you."[54] "He is within you, in your own

---

[48] *Sathya Sai Speaks, Vol. 34: Discourses of Bhagavan Sri Sathya Sai Baba, Delivered during 2001*, (Prasanthi Nilayam: Sathya Sai Books and Publications Trust, n.d.), p. 30; *Sathya Sai Speaks, Vol. 24*, p. 15.

[49] *Sathya Sai Speaks, Vol. 31*, p. 123.

[50] *Summer Showers in Brindavan 1974, Part – I: Discourses by Bhagavan Sri Sathya Sai Baba on Brahman*, (Prasnathi Nilayam: Sri Sathya Sai Books and Publications Trust, 2004), pp. 132-133.

[51] *Voice of the Avatar: Extracts from the Divine Discourse of Bhagavan Sri Satha Sai Baba, Part I*, compiled by D. Hejmadi, (Prashanthi Nilayam: Sri Sathya Sai Books and Publications, 1980), p. 1.

[52] *Sathya Sai Speaks, Vol. 4: Discourses of Bhagavan Sri Sathya Sai Baba*, (Downloaded in a *pdf* format from the official website of Sri Sathya Sai Sadhana Trust, Publications Division - *http://www.sssbpt.info/english/sss.htm*, 10.8.2012), p. 44.

[53] *Sathya Sai Speaks, Vol. 33*, p. 39.

[54] *Voice of the Avatar*, pp. 25-26.

inner altar….The attention has to be fixed on God, the God within."[55] All these explanations of God, human and creation is a clear reflection of Śaṅkara's Advaita Vedānta.

2.3. Paths of Liberation

Sathya Sai Baba explicitly states that Liberation cannot be achieved by rituals, sacrificial actions or good deeds or going to forest and undertake penance though these help to achieve purity of heart and mind. It is only by dispelling the darkness of ignorance from within and realizing his/her true nature, that one gets liberation.[56] As achieving this realization is not easy for the human beings, Swami prescribes to proceed from lower consciousness to higher consciousness – "Proceed from *Dvaita* (Dualism) to *Viśiṣṭādvaita* (partial non-dualism) and reach the stage of Advaitic (non-dual) Consciousness."[57] He harmonises the three schools of Vedānta – *Advaita* of Śaṅkara, *Viśiṣṭādvaita* of Ramanuja and *Dvaita* of Madhva saying that these are not different things. He says, referring to these *ācāryas*, that they spoke not of different things but there is underlying unity which we should acknowledge.[58]

Likewise, Sathya Sai Baba acknowledges the integral relationship between the three traditional ways of liberation – *Jñāna*, *Karma* and *Bhakti*. As ignorance is the basic cause of bondage, knowledge (*jñāna*) is the final path for liberation; nevertheless, *karma* and *bhakti* help one to tread the path of *jñāna*, because, "through devotion to God alone can that knowledge be attained."[59] Identifying the interconnectedness of these three, Baba says,

---

[55] *Sathya Sai Speaks, Vol. 7: Discourses of Bhagavan Sri Sathya Sai Baba*, Downloaded in a *pdf* format from the official website of Sri Sathya Sai Sadhana Trust, Publications Division - *http://www.sssbpt.info/english/sss.htm*, (10.8.2012), p. 3; cf. *Sathya Sai Speaks, Vol. 40: Discourses of Bhagavan Sri Sathya Sai Baba, Delivered during 2007*, (Prashanti Nilayam: Sri Sathya Sai Books and Publications Trust, 2008 – where Bhagavan Baba explains the indwelling God as – God, the indweller of all beings, every living being is an *amsa* (part) of God, p. 6; humans as embodiment of God, p. 17; not only Sai is God, but all are divine, p. 27; God does not exist outside of us, God is inside of us, p. 150, so, we should show respect to everyone, p. 155. See also *Sathya Sai Speaks, Vol. 1: Discourses of Bhagavan Sri Sathya Sai Baba*, Downloaded in a pdf format from the official website of Sri Sathya Sai Sadhana Trust, Publications Division - http://www.sssbpt.info/english/sss.htm, (10.8.2012), pp. 48, 96; also *Sathya Sai Speaks, Vol. 2: Discourses of Bhagavan Sri Sathya Sai Baba*, Downloaded in a *pdf* format from the official website of Sri Sathya Sai Sadhana Trust, Publications Division - *http://www.sssbpt.info/english/sss.htm*, (10.8.2012), p. 8.

[56] *Sathya Sai Speaks, Vol. 20*, p. 53.

[57] *Ibid.*, p. 59.

[58] *Summer Showers in Brindavan 1974, Part – I*, p. 247. *cf. Sathya Sai Speaks, Vol. 5*, pp. 64-65 where Baba explains the unity of the three Advaitic schools.

[59] *Sathya Sai Speaks, Vol. 4*, p. 39.

> Base your action on knowledge... Let action be suffused with *bhakti*; that is to say, humility, love, mercy and non-violence. Let *bhakti* be filled with knowledge... Mere knowledge will make the heart dry; *bhakti* makes it soft with sympathy, and *karma* gives the hands something to do, something which will sanctify every of the minutes that have fallen to your lot to live.[60]

For Baba *bhakti* is not simply worshipping some idols and observing certain vows and performing some rituals. It is not as simple as that. "The foremost duty of a devotee, especially of the *Bharatiyas*, is observing the quality of forbearance in practice."[61]

P.P.S. Sarma comments thus, "All three aspects of *Karma, Bhakti* and *Jñāna* (Service, Devotion and Knowledge) are unified"[62] in the philosophical exhortation of Sathya Sai Baba. However, he always emphasized the power of love for liberation saying, "There is nothing that can liberate you easily than pure and selfless love."[63] He maintains that Love and Service to the society is the best path for Liberation. "Just as two wings are essential for a bird to soar high in the sky, and two wheels for a bicycle to move, *prema* (love) and *seva* (service) are essential for man (*sic*) to reach his destination."[64] So, Sathya Sai Baba integrates various methods in accordance with the spiritual ability of the seekers for liberation. For some, rites and rituals are helpful to move on to the higher plane of spirituality. Thus, *Bhakti, Karma* and *Jñāna* have their own unique place and role to play; similarly, *dvaita*, *Viśiṣṭādvaita* and *advaita* are working together to help human beings to reach their final spiritual destiny. However, without love and service to fellow human beings, liberation is considered unattainable.

2.4. The Five Primary Human Values

Corresponding to the five basic elements (*pañcabhūtas*) that constitute the universe including human, there are five primary human values which are central to Baba's teaching and popularly known as 'the five pillars.' They are

[60] *Howard Murphet, Sai Baba: Invitation to Glory*, (Delhi: Macmillan India Limitted., 1982), p. 195.

[61] *Sathya Sai Speaks, Vol. 37: Discourses of Bhagavan Sri Sathya Sai Baba, Delivered during 2004,* (Prasanthi Nilayam: Sri Sathya Sai Books and Publications Trust, n.d.), p. 152.

[62] P.P.S. Sarma, *Bhagawan Baba's Glory of Unity*, (Prasanthi Nilayam: Sri Sathya Sai Sadhana Trust, Publications Division, 2010), p. 96. In this book the author presents how Bhagavan Baba unified thought, word and deed; science and spirituality; three tradition ways of salvation – *karma, bhakti and jñāna*; various religions of the world.

[63] *Sathya Sai Speaks, Vol. 37,* p. 159.

[64] *Sathya Sai Speaks, Vol. 32 (Part 2): Discourses of Bhagavan Sri Sathya Sai Baba*, Delivered from July 1999 - December 1999, (Prasanthi Nilayam: Sri Sathya Sai Books & Publications Trust, 2001), pp. 44, 94.

- *Sathya, Dharma, Śānthi, Ahiṃsā* and *Prema*.[65] These are not only the five primary human values, but "they are all facets of the foundational humanness."[66] Truth (*Sathya*) is that which is changeless, *Dharma* or right actions is what is based on truth. *Śānthi* or peace, in its lower aspect, is the equal state of mind which remains unaffected either by joy or sorrow. Peace, in its higher aspect, is experienced when we apprehend the prevalence of God everywhere – the entire manifestation appears as the projection of divinity. *Ahiṃsā* is the feeling of loving compassion to all beings. *Prema* – love is nothing other than the flow of the soul itself.[67] According to Baba Love (*Prema*) is the common denominator for all these values and the foremost one; it is *Prema* that flows as the under-current for the other four values.[68] In other words, Love is the uniting string of these five pillars:

> *Love as thought is 'Sathya' (Truth)*
> *Love as action is Dharma (Righteousness)*
> *Love as feeling is 'Śānthi' (Peace)*
> *Love as understanding is 'Ahiṁsā' (Non-violence).*[69]

2.5. Emphasis on Love

Sathya Sai Baba's emphasis on 'love' is well attested. He equates 'love' with God. Love is not the attribute of God but it is the essential nature of God.[70] One of the most popular line of Bhagavan Baba which he utters very often runs – "Love is God, God is love. So, live in love."[71] For him, holding on love is the way to reach *mokṣa*:

---

[65] *Sathya Sai Speaks, Vol. 17: Discourses of Bhagavan Sri Sathya Sai Baba*, Downloaded in a *pdf* format from the official website of Sri Sathya Sai Sadhana Trust, Publications Division - *http://www.sssbpt. info/english/sss.htm*, (10.8.2012), p. 98; *Sathya Sai Speaks, Vol. 18: Discourses of Bhagavan Sri Sathya Sai Baba*, Downloaded in a *pdf* format from the official website of Sri Sathya Sai Sadhana Trust, Publications Division - *http://www.sssbpt. info/english/ sss.htm*, (10.8.2012), pp. 3, 19.

[66] *Sathya Sai Speaks, Vol. 17*, p. 98.

[67] Ratan Lal, "Sri Sathya Sai Baba", in *Gurus, Godmen and Good People*, Edited by Khushwant Singh, Bombay: Orient Longman Ltd., 1975, p. 4. Cf. Daniel E, Bassuk, "Six Modern Indian Avatars and the Ways They Understand Their Divinity", p. 88 where he says: "The five pillars which undergird his (Baba's) message are truth, righteousness, peace, love, and nonviolence, but the greatest of these is love."

[68] *Sathya Sai Speaks, Vol. 18*, pp. 3, 19.

[69] *Ibid*., p. 3, cf. Kailash Kumar & Jorgen Hovgaard, *Sai Baba: The Source of Light, Love and Bliss*, p. 51.

[70] *Sathya Sai Speaks, Vol. 33*, p. 127.

[71] *Sathya Sai Speaks, Vol. 33*, pp. 64, 80, 96, 157, 231, 275, 307, 396, 397; *Sathya Sai Speaks, Vol. 39*, p. 200; *Sathya Sai Speaks, Vol. 40*, pp. 42, 168; *Sathya Sai Speaks, Vol. 1*, pp. 58, 126; *Sathya Sai Speaks, Vol. 5*, p. 56, *Sathya Sai Speaks Vol. 7*, p. 12; *Sathya Sai Speaks Vol. 10*, p. 17.

Love is God, God is love. Cultivating love is the true spiritual practice.

If one holds on to the principle of love firmly
One becomes eligible to attain the state of non-dual.[72]

"Love all, Serve all", therefore, is the hallmark of Baba's religious teaching. He has a famous principle which reads –

There is only one religion, the religion of love.
There is only one language, the language of the heart.
There is only one caste, the caste of humanity.
There is only one God, and He is omnipresent.[73]

2.6. Emphasis on Service (*Seva*)

'Service' (*seva*) occupies one of the most important places in the religious and philosophical teaching of Bhagavan Baba. This is the outcome of his emphasis on 'love'. Love and Service are considered as the two essential spiritual things, obligatory for anyone to undertake as these two are the prime components of divine life and they help in the realization of the Divine.[74] For Baba, service to humanity is so important that he goes beyond the general understanding of service as 'service to human is service to God'[75] and says, "Service is God. Divinity can be experienced only through service."[76] However, Bhagavan is very specific that service should be done without any string attached to it, like 'I am serving others' but it should be done with divine feelings, forgetting oneself and done as an offering to God,[77] an act of worship to the Divine,[78] and without expecting any return.[79]

Stressing the importance of service to humanity, Baba goes on to the extent of saying that service to humanity is the sure way to redeem oneself:

---

[72] *Sathya Sai Speaks, Vol. 33*, p. 157.

[73] See *Sathya Sai Speaks, Vol. 31*, p. 153, also *Sathya Sai Speaks, Vol. 32* (Part 2), p. 134; *Sathya Sai Speaks, Vol. 11: Discourses of Bhagavan Sri Sathya Sai Baba*, Downloaded in a *pdf* format from the official website of Sri Sathya Sai Sadhana Trust, Publications Division - *http://www.sssbpt. info/english/sss.htm,* (10.8.2012), p. 177.

[74] *Sathya Sai Speaks, Vol. 31*, p. 132.

[75] However, Sathya Sai Baba also speaks Service to human as service to God. Cf. *Sathya Sai Speaks, Vol. 10*, p. 18; Sathya Sai Speaks, Vol. 32 (Part 2), pp. 94, 113.

[76] *Sathya Sai Speaks, Vol. 33,* p. 39.

[77] *Sathya Sai Speaks, Vol. 35: Discourses of Bhagavan Sri Sathya Sai Baba, Delivered during 2002,* (Prasanthi Nilayam, Sri Sathya Sai Books and Publications Trust, 2003), p. 35; cf. *Sathya Sai Speaks, Vol. 32* (Part 2), p. 215; *Sathya Sai Speaks, Vol. 36*, p. 5.

[78] *Sathya Sai Speaks, Vol. 7*, pp. 47, 58; *Sathya Sai Speaks, Vol. 32* (Part 2), p. 215.

[79] *Sathya Sai Speaks, Vol. 32*, Part 2, p. 45.

> *Neither by penance nor by pilgrimages*
> *Nor by going through sacred texts*
> *Can one cross the ocean of Saṃsāra.*
> *Only through service can one redeem oneself.*[80]

Sai Baba summarizes the importance, the necessity, the consequences of Service and the attitude one should posses while serving others in the following lines:

> Service is the life breath of the Sathya Sai Organization. Remember the truth that you are born to serve society. Make no distinction whatsoever in rendering service. Serve your parents, brothers, friends, and even beggars alike. Divine grace will flow in abundance only when you serve with the spirit of humility and equality. Service is the easiest path to attain divine grace. Offer service and receive the love of God. Love and service are like two wings by which man (*sic*) can soar to higher levels of consciousness. If you have the spirit of love and service, divine grace will follow you like a shadow wherever you may be.[81]

2.7. Emphasis on Togetherness

In accordance with his primary message – unity of religions, Sathya Sai Baba stresses the importance of togetherness. He states, "Go on adding 'I plus you, I plus you,' and it will become 'We'. Then go on adding 'We plus W'(*sic*) - we are all one. All are children of God. This is brotherhood of man (*sic*) and fatherhood of God;"[82] because human being "cannot be alone, separate from the rest. Like drop of oil on water, he (*sic*) spreads; he (*sic*) reaches out for far. 'I' seeks other 'I's and seeks to become We. Life is a march from I to We. But it usually strays from I to they. And does not reach the God, We."[83] So, we should consider others as belonging to us because the same *Ātman* resides as the indweller in all people.[84] Delivering what he calls a special message on the occasion of *Navaratri*, Baba says, "People keep distance from one another due to differences of opinion. In fact, you are not different from others… All are

---

[80] *Ibid.*, pp. 164-165, 128; also *Sathya Sai Speaks, Vol. 35*, p.145; *Sathya Sai Speaks, Vol. 36*, p. 96. *Sathya Sai Speaks, Vol. 32*, Part 2, p. 94.

[81] *Sathya Sai Speaks, Vol. 32*, Part 2, p. 94.

[82] *Sathya Sai Speaks, Vol. 31*, p. 127.

[83] *Voice of the Avatar*, p. 29.

[84] *Sathya Sai Speaks, Vol. 42*, p. 13.

brothers and sisters! Hence, all should live like brothers and sisters with love and unity. '**All are one; be alike to everyone**.'"[85]

"Therefore", he says. "no one should have feelings of differences or even entertain ill-will towards others, cultivate the feeling of fatherhood of God and brotherhood of Man (*sic*). Bear no ill-will towards anyone."[86] In the same manner, great religious figures of the world belonged to all people. Baba says, "To accept one of them as one's own and discard the rest as belonging to others, is a sign of pettiness. Christ, Rāmā, Kṛṣṇa - they are for all men (*sic*) everywhere."[87] Swami used Jesus' name to strengthen his position:

> The message of 'Fatherhood of God and the Brotherhood of Man,' (*sic*) which Jesus Christ proclaimed 2000 years ago, should become a living faith for the achievement of real peace and the unity of mankind (*sic*). The oneness of all creation affirmed by the ancient seers and sages must be expressed in a transcendental love which embraces all people regardless of creed, community or language.[88]

Sathya Sai Baba is different from most of the contemporary gurus. Unlike most of them, there is nothing to trace his spiritual legacy in term of human guru as seen in the case of Yogananda and Ravishankar and others. In short, he was a guru by birth. And as such his philosophy and religious teachings seem to be the out pouring of his essence as an *avatāra* rather than a result of gathered information from which he builds up his teaching. He teaches authoritatively just like Lord Kṛṣṇa or Jesus – for example, he says, "My power is immeasurable; My truth is inexplicable, unfathomable. I am announcing this about me...What I *will* must take place; what I plan *must* succeed. I am Truth... My Grace is ever available... intellectuals are unable to grasp My Truth, My Power, My Glory, or My real Task as Avatār."[89] However, his uniqueness lies not on the quality and content of his numerous discourses, but on his charm, mystique power and an ability to perform miracles. In spite of mounting allegations piling up against him, he is still as popular as before.

---

[85] *Sathya Sai Speaks, Vol. 41: Discourses of Bhagavan Sri Sathya Sai Baba, Delivered during 2008,* (Prasanthi Nilayam: Sri Sathya Sadhana Trust, Publications Division, 2009), p. 8.

[86] *Sathya Sai Speaks, Vol. 27: Discourses of Bhagavan Sri Sathya Sai Baba,* Downloaded in a *pdf* format from the official website of Sri Sathya Sai Sadhana Trust, Publications Division - *http://www.sssbpt. info/english/sss.htm*, (10.8.2012), p. 58.

[87] *Sathya Sai Speaks, Vol. 11*, p. 173.

[88] *Sathya Sai Speaks, Vol. 15: Discourses of Bhagavan Sri Sathya Sai Baba,* Downloaded in a *pdf* format from the official website of Sri Sathya Sai Sadhana Trust, Publications Division - *http://www.sssbpt. info/english/sss.htm*, (10.8.2012), p. 55.

[89] *Sathya Sai Speaks, Vol. 9*, pp. 83-84.

Insofar as his philosophical and religious teaching is concerned, he has hardly any things totally new. He followed Hindu *śastras* comprehensively; his teaching has a semblance of Śaṅkara's Advaita Vedānta but does not limit himself to it. He integrates the three Vedāntic schools as much as the three traditional paths of liberation. His theology of religions can be put in the category of the school of pluralism but he moves beyond a mere acceptance of other religions as valid path and come to the acknowledgement of oneness of God, humanity and religions. He never asks his devotees to leave their faith but encourages them to see God who is one and the same in and through their own tradition. His emphasis on love and service as another name of God is innovative, his concept of belongingness and togetherness of all human beings is significant in our contemporary context of conflicts and discords between religions. His positive attitude towards other religions is laudable and his teaching on Jesus Christ is all the more arresting at the same time disturbing as well, as we shall see in the next two sections when I discuss Baba's interpretation of Jesus Christ.

3. Sathya Sai Baba and Jesus Christ

Bhagavan Baba and his devotees speak of a close relationship that exists between Swami and Jesus Christ. In the earliest exclusive discourse on Jesus Christ, in 1972, Swami claims himself as having a close connection with Jesus by saying that he is the incarnation of the God who incarnated in Jesus Christ.[90] In connection with the relationship between Baba and Jesus, it is said that the name '*Isa*' (Sanskrit name for Jesus) and '*Sai*' both mean 'Divine Mother'; when Jesus said as the Spirit of truth comes, he will guide you into all the truth, it refers to '*Sathya*' (truth) Sai Baba. Again, 'Baba' means father which is the same word Jesus used to address his father – '*abba*'.[91] Bhagavan Baba himself states that *Isa* by which Jesus was known in India, when repeated several times is *Sai*, both mean *Īśwara* (God).[92] Sreejith Narayan maintains that the second coming of the Son of Man mentioned in the Bible (especially the Book of Revelation) is exactly matched with the appearance of Sathya Sai Baba indicating that Swami is the one predicted by Jesus as to come again.[93]

---

[90] *Sathya Sai Speaks, Vol. 11*, p. 177.

[91] Peter Phipps, *Greater than You Know: Sathya Sai Baba, Jesus Christ and Christianity*, (Auckland: Sathya Sai Publications of New Zealand, 1997), p. 33. The author gives many parallels between Jesus Christ and Sathya Sai Baba, cf. pp. 33-52. Cf. Peter Phipps, *Sathya Sai Baba and Jesus Christ: A Gospel for the Golden Age*, (Auckland: Sathya Sai Publications of New Zealand, 1996, Third Edition, first published in 1994), Chapter 9 – "The teachings of Jesus and Sai Baba Compared", pp. 107-117.

[92] *Sathya Sai Speaks, Vol. 14*, pp. 58-59.

[93] See Sreejith Narayan, *Sai, Thy Kingdom Come: A Deliberation on the Possibility of Sri Sathya Sai Baba's "Return"*, (New York: Premjith Narayan, 2012), pp. 117-123.

Don Mario Mazzoleni, a Roman Catholic Priest considers Jesus and Sathya Sai Baba as the incarnations of the same God – "two temples of the Supreme Spirit."[94] Luc J. Courtois on the other hand, recognized Sai Baba as the Father who incarnated in Jesus as he said: "He who sent me will come again." So, Sathya Sai Baba is the incarnation of the Father whereas Jesus Christ is the Son.[95]

Those who are trying to link Jesus and Baba are people who are not ready to deny either of them but try to hold both of them as authentic incarnations of God. They put forwards similarities between the two without finding the differences between them which are more obvious than the former. Few examples may be given here - Jesus was crucified on the cross and died whereas Baba died a natural death in the Hospital; Jesus was materially poor leaving no possession at death but Baba died a billionaire; Jesus resurrected bodily which Baba even accepted whereas no one claims the same for Baba; Jesus' main mission was to save humanity from sin whereas Baba's main mission was to lead people to their real identity which is divine, and so on. It is not difficult to find ambiguity in their attempt to connect Baba with Jesus as there is no systematic, rational consistency in their interpretations of the Bible or the life of Baba. Basing their assumption on the words of Baba while taking the Biblical witness of Jesus as a distorted version, they come out with this suggestion concerning the Second Coming of Christ and postulate that Sathya Sai Baba is the one whom Jesus predicted as to come again. To recognise Jesus Christ and Sathya Sai Baba as two separate distinct Masters, having separate roles in a separate time and space rather than trying to connect them with so many inconsistencies may be more appropriate and laudable.

Nevertheless, it may be recognized that Sathya Sai Baba paid more attention to Jesus Christ than to other religious Masters such as Muhammad, Buddha, Mahavira, Zoroaster or Guru Nanak. He talks more about Jesus, materializes the pictures of Jesus, Cross, the crucifix, a miniature Bible which is said to contain the life and teaching of Jesus not to be found in the Bible, etc.[96] Definitely, Baba makes attempt to reveal his connection with Jesus Christ, but for what purpose, it is difficult to ascertain. Is there an authentic relationship between these two in spiritual ontological level as claimed by Baba or Is it done just to appease the numerous Christian admirers? This is a difficult question to answer at this stage.

---

[94] Mazzoleni, *A Catholic Priest Meets Sai Baba,* p. 114.

[95] Luc J. Courtois, *The Promise Fulfilled,* (Bangalore: Message Publications, 2008), p. 1.

[96] Black and white pictures are provided in the Appendix – 3.

4. Sathya Sai Baba's Interpretation of Jesus Christ: *Jesus, the Kārana-Janma*

Our source for constructing Baba's Christology is the numerous discourses delivered mainly on the Christmas day during the past forty years. Since Baba mentioned Jesus and his teaching quite often in his other discourses as well, I will also make use of them. The discourses on Jesus are available in the various volumes of *Sathya Sai Speaks* and for the benefit of the general readers, discourses on Jesus Christ were compiled in a book form under the title – "*Be Like Jesus*": *The Good News of Jesus*.[97] The first exclusive discourse on Jesus happened in the year 1972 on the Christmas day. By this time, Sathya Sai Baba had numerous Christian devotees and admirers who gathered to hear his talk and to see him face to face. His last discourse on Jesus was delivered in the year 2009 where he made a brief reference to Jesus.

Since 1972 Sathya Sai Baba delivered his regular Christmas message. However, he mentioned the name of Jesus several times in his earlier discourses, for example, he mentioned Jesus as one of the names by which one can call on God;[98] he said, "Jesus took a child up and fondling it, carried it on his shoulder,"[99] "He will be welcomed by the Divine, only when, as Jesus said, he becomes a child,"[100] also "'Give up; I shall fill the gap' says Jesus."[101] Baba maintained, "Jesus who attempted to rebuild mankind (*sic*) on the basis of Love was crucified by little men (*sic*) who feared that their tiny towers of hate and greed will be toppled by his teaching."[102] On the Christmas Day of 1970, Baba said, "This Day marks the beginning of the Christian Era, the year of Christ. Christ sacrificed his life for the sake of those who put their faith in him. He propagated the truth that service is God, that sacrifice is God."[103]

---

[97] Sri Sathya Sai Baba, *"Be Like Jesus": The Good News of Jesus*, compiled by Debra and William Miller, (Prashanthi Nilayam: Sri Sathya Sai Sadhana Trust, Publications Division, 2009).

[98] In 1963 Discourse, *Sathya Sai Speaks, Vol. 3*, p. 53.

[99] In 1967 Discourse, *Sathya Sai Speaks, Vol. 7*, p. 67.

[100] In 1967 Discourse, *Ibid.*, p. 69.

[101] In 1967 Discourse, *Ibid.*, p. 122.

[102] In 1968 Discourse at Bombay, *Sathya Sai Speaks, Vol. 8: Discourses of Bhagavan Sri Sathya Sai Baba*, Downloaded in a *pdf* format from the official website of Sri Sathya Sai Sadhana Trust, Publications Division - *http://www.sssbpt. info/english/sss.htm.* (10.8.2012), p. 47.

[103] *Sathya Sai Speaks, Vol. 10*, p. 142. Apart from these, Baba very often cited Jesus life, works and message in several of his discourses to strengthen his message. See *Sathya Sai Speaks, Vol. 12: Discourses of Bhagavan Sri Sathya Sai Baba*, Downloaded in a *pdf* format from the official website of Sri Sathya Sai Sadhana Trust, Publications Division - *http://www. sssbpt. info/english/sss.htm.* (10.8.2012), pp. 72, 109; *Sathya Sai Speaks, Vol. 13: Discourses of Bhagavan Sri Sathya Sai Baba*, Downloaded in a *pdf* format from the official website of Sri Sathya Sai Sadhana Trust, Publications Division - *http://www.sssbpt. info/english/sss.htm.*

Sai Baba does not follow the Biblical witness to Jesus. He appears to have a comprehensive knowledge of Jesus, but many of what he says concerning Jesus Christ is not to be found in the Bible. For his devotees, stories of Jesus and his teachings which are either absent in the Bible or different from the biblical witness are more important as these are coming out of the Omniscient God – Bhagavan Baba, and thus should be viewed as supplementary notes rather than contradictory ones, because, "He is aware of everything, even things which are not there in the Bible are talking about by Bhagavan Baba. Even facts which are not known by the best Christian in the world about Christ are revealed by Bhagavan Baba."[104] It is claimed that his knowledge of Jesus is not from the reading of the Bible or Christian literature or learning from other sources, but from his own self-knowledge as "he is awareness himself."[105] So, he explains Jesus' life and teachings in his own way without considering the Biblical narratives.

4.1. The Person of Jesus

Swami uses various epithets for Jesus and these are mostly put in a plural form as most of the time he refers Jesus together with other great saints. Expressions like 'Great Sages', 'Great Teachers', 'Teachers of Divinity', 'Divine Messengers', 'Divine Incarnations', 'Divine Persons', 'Divine Saviours', etc. are used by Baba for Jesus Christ together with a number of spiritual giants such as Buddha, Muhammad, Zoroaster, Guru Nanak, Mahavir, etc.[106] There is no doubt that he has high regard for Jesus which is seen from the way he talks

(10.8.2012), pp. 57, 61; *Sathya Sai Speaks, Vol. 14,* p. 148; *Sathya Sai Speaks, Vol. 15*, pp. 55, 151, 166, 187; *Sathya Sai Speaks, Vol. 18*, p. 5; *Sathya Sai Speaks, Vol. 19: Discourses of Bhagavan Sri Sathya Sai Baba,* Downloaded in a *pdf* format from the official website of Sri Sathya Sai Sadhana Trust, Publications Division - *http://www.sssbpt. info/english/sss.htm.* (10.8.2012), p. 72; *Sathya Sai Speaks, Vol. 21*, p. 5; *Sathya Sai Speaks, Vol. 22*, p. 72; *Sathya Sai Speaks, Vol. 25: Discourses of Bhagavan Sri Sathya Sai Baba*, Downloaded in a *pdf* format from the official website of Sri Sathya Sai Sadhana Trust, Publications Division - *http://www.sssbpt. info/english/sss.htm.* (10.8.2012), p. 17; *Sathya Sai Speaks, Vol. 26: Discourses of Bhagavan Sri Sathya Sai Baba,* Downloaded in a *pdf* format from the official website of Sri Sathya Sai Sadhana Trust, Publications Division - *http://www.sssbpt. info/english/sss.htm.* (10.8.2012), pp. 5, 135; *Sathya Sai Speaks, Vol. 27*, pp. 53, 67, 79; *Sathya Sai Speaks, Vol. 28: Discourses of Bhagavan Sri Sathya Sai Baba*, Downloaded in a *pdf* format from the official website of Sri Sathya Sai Sadhana Trust, Publications Division - *http://www.sssbpt. info/english/sss.htm.* (10.8.2012), pp. 7, 74, 115; *Sathya Sai Speaks, Vol. 29: Discourses of Bhagavan Sri Sathya Sai Baba*, Downloaded in a *pdf* format from the official website of Sri Sathya Sai Sadhana Trust, Publications Division - *http://www.sssbpt. info/english/sss.htm.* (10.8.2012), pp. 27, 53-54, 153-154.

[104] Gangadhar Shastri in a personal interview.

[105] *Ibid.*

[106] See Luc J. Courtois, *Sai Baba Speaks of Jesus,* (Bangalore: Message Publications, 2008), pp. 83-84.

about him. He says, "All the acts of Jesus were pure and holy, and filled with selfless love."[107] "He had no envy or hatred, and was full of love and charity, humility and sympathy,"[108] because "Jesus was the personification of self-sacrifice,"[109] who "attempted to rebuild humankind on the basis on love."[110] In 1978 Christmas Discourse, Sathya Sai Baba said:

> Jesus was *kārana-janma,* a Master born with a purpose, the mission of restoring love, charity and compassion in the heart of man (*sic*). He had no attachment to the self, nor paid any heed to joy or sorrow, loss or gain. He had a heart that responded to the call of anguish, and he went about the land preaching the lesson of love. His life was a libation for the upliftment of humanity.[111]

When narrow pride and thick ignorance defiled humankind, Jesus came to this world, two thousand years ago, as the embodiment of love and compassion and lived among humans, holding forth the highest ideals of life.[112] He was a person whose only joy was in spreading Divine Love, offering Divine Love, receiving Divine Love and living on Divine Love.[113] Jesus was compassion (*karuṇā*) in human form. He spread the spirit of compassion and conferred solace on the distressed and the suffering, including the sufferings of birds and beasts.[114] Such words of admiration flow from the mouth of Swami when he talks about Jesus Christ.

4.1.1. Jesus as *Kārana-Janma*

Sai Baba does not consider Jesus as a true *avatāra* of the rank of Kṛṣṇa or himself. Jesus is Kārana-Janma – a master born with a purpose.[115] However, he accepts Jesus as a lower form of avatāra – i.e. *amsāvatāra* or fractional *avatāra* in which category are sages like Śaṅkara, Ramakrishna, Aurobindo, and the likes whereas he claims himself to be a full and integral *avatāra* - a *purnāvatara* just like Lord Kṛṣṇa.[116] Baba maintains that Jesus never considered himself as God and never claimed that he is the truth, the path, the saviour and the redeemer. "Only a Divine Incarnation (*Avatār*) can give such an assurance...

[107] *Sathya Sai Speaks, Vol. 14,* p. 148.

[108] *Ibid.*, p. 58.

[109] *Sathya Sai Speaks, Vol. 19*, p. 72.

[110] *Sathya Sai Speaks, Vol. 27*, p. 79.

[111] *Sathya Sai Speaks, Vol. 14*, p. 58; *Sathya Sai Speaks, Vol. 15,* p. 118.

[112] *Sathya Sai Speaks, Vol. 14*, p. 206.

[113] *Ibid.*, p. 153.

[114] *Sathya Sai Speaks, Vol. 15*, p. 118; *Sathya Sai Speaks, Vol. 13,* p. 82.

[115] *Sathya Sai Baba, "Be Like Jesus",* p. 7. Cf. *Sathya Sai Speaks, Vol. 14,* p. 58.

[116] V.K. Gokak, *Bhagavan Sri Sathya Sai Baba,* p. 15.

Jesus never said this. It was the work of the compilers of the Bible that led to this mistaken notion."[117] However, this does not mean that Baba plays down the importance of Jesus for he says that the lives of Divine personalities such as Jesus are lived out in order to establish the welfare, peace and prosperity of humanity and individual liberation from bondage,[118] indicating the capability of Jesus Christ in bringing salvation to anyone who follows him.

4.1.2. Jesus' Self Understanding

According to Sai Baba, Jesus understood himself in three progressive stages – Jesus first considered himself as the 'Messenger of God'. Later on, after years of contemplation and meditation, Jesus realized that he is more than a 'Messenger of God' and could declare to the people, "I am the Son of God." As the awareness of God developed in him more and more through contemplation and meditation, he realized his oneness with God and therefore towards the end of his life Jesus could declare, "I and my Father are one." Sai Baba concludes, "He is the one who comprehends the purpose of his life. The 'Son of God' is one who appears as Divine to others. 'I and my Father are one' signifies the true nature of the individual, his (sic) identity with Divinity."[119] According to Sai Baba these three progressive identities of Jesus is corresponding to the three Vedānta schools of thought – Dvaita, Viśiṣtādvaita and Advaita Vedānta. In the first stage the messenger and master are separate so this stage is that of dualism (*dvaita*). In the second stage, the son and the father, though they have separate entity, are bound by a bond of relationship, feelings and attitudes. This stage is called qualified non-dualism (*viśiṣtādvaita*). In the last stage Jesus attained mergence (*sāyujya*) – oneness with God. This stage is of non-dualism (*advaita*).[120] This indicates that though Jesus showed divine trait right from his childhood, he experienced spiritual growth, through long struggle and contemplation, and finally reached the highest spiritual attainment – oneness with God. May be because of this that Sathya Sai Baba does not consider Jesus as a full flagged *avatāra* like Kṛṣṇa or himself.

4.1.3. The Birth of Jesus

In 1978 Christmas Discourse, which may be considered as one of the most important Christmas discourses of Baba, he says that God incarnated in the form of Jesus Christ to elevate humans, to raise the level of their consciousness,

---

[117] Sai Baba, *"Be Like Jesus"*, pp. 125-126.

[118] *Ibid.*, p. 6.

[119] *Ibid.*, pp. 25-26, 19-20; 29-30. Cf. *Sathya Sai Speaks, Vol. 13,* p. 82; *Sathya Sai Speaks, Vol. 14,* p. 58; *Sathya Sai Speaks, Vol. 20,* p. 128; *Sathya Sai Speaks, Vol. 27,* p. 148; *Sathya Sai Speaks, Vol. 31*, pp. 470-471.

[120] Sai Baba, "*Be Like Jesus*", *op,cit.*, pp. 25-26. Cf. *Sathya Sai Speaks, Vol. 13,* p. 57; also *Sathya Sai Speaks, Vol. 29,* p. 153.

to speak to them in their own style and language and to teach them the methods that they can adopt and practise.[121] Sai Baba told many stories about the birth of Jesus. Some of these stories are in line with the Biblical narratives whereas some are not. In any case it is evident from his discourses that he believed in most of the fundamental Christian doctrines such as the virgin birth, the appearance of a star but he holds that this has nothing to do with the birth of Jesus, the visit of three kings from the east, they were Arabian kings, the census, baby Jesus laid in the manger, heavenly herald singing song, etc. The three Arabian kings who came to see Jesus said something highly significant. The first king said to Mary, "Mother, you have given birth to a child who loves God," which means he is the Messenger of God; the second king said, "Mother, you have given birth to a child who will be loved by God," signifying that he is the Son of God; the third king said, "Mother Mary, your child is not different from God; both are one and the same," which means that he is God himself as they are one.[122] The prophetic pronouncement of the three kings from the east confirmed the three progressive identity of Jesus Christ and possibly Swami has this story to support his claim of Jesus' progressive identity.

4.1.4. Christmas Celebration

Baba emphasizes spiritual way of celebrating Christmas. In fact, every year Christmas is celebrated with solemnity and holiness, as they claimed, at Prasanthi Nilayam. Christmas celebration at Prasnathi Nilayam usually includes among others some carol singing by Western devotees, speeches by Sai devotees of Christian background, a special discourse on Christmas by Sathy Sai Baba.[123] According to Baba, Christmas celebration must take the form of adherence to the teachings, loyalty to the principles, practising the disciplines and experiencing the awareness of the Divine that Jesus sought to arouse.[124] Singing carols, burning of candles, reading from the Bible and acting out the incidents that surrounded Jesus' birth are not enough to celebrate the birth of Jesus, it should be celebrated by putting into practice at least one of the ideals he enunciated. By practicing the ideals he taught like to love all beings and serve all with compassion, one can truly celebrate Christmas. The best way to celebrate Jesus' birth is to possess a pure heart, to have holy activities and to harbour feelings beneficial to all.[125] Swami asks people to give up two evils such as self praise and talking scandal and adopt one good habit

---

[121] *Sathya Sai Speaks, Vol. 14,* p. 60.

[122] *Sathya Sai Speaks, Vol. 31,* pp. 465-466.

[123] Cf. Murphet, *Sai Baba: Invitation to Glory*, p.134.

[124] *Sathya Sai Speaks, Vol. 11,* p. 174.

[125] Sathya Sai Baba, *"Be Like Jesus"*, pp. 15-16.

– the habit of loving service to the weak, the helpless, the distressed and the disconsolate in honour of Christmas.[126]

4.1.5. Jesus in India

Sathya Sai Baba says that Jesus, after the death of his earthly father Joseph, declining his mother's plea to continue his father's profession to earn a livelihood, set out to do ministry and came to India. He perfected himself during his stay in India. Jesus, like most seekers, started seeking God in the objective world. But he soon realized that the world was a kaleidoscopic picture created by one's own imagination, and sought to find God within himself. He stayed in the Himalayan monasteries in Kashmir, and in other centers of Eastern asceticism. Philosophical enquiry coupled with much contemplation, gave him great awareness. It grew in him by stages.[127] In India Jesus was known by the name Isa; and Swami testifies that in the Tibetan manuscript, at the monastery where Isa spent some years, his name is written as Isa.[128] Jesus' stay in India is important for Baba to explain how he achieved oneness with God by a progressive growth from dualism via qualified non-dualism to non-dualism. Luc J. Courtois comments, "This period in Jesus' life is of monumental importance to throw light on the spiritual evolution Jesus went through."[129]

4.1.6. The Uniqueness of Jesus Questioned

Like other Hindu spiritual leaders who on one hand show genuine respect and adoration to Jesus, but on the other hand denied his uniqueness as the only saviour, Baba also denies the message propagated by Christians that Jesus is the *only* way to God. He narrated a story - Once a priest told Jesus, "You are telling them that everyone can enter heaven only through you," to which Jesus reply, "The kingdom of heaven is within you, within everybody. When this is my teaching, how can I be accused of claiming that the kingdom of heaven can be attained only through me?"[130] With this Baba concludes that Jesus never say that he is the only way. He states, "Jesus was never egoistic at any point of time. Nowhere did Jesus ever state that he was God or the Master. Jesus was a noble soul and declared that he was the son of God, but he never said that he was God. He always addressed God as his Father."[131] Baba even goes further by saying that Jesus is not a real *Avatāra* who can save people. "Never

---

[126] *Ibid.*, p. 16.

[127] *Ibid.*, p. 19.

[128] *Sathya Sai Speaks, Vol. 14,* p. 59.

[129] Courtois, *Sai Baba Speaks of Jesus*, p. 45.

[130] Sai Baba, "*Be Like Jesus*", p. 79.

[131] Sai Baba, "*Be Like Jesus*", p. 125. Cf. *Sathya Sai Speaks, Vol. 34,* pp. 371-372.

did Jesus declare that he was the truth, the path, the savious and redeemer. Only Divine Incarnation (*Avatār*) can give such an assurance… Jesus never said this."[132] Even though Swami mentioned the name of Jesus in affirmative sense in a number of his discourses and celebrated with his devotees the birth of Jesus in his *āśram* for nearly forty years where he used to give Christmas Discourses, he always puts himself as superior to Jesus Christ.

4.2. The Work of Jesus Christ

It is apparent that for Bhagavan Baba the work of Christ is less important than his teaching though he mentioned miracles, cross, resurrection, etc. His main focus in the ministry of Jesus is the message he preached to the people rather than what he had accomplished with his earthly body.

4.2.1. Miracles

For Bhagavan Baba, miracles are not what is most important, they are just like a 'Visiting Card,'[133] but he acknowledges that Jesus performed many miraculous deeds, relieved the suffering of many distressed people, preached sublime truths to the people, and ultimately sacrificed his life. He spread the spirit of compassion and conferred solace on the distressed and the suffering.[134] He attracted people by his miracles and transformed them into apostles and exemplary servants of humans.[135] Baba cites Jesus' acts of helping the needy as a model to follow in the service of the society.[136]

4.2.2. The Crucifixion

Sai Baba accepts the crucifixion of Christ but does not believe in the atonement theory propagated by the Church. However, he mentions that Christ sacrificed his life for the sake of those who put their faith on him,[137] without elaborating in what way Jesus' death on the cross would benefit his followers. He says that Jesus earned a good name by sacrificing his body on the cross. Suffering on the cross is more of an example set by Jesus for his followers. Jesus' crucifixion was mainly because of three things - His sacred teachings, jealousy due to his popularity, and the cleansing of the Jerusalem temple where

---

[132] Sai Baba, "*Be Like Jesus*", pp. 125-126.

[133] *Sathya Sai Speaks, Vol. 12*, p. 124.

[134] *Sathya Sai Baba, "Be Like Jesus*", pp. 48-49.

[135] *Sathya Sai Speaks, Vol. 13*, p. 82.

[136] Cf. Sathya Sai Baba, "*Be Like Jesus*", p. 49.

[137] *Sathya Sai Speaks, Vol. 10*, p. 143; *Sathya Sai Speaks, Vol. 18*, p. 5.

he condemned blood sacrifice.[138] Swami's version of crucifixion also includes the following:[139]

Jesus as complaining his suffering, says, "O God, why do you punish me like this", "O Father, why are you not coming to save me?"[140]

- The unseen voice from heaven said: "Death is the dress of life," "All life is one, my dear son. Be alike to everyone."
- Jesus then said: "O God, let your will prevail..."
- Jesus interceding with God for his persecutors to pardon them.

It is mission accomplished – the mission of crucifying the ego on the cross of compassion. The Christian cross is a symbol for the elimination of the ego. When the feeling of "I" is eliminated, the ego vanishes and you become God.[141] He reached the stage of unity with God at the cross and felt no pain. "Even at the time of crucifixion, Jesus was smiling, because he realized that he was not the body."[142] Thus, "Christ became a glorious figure in the moment of his crucifixion."[143]

For Sathya Sai Baba crucifixion is not the greatest sacrifice Jesus paid because this is something imposed forcibly by the crowd and the government officials; "a person bound and beaten by police cannot say that he has sacrificed anything, for he is not a free man."[144] The real sacrifice that Jesus made is what he did voluntarily, out of his own volition. "He sacrificed his happiness, prosperity, comfort, safety and position; he braved the enmity of the powerful. He refused to yield or compromise. He renounced the 'ego' which is the toughest to get rid of... He willingly sacrificed the desires with which the body torments man (sic); this is sacrifice greater than the sacrifice of the body under duress."[145]

4.2.3. The Resurrection

Sathya Sai Baba accepts the bodily resurrection of Jesus Christ, but he rarely speaks about it. In his discourses only two times, i.e. 1992 and 2001 Christmas discourses that he mentioned about the resurrection of Jesus Christ. "Jesus

---

[138] Sathya Sai Baba, "*Be Like Jesus*", p. 116.

[139] Cf. *Ibid.*, pp. 121-122.

[140] Sathya Sai Baba says, "When he was crucified, God did not come to his rescue. Christ even cried out in anguish: 'Oh Father, Why are you not coming to save me?'" *Sathya Sai Speaks, Vol. 26,* p. 135.

[141] Sathya Sai Baba, "*Be Like Jesus*", p. 123.

[142] *Ibid.*

[143] *Sathya Sai Speaks, Vol. 26,* p. 135.

[144] Sai Baba, "*Be Like Jesus*", p. 124.

[145] *Ibid.*

was crucified on a Friday and He rose from the tomb on a Sunday. That is why Sunday is taken as the day of worship and service in churches,"[146] and "It was decided that Jesus should be crucified... When Jesus rose from the cross, he went on propagating the glory of Jesus."[147] One source testifies Baba as saying that after Jesus was resurrected he continued his mission and even visited places like India, Malaysia, visiting Kolkata and Kashmir and finally died in Kashmir.[148] So, the traditional doctrine of Christianity concerning Jesus' death and resurrection as having salvific power in cleansing and redeeming the sinful humans, is not to be found in Baba's Christology. His advaitic worldview which takes human soul as identical with God but in bondage due to ignorance, does not permit him to take Jesus' death and resurrection as a solution to the problem of human being.

4.2.4. Jesus' Second Coming

Having aware of Christians giving so much importance to the second coming of Jesus, Swami tries to throw some light on this issue also. He said in 1972, in his first exclusive Christmas discourse, that when Jesus was merging in the Supreme Principle of Divinity, he promised his second coming:

> The statement of Christ is simple: 'He who sent me among you will come again!' and he pointed to a Lamb. The Lamb is merely a symbol, a sign. It stands for the Voice - Ba-Ba; the announcement was the Advent of Baba. 'His Name will be Truth', Christ declared. *Sathya* means Truth. 'He will wear a robe of red, a blood red robe', (Here Baba pointed to the robe He was wearing!). 'He will be short, with a crown (of hair). The Lamb is the sign and symbol of Love." Christ did not declare that he will come again. He said, "He who made me will come again'. That Ba-ba is this Baba and Sai, the short, curly-hair-crowned red-robed Baba, is come.[149]

According to Baba, it is not Christ, the son that will come again, because Jesus said that he who sent me will come again; so, the Father, that is Sai, is foretold here as the one to come again. Though Swami believes that Jesus

---

[146] *Sathya Sai Speaks, Vol. 25,* p. 192.

[147] *Sathya Sai Speaks, Vol. 34*, p. 373.

[148] Peggy Manson & Ron Laing in their book *Sathya Sai Baba: The Embodiment of Love*, reported a conversation between them and Sri Baba where they asked whether Jesus was resurrected bodily. Baba said that Jesus was resurrected with physical body and travelled to various places and continued his mission, he died in Kashmir and was buried there. As cited in Sreejith Narayan, *Sai, Thy Kingdom Come,* p. 141. Cf. Peggy Manson & Ron Laing in their book *Sathya Sai Baba: The Embodiment of Love*, (London: Sawbridge, 1982), pp. 48-49.

[149] Sai Baba, "*Be Like Jesus*", pp. 126-127. Cf. *Sathya Sai Speaks, Vol. 11*, p. 177.

was resurrected bodily, he is silent about the ascension of Jesus into heaven in order to come again, rather, he admits that Jesus after his resurrection, traveled far and wide and finally died and buried in Kashmir, India.[150] With this Baba tries to nullify the possibility of Jesus' second coming by projecting that what is to come has already come in his personal form.

4.3. The Teachings of Jesus Christ

The teachings of Jesus Christ as presented by Sathya Sai Baba are discussed as follows:-

4.3.1. The Basic Teaching of Jesus Christ

According to Sathya Sai Baba, "Christ's basic teachings were related to promotion of compassion, sympathy, love, sacrifice and fellowship among human beings."[151] He repeatedly says that Jesus taught the 'Fatherhood of God and the brotherhood/sisterhood of human.'[152] Jesus Christ pronounced to the world three important things – (1) God is one, (2) God is omnipotent, and (3) do not hurt anyone. Christ embarked on his mission and went about calling upon people to earn the love of God by developing love towards God.[153] The most vital and the greatest message of Jesus, according to Swami is, "God is in everyone. Do not revile anyone. Do not cause harm to anyone."[154] Elsewhere, he also says that one of the most important messages of Jesus was the establishment of 'peace on earth and goodwill among men.'[155] So, the Jesus Christ we see in Baba's exposition is the one whose central message is that of oneness of God and humanity, the divinity of human and the need to develop brotherly/sisterly love towards all in order to establish harmonious co-existence. In other words, Baba's Christ did not go beyond Advaitic tradition and its vision of oneness of existence.

Looking at Jesus from the perspective of Advaita Vedānta, Baba said that Jesus' message is universal. He taught that God is one and that the Divine dwells in every being. You can realize this truth only when you experience non-dualism – seeing the same God in all beings in the true spirit of non-dualism.[156]

---

[150] Though he did not mention this in his public Discourse, he disclosed it to the devotees, cf. Sreejith Narayan, Sai, Thy Kingdom Come, p. 141.

[151] *Sathya Sai Speaks, Vol. 24,* p.158.

[152] Sai Baba, "*Be Like Jesus*", p. 64. Cf. *Sathya Sai Speaks, Vol. 12*, p. 109; *Sathya Sai Speaks, Vol. 14*, p. 153; *Sathya Sai Speaks, Vol. 15*, p. 55; *Sathya Sai Speaks, Vol. 17*, p. 95.

[153] Sai Baba, "*Be Like Jesus*", p. 22.

[154] *Ibid.*, p. 103.

[155] *Ibid.*, p. 85.

[156] *Ibid.*, pp. 32-33.

Baba claims Jesus Christ as declaring, "All are One; be alike to everyone,"[157] which definitely goes together with the advaitic tradition advocated by him.

4.3.2. Inherent Divinity of Human

It is apparent that Baba tries to make Jesus endorse Advaitic worldview when he says that the first message of Jesus was the inherent divinity of human being and the importance of striving to realize our divine nature.[158] He preached the omnipresence of God in all living beings. Jesus proclaimed that there is Divinity in everyone, Divine Spirit in everybody. "On listening to the teachings of Jesus, the people of Rome realized that Divinity was present in every human being in a hidden way."[159]

4.3.3. The Kingdom of God

For Sai Baba's Jesus, the kingdom of God is within everybody, suggesting that everybody is capable of entering the kingdom of God. The kingdom of God, for Jesus, is the realm of pure equanimity that is far beyond the reach of the mind. While the earthly kingdom is spoken of as the scene of the ever-changing, the kingdom of God is spoken of as the everlasting glory of the Divine.[160] Kingdom of God is spoken of as a state of human awareness. There are three levels of consciousness – in the lowest level (*Vaasana thathwa*), a person has little or no idea of God; in the second level (*Mishra thathwa*) a person divides his/her time between worldly pursuit and spiritual exercise. The third phase (*Shuddha thathwa*) of awareness is referred to by Jesus as the 'Kingdom of God' or 'Kingdom of heaven'. This level is a realm of pure equanimity. One is in constant harmony with God's unending glory.[161] Jesus taught that to enter that Kingdom of God one humans have to cultivate loving hearts. Then, their hearts would become the Kingdom of Heaven.[162]

4.3.4. Jesus Endorses the Doctrine of Transmigration of Soul

In the words of Bhagavan Baba, Jesus endorses the Hindu doctrine of transmigration of soul. He narrates Jesus as consoling Peter's mother due to the demise of her husband by telling her, "Death is but a dress of life. Wherefore do you shed tears? Death is like changing one's dress. Therefore, stop grieving. These physical bodies come and go, so do not waste your thought on these ephemeral things. The indweller (*dehi*) who lives inside this body is the true

---

157 *Sathya Sai Speaks, Vol. 12,* p. 72; *Sathya Sai Speaks, Vol. 31*, p. 466.

158 Sai Baba, "*Be Like Jesus*", pp. 32, 97.

159 *Ibid.*, pp. 61-62.

160 *Ibid.*, pp. 79, 81.

161 *Sathya Sai Speaks, Vol. 13*, p. 43; cf. Courtois, *Sai Baba Speaks of Jesus,* p. 130.

162 *Sathya Sai Speaks, Vol. 27,* p. 148.

divinity."[163] At the time of crucifixion Jesus said to her wailing mother that death is the dress of life, just as one change his/her dress, he/she changes the body from birth to birth. So, Jesus concluded that the Spirit is immortal and non-dual, to realise the non-dualistic nature of the Spirit is true wisdom.[164]

4.3.5. The Real Meaning of the Last Supper

Sai Baba has an interesting interpretation of Jesus' last supper from Advaita Vedānta perspective. When Jesus said that the bread taken in the last supper was his flesh and the wine his blood, he means to say that:

> all beings alive with flesh and blood are to be treated as he himself and that no distinction should be made of friend and foe, we or they. Everybody is his body, sustained by the bread; every drop of blood flowing in the veins of every living being is his, animated by the activity that the wine imparted to it. This is to say, every man (*sic*) is Divine and has to be revered as such.[165]

4.3.6. Ethical and Moral Teachings

According to Bhagavan Baba, Jesus taught about truth, righteousness, peace, love, non-violence, selfless service.[166] Jesus propagated the truth that service is God, that sacrifice is God.[167] Jesus paid special attention to service and he even said that the life of an individual is useless if he/she does not realise his/her duties toward society.[168] One interesting thing about Baba's presentation of Jesus' teachings is that in all these he quotes Jesus as saying something connected to the themes like love, truth, selfless service, etc., but these quotations are mostly not from the Bible. Did Swami put into the mouth of Jesus whatever he wants or did he bring out from his infinite knowledge about Jesus which were not known before or are not to be found in the Bible, is a question which is difficult to answer. Some of Jesus' ethical and moral teachings that are unique to Baba's interpretation are given below:

- Jesus advised the grownups to become like children so that they may be saved. Jesus declared: "If I were to be a child everyday for a while, with full faith in my mother, how happy I would be!" Christ

---

[163] *Sathya Sai Speaks, Vol. 35,* p. 361. Cf. *Sathya Sai Speaks, Vol. 14,* p. 206.

[164] *Sathya Sai Speaks, Vol. 35,* p. 370. Cf. *Sathya Sai Speaks, Vol. 31,* p. 471.

[165] Sathya Sai Baba, "*Be Like Jesus*", pp. 119-120. Cf. *Sathya Sai Speaks, Vol. 14*, p. 59.

[166] See Sai Baba, "*Be Like Jesus*", pp. 32-39.

[167] *Sathya Sai Speaks, Vol. 10,* p. 142.

[168] *Sathya Sai Speaks, Vol. 34,* p. 366.

said once that bliss is playing around the tender cheeks of Children in whom there are no desires.[169]

- Jesus said that the life of an individual was useless if one did not realize their duties toward society. Jesus preached that helping others in time of need is the greatest virtue of a person.[170] Baba takes Jesus' washing of his disciples' feet as a model for selfless service. When the disciples asked him why he washed their feet, "Jesus answered: 'I am washing your feet as your servant, so that you may learn to serve the world.'"[171]
- It was the teaching of Jesus that one has to overcome difficulties to be successful in life. At the time of his crucifixion Jesus complained saying, "Oh Father, what sin have I committed? Why do you make me suffer?". God answered him, "It is not suffering, whatever happens is good for you. So, accept it cheerfully." Baba concludes that Jesus bore all difficulties with fortitude, an ideal model for all of us to follow.[172]
- According to Sai Baba, Jesus set no value on wealth and position. He advised a rich man to distribute his wealth among the poor and the needy and accumulate the wealth of God's grace through love of fellow human beings. Jesus said, "Give up; I shall fill the gap" – this is the golden key of non-attachment which opens the door to heaven. Though accumulation of wealth is sinful, Jesus taught humans to be self-reliant. He gave a starving man a fish; and the next day he saw the same man starving. Jesus then rebuked him saying that he cannot give fish every day and advised him to work for his food instead of depending on others.[173]
- Jesus, according to Baba, declared: "You must face with courage the vicissitudes of life. For this, love is the supreme virtue."[174] Jesus wished well for those who insulted and injured him, he was un affected by the persecution to which he was subjected, instead he gave a pleasing smile to those who persecuted him.[175]
- One of the most important teachings of Jesus, according to Sai Baba, is the greatness of love. St. Paul who was originally an inveterate critic of Jesus was transformed into the greatest apostle by Jesus'

---

[169] *Sai Baba, "Be Like Jesus"*, p. 42.

[170] See *Ibid.*, pp. 47, 49.

[171] *Ibid.*, p. 39.

[172] See *Ibid.*, pp. 44, 50-51.

[173] *Ibid.*, pp. 53, 57, 59.

[174] *Ibid.*, p. 94.

[175] *Ibid.*, pp. 93-95, 99.

love.[176] Jesus advised one of his foremost disciples, Peter, to live in love, for love is God.

Most of the ethical and moral teachings of Jesus narrated by Sai Baba are not to be found in the Bible. For those who accept Sai Baba as God in human form who is omniscient, these are invaluable contribution towards the knowledge of Jesus Christ as they contain a number of things that are missing in the Bible. However, looking at him and the way he interpret objectively, it is apparent that Sai Baba is simply creating his own story around him, using the name and form of Jesus to propagate his own theology and philosophy. Baba narrated a story as to how Peter found new meaning of the word 'joy' after listening to Jesus' teaching on the important of love where "J" stands for Jesus who is to love first, "O" stands for others who are to love next and "Y" means you who ought to be loved only last.[177] Narrations such as this and several more on the same line make us assume that these are not Jesus' genuine teachings, but Baba's own words put in the mouth of Jesus, done to entertain the Western devotees and admirers who are predominantly practicing Christians.

4.4. Merging with Jesus Christ

Christ identified his body as having been given to him for serving others. We must follow Jesus. "The heart of Jesus is pure… We must make our hearts sacred so that either we merge in Jesus or Jesus merges in us. When we merge, it is called devotion (*bhakti*); to have Jesus awakened in us is the path of wisdom (*jñāna*)."[178] Bhagavan Baba with his Advaita Vedānta world-view, says, "The human body is not you, it simply houses the soul, or the spark of Divinity within."[179] Therefore, Baba advices: "You should constantly remind yourself, 'I am God', 'I am God', 'I am God'. The day you see yourself as God, you become God. Finally you should realize that you are Jesus and that you are God."[180]

4.5. Some Problems with Baba's Version of Jesus Christ

Sathya Sai Baba's explanation of Jesus can be put into three categories – *first*, some of the stories he tells of Jesus, the incidents in the life of Jesus he narrates and the teachings of Jesus he quotes are accurately as written in the Bible. *Second*, some of the incidents he narrates and Jesus' words he quotes are not exactly similar with Biblical narratives but are the rephrased of Biblical verses.

---

[176] *Sai Baba, "Be Like Jesus"*, p. 36.

[177] *Ibid.*, p. 109.

[178] Sai Baba, "*Be Like Jesus*", p. 171.

[179] *Ibid.*

[180] *Ibid.*, pp. 172-173.

Third, many of Baba's words on Jesus – stories, incidents and teachings of Jesus Christ, are not found in the Bible. Few examples may be given:

- Jesus declared, "All are one my dear son, be alike to everyone."[181]
- Then Jesus said, "Peter, why are you giving fish to the needy? If you give him a net, he will be able to catch fish for himself."[182]
- Once a young disciple asked Jesus, "O Master, when I am faced with some problems, how am I to solve them? Jesus replied, "O simpleton, do not seek solutions to your problems. Love God, who is installed in your heart."[183]
- When Mother Mary was shedding tears, Jesus told her, "Death is the dress of life."[184]
- Once an old woman went in search of Jesus. When she met him, she asked, "Are you Jesus?" Jesus replied, "That is the name given to me. But you can call me by any name, I shall respond."[185]
- Mary then told him, "Are you not the son of this body?" Jesus replied, "Of course! I am related to you at the physical level, as a son. But, 'I am I' only. You are all like children to me. You are all embodiments of Divinity."[186]
- "Jesus also proclaimed this truth that the one Spirit resides in all beings."[187]
- "St. John… one occasion punished one brother. Jesus appeared in his dream and questioned him, 'Do you think you are hurting that man? No, you are hurting me.'"[188]

It is noticeable that Jesus' teachings put forward by Swami, which are non-biblical, are somehow connected with the Hindu religious worldview in general and Advaita Vedānta in particular.

Again, there are a numbers of discrepancies in his presentation of Jesus Christ that can create uneasiness to those who study Swami's interpretation of Jesus. Few examples may be given:

---

[181] *Sathya Sai Speaks, Vol. 32,* Part 2, p. 151, *Sathya Sai Speaks, Vol. 39*, p. 273.

[182] *Sathya Sai Speaks, Vol. 33*, p. 372.

[183] *Ibid.*, p. 395.

[184] *Sathya Sai Speaks, Vol. 34,* p. 370.

[185] *Sathya Sai Speaks, Vol. 38: Discourses of Bhagavan Sri Sathya Sai Baba*, Delivered during 2005, (Prasanthi Nilayam: Sri Sathya Sai Books and Publications Trust, n.d.), p. 141.

[186] *Sathya Sai Speaks, Vol. 40,* p. 254.

[187] Sai Baba, "*Be Like Jesus*", p. 32.

[188] *Ibid.*, p. 38.

- *The year of the passing away of Joseph* - "Joseph passed away when Jesus was thirty."189 "His father passed away when Jesus was ten years old."[190] Joseph died after they returned from Jerusalem, that is after he was twelve years of age.[191]
- *The exact date of Christmas* – "Christmas falls in the month of March, not in December… Actually, Jesus was born in the month of March."[192] "He was born at 3-15 a.m. (early morning) on December 28 (sic), 1980 years ago. It was Sunday."[193]
- *The lost year of Jesus* – "Jesus grew up at Nazareth till he reached thirty."[194] "In the Tibetan manuscript, at the monastery where Isa spent some years"[195] "Jesus spent twelve long years wondering alone in deserts…He spent these many years in austerities…"[196] "For eight years following his sixteen birthday he travelled in India, Tibet, Iran and Russia…Jesus lived for five years in Himalayan region of Bharat."[197]

Such contradictory information as these and many more make Baba's witness to Jesus weak and suspicious of human creation rather than things coming from the omniscient God as it is claimed.

However, unlike most of the Hindu interpreters of Jesus Christ, Sai Baba mostly accepts Jesus' life, work and message depicted in the Bible and propagated by the Church but with different interpretations. He accepts Jesus' virgin birth and things connected to it like appearance of the angels and star, three wise men, a manger; he accepts the story of Jesus being left with the priest at Jerusalem temple at the age of twelve, Jesus' Baptism and forty days in the wilderness, Jesus' miracles, the twelve disciples, one of the disciples Judas betraying Jesus, Jesus as the incarnation of God, the Son of God and one with God, the last supper, his crucifixion and bodily resurrection. Baba seems to have been drawn to the exemplary life Jesus had led, the message of love he propagated and the moral and ethical ideals in the teaching of Jesus and accepts them uncritically.

---

[189] *Sathya Sai Speaks, Vol. 27,* p. 148.

[190] *Sathya Sai Speaks, Vol. 28,* p. 188.

[191] *Sathya Sai Speaks, Vol. 35,* p. 360.

[192] *Sathya Sai Speaks, Vol. 31,* p. 472.

[193] *Sathya Sai Speaks, Vol. 14,* p. 153. 'December 28' seems to be typing mistake, it should be December 24, cf. Courtois, *Sai Baba Speaks of Jesus*, p. 33.

[194] *Sathya Sai Speaks, Vol. 21,* p. 130.

[195] *Sathya Sai Speaks, Vol. 14,* p. 59.

[196] Sai Baba, "*Be Like Jesus*", p. 19.

[197] Quoted in Courtois, *Sai Baba Speaks of Jesus*, p. 51.

Sathya Sai Baba puts many things as said by Jesus which are by and large not to be found in the Bible. His followers claim that as he is omniscient, he knows many things about Jesus which has never been written and believe that whatever he said of Jesus is true. More importantly, such statements of Jesus are very often supportive of the Advaita Vedānta school of thought and other Hindu doctrines. It is not possible to provide a substantial scientific proof to ascertain the correctness or falsity of what Baba has said of Jesus, but due to the discrepancies and contradictory statements intertwined in his presentation of Jesus Christ, it cannot be ruled out that Baba might have created some of these stories in order to communicate his message more meaningfully.

Concluding Remarks

A very different and peculiar boy Raju left school education at the age of fourteen to be 'Sai Baba' as he was clear of himself being no ordinary human being, but the incarnation of God with a specific mission to fulfill. Endowed with extraordinary intelligence and miracle-working power, he rose to fame within no time, gathering a multitude of followers. Right from the beginning he preached 'unity of religions', oneness of God and the inherent divinity of human being. He managed to pull together the diverse and seeming contradictory theological and philosophical traits of Hinduism by finding the integral relationship between them. The six schools of Hindu philosophy (*sad darśan*) are not contradictory but supportive of one another, likewise, the three Vedāntic schools – dvaita, viśiṣṭādvaita and advaita are complementary. Sathya Sai Baba held that *Bhakti*, *Karma* and *Jñāna* yogas are all important for individuals according to their stages of spiritual development and are to be treated as complementary, rather than contradictory distinctive separate paths. Similarly, the diverse religious traditions of the world have their underlining unity behind their visible structural and perspectival differences. So, all religions should be respected and treated as authentic. His respect for other religions and love for harmony of religions is exemplary. Any one belonging to any religion would be feeling at home at the Prasanthi Nilayam – the *āśram* of Baba as the atmosphere looks like 'parliament of religions' with '*sarva dharma symbol*' to be found in every nook and corner of the *āśram*, with images and statues of founders of major religions of the world, and celebration of religious festivals of various religions and people from all over the world belonging to various religions.

Having stressed the importance of love and service to humankind, Bhagavan Baba exalted these two to the level of God. Truth, Peace and Non-violence also get so much attention in his teaching. His emphasis on love, service, peace, truth and non-violence appears to be the outcome of his theology of religion – oneness of reality, belongingness to one another, unity and brotherhood/sisterhood of humankind. For this he is indebted to Śaṅkara's

Advaita Vedānta, though he and his followers claimed that Sai Baba is influenced by none, because he is omniscient God who receives no sustenance from *pañcabhūtas* but on the contrary *pañcabhūtas* receive sustenance from him. Such was his self-understanding that makes him teach authoritatively without relying on any other authority. From this perspective Swami looks at Jesus Christ and tells of his story without relying on the Bible, bringing out new dimensions of Jesus which are quite unknown to the world.

His acceptance of some of the most prominent Christian doctrines of Christ such as the virgin birth, the visits of the three wise men, the baptism, Jesus' miracles, the cleansing of temple, the last supper, the crucifixion and resurrection would be welcomed by most Christians. However, he does not follow traditional interpretations in treating these subjects but fosters new and revelatory interpretations which most of the time contradicts the traditional interpretations. Inconsistencies and contradictory statements Baba made on Jesus are also disturbing as they betray Baba's identity as omniscient God. However, modern godmen/women in general are less interested in giving accurate-factual information; they rather stick to the issues and message conveyed by those facts. Sathya Sai Baba also appears to have fallen into this stream even though there is room for doubting the reliability of his interpretation of Jesus on account of discrepancies.

The main drawback seems to be his attempts to drag Jesus and his message into the fold of Advaitic tradition instead of interpreting Jesus Christ in relation to Advaita Vedānta. Looking at Jesus in the light of Advaitic worldview may be welcomed, but trying to put Jesus into it, cutting him off from the contextual realities of his world is presumptuous. But, that is what Baba is doing. As Biblical records of Jesus are not helpful for this purpose, Baba makes Jesus as saying so many things which are not to be found in the Bible, but which support his advaitic stand. He even attempts to connect himself with Jesus which is all the more less convincing and unreasonable. Things like "*Isa* (name of Jesus) when repeated is *Sai*, both mean *Īśwara* (God)", "'He who sent me among you will come again!' and he pointed to a Lamb. The Lamb is merely a symbol, a sign. It stands for the Voice - Ba-Ba; the announcement was the Advent of Baba.", etc. are not convincing enough to prove the connection between Baba and Jesus, but rather hilarious. Irresponsible and untenable statements like these are rather tarnishing the image of him and his interpretation of Jesus. It is understood that the four Gospels of the Bible do not exhaust all the things Jesus had done and said. Still, it is not possible to ascertain what Baba had said of Jesus is true or not. Sai Baba may be true in his presentation of Jesus or may be utterly wrong, but his interpretation of *the* Jesus he knew still stands as an important mile stone in providing yet another face of Jesus which has not been recognized through the ages, thereby enriching our knowledge of Jesus. In other words, the falsity or correctness of his story of Jesus does not dictate the value of his interpretation. In either of the case, Baba's interpretation of Jesus could serve as a useful agent in bringing cordial interreligious relations in India.

Sai Baba's interest in Jesus seems to be primarily because of his theology of religions that emphasizes oneness, unity, brotherhood/sisterhood, love, service, belongingness and togetherness, on one hand; and on the other hand, it is his methodological tool to entertain Christian audiences. He interprets Jesus as belonging *not* to the Christians only but to the whole humanity irrespective of their religious affiliations, his teaching as relevant even to the hard-core Hindus as much as it is for Christians. So, he asks his devotees to follow Jesus and try to be like him, worshipping him by following his ideals. Baba's presentation of Jesus may be contentious and even doubtful but his attitude towards Jesus and his message is definitely heartening. It is presumed that such positive attitude shall produce a far-reaching effect towards building cordial inter-religious relations in India.

Chapter 6

Osho Rajneesh's Interpretation of Jesus Christ

Osho may be the most controversial of all the contemporary gurus. He is one of the most philosophical in dealing with and presentation of any subject but he is the one most against philosophy. He is considered as one of the most intellectual persons India has ever produced but he is probably the one propagating the most anti-intellectualism. He is a mystic, but based his mysticism on science. This man is full of paradoxes! Owing to his varied nature he earned negative appellations such as 'Sex Guru', 'Con Man', 'Self-Appointed Bhagavan', 'The Rich Man's Guru', 'The Joker', 'The Rolls-Royce Guru', etc. He is often described as a rebel, an iconoclast, spiritual terrorist and anarchist.

Osho is not easy to understand mainly due to his contradictory teaching which is apparently done consciously and intentionally for some deeper purposes. Some people hailed him as an enlightened man whereas for some he is a narcissistic patient in need of psycho-medical treatment. Some people regarded him as the most original guru but some alleged him as syncretistic, being influenced by a number of persons and their thoughts – such as Gautama Buddha, Jesus Christ, Maharishi Raman, Krishnamurti, Nietzsche, Gurdjieff, Zen Masters and Śaṅkara. His liberal view on sex and individual freedom earned him many enemies, but attracted thousands of upper-class men and women who thronged the ground to listen to his discourses in hoping to get *authentic individuality* and *spiritual freedom* which are the main ends of his spiritual endeavour.

Osho speaks on a wide variety of subjects that includes discourses on Hindu religious tradition, Jainism and Buddhism, on Jesus, Buddha, Zen Masters, on Himself, etc.[1] He speaks a lot on Jesus and his teachings. There

[1] Books that bear his name as the author numbered to more than 600, of which nearly half of them are in English. These books are the transcribed of his numerous lectures, discourses and

are seven volumes of books that contain Osho's discourses on Jesus and apart from this, Osho mentions, discusses and makes use of Jesus and his teachings in almost all of his books. The main purpose of this Chapter is to discuss Osho's interpretations of Jesus Christ. I begin my discussion with his life and influences on him in brief, and then move on to discussing Osho's methodological framework as well as a brief discussion on his philosophical and religious teachings. The final section deals with his interpretation of Jesus Christ and I close the Chapter with concluding remarks.

1. A Brief Life Sketch of Osho Rajneesh

Osho Rajneesh (1931-1990)[2] was born in a Jain business family as Rajneesh Chandra Mohan on 11 December 1931 in Kuchwada in Madhya Pradesh. It is said that Osho's birth was not ordinary. When his mother carried him in her womb, a flooded river detained them for three days on their journey. No boatman had the courage enough to take them across the river due to the flood. But a Monk told one of the boatmen to carry them across saying that they would be safe because of the baby in the womb. Trusting in the Monk, one boatman agreed to sail through the flooded river. As the Monk predicted, they went through without any difficulty. Again, when Osho was born, unlike other new-born babies, he did not cry and did not take milk for three days. Such extraordinary things are reported of Osho.[3] In one of his discourses, Osho said that the Monk who told a boatman to carry her mother across the river was Sai Baba.[4] But it cannot be Sathya Sai Baba of Puttaparthi as he would be only 4 years old by this time.

He happened to be the eldest of eleven children born to his parents Babulal and Saraswati Jain. He was reared by his maternal grandparents in a remote village, which had hardly two hundreds inhabitant, with so much love and understanding plus extraordinary freedom given to him till he reached the age of seven. With the influence of his grandmother, this old couple looked after Rajneesh, helping him to be himself without giving him any guidance, advice, education, and the like. He was made free to do whatever he liked,

interactions with his disciples.

[2] There are two books which are the records of Osho's lecturer on his life – Osho, *Autobiography of a Spiritually Incorrect Mystic,* (New York: Osho International Foundation, 2000), and Osho, *Glimpses of a Golden Childhood: The Rebellious Childhood of a Great Enlightened One*, (Pune: Osho Media International, 2010). These books are also available in the Osho International On-line Library at *http://www.osho.com/library/the-books.aspx.*

[3] Vasant Joshi, *The Luminous Rabel: Life Story of a Maverick Mystic*, (New Delhi: Wisdom Tree 2010), pp. 28, 30.

[4] Cf. Osho, *From Misery to Enlightenment*, downloaded in a *pdf* format from *http://www.messagefrommasters.com/Ebooks/Osho_Discourse_Series.htm* (09.04.2013), pp. 229-230.

without friends, without a company, with himself alone in silence.[5] Though his grandfather was a devout Jain, Osho, like his maternal grandmother, right from his childhood, belonged to no religion but always in desire of and in pursue of spiritual enlightenment. He testifies, "I have been looking for the door to enlightenment as long as I remembered... I don't remember a single day in my childhood in this life that I was not looking for it."[6]

After the death of his maternal grandfather, he and his grandmother shifted to Gadarwada and he lived with his parents there. He started his education, became more mischievous, independent - challenging anything he considered wrong including people who were in authority. His spiritual hunger became more and more in spite of his regular visit to Church, and Mosque, Gurudwara, Hindu and Jain Temples.[7] He tried every possible way within his reach and capability to get enlightenment but to no avail. He even had nervous breakdown may be due to this intense mental unrest or may be because of the death of his beloved girlfriend. M.L. Ahuja records, "The death of his childhood girlfriend in 1947 reportedly sent him into deep depression after which he lapsed into a silence and would seldom speak."[8] According to one of his close friends, after the death of his girlfriend Shashi, Osho became more distant and detached, keeping complete silence for many days.[9] It is claimed that on the 21st March, 1953, at the age of 21, Osho experienced death and deathlessness. His worldly connections and desires, and his past died but he was reborn. He experienced enlightenment! He narrated this incident:

> I went to sleep. It was a very strange sleep. The body was asleep, I was awake...Nearabout twelve my eyes suddenly opened – I had not opened them. The sleep was broken by something else. I felt a great presence around me in the room...I felt a throbbing life all around me, a great vibration – almost like a hurricane, a great storm of light, joy, ecstasy, I was drowning in it. It was so tremendously real that everything else became unreal...There is an awakening – compared to the reality of that awakening, this whole reality becomes unreal.[10]

He says that that state, the awakening, the state of enlightenment, cannot be understood by intellect, nor can it be explained by academic categories, it

---

[5] Osho, *Autobiography of a Spiritually Incorrect Mystic,* pp. 6-7.

[6] *Ibid.*, p. 61.

[7] *Ibid.*, p. 39.

[8] M.L. Ahuja, *Gurus: Ancient, Medieval and Modern,* (New Delhi: Rupa & Co., 2009), p. 205. Vasant Joshi, *The Luminous Rebel,* p. 57.

[9] Vasant Joshi, *The Luminous Rebel,* p. 57.

[10] Osho, *Autobiography of a Spiritually Incorrect Mystic,* pp. 72-73.

is only understood by experiencing it. That enlightenment gave him totally new perspective. He felt that he was not in the body, but hovering around the body;[11] so he observes, "I died and was reborn. But the one that was reborn has nothing to do with the one that died, it is a discontinuous thing. On the surface it looks continuous, but it is discontinuous."[12]

After the experience of enlightenment, he continued his education, graduated in 1955 and received master degree in 1957. He worked as a lecturer at Sanskrit College, Raipur and then a Professor of philosophy at the University of Jabalpur in 1960 where he taught till he left the University in 1966. His rebellious and unnatural nature and uncontrollable behavior made him unwelcome in institutions and other organizations where one has to follow prescribed rules and regulations. In 1940s Osho joined two prominent organizations, such as Rashtriya Swayamsevak Sangh (RSS) and Indian National Army (INA) led by Subhas Chandra Bose and began to involve in freedom movement; but soon he left both INA and RSS because he could not accept any external discipline, ideology, or system to have control over him. He could not work for long in the college and University where he taught due to conflict between him and the authority as he is un-controllable. It is said that though he was awarded a Gold Medal for being stood first in the university, he dropped the medal in the University well in order to show that no one is inferior to him and that he is nobody.[13] Apart from his teaching engagement, he began his active public ministry, meeting people as he travelled far and wide within the country, organizing meditational camps, addressing big gatherings. He was, then, popularly known as 'Ācārya Shree Rajneesh'. His popularity grew as more and more controversies surround him. His meditation camps earned him popularity as well as controversy. For instance, in 1968 he was invited to give a series of five talks on 'love' in the prominent Bharatiya Vidhya Bhavan Auditorium in Bombay. In the first talk, he referred sex as a possible step towards superconsciousness which aroused anger among the audience, resulting into the cancellation of the rest of the talks. But after a month, he was invited again to talk on the same subject where he addressed 50,000 odd crowds in an open field. Since then he was given an appellation 'Sex Guru.'[14]

---

[11] *Ibid.*, p. 75. According to him when the really real is dawn, all others which we considered as real reduced to the state of *māyā*. He confesses: "That night for the first time I understood the meaning of the word *māyā*." *Ibid.*, p. 73.

[12] *Ibid.*, p. 77.

[13] See Vasant Joshi, *The Luminous Rebel,* pp. 49, 82, 91, 97; "Osho Rajneesh" *The Famous People website*, 2013, in *http://www.thefamouspeople. com/profiles/osho-rajneesh-23.php* (13.02.2013).

[14] Vasant Joshi, *The Luminous Rebel,* p. 101; Osho, *Autobiography of a Spiritually Incorrect Mystic*, p. 226.

A number of years of active travelling came to an end when he settled in Bombay from 1970-1974 and used to address small group who gathered for his talks, and started to initiate disciples called '*Neo-sannyāsins*'. Few months before he moved to Bombay (Mumbai) he introduced in April, 1970, in one of his meditation camps, what has become the most popular meditational technique among the several techniques he developed, the *Dynamic Meditation*.[15]

In May 1971 Osho changed his name from 'Ācārya Shree Rajneesh' to 'Bhagavan Shree Rajneesh'. For Osho, *Bhagavan* does not mean God, but it means 'the blessed one', 'one who is at home', 'one who has found', 'one who has arrived' or 'one who has encounter himself/herself'. It does not mean God for him; rather it refers to a state of experience, a state of experience of bhagavatta, of godliness.[16] According to Vasant Joshi changing of his name indicates that Osho wants to change his way of communication from intellectual communication in the capacity as Acharya to a heart to heart communication as Bhagavan.[17] He also for the first time declared publicly that he is enlightened. He kept secret about his enlightenment for almost twenty years, disclosing only to few individuals who suspected it as they observed him.[18] Few years after this, in 1974 exactly twenty one years after his enlightenment he moved from Bombay (Mumbai) to Koregaon Park in Pune where the present Osho Commune International is located. His followers give Bombay's climate that affects Osho's health as the reason for shifting his base whereas other sources give opposition of the local residents to his movement as the primary reason that made Osho leave Mumbai.[19]

At Pune *āśram*, Osho used to give discourse every morning and in the evening he used to answer personal questions of the devotees. The Pune *āśram* attracted more and more people especially the Western elite urbanites and it is said that by 1981 the *āśram* received 30,000 visitors per year.[20] Bob Mullan records that from 1974 there are about 6,000 rajneeshees (followers of Rajneesh)

---

[15] See Vasant Joshi, *The Luminous Rebel*, p. 103.

[16] Osho, *The Last Testament, Vol.1*, retrieved from Osho Internationals official website online - Library *http://www.osho.com/library/online-library-blessed-moment-followers-9c6fd47a-413.aspx*, (16.04.2013), Chapter 1, p. 3. [In the Online-Library each chapter starts with page number 1, so we mention '*chapter number*' in order to avoid confusion]; also Osho, *Autobiography of a Spiritually Incorrect Mystic,* pp. 140, 142.

[17] Vasant Joshi, *The Luminous Rebel,* p. 116.

[18] Osho, *Autobiography of a Spiritually Incorrect Mystic,* p. 231.

[19] See M.L. Ahuja, *Gurus: Ancient, Medieval and Modern*, p. 208.

[20] Lewis F. Carter, "The 'New Renunciates' of Bhagavan Shree Rajneesh: Observations and Identification of Problems of Interpreting New Religious Movements", in *Osho Rajneesh and His Disciples: Some Western Perceptions*, edited by Harry Aveling, (Delhi: Motilal Banarsidass Publishers, 1999), p. 194.

in Pune.[21] As Osho's movement expanded more and more, opposition from the local people and religious leaders grew stronger and stronger. May be due to pressure from the local residents and religious leaders, the Government of India cancelled the tax evasion status of the *āśram*. Meanwhile Osho decided in April, 1981 to observe silence and to communicate to his followers only through silence. In the month of June, the same year, Osho left Pune *āśram* for USA. His supporters give Osho's frail health that needs better medical treatment as the reason for his US trip, while others give the growing opposition to his movement as the primary reason for which he left India.[22]

In USA a vast land, 64,000 acre spread was bought by his secretary Ma Anand Sheela in the middle of Oregon, twenty miles from the nearest town of Antelope which was formerly a cattle ranch called 'Big Muddy Ranch' where a new city named after Osho – Rajneeshpuram was built. The new city included a hotel, airport, casino, Rajneesh International Meditation University, city hall, post office, discotheque and a shopping centre with restaurants, a beauty shop, a book and record store, a clothing store and a bar.[23] It is again 'the controversy' which surrounds Rajneeshpuram that made Osho movement gain rapid popularity as *sannyāsins* and visitors poured in thousands daily. Within no time Rajneeshpuram became the largest spiritual centre ever created in USA. Carl A. Latkin and his friends who did a research on Rajneeshpuram mentioned that Osho's movement was a regular feature on both national and local television and "rarely a day went by that a major article did not appear in the state's largest newspapers."[24] According to Lewis F. Carter at the peak around October 1984, Rajneeshpuram had approximately 5,700 residents.[25]

However, the honeymoon period of Osho and his people was a short one. A number of internal conflicts and outside pressure from religious leaders and the government brought about the downfall of Rajneeshpuram. Controversies include use of land, the raising city taxes and gaining control of Antelope town and its public school. Again, Ma Anand Sheela, the main person in establishing the city, revolted against her master, Osho and finally left the commune with some 15-20 top leaders in September, 1985. Osho charged them of perpetrating

---

[21] Bob Mullan, *Life as Laughter: Following Bhagavan Shree Rajneesh*, (London: Routledge & Kegan Paul plc, 1983), p. 23.

[22] *Ibid.*, pp. 194-195.

[23] Lewis F. Carter, "The 'New Renunciates' of Bhagavan Shree Rajneesh", p. 196.

[24] Carl A. Lsatkin, et.al. "Who Lives in Utopia?: A Brief Report on the Rajneeshpuram Research Project" in *Osho Rajneesh and His Disciples: Some Western Perceptions*, edited by Harry Aveling, (Delhi: Motilal Banarsidass Publishers, 1999), p. 220; cf. Carl A. Latkin, "Seeing Red: A Social-Psychological Analysis of the Rajneeshpurum Conflict" in *Ibid.*, p. 337.

[25] Lewis F. Carter, "The 'New Renunciates' of Bhagavan Shree Rajneesh", p. 196. Vasant Joshi also says that by 1985, Rajneeshpurum was almost 5,000 strong. Joshi, *The Luminous Rabel,* p. 164.

crimes inside and outside the city like wiretapping, poisonings, arson and attempted murder.[26] Osho gave up his silence after three and half years in October, 1984. His discourses bear quite a different tune. As Joshi puts it, "God, heaven, hell, Jesus, figures on whom he had talked highly in the past, along with all the religions and societies now came under severe criticism."[27] Just like he criticized Indian politicians, he did with US politicians and government officials. This aggravated the flame of controversy that engulfed Rajneeshpurum. Osho himself was charged with 'immigration violation' and 'arranging sham marriages' in order that foreign disciples could evade visas restrictions and stay on in USA. He was arrested on October 1985. Osho left the country for good after giving a fine of $ 4,00,000 on 14 November 1985.

Osho came to Delhi and announced his plan for a world tour. However, his 'world tour' was not at all smooth, no country could give him a stay more than few days and a number of countries declined visa permit. According to Joshi twenty one countries had either deported Osho or denied him entry.[28] So, after a failed[29] and controversial 'world tour', Osho finally landed in Mumbai and then Pune *āśram* in the middle of 1986 where he remained till he died in 1990. Osho changed again his name from 'Bhagavan' to 'Osho' in the year 1989. He explains that his name 'Osho' is derived from William James' 'oceanic' signifying 'that which dissolves into the ocean'. Later he found out that the word 'Osho' has been used in the Far East meaning 'the Blessed One, on Whom the Sky Showers Flowers'.[30] The last few years of his life was spent on discoursing on the life of Gautama Buddha and Zen Buddhism.[31]

---

[26] See Latkin, "Seeing Red: A Social-Psychological Analysis of the Rajneeshpurum Conflict", pp. 339-341; also Osho, *Autobiography of a Spiritually Incorrect Mystic*, p. 254.

[27] Vasant Joshi, *The Luminous Rebel*, p. 171.

[28] *Ibid.*, p. 208. For details of the controversies during the World Tour, ref. Chapter 11, pp. 192-210; also Osho, *Autobiography of a Spiritually Incorrect Mystic*, pp. 260-265.

[29] Osho seemed to be dejected as he said after the world tour: "I have come home with dreams broken, fictions destroyed, hopes shattered. What I have seen is the reality, and what I had been thinking all my life about man (*sic*) was only his mask." Osho, *Last Testament, Vol.* 6, downloaded in a *pdf* format from *http://www.oshorajneesh.com/osho-personal-glimpses.htm* (09/04/2013), p. 47.

[30] Joshi, *The Luminous Rebel,* p. 221.

[31] According to him, Buddha said that he will come again after twenty five centuries in the name of *Maitreya* and he will be called 'The Friend'. Osho claims that Gautama the Buddha has taken shelter in him, "I am the host, he is the guest", because he (Osho) does not consider himself as a guru, but a friend, he claims that he is the fulfilment of that prophesy. Osho, *Autobiography of a Spiritually Incorrect Mystic,* p. 276.

2. Influences on Osho

There may be no modern guru who read more books than Osho; he is reported to have read many thousands of books of all kinds during his life time.[32] It can be, therefore, assumed that he might have been influenced by those readings. Ram Chandra Prashad, who is considered as an official biographer of Osho, discusses similarities of Rajneesh's teaching with that of Gurdjief, Krishnamurthi and Zen Buddhism which suggests a possibility of him being influenced by them. Prasad mentions that Krishnamurthi and Osho emphasize freedom of individuals and were both negative towards tradition, orthodoxy and dogmas. Both decline to be known as 'guru' having disciples as they stick to giving freedom to each individual. Both refuse to organize their teaching and movement.[33] Prasad also points out that Rajneesh's conception of the 'unawakened human' bears a close resemblance to Gurdjieff's description of humans as machines. Both aim at achieving a synthesis of Western science and Eastern spirituality.[34] Osho's teaching on inner void and throwing away the mind or transcending the mind is similar with Zen Buddhism.[35] His view on sex and mysticism resembles an amalgamation of tantricism and modern psychology and in the words of Uday Mehta, P.D. Ouspensky's stressed on the kinship between sex and mysticism had a far reaching influence on Rajneesh.[36]

As Osho exhibits familiarity with the teachings of Upanishad, Zen Masters, Tantricism, Buddha, Christ, Krishnamurthi, Gurdjieff, etc. it can be assumed that their thoughts might have a deep impact upon him, but we should not be so quick to conclude that Osho's religious and philosophical teachings are an eclectic combination of these. Authors who wrote on Osho's life and teaching seem to have missed the importance and role of his first seven years spent with his maternal grandparents and a deep influence his maternal grandmother had on him.[37] His maternal grandmother was a liberated woman,

[32] One of his biographers testifies that he read more than 80,000 books on almost 400 different subjects. Joshi, *The Luminous Rebel,* p. 81.

[33] Ram Chandra Prasad, *Rajneesh: The Mystic of Feeling*, (Delhi: Motilal Banarsidass, 1978, Revised Edition), pp. 43-45.

[34] *Ibid.*, p. 16.

[35] *Ibid.*, p. 95.

[36] See Uday Mehta, *Modern Godmen in India: A Sociological Appraisal*, (Bombay: Popilar Prakashan, 1993), p. 85.

[37] A number of books on Osho miss to mention this, to mention few - Ram Chandra Prasad, *Rajneesh: The Mystic of Feeling, op.cit.;* Harry Aveling (ed.), *Osho Rajneesh and His Disciples, Bob Mullan, Life as Laughter: Following Bhagavan Shree Rajneesh, op.cit.;* M.L. Ahuja, Gurus*: Ancient, Medieval and Modern*,; Khushwant Singh, *Gods and Godmen of India,* (New Delhi: HarperCollins Publishers & India Today Group, 2003); Uday Mehta, *Modern Godmen in India, op.cit.*; Peter Brent, *Godmen of India*, (Middlesex: Penguin Books, 1972); Vishal

a rebel who believes in no religion and in no God. She let Rajneesh grew up with utmost freedom to do whatever he likes and just to be 'himself' without any interference or restriction from outside. He acknowledges her influence upon him. He lovingly confesses, "All that is beauty in my vision somewhat comes through her. She helped me in every way to be the way I am. Without her I may have been a shopkeeper or perhaps a doctor or an engineer."[38] So, it may not be too much to say that Osho is influenced most deeply by his grandmother because his rebellious nature, his rejection of any codified religion, God, dogmas, tradition and his emphasis on individual freedom, personal experiencing and the likes had been obtained when he was under her care. When he left her at the age of seven, Osho already held all these firmly to never abandon them.

3. Glimpse of Osho's Methodological Framework

A brief discussion on the method Osho employs in his attempt to attract people and disseminate his teaching is vital due to its peculiarity and uniqueness. He is a man of protest and a rebel who, from his childhood, was against anything that does not fit into his pattern of logic and thinking. In his approach, his nature as a rebellious thinker has the upper hand. Having fully aware of the importance of drawing crowds in order to move on in his mission, he creates confusion and annoyance by discriminately attacking and outrageously criticizing religions, traditions and religious leaders and political figures. This method makes him controversial and different from others that give rise to inquisitiveness in many well-to-do and educated urbanites who have had enough of the traditional droning religious practices. At the end this method only adds to his popularity.

Osho changes his position frequently, giving contradictory teachings and as by doing so he apparently wants to communicate three things – *Firstly*, for him information is not the primary, instead, he wants to make people experience things by themselves since intellectual-academic knowledge is not sufficient. *Secondly*, Osho gives contradictory teaching so that it will not be possible to create dogma out of it. *Thirdly*, Osho addresses his audiences in two levels, viz. *their* level and *his* level, or we may say, in the 'phenomenal level' and 'transcendental level'. For examples, though he did not believe in God, he talks so much about God as his audience are at the level of believing in God. He talks about Jesus, Buddha and others great Masters as the audience are at that level of somewhat attaching themselves with these Masters even

Mangalwadi, *The World of the Gurus: A Critical Look at the Philosophies of India's Influential Gurus and Mystics*, Revised Edition, (Chicago: Cornerstone Press, 1992); Kushwant Singh, *Gurus, Godmen and Good People*, (New Delhi: Orient Longman Ltd., 1975).

[38] Osho, *Autobiography of a Spiritually Incorrect Mystic*, pp. 22-23.

though he does not believe in them. This is his way of addressing people in the 'phenomenal level'. Again, Osho also said things in the 'transcendental level' or 'his own level' where he bashes aside all the things he had said in the 'audience level' or 'phenomenal level' and teaches totally contradictory things. For him things said in the 'transcendental level' is what is really true and it is to this level that he wants to drive his audience. As the levels are different, these two are always contradictory. He says,

> I have to work on two levels: one is the level where you live, where you are, and one is the level where I am and I want you also to be.
>
> From the top of a hill I have to come into the valley where you are; otherwise you won't listen, you won't believe the sunlit top. I have to take your hand in my hand and persuade you – and on the way, tell stories that are not true! But they keep you engaged, and don't create any trouble in walking; you go on, engaged with the story. And when you have reached the hilltop, you will know why I was telling long stories, and you will feel grateful that I told those stories; otherwise you would not have been able to travel that long, that far uphill.[39]

As all of his audiences have their religious affiliation, in order to attract them and make them listen, he felt that he has to use their religious doctrines though he did not believe in them. He says that this 'game' is a 'necessary evil' to draw people to him so that he can tell his own truth, the truth which according to him is the real one.[40] Elsewhere he also says to his own selected people, "To the Hindus I had to speak through Krishna, and I was not happy about it. But there was no other way, it was a necessary evil. To Christians I could speak only through Jesus. I was not at ease about it, but there was no other way.[41]

So, we should understand that discourses on religious figures, commentaries on scriptures of various types and the like are just the 'untrue stories' narrated to engage people in their level so that they remain with him till they realise what really is. Osho says that speaking on some religious figures whom he does not agree with, or discoursing on some religious doctrines just for the sake of his audiences, is very depressive: "So I have been carrying a

---

[39] *Ibid.*, p. 136.

[40] Osho, *From Personality to Individuality*, downloaded in a *pdf* format from *http://www.messagefrommasters.com/ Ebooks/Osho_Discourse_Series.htm*, (09.04.2013), p. 248.

[41] Osho, *From Unconsciousness to Consciousness*, retrieved from Osho Internationals official website online Library, *http://www.osho.com/library/online-library-brainwashing-mahavira-points-b58e703c-4d4.aspxp*, (16.04.2013), Chapter 1, p. 4.

heavy weight on me, on my heart. My health has been destroyed for many reasons... that I have been speaking on people with whom I do not agree at all. I disagree – not only disagree, but I find them basically psychotic, neurotic, schizophrenic, anti-life."[42] Osho used this approach mainly before the period of three and half years silence, and after the silence, he spoke mostly to his people, the *sannyāsins* and spoke directly to them. So, when speaking to his loyal *sannyāsins*, he says that such 'game' is no longer necessary. The tune is also very different now:

> I am continually telling you to flush God down the toilet, to forget all about heaven and hell, and that the law of karma is nothing but boo-boo. And I am no longer showing any respect to Jesus, or Buddha, Mahavira, Krishna. I am just treating them as a headmaster treats his children. If they behave rightly then they will not be punished, that's all. If they don't behave rightly, then I am going to give them real hits that they will never forget. Now I have no need for any camouflage.[43]

Therefore, any attempt to unfold Osho's religious teaching and locate him in a right perspective, should take into consideration the peculiar methodological framework under which he operates. His words at 'phenomenal level' should not be taken as having 'his' ontological truth as they are not always his 'intended message'. It is imperative to differentiate between 'the truth that is mine' (to borrow his expression), which, according to him, is the real truth and 'truth of the other Masters' which is a distorted one.

4. Philosophical and Religious Teaching: An Overview

Any researcher who tries to understand and present systematically Osho's teachings will find himself or herself struck by the utmost difficulty of doing so due to his contradictory teaching, inconsistencies and unsystematic presentation of his message as underlined above. What he said holds some water: "I am a man who is consistently inconsistent. It will not be possible to make a dogma out of my words; anybody trying to make a creed or dogma out of my words will go nuts!... When I am gone there will be few fools who will try to figure it out, to make a system, although I am making it almost impossible."[44] But, here we are, trying to make some system on Osho's teaching, to figure it out what is the main content of Osho's message and locate him in a right perspective, because we feel that it is possible, though not easy, to do so because he is not consistently inconsistent as he claims himself to be.

---

[42] Osho, *From Unconsciousness to Consciousness,* Chapter 1, p. 7.

[43] Osho, *From Personality to Individuality*, p. 249.

[44] *Ibid.*, p. 156. Cf. Osho, *Autobiography of a Spiritually Incorrect Mystic*, p. 171.

4.1. Religionless Religion

Osho's teaching in its totality is a negation of the validity of any codified religion of the world. This is not something he picked up as he travels in his spiritual journey or gained at the time of his enlightenment, but rather inherited from his maternal grandmother which was fully developed when he reached the age of seven. According to him religion is the past thing which is no longer relevant for today's generation. It has done enough damage to the human civilization. "The organized religions are all dead; the churches, the temples, the mosques, the synagogues... they are all graveyards of the past…They have crippled everybody, poisoned everybody; their destruction is uncountable."[45] To a question – 'Is there any part of Christianity, Hinduism, Buddhism, any of the established religions that you think are good?' Osho replies, "Nothing is. I want to be finished with the whole past completely... I want a discontinuity with the past. Only then the new humanity is possible, a new world, a new man (*sic*). So I categorically say everything is wrong. And the proof is there: the whole world is in a mess. These are the people who have given the world principles how to live, ideologies, systems. This is the outcome of Buddhism, Hinduism, Christianity, Mohammedanism.[46] Religions are useless because they were made by somebody else for somebody else far back – centuries before and not for today's generation.[47] Furthermore, religion is the business of the priest; it has nothing to do with religiousness. It is a profession, pure and simple, of exploiting the ignorance and the helplessness of humankind. It is exploiting the fear of death, the fear of the unknown, the fear of the responsibilities of life.[48] In contrast to this, Osho calls his religion 'religionless' to avoid the misconception of the term 'religion' which means 'to bring all the parts together, to make it whole.'[49]

4.2. Godless Spirituality

Osho talks much about God in his numerous discourses and it is very easy to conclude that he believes in God. However, Osho right from his childhood till his death, never believes in God. His references to God are all his methodological game to meet people in their level. He declares to his *sannyāsins*, "I am calling my religion godless."[50] Adinatha, the first of the twenty-four *tirthankaras* in Jainism is the first to organize Godless religion; Gautama Buddha is again

[45] Osho, *The Rebel*, downloaded in a *pdf* format from *http://www.messagefrommasters.com/Ebooks/Osho_Discourse_Series.htm* (09.04.2013), p. 93.

[46] Osho, *The Last Testament, Vol. 1,* Chapter 1 p. 6.

[47] Osho, *The Rebel,* p. 95.

[48] *Ibid.*, p. 92.

[49] Osho, *From Personality to Individuality*, pp. 249-150.

[50] *Ibid.*, p. 294.

another Master who proclaimed a religion without God. Adinatha dropped God but did not give a substitute. Buddha dropped God and gave a substitute – meditation. However, his weakness, according to Osho, is that he organized his religion with priests in between individuals and meditation. Osho also drops God and substituted with meditation and takes one more step ahead - he also drops organization, priesthood, and the like. He leaves his people alone with meditation, with no mediators in between them and existence.[51] Osho emphatically states, "There is no God…God is the greatest lie invented by man."(*sic*)[52] However, Osho acknowledges the presence of godliness. There are theists, atheists and agnostics; Osho claims to belong to none of these. "I belong to the fourth, the unnamed category. I have looked, searched, I have not found God, true, but I have found something far more significant: godliness," states Osho.[53] Thus, he claims that he is not an atheist when he denies the existence of God, because he believes in the existence of an impersonal, pure energy which he calls godliness.[54]

Just like Sigmund Freud's theory of the origin of religion as illusory, the fulfilment of the oldest, strongest and most urgent wishes of human being,[55] Osho says that religion "is a simple psychological projection of a child. It has no basis in reality."[56] As Freud reduces religion to the level of infantile neurosis, a projection of infantile dependencies upon imagined superhuman beings, Osho says that human feels so helpless, so afraid of death, etc. and is in need of somebody to take care of him/her. "That psychological childhood is projected into all the religions."[57] So, God is just an illusory mental projection of a weak mind, because "Not a single religion has been able to prove God's existence."[58] He goes further than Friedrich Nietzsche's 'God is dead' theory and says, "'God is dead' is to accept that once he was alive. I say there has been never a God; he is the invention of the priests to exploit humanity."[59]

---

[51] See Osho, *Autobiography of a Spiritually Incorrect Mystic*, pp. 176-177.

[52] Osho, *The Last Testament, Vol. 1*, Chapter 1, p. 4; cf. Osho, *The Last Testament, Vol. 3*, downloaded in a *pdf* format from *http://www. oshorajneesh.com/osho-personal-glimpses.htm* (09.04.2013), p. 33.

[53] Osho, *Autobiography of a Spiritually Incorrect Mystic*, p. 140.

[54] Osho, *From Unconsciousness to Consciousness*, chapter 3, p. 1.

[55] See Jacques Waardenburg, *Classical Approaches to the Study of Religion: Aims, Methods and Theories Research* (The Hague: Mouton & Co., 1973), p. 361.

[56] Osho, *The Last Testament, Vol. 1*, Chapter 1, p. 6.

[57] *Ibid.*

[58] *Ibid.*, Chapter 2, p. 10.

[59] Osho, *The Last Testament, Vol. 6*, p. 91; cf. Osho, *I Celebrate Myself: God is No Where,* Life is Now Here, retrieved from Osho Internationals official website online Library *http://www. osho.com/library/online-library-celebrate-nietzsche-cleans-9b073fa4-46a.aspx,* (16.04.2013), Chapter 1, p. 1. Cf. Osho, *From Misery to Enlightenment*, p. 197.

However, he projected 'Existence' in place of God. He makes references to 'Existence' in much a similar fashion as theists would do to God. Existence is the indwelling presence, a pure consciousness that surrounds human being and the universe, which is not personal, but a life force.[60] Though Osho declines to believe in God, still he teaches 'godliness' which he says is a totally different conception,[61] and he refers it as 'Existence'.

4.3. Human Being

Osho time and again reminds us that human being is not a person, because personality is not a permanent thing or an original thing, but it is something imposed upon individual by the society. So, we are individuals, which is our intrinsic nature.[62] He observes, "Individuality is not personality. Personality is given by the society to you. Individuality is your intrinsic nature... Individuality is...your innermost enlightenment, your innermost door to the divine."[63] Human is not the body, not the mind, but soul, pure consciousness. With much reservation, as no definition is enough to really define soul, Osho attempts to define soul as "being totally conscious, totally alive, totally blissful, without being bound by anything... That feeling, that state when nothing is there, but you are in your total aliveness, in your total consciousness, is the soul."[64] This pure consciousness separates us from the body and the mind, and ultimately only we are there as pure consciousness, as pure awareness.[65] Osho has high regard for human being, which has the seed of *buddhahood*, capable

---

[60] Osho makes a number of references to Existence in his discourses in the same manner the theist would refer to God. Few examples may be given here – "Existence is very compassionate." Osho, *The Last Testament, Vol. 1,* Chapter 3, p. 16. "You will never know the beauty and the splendor of this existence that surrounds you." Osho, *This, This, A Thousand Times This: The Very Essence of Zen*", downloaded in a *pdf* format from *http://www.oshorajneesh.com/osho-zen-books.htm* (09.04.2013), p. 12. "Man (*sic*) can directly connect with existence," "Existence has no need of your sacrifices, existence has no need of your dances," "But when existence overwhelms you, showers all its blessings on you," "you become one with existence". Osho, *From Misery to Enlightenment,* pp. 28, 94, 132, 151, "Then between you and existence there is no question, there is no answer, but there is a communion." Osho, *From Death to Deathlessness*, downloaded in a *pdf* format from *http://www.messagefrommasters.com/ Ebooks/ Osho_Discourse_Series.htm* (09.04.2013), p. 15.

[61] Osho, *The Last Testament, Vol. 6*, p. 91.

[62] Osho, *The Path of the Mystics*, downloaded in a *pdf* format from *http://www.oshorajneesh.com/osho-world-tour-discourses.htm* (09.04.2013), pp. 5-6.

[63] Osho, *Christianity: The Deadliest Poison and Zen: The Antidote to All Poisons*, retrieved from Osho Internationals official website online Library, *http://www.osho.com/library/online-library-tozan-yakusan-finger-48bf6651-269.aspx*, Chapter 1, p. 1. There is even a book authored by Osho named – *From Personality to Individuality, op.cit.*

[64] Osho, *Meditation: The Art of Ecstasy,* (Pune: Osho Media International, 2009, first published in 1973), pp. 182-183.

[65] Osho, *The Path of the Mystics*, pp. 7, 11.

of attaining enlightenment by himself or herself – the treasure is already there in each individual, the key to unlock that treasure is also with him/her. Every human is unique, extraordinary, and exceptional; having been born alike, no one is higher or lower, all have potential to be a *buddha*.[66]

Osho is apparently influenced by Buddhist concepts of *no-soul* where the existence of a permanent, unchangeable, eternal soul or jīva as in the case of Hinduism is denied. He says in the series of his last discourse given in the last part of 1989, "As you go deeper in your interiority, you suddenly find yourself disappearing into the oceanic consciousness. There is no self as such. You are no more, only existence is."[67] This is what he calls the 'Zen manifesto' – freedom from oneself. He further clarifies this concept: As you go beyond the mind, even the idea of "I am" disappears. When the "I" also disappears and you start feeling a deep involvement in existence, with no boundaries, then only has Zen blossomed in you. In fact, that is the state, the space of the awakened consciousness. But it has no "I" at the center, no *ātman*, no self.[68]

4.4. On Sex and Sexuality

Osho is well known for his liberal teaching on sex as natural, the essential practice for attaining super-consciousness. He endorses sex between any two agreeing individuals as a natural act which is good and should not be criticized. He says in his discourse in 1979 that sex is not a sin, it is natural; there is no need to make any effort to get rid of it, although it can be transcended. It is a fun, a sport, a best exercise, a healthy practice - no man/woman has ever had a heart attack while making love. Any repression of it will result into homosexuality which is happening in monasteries, army and boys' and girls' hostels where men and women are not allowed to mix.[69] In a series of discourses on love and sex delivered in 1969 which was published as *From Sex to Superconsciousness*, he maintains that all life, all expression, all

---

[66] Osho, *Be Still and Know,* (Pune: Osho Media International, 2010, first published in 1979), pp. 14-15, 17-18.

[67] Osho, *The Zen Manifesto: Freedom from Oneself,* retrieved from Osho Internationals official website online Library, *http://www.osho.com/library/online-library-ego-self-mirrors-80a24f5d-6d5.aspx*, (17.04.2013), Chapter 1, p. 6.

[68] *Ibid.*

[69] See, Osho, *Be Still and Know,* pp. 18-20; Osho, *Come, Come Yet Again Come*, downloaded in a *pdf* format from *http://www.oshorajneesh.com/osho-discourses.htm* (09.04.2013), pp. 64-66; also Roy Wallis, "Religion as Fun? The Rajneesh Movement" in *Osho Rajneesh & His Disciples: Some Western Perceptions*, edited by Harry Aveling, (Delhi: Motilal Banarsiadss, 1999), p.133; Osho, *The Mustard Seed – The Revolutionary Teachings of Jesus: Commentaries on the Gnostic Gospel of Thomas,* (Mumbai: Osho Media International, 2009, first published in 1975), p. 65.

flowering is basically sex energy.[70] Sex is the greatest energy in human, the most powerful pull of nature and biology. There is no way to destroy it. Either you can condemn and repress it, or you can understand and transform it.[71] Though Osho accepted sex as a natural phenomenon, he rejects sexuality as something unbeautiful. By Sexuality he means thinking about sex, planning it, manipulating it, sex in the mind. When the mind has nothing to do with sex, then it is pure, innocent sex which is natural.[72] So, sex is nature and good, sexuality is unnatural and sinful.

Osho stresses the possibility of going from sex to superconsciousness and says that sexual orgasm gives us the first glimpse of meditation because during this few moments, the mind stops, time stops and we are just utterly silent and blissful. So, sexual enjoyment is not the goal, but can be a mean to the goal, effort should be made to transform sexual energy into spiritual energy.[73] Osho, therefore, does not end in sexual enjoyment, but teach transcending sex to reach superconsciousness. There is a bridge, a route between sex and superconsciousness where superconsciousness is the final rung of the same ladder of which sex is the first rung. Once we transform sex, we become asexual – we are free from sex in the sense that sexual urges do not disturb us any longer, we have sex or we can drop it, in both the cases it has no hold in us, it has lost all the old meaning and all the old implications, all the old bondage.[74] Osho believes that it is possible to reproduce a new man whom Nietzsche and Sri Aurobindo call 'Superman' by rightly understanding sex and sexual activities. The day humanity becomes thoroughly acquainted with the entire science of sex, the entire art of sex, they will be able to give birth to a superior human being.[75]

4.5. Meditation and Enlightenment

According to Osho enlightenment is the birthright of every individual; it is not something we gain, but it is what we really are. In enlightenment nothing is added to us, we only discover ourselves. He prescribes nothing but meditation as the only possible way for enlightenment or awakening.

---

[70] Osho, *From Sex to Superconsciousness,* (Pune: Osho Media International, 2011, first published in 1973), p. 19.

[71] Osho, *From Unconsciousness to Consciousness,* Chapter 6, p. 2.

[72] Osho, *A Rose is a Rose*, downloaded in a *pdf* format from *http://www.messagefrommasters.com/Ebooks/Osho_Darshan_Diaries.htm* (09.04.2013), p. 99.

[73] Osho, *Autobiography of a Spiritually Incorrect Mystic*, p. 130-132; cf. Osho, *Beyond Psychology*, downloaded in a *pdf* format from *http://www.oshorajneesh.com/osho-world-tour-discourses.htm* (09.04.2013), p. 334, where he explains how for ten thousand years people have experimented with how sexual energy can become your spirituality.

[74] See Osho, *From Sex to Superconsciousness*, p. 171; Osho, *Beyond Psychology*, p. 172.

[75] Osho, *From Sex to Superconsciousness*, p. 176.

Meditation is not contemplation, it is not thinking but "looking inside is meditation – just pure looking inward, a turning of the eyes inward... Meditation can be called awareness, watchfulness, witness,"[76] it is a non-doing, it is not a task, but a state of non-occupation, a naturalness.[77] As long as there is desire, searching, activity, enlightenment is not achieved. "Drop all searching and see who resides in you. Wake up the one who is. This is possible only by non-searching. It is possible only by stopping, not by running... Stop and see who the "I" is.[78] He explains the connection between meditation and enlightenment as follows:

> Meditation is nothing but withdrawing all the barriers – thoughts, emotions, sentiments – that create a wall between you and existence. The moment you drop, you suddenly find yourself in tune with the whole...you really find you *are* the whole. When the dewdrop slips from a lotus leaf into the ocean it does not find that it is part of the ocean, it finds it is the ocean. And to find it is the ultimate goal, the ultimate realization. There is nothing beyond it.[79]

Being in that state, a moment comes when all thinking disappears – just by watching, mind disappears, "and the disappearance of the mind is the beginning of knowing yourself"[80] which is enlightenment. As we grow in meditativeness and go on growing, there comes a moment when we have reached the very peak of our potentiality – we may call it buddhahood, enlightenment, *bhagwatta*, godliness – name is not important.[81]

What is vital for anyone to get enlightenment is the *absence* of all that is *not* you – the absence of your ego, the absence of your mind, the absence of your prejudices, your borrowed knowledge. "You disappear as a personality and there remains only a pure presence. So it is absence on one side of all that is false in you, and it is presence on the other side of all that is real in you."[82]

---

[76] Bhagawan Shree Rajneesh, *The Great Pilgrimage from Here to Here,* (Cologne: The Rebel Publishing House, 1988), p. 51. Osho also defines meditation – "Meditation is nothing but coming to terms with your inner emptiness", Osho, *The Mustard Seed.*, p. 50.

[77] Osho, *The Perfect Way,* (Pune: Osho Media International, 2008, first published in 1975), p. 38.

[78] *Ibid.*, p. 50.

[79] Osho, *Autobiography of a Spiritually Incorrect Mystic,* p. 178.

[80] Bhagawan Shree Rajneesh, *The Great Pilgrimage from Here to Here,* p. 52.

[81] Osho, *Autobiography of a Spiritually Incorrect Mystic,* p. 179.

[82] Osho, *Satyam Shivam Sundaram,* downloaded in a *pdf* format from *http://www.messagefrommasters.com/Ebooks/Osho _Discourse_Series.htm* (09.04.2013), p. 3.

Osho explains an enlightened man/woman as follows:

> An enlightened man/woman is all emptiness. It has no 'constitutes' in it; hence it is empty. A man/woman who is enlightened has no character. He/she lives from moment to moment, having no character to follow, no structure around him/her. A character is a structure, an enlightened person has no character. He/she has no structured consciousness. He/she has consciousness but the structure has been dropped. He/she is neither Hindu nor Mohammedan nor Christian, neither good nor bad, neither moral nor immoral, neither this nor that. He/she simply is. All duality has disappeared. You cannot evaluate him/her; you cannot categorize him/her; you cannot put him/her into any pigeon-holes of your logic. He/she exists like an emptiness. Nothingness he/she is. He/she goes on flowing without any mask or rule to follow.[83]

Though Osho developed a number of meditation methods, he insists that we cannot do meditation, but can only be in meditation, it is not an act or a doing, but a state, a being. According to him, the Sanskrit word for meditation 'dhyana' also suggests the dropping of all contents of the mind and just being. When all thoughts are eliminated, the only thing left is 'self' – the 'you', the 'I', godliness.[84] So, all his meditation methods concentrate on throwing away the repressive things from human being that have been accumulated for ages, and not taking in any new thing. Osho develops several meditation methods of which *Dynamic Meditation* is the most popular one.

'Rajneesh Dhyana Yoga' or popularly known as 'Dynamic Meditation' or 'The Chaotic' consists of elements from Yoga, Sufi, Tibetan tradition as well as findings of contemporary psychology modified and blended wisely by Osho to suit the need of the contemporary society. It has four stages, each lasting for ten to fifteen minutes. The *first stage* involves 10 minutes of fast, deep, vigorous breathing while standing with loose fitting or no clothes without any rhythm. The *second stage* is also 10 minutes of deep catharsis and 'let-go' – "to be consciously insane" where the practitioner expresses himself/herself in whatever way he/she chooses like shouting, screaming, dancing, crying, laughing, any kind of body movement, etc. holding nothing back in order to get rid of tension within him/her. The goal is to be empty of all repression. The *third stage*, again 10 minutes, consists in jumping vigorously up and down with the shouting of the Sufi mantra 'Hoo-Hoo-Hoo' with deep inhalation and

---

[83] Osho, *Come Follow to You: Reflection on Jesus of Nazareth, Vol. 3*, downloaded in a *pdf* format from *http://www.oshorajneesh.com/osho-books-on-jesus-christ.htm* (8.03.2013), pp. 78-79.

[84] See Osho, *Autobiography of a Spiritually Incorrect Mystic*, pp. 183-184.

exhalation which ends in a sudden stop. The *fourth stage* is a stage of silence and motionlessness where the practitioner stops all movements suddenly, remaining motionless for fifteen minutes. In this stage, one is just to be a witness – a conscious alertness, not doing anything, without desire, without becoming but just remaining then and there, silently witnessing whatsoever is happening. The purpose is to witness the energy that comes up in stillness. This is followed by dancing and celebration in the tune of a soft music for fifteen minutes.[85]

4.6. A New Creation – Zorba the Buddha

In order to create a new human community, a totally new human needs to be created. That is how Osho perceives as he initiated disciples whom he called *Neo-sannyāsins*. As the name indicates his disciples are totally a new type of *sannyāsins* who are distinctly different from the Hindu traditional sannyāsins where a seeker is considered as a renouncer of all the worldly pleasures including home, family and social connections, sumptuous food, sexual pleasure and the likes. The *neo-sannyāsin*, instead of renouncing the world, embraces the world but renounces all the conditions the world has imposed on the individuals. Osho says,

> I mean renouncing all the condition that the world has given to you – your religion, your caste, your Brahmanism, your Jainism, your Christianity, your God, your holy book. To me *sannyās* means a commitment that 'I am going to clean myself completely of all those things that have been imposed upon me, and I will start living on my own – fresh, young, pure, unpolluted.[86]

For Osho giving up the world is not sannyās, but the awakening of self-knowledge is *sannyās*. This awakening leads to the renunciation not of the world but of the attachment to it. It is the transformation of the way we look at the world.[87] The *neo-sannyāsins* are asked to wear red or orange robe, a necklace known as *mala* which consists of one hundred and eight beads plus

---

[85] See, Osho, *Meditation: The Art of Ecstasy,* pp. 45-52; Ma Ananda Prem, "Bhagavan Shree Rajneesh: The Modern Buddha", in *Gurus, Godmen and Good People*, edited by Khushwant Singh, (New Delhi: Orient Longman Ltd., 1975), p. 10; Swami Prem Amitabh, "Shree Rajaneesh āśram Poona: A Provocative Community", in *Osho Rajneesh & His Disciples: Some Western Perceptions,* edited by Harry Aveling, (Delhi: Motilal Banarsiadss, 1999, pp. 108-111 and Osho, *Autobiography of a Spiritually Incorrect Mystic*, pp. 188-191; and also Osho, *The Orange Book: The Meditation Techniques of Bhagavan Shree Rajneesh*, (Pune: Rajneesh Foundation, 1980), pp. 31-32.

[86] Osho, *Autobiography of a Spiritually Incorrect Mystic,* p. 228.

[87] Ma Ananda Prem, "*Bhagavan Shree Rajneesh: The Modern Buddha*", p. 11.

a locket with Osho's picture. Osho gives them a new name having a common prefix '*swami*' for male and '*ma*' for female.[88]

The *neo-sannyāsins* are designed to be a new kind of human being, *homo novus* which he calls '*Zorba the Buddha*', a combination of sensual and down to earth aspect of Nikos Kazantzakis' novel - 'Zorba the Greek' and the spirituality of Gautama Buddha. Osho finds the old concept of human being absurd as it was characterized by division - materialist or spiritualist, moral or immoral, sinner or saint. It was based on division and split. It created a schizophrenic humanity.[89] On the contrary, his concept of new human being, Zorba the Buddha is a beautiful blend of the sensuous Zorba and spiritual Buddha - he/she will be Zorba the Greek and he/she will also be Gautama the Buddha. He/she will be sensuous and spiritual, physical, utterly physical, in the body, in the senses, enjoying the body and all that the body makes possible, and still a great consciousness, a great witnessing will be there.[90] According to Osho, Zorba represents all that has been condemned upon centuries by all religions, full of life, love, laughter. Eat, drink, and be merry is his whole religion, perfectly happy in those things. Buddha represents the purity of the highest conceivable spirituality, denying everything that life is – love, sensual enjoyment. Zorba represents the materialist in its best form whereas Buddha represents the spiritualist in its best form.[91] Osho intends to combine these two in a person to produce a totally new human. This movement grows rather fast and according to Swami Prem Amitabh, by the fall of 1979 there were over 100,000 *neo-sannyāsins* throughout the world.[92] With this institution, Osho tries to build a new community on this earth.

4.7. Osho's Vision for Oneness of Human Beings

Osho was quite opposed to the idea of religious toleration because for him tolerance is ugly,[93] instead he teaches freedom from being Hindu, Muslim, Christian, etc. We have been brought up as Hindus, Muslims, Christians and we became fascists and fanatics. We should have been brought up as human beings.[94] "Be free from all prejudices, be just a human being" is his slogan.[95]

---

[88] Osho, *Autobiography of a Spiritually Incorrect Mystic,* p. 228.

[89] Osho, *Zorba the Buddha*, downloaded in a *pdf* format from *http://www.messagefrommasters.com/Ebooks/Osho_Darshan_Diaries.htm*, (09.04.2013), p. 2.

[90] *Ibid*., p. 3. Cf. Osho, *Socrates Poisoned Again After 25th Century*, retrieved from Osho Internationals official website online Library *http://www.osho. com/library/online-library-foundation-zorba-the-buddha-man-72e3a20b-1ac.aspx*, Chapter 5, p. 5.

[91] Osho, *The Last Testament, Vol. 1,* Chapter 22, p. 1.

[92] Swami Prem Amitabh, "*Shree Rajaneesh āśram Poona: A Provocative Community,*" p. 97.

[93] Osho, *Be Still and Know,* p. 54.

[94] *Ibid*., p. 47.

[95] *Ibid*., p. 55.

When one is free from being a member of a particular religion, he/she starts to feel love for other human beings. "You will start feeling the whole universe as your family, your commune... you will even have a communication with the trees and the birds and the animals."[96] As religion creates fascism in us, one who adheres to any particular religion murders the feeling of love, compassion and oneness towards others.[97] He says, "I conceive of a world without poverty, without classes, without nations, without religions, without any kind of discrimination. I conceive of a world which is one, a humanity which is one, a humanity which shares everything – outer and inner – a deep spiritual brotherhood (*sic*)."[98] For him religion is the cause of inter-religious conflicts and religionless spirituality is the answer to that problem. He feels that his concept of 'New humanity' is sailing towards this –

> I would like a new man (*sic*) to be born, a new humanity, where ugly discriminations disappear, where there are no wars, no atomic or nuclear weapons, no nations, no races; where man (*sic*) can share all the bounties of existence and all the experiences of his/her inner being. I want this whole humanity to be one ocean of consciousness.[99]

Thus, his message is to create a world without the boundary of nations, without the boundary of religions; his effort is to expose our barbariousness in nationalism, in different groups, calling them religions; in different political ideologies, because it is the time to drop all the boundaries, all the distinctions of colour and race, and bring the whole humanity as one, undivided whole.[100] He hopes that this will mark the beginning of a new civilization.

4.8. Key Terms in Osho's Teaching

There are some 'key terms' which Osho repeatedly uses in his discourses. Some of them may be mentioned here briefly.

Celebration is his message and his approach to life. His religion is characterized by celebration not renunciation.[101] Experience is another key term.

---

[96] *Ibid.*

[97] *Ibid.*, p. 53.

[98] Osho, *The Rebellious Spirit*, retrieved from Osho Internationals official website online Library, h*ttp://www.osho.com/library/online-library-revolution-centeredness-first-44ba8ff4-42a.aspx*, (20.04.2013), Chapter 3, p. 6.

[99] *Ibid.*, p. 7.

[100] Osho, *The Last Testament, Vol. 6,* p. 45.

[101] See Osho, *Unio Mystica, Vol. 1,* downloaded in a *pdf* format from *http://www.oshorajneesh.com/osho-books-on-sufi.htm* (10.04.2013), p. 153; Osho, *Dance your Way to God*, retrieved from Osho Internationals official website online Library, *http://www.osho. com/library/online-*

Truth can be possessed by experience alone; religion is experience, without experiencing there can be no enlightenment.[102] Silence is important for Osho in many ways: he experienced it,[103] it is the beginning of everything,[104] it is the nature of existence,[105] the moment you attain silence you attain paradise.[106] Your own being is available only in silence, not in intellectual activity, in silence you come close to the point from where you can go only beyond... If you are silently waiting – with no desire, no expectation – there comes one moment when your silence is so total and your waiting is so unpolluted that the doors open. You are taken into your own, innermost shrine.[107] Individual Freedom is given a high place in Osho's movement to the extent that he even denies himself being the Master of his disciples, rather he refers to himself as 'the friend' and his disciples 'fellow travellers.'[108] For him individual freedom is absolute, should be absolute. Nobody should interfere.[109] When Osho gets enlightenment it is reported that there is discontinuity with the past or the past has no hold on him.[110] Since then Osho consistently stresses the importance of the Present, the Moment. He says, "This moment is all

---

library-revolution-centeredness-first-44ba8ff4-42a.aspx, (20.04.2013), where he explains in details the usefulness of dance and celebration in Chapter 1; Osho, *From the False to the Truth*, retrieved from Osho Internationals official website online Library, *http://www.osho.com/library/online-library-enquiry-eve-eternal-60a0b539-500.aspx, (20.04.2013)*, Chapter 4, p. 1; Osho, *Until You Die*, downloaded in a pdf format from *http://www.oshorajneesh.com/osho-books-on-sufi.htm* (10.04.2013), p. 72; Osho, *Autobiography of a Spiritually Incorrect Mystic,* p. 18; Osho, *The Great Pilgrimage from Here to Here*, pp. 19, 86, 90.

[102] See Osho, *Zorba the Buddha,* p. 29; Osho, *The Rebel,* p. 91; Osho, *Dance Your Way to God*, downloaded in a *pdf* format from *http://www.messagefrommasters.com/Ebooks/ Osho_Darshan_Diaries.htm* (09.04.2013), p. 38.

[103] Right after his enlightenment for two years he almost stopped speaking to anyone and also he observed three and half years silence. Cf. Osho, *The Path of Mystic,* downloaded in a *pdf* format from *http://www.oshorajneesh.com/osho-world-tour-discourses.htm* (09.04.2013), pp. 292-293.

[104] *Ibid.*, p. 407.

[105] *Ibid.*, p. 408.

[106] Osho, *Zorba the Buddha*, p. 29. He states that his religion is basically centered around consciousness, silence, Osho, *The Last Testament, Vol. 1,* Chapter 1, p. 2.

[107] Osho, *The Path of Mystic,* pp. 13-14, 29, 301, cf. pp. 319, 337.

[108] Osho, *From the False to the Truth,* Chapter 33, p. 4; cf. Osho, *Dance Your Way to God*, p. 102.

[109] Osho, *Blessed are the Ignorant,* downloaded in a *pdf* format from *http://www.messagefrommasters.com/Ebooks/Osho_Darshan_Diaries.htm* (09.04.2013), p. 7. Cf. for more on Individual freedom Osho, *My Way the Way of the White Clouds,* downloaded in a *pdf* format from *http://www.messagefrommasters.com/Ebooks/Osho_Discourse_ Series.htm* (09.04.2013), p. 137; Osho, *From Darkness to Light*, downloaded in a *pdf* format from *http://www.messagefrommasters.com/Ebooks/Osho_Discourse_Series.htm* (09.04.2013), p. 227.

[110] Osho, *Autobiography of a Spiritually Incorrect Mystic*, p. 77.

there is and just this moment is god."[111] He asks his *sannyāsins* to live and act moment to moment with no commitment to the past.[112] Love is another key term. For him God is not needed, love is enough, love surrounds us, fills us completely,[113] love without attachment is divine in itself,[114] love is inside us, it is our intrinsic nature,[115] love plus meditation is equal to godliness,[116] there is no God, love itself becomes God, the whole existence is made up of the stuff called love.[117] For Osho 'Mind' is the primary problem of human, it is what Christian called Devil or Satan.[118] From the mind comes ego and all problems. Enlightenment is achieved when mind is transcended or when the state of No-Mind is reached.[119]

A brief survey on Osho's religious and philosophical teachings reveals that though he said making dogma out of him is almost impossible due to his inconsistency, Osho is not inconsistent at the core of his teaching. Contradictory statements we find in him are negligible considering his real message which is unaltered through and through. He is consistently consistent in his emphasis on feeling and experience, silence, individual freedom, celebration, living in the present moment, love and sex as natural phenomena to be welcomed. His rejection of all established religions and existence of God, a personal being, and his utter denunciation of moral code of conduct based on written scripture and unwritten tradition, and his downright rejection of the mind which for him

---

[111] Osho, *The Madman's Guide to Enlightenment,* downloaded in a *pdf* format from *http://www.messagefrommasters.com/Ebooks/Osho_Darshan_Diaries.htm*, (09.04.2013), p. 2.

[112] Osho, *Meditation: The Art of Ecstasy*, p. 142; cf. *The Last Testament, Vol. 1*, Chapter 1, p. 3, also Chapter 8; also Osho, *Blessed are the Ignorant*, pp. 72, 86, 124.

[113] Osho, *Yoga: The Science of Living,* retrieved from Osho Internationals official website online Library, *http://www.osho.com/library/online-library-love-indivisible-fasting-38173b16-34e.aspx*, (20.04.2013), Chapter 8, p. 13.

[114] Osho, *Showering Without Clouds*, retrieved from Osho Internationals official website online Library, *http://www.osho.com/library/online-library-love-passion-attachment-5de53298-b88.aspx*, (20.04.2013), Chapter 2, p. 8.

[115] Osho, *From Sex to Superconsciousness,* p. 12.

[116] *Ibid.*, p. 143.

[117] Osho, *Be Still and Know,* p. 266. In another place Osho equates love with God "You can say 'love' or you can say 'God', they both mean the same. God is not loving; God is love itself. Osho, *Vigyan Bhairav Tantra, Vol 2*, downloaded in a *pdf* format from *http://www.messagefrommasters.com/Ebooks/Osho_Books_on_Tantra_&_Mantra.htm* (09.04.2013), p. 46.

[118] Osho, *The Madman's Guide to Enlightenment*, p. 65; Osho, *Come Follow to You: Reflections on Jesus of Nazareth, Vol. 2*, (Pune: Tao Publishing Pvt. Ltd., 2003, first published in 1977 as Come Follow Me, Volume 2), p. 252; Cf. Osho, *The Mustard Seed*, p. 67.

[119] See Osho, *From Bondage to Freedom*, retrieved from Osho Internationals official website online Library, *http://www.osho.com/library/the-books.aspx*, (22.04.2013), Chapter 38, p. 4, Chapter 39, pp. 1, 5, Chapter 43, pp. 1, 3 ; also Osho, *Beyond Psychology,* pp. 30, 341; Osho, *From Death to Deathlessness,* p. 2.

is the cause of all trouble, are all constantly maintained throughout his life and teaching. So, Osho, as we find him, is consistent though there are a number of contradictory teachings which is understood as his methodological game. His wide reading appears to have a deep impact upon his life and teaching which makes it easy to conclude that his teaching is but a combination of Western and Eastern religious and philosophical thought. There is practically nothing in Osho's message that had never said or wrote before. However, this does not make him an un-original necessarily. The ability to combine, reinterpret, develop and contextualize diverse thoughts into a system itself is creativity and innovative. So, in this sense Osho is not un-original. Again, like most of the contemporary gurus whose teaching is secondary to their 'being', it is not his teaching that attracts people but himself as an enlightened being.

Osho's approach to religion is philosophical though he utterly denies philosophy as ineffectual in dealing with spiritual matter. He suggests feeling and experiencing the reality within us rather than philosophizing, but in Indian understanding of philosophy – *darśana* (from Sanskrit root *dṛś* – 'to see') feeling and experiencing is very much within philosophical ambit. Again, Osho discards all form of organisation, rules and regulations but he and his *sannyāsins* are also following the same path, they organised themselves with rigid rules and regulations, even going to the extent of dictating what colour of cloth to wear and a new name to bear. While he emphasizes individual freedom, his people have to follow timings set by the *āśram* authority – all indicate freedomlessness. He claims to be an enlightened man who has no ego, but his egoistic tendency is visible in many cases – the *sannyāsins* are required to wear a mala with a locket having *his* picture; the books published by his organisation should contain *his* image; from the honorific titles *he* assumed like Ācārya, Bhagavan and Osho; from a stylistic costume with which he covers himself and an extraordinary luxurious living - are all indicative of an ego that remains within. Therefore, in short, Osho is a negation of himself.

5. Osho's Interpretation of Jesus Christ: *Jesus, the Christified*

Osho is somewhat attracted to Jesus. His discourses hardly end without referring to him. Almost all of his numerous books contain discussion on Jesus. Apart from this, there are seven books exclusively on Jesus authored by Osho which all belong to 'the old book' (to use his expression) as they were the product of his 'before silence' period.[120] In my discussion I will take all of these into consideration and try to arrive at Osho's interpretation of Jesus Christ.

[120] Six out of the seven books are mainly commentary on select passages from the four Gospels and one is a commentary of the Gospel of Thomas, a non-canonical work.

5.1. Osho's Approach to Jesus Christ

Negating the validity of the Christian representation of Jesus Christ, Osho fosters his own interpretation which according to him is more authentic than Christian interpretation because it is not based on any academic knowledge but on the direct experience of Jesus. "I know Jesus because I know meditation. My knowing of Jesus is not through the Bible, it is not through Christian theology. I know Jesus directly," claims Osho.[121] Though most of his talks on Jesus are nothing but a commentary on the Bible, he denies the possibility of valid knowledge of Jesus in and through the written scripture. He is less concerned with what exactly is written in the book, but more on what happened to Jesus in his innermost core which he knows as an enlightened person who has Christ-consciousness.[122] In spite of his heavy dependence on the written scripture, Osho does not shy away to state, "There is only one way to see Jesus, and that is to see him as he is; directly. No scriptures are needed to interpret him. He has to be seen untranslated. He has to be seen directly - he has to be faced and encountered, eye to eye, heart to heart."[123] He says, "When I talk about Jesus, it is not that I am talking about him, rather, he talks himself. I give him way, I become a passage. All that I do is that I don't hinder him. That is the only way to talk about Jesus or Buddha or Krishna."[124] He recognizes his oneness with Jesus where boundaries completely merge. He testifies, "Then Jesus talks through me; then I can become a vehicle. Because I have no prejudice for or against, and I have no dogma to preach, Jesus can come in his crystal purity to you."[125]

According to Osho, Jesus can be known only through a person who has attained Christ-consciousness or Buddha-consciousness or Kṛṣṇa-consciousness - which are all the same.[126] Elsewhere he says that he is not commenting on Jesus, but simply responding to him. "I read his words, something echoes in me... My heart throbs with him, something parallel echoes in me, and I tell you what it is... I am not trying to explain Jesus to you... I am simply mirroring – I am telling you my heart. I am telling you what happens to me when I am listening to Jesus."[127] The undistorted Jesus can be known,

[121] Osho, *The Mustard Seed,* p. 7; Osho, *Be Still and Know*, p. 38.

[122] Osho, *I Say Unto You: Talks on the Sayings of Jesus, Vol. 1*, (New Delhi: Diamond Pocket Books, Pvt. Ltd., 1996), p. 99.

[123] Osho, *Come Follow to You, Vol. 3*, p. 35.

[124] *Ibid.*, p. 3.

[125] *Ibid.*, p. 115.

[126] Osho, *I Say Unto You, Vol. 1*, pp. 34-35.

[127] Osho, *Come Follow to You: Reflections on Jesus of Nazareth, Vol. 1,* (Pune: Tao Publishing Pvt. Ltd., 2003, first published in 1976 as Come Follow Me, Volume 1), p. 100.

according to Osho, only by knowing our innermost nothingness.[128] "You can recognize Jesus only if you have recognized something of the beyond within yourself; otherwise not."[129] Christians or Hindus cannot understand because Christianity or Hinduism becomes an obstruction, a hindrance.

> You can understand Christ only if you are nobody… When you are nobody, when you drop all the curtains and you start moving in that reality called Christ without any preoccupied mind – empty, clean, clear, no smoke around you... Only if you are a nobody can you meet with Christ or Buddha or Kṛṣṇa. And these are different names for the same state of consciousness.[130]

Jesus is known not by gaining information about him, but by dropping layers of clothing and become naked, pure and original; by discarding all the borrowed masks, all falsities.[131] To understand Jesus one needs to attain Christ consciousness – at least a little bit.[132] Osho claims that his approach to Jesus Christ is not academical or philosophical but experiential, but it is questionable whether he really experience Jesus or he interprets him philosophically in relation to his own philosophy of life.

5.2. Jesus' Methodology

Osho maintains that Jesus' method to transform people is different from other Masters like Buddha, Kṛṣna and Muhammad. He puts the whole alchemy of Christ into seven categories:[133] *First: Catalytic* - Jesus' work is that of a catalytic agent. His main work is to be with people, to come in contact with them. This is what Hindus call *Satsang* – to be in the presence of the Master. He transforms people just by his touch, he overpowers them, surrounds them, his energy starts dancing around them, he pulsates people through his pulse, magnetizes people through his magnetism, his presence is with them.[134] Though Jesus is not a great philosopher like Buddha nor is he a great scientist like Patanjali, nor a singer like Kṛṣna but he has something special – to be a catalytic agent. The catalytic agent does not do anything to us, but something happens to us; the catalytic agent does not go into us, but just the presence,

---

[128] Osho, *I Say Unto You, Vol. 1*, p. 35.

[129] Osho, *Come Follow to You, Vol. 3*, p. 30.

[130] Osho, *I Say Unto You: Talks on the Sayings of Jesus, Vol. 2*, downloaded in a *pdf* format from *http://www.oshorajneesh.com/osho-books-on-jesus-christ.htm* (8.03.2013), p. 24.

[131] Ref. Osho, *The Mustard Seed*, pp. 15, 61, 69, 72-73 for more on this.

[132] Osho, *Sufis: The People of the Path, Vol. 2,* downloaded in a *pdf* format from *http://www.oshorajneesh.com/osho-books-on-sufi.htm* (10.04.2013), p. 106.

[133] Osho, *I Say Unto You, Vol. 2,* p. 92.

[134] *Ibid.*

just the very presence provokes us, inspires us, and something starts growing in us. That is Jesus' method.[135] *Second: Catalepsy* – the suspension of your old being. When we are in contact with a Christ or a Buddha, our old being is immediately suspended; we cannot function as we used to function before. The very presence of Christ is such a shock that everything is suspended. For a moment all thoughts stop, all feelings disappear, and we may miss a heartbeat. So, before Jesus, in his powerful presence people are catalepsized.[136]

Third: Catharsis – With Catharsis the repressed emotions and feelings explode and burst out, the control is lost, the prisoner is free. Before Jesus such a strong quake used to happen.[137] *Fourth: Catastrophe.* When reason is gone and the heart goes mad, ego starts falling into pieces - it is catastrophe. All is lost, chaos arises and now one feels that one has really gone mad. One cannot look beyond it. This is what Christian mystics call 'the dark night of the soul', a kind of hopelessness where one is utterly lost and there seems to be no possibility of getting out of it.[138] *Fifth: the cross* - The ego dies on the cross, completely eradicated on the cross. The self has no more identity with body or mind, a state of negation, death, emptiness. Great trembling, fear, one is on the verge of the abyss called God. That was the experience of Jesus on the cross. That cross has to come to everybody. Jesus says everybody has to carry his/her cross.[139] *Sixth: Conversion* - Only when you are dead does God become alive in you. Only when the seed dies does it become a tree, only when the river disappears into the ocean does it become one with the ocean, that is Conversion. Jesus becomes Christ.[140] Osho maintains that Conversion is not changing of religion, rather, conversion happens only when the ego dies and God is born in us, conversion is when the human becomes divine, not when a Hindu becomes Christian. When the human becomes divine, when Jesus becomes Christ, then there is conversion. At this stage all differences are gone, one is neither Christian nor Hindu nor Muslim nor Communist not fascist. One is simply is – a purity, is-ness. In this stage what Hindus call *Satyam, Shivam, Sundaram* – truth, good, beauty is felt.[141] Seventh: Christ-consciousness – At this stage we are no more away from the peaks, but rather we have become the peaks! Christ-consciousness is born: one becomes one with the whole.

---

[135] *Ibid.*, p. 93.

[136] *Ibid.*, p. 94.

[137] *Ibid.*, p. 95.

[138] *Ibid.*, pp. 95-96.

[139] *Ibid.*, p. 96.

[140] *Ibid.*

[141] *Ibid.*

One becomes that which one really is. Buddha calls it *Nirvāṇa*, Christ calls it *Kingdom of God*, and Hindus call it *Satchitānanda*.[142]

Osho projects the above seven states as the methodological tools employed by Jesus to transform his followers, nevertheless, the authenticity is questionable; it appears that Osho is narrating his own experience and ideas in the name of Jesus, because what he said of Jesus is quite similar with the way he had experienced enlightenment.

5.3. The Real Jesus Lost in Christianity

Like other contemporary gurus and other Hindu interpreters of Jesus Christ, Osho starts with a negative note that Christians do not understand Jesus Christ and that Christian theology misses the real Jesus. He maintains throughout his career that "Christianity has nothing to do with Christ,"[143] "In fact, Christianity is anti-Christ."[144] Osho maintains that Christ is totally different from Christianity and whatever Christians have been teaching about Jesus is not the real Jesus. To know the real Jesus, we need to go directly, immediately not via Christianity.[145] He even says that Christianity kills Jesus, they killed him through dogma; they killed him through organization. Jews crucified him, but he survived, resurrected, but Christianity succeeded.[146] The 'Jesus' represented in Christianity is erroneous because it depends on three things: a virgin birth; a non-laughing, non-enjoying monotonous, sad life; and a resurrection. These are the three things that seem to be vital to them, and these are all useless because they miss the whole point. Without properly understanding the real message, a myth is created around these, and because of this myth the real Jesus is lost.[147] Jesus is murdered again at the hands of Christians at Vatican and unlike the first murder he has not been able to resurrect again this time.[148]

When Jesus is gone Christianity came up as an establishment and organization with doctrines and dogmas where the doctrines and the dogmas become more important. This new religion is diametrically opposed to Jesus'

---

[142] *Ibid.*, p. 97.

[143] Osho, *Come Follow to You: Reflections on Jesus of Nazareth, Vol. 4*, downloaded in a *pdf* format from *http://www.oshorajneesh.com/osho-books-on-jesus-christ.htm* (8.03.2013), p. 173. Cf. Osho, *Come Follow to You, Vol. 2,* p. 13 where he says, "The real Jesus is completely lost in the desert of Christian theology", etc.

[144] Osho, *Come Follow to You,* p. 4.

[145] *Ibid.*, pp. 92-93. Cf. Osho, *The Mustard Seed*, p. 7.

[146] Osho, *Until You Die*, p. 4.

[147] Osho, *I Say Unto You, Vol. 2,* p. 89; cf. Osho, *Yoga: The Alpha and the Omega, Vol. 3,* downloaded in a *pfd* format from *http://www.oshorajneesh. com/osho-yoga-books.htm* (10.04.2013), p. 132.

[148] Osho, *Come Follow to You, Vol. 4,* p. 173.

being because it is based on sadness whereas Jesus is for celebration.[149] The message of love propagated by Jesus was gone as Christianity is ready to fight whoever opposes. "No other religion has created as many wars as Christianity, and all its preaching is about love...The whole of Christianity is based on a single word 'love', but the ultimate result is crusades, wars, murders."[150] Osho states that Christians are not in love with Jesus, they are in love with the cross and Christianity is born not because of Christ, but because of the cross, "That's why I call Christianity 'Crossianity'. It has nothing to do with Christ."[151] So, Osho suggests that in order to know Jesus Christ we have to go beyond Christianity because Christ is beyond churches.[152]

5.4. Jesus a Real Human

The distinctiveness of Osho's interpretation of Jesus Christ may be his emphasis on Jesus' humanity. According to him Jesus is a real human, an authentic human who lived like a human just like us, of blood and bone, as human as we are, rooted in earth as we are. He laughs, he cries, he loves, he lives in all the dimensions of humanhood.[153] In contrast to Buddha who is highly philosophic and refined, Jesus is plain and simple who speaks like a villager, a farmer, a fisherman. But as he speaks the way common people speak, his words have solidity, concreteness and a reality.[154] "Jesus' words are very very earthbound, rooted in the earth. He is an earthly man, and that is his beauty. Nobody else can be compared with that beauty."[155]

Jesus' real humanity is seen in the way he deals with people. He walked with the fisherman, the woodcutter, the shoemaker; he moved and talked with very ordinary people: the downtrodden, oppressed, poor, labourers, farmers, gamblers, prostitutes and drunkards. Jesus stayed with prostitutes, he stayed with anybody and ate with anybody. On the surface, to all appearances he looked like a fallen human. Again, he was very ordinary, not the son of a king but a carpenter's son. Unlike Buddha whose message is like a classical music, silent, beautiful, but no revolution in it, Jesus' message is a slogan delivered in a raging voice, in anger, because Jesus, as a real human, used to get angry

---

149 See Osho, *Come Follow to You, Vol. 2,* p. 15; Osho, *Come Follow to You, Vol. 3*, pp. 58-59.

150 Osho, *Come Follow to You, Vol. 3*, p. 60.

151 Osho, *I Say Unto You, Vol. 1,* pp. 32, 281; Osho, *From Darkness to Light,* p. 211.

152 Osho, *Come Follow to You, Vol. 1*, p. 4.

153 Osho, *I Say Unto You, Vol. 2*, p. 89; Osho, *Come Follow to You, Vol. 3*, p. 3; Osho, *Come Follow to You, Vol. 1*, p. 283; Cf. Osho, *Come Follow to You, Vol. 4*, pp. 77-78, 81; cf. Osho, *Yoga: The Alpha and the Omega, Vol. 10,* downloaded in a *pfd* format from *http://www.oshorajneesh.com/osho-yoga-books.htm* (10.04.2013), p. 86.

154 Osho, *I Say Unto You, Vol. 1,* p. 4.

155 *Ibid.*, p. 5.

whereas in Buddha no such anger is to be seen.[156] However, Osho never stops at Jesus humanity, he also talks about his divine nature as an enlightened person. It can be said that Osho tries to project Jesus as a combination of Zorba the Greek and Buddha – a new human, *Zorba the Buddha.*

5.5. Jesus a Rebel

Osho demonstrates that Jesus is of the *present* that does not belong to any tradition; he is a rebel.[157] Jesus does not bring revolution because revolution is political, a social phenomenon where the goal is to change others and the surroundings. Rebellion is unorganized, individual in nature, coming out of the authenticity of a single being. It a non-political, religious phenomenon and the goal is to change oneself. Rebellion is again non-ideological and spontaneous, like love rebellion is a happening.[158] Jesus belongs to this category. As a rebel, Jesus was not diplomatic, but simply lived out his spontaneity; acting out of his understanding; he responded to a situation, and something starts happening.[159] He was un-compromising, destroying the old morality, creating chaos, destructing the existing structure, replacing with the new one. If he had diluted his message, if he had kept himself within the imprisonment of tradition, he would not have been crucified but then there would have been no Christ either.[160] As a rebel "Jesus brings disorder, chaos, because he knows that unless your periphery is in disorder, you will not be able to move towards your innermost core… Only when the outside life is in chaos is the inner life born."[161] Osho himself is a rebel, always rebellious against the existing socio-political and religious orders and it is evident that his projection of Jesus as a rebel is apparently the product of his understanding of himself.

5.6. Jesus a Man of Celebration

Osho is a man of celebration – dancing, celebration, enjoyment and the likes never leave his life and teaching. He puts Jesus in the same category - "He had enjoyed a thousand and one enjoyments…He loved eating, he loved wine, he loved women; he loved the small joys of life."[162] Osho maintains that while

---

[156] Osho, *I Say Unto You, Vol. 2,* pp. 134-135; cf. Osho, *The Mustard Seed,* p. 47; cf. Osho, *Come Follow to You, Vol. 1,* p. 97.

[157] Osho, *Come Follow to You, Vol. 3,* p. 32. Cf. Osho, *Come Follow to You, Vol. 2,* p. 10; Osho, *Be Still and Know,* p. 38.

[158] Osho, *Come Follow to You, Vol. 3,* p. 58.

[159] *Ibid.* Cf. Osho, *The Mustard Seed,* p. 7.

[160] Osho, *Come Follow to You, Vol. 2,* pp. 93-94, 97; cf. Osho, *I Say Unto You, Vol. 1,* pp. 19, 153; also Osho, *Come Follow to You*, Vol. 4, p. 107.

[161] Osho, *Come Follow to You, Vol. 4,* p. 126. For more discussion on Jesus as a rebel, see Osho, *Come Follow to You, Vol. 4,* pp. 107-108; Osho, *I Say Unto You, Vol. 2,* pp. 124, 127, 130, 135.

[162] Osho, *Come Follow to You, Vol. 4,* p. 78.

'feasting' is not suitable with Mahavira and Buddha, with Jesus it is always feasting, not fasting. It is always celebration. He even celebrates his death with his disciples.[163] Osho argues, "Jesus was a very joyous man but Christians say he never laughed. It is impossible to conceive of Jesus never laughing. He enjoyed eating, he even enjoyed drinking... he enjoyed company, friends. It is impossible to conceive of him never laughing, but the way Christians have been painting him is as a very serious, long-faced man."[164] We cannot think of Mahavira or Buddha drinking wine, Jesus is perfectly all right with wine. Jesus' renunciation is positive, whereas Buddha's renunciation is negative. It is like Buddha said 'God minus the world', whereas Jesus said 'God plus the world'.[165] Osho completely rejects the idea that 'Jesus never laugh'. "Christians have depicted Jesus as very sad, with a long face, in great misery as if he is being tortured. This is false, this is not true about Jesus! It cannot be true about Jesus! Otherwise who else will laugh, and who else will love, and who else will celebrate? Jesus is a celebration of being, and the highest celebration possible."[166] A man like Jesus who is always moving with people, celebrating feasts, eating with friends should be always laughing. Again, a man like Jesus who has attained to ultimate consciousness will be completely blissful, cheerful. His life will be a song and a dance. It will have the quality of flowers and stars. It can't be sad.[167] He says that Jesus committed a sin because of which he was crucified, that is a sin of being happy – the crime of being happy – this was his only crime![168]

He claims that Jesus must have had something of the quality of Zorba the Greek, "a tremendous capacity to enjoy life, an infinite trust in life, a deep attunement with the present… He has – I can't help it – a spiritual hedonism."[169] His message is 'Be of good cheer! Be happy! Dance! Celebrate!'[170] Osho states:

> Even on the last night Jesus is breaking bread, filling cups with wine for his disciples. They are enjoying, they are eating, they are

[163] Osho, *The Mustard Seed,* p. 7.

[164] Osho, *God's Got a Thing About You*, downloaded in a *pdf* format from *http://www.oshorajneesh.com/osho-darshan-diaries.htm* (07.05.2013), p. 173.

[165] Osho, *Come Follow to You, Vol. 4, op.cit,* p. 14; Osho, *I Say Unto You, Vol. 1*, pp. 34, 61; cf. Osho, *Come Follow to You, Vol. 4,* p. 160; Osho, *I Say Unto You, Vol. 2*, p. 88.

[166] Osho, *I Say Unto You, Vol. 1,* pp. 34, 61; cf. Osho, *Come Follow to You, Vol. 4*, p. 160; Osho, *I Say Unto You, Vol. 2,* p. 88.

[167] Osho, *I Say Unto You, Vol. 2,* p. 88; Osho, *I Say Unto You, Vol. 1*, p. 34; also Osho, *Come Follow to You,* Vol. 2, pp. 7, 70.

[168] Osho, *Come Follow to You, Vol. 2*, pp. 8-9.

[169] *Ibid.*, p. 19.

[170] Osho, *Come Follow to You, Vol. 3*, p. 12.

> in a merry mood. Death is coming close, but celebration has not to stop for it because Jesus knows that this death is going to be the greatest celebration. He wants to leave his disciples in celebration. He wants it to be imprinted on their consciousnesses that Jesus was a celebrant, that he was a man of feasting not of fasting; that he was a man who was thrilled by the small joys of life – the flowers, the birds, the rivers – that he liked the lilies in the field; that he liked people, that he was immensely thrilled – always immensely thrilled when looking into people's eyes; that he loved, that he was not against life.[171]

Therefore, Osho's Jesus is not an ascetic who teaches renunciation of the world, rather he embraces the world, enjoys whatever the world is giving him with utmost gratitude. Osho's emphasis on celebration is well known, by rendering Jesus as a man of celebration, it can be assumed that Osho puts his words in the mouth of Jesus, his nature in Jesus' nature and proclaims – 'Jesus is like me, a man of celebration.'

5.7. Jesus Christ – the Son of Man and the Son of God

Osho acknowledges Jesus as having dual identity or paradoxical identity – Son of man and Son of God. He approves that Jesus used the Son of Man title for himself much more frequently than 'Son of God' title. He called himself the 'Son of Man' more often because it is more comprehensible for the un-enlightened people.[172] For Osho 'Son of Man' indicates Jesus body and mind whereas 'Son of God' implies his spirit, his consciousness.[173] Like Jesus we are also both Sons of Man and Sons of God. We are also both 'Sons of Man' and 'Sons of God' in the sense that we are born to a human, but we are also born to be a god. "Humanity is your form, divinity is your being. Humanity is your clothing, divinity is your soul."[174] The only different we have with Jesus is that while we are still on our way to the shore, Jesus has already reached the shore.[175] Osho links the concept of the Son of Man and the Son of God with Jesus and Christ saying, "Christ is the son of God, Jesus the son of man."[176] The next point further explicates this.

---

[171] Osho, *I Say Unto You, Vol. 2*, p. 169.

[172] Osho, *Come Follow to You, Vol. 2,* pp. 248-249; Osho, *Come Follow to You, Vol. 1,* pp. 256-257.

[173] Osho, *I Say Unto You, Vol. 1,* p. 9.

[174] Osho, *Come Follow to You, Vol. 1,* p. 257, cf. Osho, *Come Follow to You, Vol. 3*, pp. 38, 114.

[175] Osho, *Come Follow to You, Vol. 3*, p. 114.

[176] *Ibid.*, p. 3.

5.8. Jesus Christ - Jesus and Christ

For Osho, Jesus Christ comprises of 'Jesus' and 'Christ'. "Jesus and Christ are like two shores, and the river is only possible if there are two shores. Jesus is the river that flows between these two shores: both shores are his. He exists between them, he is a river... Jesus Christ is both Jesus and Christ. He is Christ in Jesus, and he is Jesus in Christ. He is the meeting point where two worlds meet, where two utterly polar worlds meet. And hence the beauty, and hence the ecstasy of Jesus."[177] On the other hand, Jesus and Christ are totally two different entities as Osho says, "To call Jesus 'Christ' is not right – because they were never together. There was a time when there was Jesus but there was no Christ. Then a time came when there was Christ but there was no Jesus. They were never together."[178] 'Jesus' is a real man with blood and flesh; his heart beats, he loves, lives and cries just like us, whereas 'Christ' is abstract principle.[179] Christ is not a person but a state of mind or more appropriately a state of no-mind, a state when thinking stops and you are simply aware. Christ is a state of consciousness, of silence, peace, bliss, of purity, innocence.[180] Osho perceives Christ as a sort of cosmic principle, an universal significance which does not confine to Jesus because Buddha and Kṛṣṇa are also Christ.[181]

Osho maintains that Christhood or Christ-consciousness is not there in Jesus from the beginning, it is something he attained in course of time. Osho maintains, when Jesus says "Before Abraham was, I am", he is not talking about Jesus – his body and mind, he is talking about Christ-consciousness which is eternal, timeless. Christ-consciousness has always been there. Jesus has participated in it now.[182] Jesus has fallen into Christ-consciousness. The moment he falls, he, the Jesus, disappears; he is no longer the son of Mary or Joseph. The body and everything attached to it has gone. Now he is the

---

[177] Osho, *I Say Unto You, Vol. 2,* pp. 85, 90.

[178] Osho, *Sufis: The People of the Path, Vol. 2,* pp. 230-231; cf. Osho, *Blessed are the Ignorant,* p. 157; also Osho, *Yoga: The Alpha and the Omega, Vol. 2,* downloaded in a *pfd* format from *http://www.oshorajneesh. com/osho-yoga-books.htm* (10.04.2013), p. 57.

[179] Osho, *Come Follow to You, Vol. 3,* p. 3.

[180] Osho, *A Rose is a Rose is a Rose,* p. 27; Osho, *Sufis: The People of the Path, Vol. 2,* p. 189.

[181] Osho explains the possible origin of the word 'Christ' saying "there is every possibility that the word 'Christ' comes from 'Kṛṣṇa'. In Bengali, Kṛṣṇa is called 'Cristo'. There is every possibility that Christ is a form of the same root, Kṛṣṇa. What does 'Kṛṣṇa' mean? The word means 'that which attracts'. Kṛṣṇa is one who has become capable of attracting the divine in him. Christ is also the same. It means the drop has become capable of attracting the ocean in him." Osho, *Come Follow to You, Vol. 3,* p. 36. Cf. Osho, *Yoga: The Alpha and the Omega, Vol. 3,* p. 131; also Osho, *Blessed are the Ignorant,* p. 116.

[182] Osho, *I Say Unto You, Vol. 2,* p. 61.

transcendental, the fourth state of consciousness: *turīya.*[183] This is the state which Buddha called *Nirvāṇa* and Jesus referred to it as 'Kingdom of God' – a state of no mind, a state of no time and space.[184] According to Osho as Jesus became Christ, we can also become Christ, in other words, we can attain Christ-consciousness.[185] When ego is destroyed and transcended a person becomes Christ.[186] Osho means to indicate that it is like a river falls into the ocean and lost it identity or a drop of water falls into the river and lost its existence as a drop, so also the moment we participate in Christ, we are lost and Christ remains.

5.9. Jesus as Love

Jesus as the manifestation or embodiment of love is emphasized by all the contemporary gurus investigated in this book. For Osho Jesus is love, a pure love. As pure love cannot be tolerated, thus Jesus was crucified on the cross. The day Jesus was crucified, love was crucified, not Jesus.[187] Jesus was a man of love, of immense love. He loved this earth, the smell of this earth. He loved the trees, the people.[188] Love is the only language Jesus understands.[189] Emphasizing the oneness of Jesus and love, Osho sometime goes to the extent that Jesus looks impersonal. He says that Jesus is a quality like love, a quality of tremendous love, a quality of tremendous perception, vision, of tremendous realisation. Jesus is a quality, but to see that quality we will have to drop our egos.[190]

The uniqueness of Osho's perception of love, to love and to be loved is that one needs to love himself/herself in order to love others, for Jesus says, "Thou shall love thy neighbour as you love yourself." Osho maintains that Christians do not interpret this passage correctly as they teach hatred towards oneself. "Unless you love yourself, you cannot love your neighbour… Self-love is the most fundamental thing - if you ever want to be religious, self-love

---

[183] *Ibid.* Cf. Osho, *The Mustard Seed,* p. 26.

[184] Osho, *I Say Unto You, Vol. 2,* p. 62.

[185] He says, "The moment you realize that your origin is shrouded in mystery, that your beginning and your end are mysterious, and there is no way to know them because you have been always and always and always.... In fact there has never been a beginning - that's the meaning, when I say they are shrouded in mystery… Once you realize this, suddenly you have become the Christ. The realization that 'I am beyond time', is the meaning of the word 'Christ'." Osho, *Come Follow to You, Vol. 3,* p. 120.

[186] *Ibid.*, p. 122.

[187] Osho, *Come Follow to You, Vol. 1,* pp. 54-55.

[188] Osho, *I Say Unto You, Vol. 1,* p. 60.

[189] Osho, *Yoga: The Alpha and the Omega, Vol. 3,* p. 77.

[190] Osho, *Come Follow to You, Vol. 3,* p. 7.

is the basis."[191] Only those who love themselves are capable of loving their neighbour.[192] To follow Christ, one has to follow love, follow love and forget everything. Everything is irrelevant; only love has relevance because only love leads you to the divine, to the temple of God.[193] Jesus gives a new commandment – to love one another just as he loves us. His love is unconditional - he loves without any expectation in return. "Jesus' 'as I have loved you' means: be in the attitude of unconditional love...only unconditional love is love. Love conditioned is love corrupted; love unconditioned is the vast sky of being. It is another word for God."[194] By saying so Osho equates Love with Jesus, with God Himself and to follow Jesus such unconditional love needs to be possessed. When Jesus says, "Love your enemies", it is not the question of loving the enemies, but it is becoming love.[195]

5.10. Cross and Resurrection

According to Osho Jesus was crucified not to redeem humanity from sin but because people detested him as he was against the existing tradition. According to Osho, Jesus was crucified because he was against the traditions, the laws. The charge was that he is corrupting people, destroying the old morality, creating conflict and chaos. He was destroying the whole structure, uprooting all that the people had been protecting for centuries. Though he did not commit any crime, he is the greatest criminal because he was bringing a revolution in the thinking of people, in their minds. The greatest revolution which Jesus brought is the revolution for love and against law.[196] Osho's separation of Jesus into Jesus and Christ is a key to understanding his concept of Cross and resurrection. He firmly asserts that the *real Jesus* was neither crucified nor died on the cross; it was the body Jesus that was crucified and died. As the real Jesus, the Christ was not killed, there is a possibility of resurrection which otherwise would not be possible.[197] He puts emphasis on the significance of the

---

[191] *Ibid.*, p. 100.

[192] *Ibid.*, p. 101.

[193] Osho, *Come Follow to You, Vol. 4,* p. 50.

[194] *Ibid.*, p. 51.

[195] Osho, *Yoga: The Alpha and the Omega, Vol. 3,* p. 21.

[196] Osho, *Come Follow to You, Vol. 4,* p. 130; Osho, *Come Follow to You, Vol. 2,* pp. 93, 97. For more on the reason why Jesus was crucified cf. Osho, *Come Follow to You, Vol. 4,* pp. 125-127, and Osho, *The Wisdom of the Sands, Vol. 2*, p. 62.

[197] Osho, *I Say Unto You, Vol. 1,* p. 32; Osho, *Come Follow to You, Vol. 2,* p. 95; Osho, *Come Follow to You, Vol. 4,* p. 135. Cf. Osho, *The Mustard Seed,* p. 37-38 where he says that the crucifixion was arranged by Jesus himself, he did not try to run away from it because he knew that though his body would be killed, the earth falling back to the earth, 'the real he' will not be killed as the separation between the body and the spirit was so total, so absolute. He allowed it to happen.

cross as a symbol of the destruction of the ego and a new life that follows in the resurrection. So, everybody has to pass that cross, to destroy the ego in order to resurrect with a new life.[198] Again, Crucifixion is a meeting point, it is a crossroad where the ego disappears and divinity takes the place.[199] Osho often says that the greatest miracle that had ever happened on this earth happened that day on the cross – it is not the show of power, but a humble man dying, saying his last prayer for those who crucified him – "Father, forgive them for they know not what they do". The ability to show love to the aggressors and pray for them while being crucified, for Osho, is to indicate where Jesus is, the heart of Jesus – what Jesus really is[200] - the greatest miracle.

One of the most important sayings of Jesus on the cross, according to Osho is, "My God, my God, why hast thou forsaken me?" which is misunderstood by Christians. It is not that Jesus doubted God or Jesus was expecting a miracle which had never happened. Osho argues that this happens to everybody who comes to the last step, to the very verge of *samādhi*, the very verge of enlightenment. Jesus is entering another life, a life of enlightenment, as a man of flesh and bone, Jesus had this awful experience - a fragile being facing eternal abyss. Everyone who experiences enlightenment will also cry, 'My God, why have you forsaken me?' It is simply an indication of fragile humanness disappearing and evaporating. It shows the authenticity of the experience because it happens only when one really faces that moment of total cessation of the ego, a total emptiness.[201] Osho concludes, "If you go deeper in meditation, one day you will find the meaning of this sentence, '*Eli, Eli, lamasabachthani.*'"[202] He argues that Jesus on the cross gets final enlightenment when he managed to relax and said 'thy will be done'. At that moment Jesus disappeared, Christ was born. It is Jesus begetting Christ; Christogenesis took place - human becomes that which he/she really is by loosing that which he/ she is not; in other words, human becomes 'Christified.'[203]

Osho affirms that in that moment the resurrection happened, not after the crucifixion. In that moment the discontinuity happened - Jesus cessed, Christ

---

[198] Osho, *Come Follow to You, Vol. 2,* pp. 318-319.

[199] Osho, *Come Follow to You, Vol. 4,* p. 48.

[200] Osho, *Come Follow to You, Vol. 3,* p. 142; Osho, *Come Follow to You, Vol. 1*, p. 231. Cf. Osho, *Come Follow to You, Vol. 4,* p. 158; Osho, *The Wisdom of the Sands, Vol. 2,* downloaded in a *pdf* format from *http://www.oshorajneesh.com/osho-books-on-sufi.htm* (10.04.2013), p. 37; Osho, *The Mustard Seed,* p. 245.

201 Osho, *Come Follow to You, Vol. 4,* pp. 132-133.

[202] *Ibid.*, p. 133.

[203] Osho, *I Say Unto You, Vol. 1,* p. 9. Cf. Osho, *Yoga: The Alpha and the Omega, Vol. 6,* downloaded in a *pdf* format from *http://www.oshorajneesh. com/osho-yoga-books.htm* (10.04.2013), p. 148; also Osho, *Blessed are the Ignorant,* p. 157.

appeared. This is the real resurrection.[204] So, the real resurrection, for Osho, is *not* the restoration of the dead body to life, it is a *new birth of consciousness* that happened at the cross in the case of Jesus.[205] However, Osho acknowledges the Biblical story of Jesus' body being laid in the tomb after crucifixion and adds that a certain sect called Essenes took care of him and preserved his body for three days after which Jesus entered his body again – the resurrection. By doing so Jesus gave a proof that nothing really dies.[206] Osho insists that Jesus' resurrection should not be taken as historical event, but should be understood as spiritual phenomenon because the one resurrected is no longer Jesus, son of Mary and Joseph, but totally new consciousness, egoless – Christ.[207]

5.11. Jesus' Enlightenment

Osho talks about three types of enlightenment – the first is called *mini-satori.* When, for the first time, for a single moment mind is not functioning, there is a gap – no thought between we and existence, the meeting, the merging with existence but for a moment. From that moment the seed will be in our heart and growing. The second is called *satori* that happens when we have become capable of retaining this gap as long as we want, but with a little effort, the moment we drop the effort, satori disappears. The third *satori* is the final one; it is a complete drop of ego, the state of no-mind. Osho refers to this as *samādhi.*[208]

Osho postulates that the first type of enlightenment, first *satori* must have happened to Jesus somewhere in India or Tibet where Jesus spent a number of years with Buddhist Masters, but he also admits that nobody can be certain of where it happened. The second *satori*, deeper enlightenment definitely happened in the river Jordan with John the Baptist when Jesus took baptism. The dove, a symbol of peace and silence, descending on Jesus is a sign of *satori.* The third and final *satori*, final enlightenment happened at the cross when Jesus finally gave up his ego. In that moment he relaxed, he surrendered – 'Thy will be done'. That moment Jesus disappeared and became God. That is the moment Buddha says, 'Gone, gone, gone beyond, gone altogether beyond'. With that experience Jesus had come home.[209] So, Osho's Jesus is a real, normal human

---

[204] Osho, *I Say Unto You, Vol. 1,* pp. 66-67. Cf. Osho, *The Mustard Seed,* p. 249.

[205] Cf. Osho, *Tantra: The Supreme Understanding,* downloaded in a *pdf* format from *http://www.messagefrommasters.com/Ebooks/Osho_Books_on_Tantra_&_Mantra.htm* (09.04.2013), p. 121.

[206] Osho, *Come Follow to You, Vol. 4,* pp. 170-171. Cf. Osho, *Come Follow to You, Vol. 1,* p. 232.

[207] Osho, *My Way the Way of the White Clouds*, p. 42 and Osho, *The Madman's Guide to Enlightenment*, p. 87.

[208] Osho, *I Say Unto You, Vol. 1,* pp. 106, 109.

[209] *Ibid.*, pp. 109-111; cf. Osho, *The Mustard Seed,* p. 219.

being who by virtue of his religious quest, with tireless attempt travelling in various places, learning from various Masters, got glimpse of enlightenment. The seed that had sprouted grew as he moved on and finally on the cross final enlightenment happened. Osho refers to it as 'the real resurrection'.

5.12. The Significance of Jesus' Baptism

Osho lays great importance to Jesus' baptism and he is the only one among the gurus investigated in this book to have paid great attention to Jesus' baptism. As mentioned above Osho argues that the baptism elevated Jesus to a new plane of consciousness, led him to a new door of existence. A new consciousness has entered. The man Jesus is no longer the Jesus who used to be because the new consciousness – Christ entered him.[210] At the river Jordan, Jesus disappeared and in that moment of nothingness, what Buddha called śūnyatā, emptiness, heaven opened, the spirit of God descended – then Jesus attained *buddhahood.* The son of a carpenter, who was busy helping his father in the workshop, suddenly became a new man and started preaching.[211] This is the significance of Jesus' baptism.

5.13. The Real Miracle of Jesus

For Osho Jesus is a poet, not philosopher or theologian; his messages are poetical in nature and therefore, should not be interpreted literally. From this perspective he looks at Jesus message and works particularly his miracles recorded in the Gospels. He denounces altogether that Jesus performs miracles like healing the sick, feeding the multitude, giving sight to the blind, reviving the dead, etc. These 'miracles' should not be read literally as something actually taking place physically, but poetically as meaning inner spiritual miracle. Spiritually blind people started seeing but not with their physical eyes, many spiritually dead people were revived and made alive. This is a greater miracle. Miracles happened around Jesus of far greater significance than physical healing and restoration of corporeal life.[212] Among the four gurus studied in this book, Osho is the only one who is not connected with miracle. There is no report of miracle being performed by him. His scientific nature and religious commitment do not allow him to give supernatural phenomenon a place in his teaching. So, considering his revulsion towards supernatural thing, it is no wonder that he denied Jesus' miracles as something actually happened.

---

[210] Osho, *Come Follow to You, Vol. 2,* pp. 130-132.

[211] Osho, *Come Follow to You, Vol. 1,* pp. 124-126, 128-129.

[212] Osho, *The Mustard Seed,* pp. 242-243.

5.14. Jesus did a Zen-Act

According to Osho, when Jesus washed the feet of his disciple he did a Zen act. A Zen act is an act by which things are communicated which cannot be said in any other way. There are things which can only be acted upon. Through action, total action, they can be said; there is no other way to say them. That was what Jesus did.[213] By touching the feet of his disciples reverently, Jesus showed them what reverence is, in its totality, what love is and how one can totally surrender. By doing this he gave them the greatest gift he could, the gift of reverence.[214] Why their feet? Feet are symbols of the lowly. Jesus touched their feet to show that God is there also; even in a thorn bush, in the lowliest depth God is there, because God is everywhere. In the darkest valley He is there. He is not only at the peaks but also in the valleys. He is not only in the saints; in the sinners also. Jesus touched the feet of the disciples to show them that nothing is lowly.[215] When Jesus touched the feet of his disciples, love touched their feet. He touched their feet to show them that they are not that which they think they are. They are that which they are seeking. The disciples were only seeds, but Jesus could see the flower. He touched their feet because of the possibility of the flowering; someday or other they would explode into beautiful flowers, they would blossom.[216]

By doing this lowly act, Jesus is telling them to be respectful to each other, and that is very difficult for disciples, because they are competitive. He knows that the moment he disappears, the religion will be forgotten and politics will enter because disciples are politicians. After Jesus left them, the disciples did not fight among themselves because Jesus touched their feet. But later on, these disciples did not continue the example Jesus had set, and did not follow what he had commanded to touch each other's feet; the result was - Christianity became divided.[217] Jesus touched the feet of his disciples because he wanted to give them an existential meaning of love. In love nobody is higher or lower, because love knows no hierarchy. By touching his disciples' feet Jesus is declaring that "You are exactly like me, there is no difference. You and I are absolutely the same. I have known it, you have not known it, that is the only difference."[218]

---

[213] Osho, *Come Follow to You, Vol. 4,* p. 36.

[214] *Ibid.*, pp. 37-38.

[215] *Ibid.*, p. 38.

[216] *Ibid.*, p. 40.

[217] *Ibid.*, pp. 44-45.

[218] Osho, *I Say Unto You, Vol. 2,* p. 168.

5.15. Some of the Prominent Christian Doctrines on Jesus Rejected

Osho rejects some of the traditional Christian doctrines including the doctrine of incarnation, virgin birth, Christological affirmation of Jesus as God, trinity, atonement and Jesus as the only begotten Son of God, the only savior. Osho utterly denounced Christian's claim that Jesus was born of a virgin woman. For him Mary was a virgin, but by 'virginity' he means that Mary must have been in a very non-sexual state, she must not have been thinking about sex. She must have made love, but that love was innocent.[219] On Mary's 'virginity' Osho says that Christian's claim of Jesus being born of a virgin woman is all foolishness. They pretend that sex was not involved in Jesus' birth. Mary must have been very pure and sexually innocent, she must have been spiritually virgin, that is true but there is no way to enter into life without the energy of sex.[220] So, for him, Jesus was born from normal human reproductive activity but of a very non-sexual, innocent woman, Mary. He maintains, [221]

> Mary, Jesus' mother, is virgin; no man has corrupted her. This is a symbolic thing. It is not that Jesus is born out of a virgin biologically. Then you miss the metaphor; the beautiful story becomes an ugly doctrine. Then you miss the poetry. And then for centuries Christians have been arguing, and trying to prove somehow that Jesus is born, really, from a virgin mother. How can theologians be so stupid?

As Osho does not believe in God, a personal being, the creator, there is no question of him believing in the doctrine of incarnation, trinity or Jesus as God. Again, like other contemporary gurus, Osho also dismissed the so called 'uniqueness of Jesus' as the only begotten Son of God, the only Saviour, the only Way.

The famous statement on which 'the only Saviour' notion is based, runs – "Jesus said to him, I am the way, the truth and the life; no man come to the Father but by me". Osho says that this statement is of immense importance, but Christians misunderstood it tremendously. When Jesus says, "I AM" Christians understand it as 'Jesus Christ, son of Mary is the only way and Christianity is the only true religion. "I AM" does not signify Jesus as a person, but it means the inner consciousness. It has nothing to do with Jesus or Kṛṣṇa, "I AM" is the way, the gate. The inner consciousness is what Jesus meant when

---

[219] *Ibid.*, pp. 49 -54. Cf. Osho, *Tantra: The Supreme Understanding*, p. 139.

[220] Osho, *The Beloved, Vol. 1: Talks on the Baul Mystics* downloaded in a *pdf* format from *http://www.oshorajneesh.com/osho-books-on-indian-mystics.htm* (08.05.2013), p. 148; cf. Osho, *The Wisdom of the Sands, Vol. 2*, p. 22.

[221] Osho, *Until You die*, p. 144. Elsewhere he says, "Jesus is born out of sex like anybody else." Osho, *The Mustard Seed*, p. 119.

he said "I AM".[222] Again, Jesus cannot be the 'only begotten Son' because all comes from God, so how can Jesus be the son of God exclusively? Everyone is the son of God and we all partake of sonhood.[223] Jesus is a savior unto himself, not others because "nobody can be the salvation of the world."[224] By discarding completely his ego, he saves himself and becomes a model for all of us. We can be like Jesus by letting go our ego, by emptying ourselves, reaching the mindless, egoless state. That shows that Jesus Christ is not unique in any sense!

5.16. Other Aspects of Jesus

Apart from what had been discussed above, Osho brings to the surface a number of innovative ideas about Jesus Christ. According to him, Jesus' words "I and my Father are one" means both the son is the father and the father is the son. It signifies that we are one with the whole and we become cosmic, which is equivalent to Upaniṣadic 'I am the Brahman'. This is the very essence of religion.[225] Again, without much elaboration Osho talks about Jesus as a messenger of Peace,[226] a medium between God and human,[227] a friend and fellow traveller,[228] the Messiah,[229] a poet, not a scientist, but the greatest artist,[230] and a wonderer, a *sannyāsin* who is not of this world.[231] Besides, Osho affirms what had been said by most of the Indian spiritual leaders that Jesus spent a number of years in India among the Hindu and Buddhist masters.[232] He also says that Jesus believes in the doctrine of transmigration of soul (*karma-saṃsāra*), but he did not teach it because he knew that people used to postpone

---

[222] Cf. Osho, *I Say Unto You, Vol. 2,* pp. 174-176.

[223] Cf. *Ibid.*, pp. 86-87. Elsewhere Osho says that Jesus is the 'only begotten Son' for those who believe in him, but this cannot be generalized, it is not for everybody. Cf. Osho, *Yoga: The Alpha and the Omega,* p. 104.

[224] Osho, *Be Still and Know,* p. 39. Cf. Osho, *The Wisdom of the Sands, Vol. 2,* p. 123; also Osho, *Sufis: The People of the Path, Vol. 2,* p. 215; Osho, *The Madman's Guide to Enlightenment,* p. 37.

[225] Osho, *Come Follow to You, Vol. 3,* p. 45; cf. Osho, *Come Follow to You, Vol. 4,* p. 34; Osho, *I Say Unto You, Vol. 2,* p. 178. See for more on this issue, Osho, *The Path of Love: Talks on Songs of Kabir,* downloaded in a *pdf* format from *http://www.oshorajneesh. com/osho-books-on-indian-mystics.htm* (08.05.2013), p. 49; Osho, *Tantra: The Supreme Understanding,* p. 153; cf. Osho, *Come Follow to You, Vol. 2*, pp. 60, 63.

[226] Osho, *Come Follow to You, Vol. 1,* pp. 80, 84.

[227] Osho, *Come Follow to You, Vol. 2,* pp. 84-85; Osho, *I Say Unto You, Vol. 1*, p. 18.

[228] Osho, *Come Follow to You, Vol. 2,* p. 113; Osho, *Come Follow to You, Vol. 4*, p. 13.

[229] Osho, *Come Follow to You, Vol. 1,* p. 32.

[230] *Ibid.*, p. 222; *The Mustard Seed,* p. 242.

[231] Osho, *Come Follow to You, Vol. 4,* p. 12; Osho, *Come Follow to You, Vol. 1,* p. 249-250.

[232] Osho, *The Mustard Seed,* p. 57; Osho, *I Say Unto You, Vol. 2,* p. 173; Osho, *The Zen Manifesto*, Chapter 7, p. 8.

their enlightenment when they know that there is still a next life.[233] He also interprets the meaning of Jesus' repentance as 'coming back to our original being or come back to our deepest core of being';[234] washing of the disciples' feet as to show that God is there also, that nothing is lowly, to show them the existential meaning of love – in love nobody is higher and nobody is lower; love knows no hierarchy.[235]

5.17. A Negative Portrayal of Jesus

The methodological frameworks of Osho discussed before becomes more vivid when we come to his interpretation of Jesus Christ. After the silence period, he speaks mainly to his own people, the *sannyāsins* and the message is significantly different. Here, he shows his true colour, no longer use indirect method, but directly speaks to his people, offering them not a commentary on some religious figures but his own experience. He confesses in his discourse in 1985, "Now it is no longer a commentary, I am telling you my experience. If Jesus or Buddha or Zarathustra agrees with me, good; if they don't agree, they can go to hell."[236] The result is - his words on Jesus before the silence period and after are totally different, sharply contradicting one another.

Since the last part of 1984, after the silence, Osho left no stone unturned to show the nothingness and falsity of Jesus and his teaching. He practically cancels all that he had said before. It is not that Osho has changes his position on Jesus after his silence period, but right from the beginning, he had never consider Jesus as an authentic Master who can lead people to enlightenment, but just a crackpot. His positive comments on Jesus are just 'a methodological game' to engage people in order to attract them to remain with him till they can be initiated into *sannyās*. So, it is not that Osho renounces his previous interpretation of Jesus for a new one, rather he never own them in the first place, but uses them as bait to catch people as he spreads his net in the religious water of Christianity.[237] As the fishing session has come to an end with a huge catch, Osho now talks to his own people, revealing his own truth, bashing aside all he had said of Jesus with totally different tone and content. He discards Jesus

---

[233] Osho, *The Mustard Seed,* pp. 55, 57.

[234] Cf. Osho, *Come Follow to You, Vol. 1,* pp. 68-69; Osho, *The Mustard Seed,* pp. 54-55; Osho, *Yoga: The Alpha and the Omega, Vol. 6,* p. 132; cf. Osho, *Come Follow to You, Vol. 4,* p. 172.

[235] Osho, *Come Follow to You, Vol. 4,* pp. 37-40; cf. Osho, *I Say Unto You, Vol. 2,* p. 168.

[236] Osho, *From the False to the Truth,* Chapter 33, p. 3.

[237] See Osho, *From Death to Deathlessness,* p. 519 where he unfolds how he played a methodological game.

as enlightened person,[238] and rejects Jesus' miracles altogether.[239] He mocks Jesus as a neurotic patient, a mental case, a fascist just like Adolf Hitler.[240] Osho ridicules Jesus in the following lines, "Jesus needs a few therapies to put him right, to put him together. A little deprogramming... 'You are not the son of God – drop this idea. This is what is making you look unnecessarily a clown. It does not prove that you are a messiah, it simply proves you are nuts…' Just a little bit of treatment here and he would have been a perfectly good *sannyāsin.*"[241] He maintains that Jesus survived crucifixion and escaped from the cross, went to Kashmir and died there.[242] He ridicules Jesus, saying that Jesus claimed the position of the Saviour of the world but could not even save himself.[243]

It may be concluded that Osho's real position on Jesus is quite negative. For him Jesus is an ordinary person, a son of an ordinary carpenter, nothing else. But crucifixion made him popular and his disciples created amazing stories around him and those stories worked perfectly and in course of time Jesus became very great. In two thousand years, scholars, professors, theologians and philosophers are increasing the greatness of Jesus by bringing out of him meanings, words, philosophies, and ideologies of which that poor fellow, Jesus, was never aware.[244] Nevertheless, the significance of those positive comments he made on Jesus is not diminished whether he really believes in them or follow them or not, because the value of truth is not nullified whether one owns it or not. Thus, his interpretation, though given non-seriously as 'a game' just to attract people, has its own value because it adds diversity to an overall Indian understanding of Jesus Christ and also has positive aspects for inter-faith relations.

Concluding Remarks

A pro-life guru, who refuses guru-ship but identifies himself as 'a friend', a fellow traveller, highly intellectual but utterly against intellectualism, highly

---

[238] Osho, *The Last Testament, Vol. 4,* downloaded in a *pdf* format from *http://www.oshorajneesh.com/osho-personal-glimpses.htm* (09/04/2013), p. 221; Osho, *The Last Testament, Vol. 5,* downloaded in a *pdf* format from *http://www.oshorajneesh.com/osho-personal-glimpses.htm* (09/04/2013), p. 76; Osho, *From Death to Deathlessness,* p. 214.

[239] Osho, *From Unconsciousness to Consciousness,* Chapter 1, p. 5. Cf. Osho, *The Zen Manifesto,* Chapter 9, p. 13; Osho, *From Misery to Enlightenment,* p. 213; Osho, *The Last Testament,* Vol. 5, p. 85.

[240] Osho, *From Unconsciousness to Consciousness*, Chapter 1, p. 5.

[241] Osho, *From Misery to Enlightenment,* p. 206.

[242] Osho, *From Personality to Individuality*, p. 39.

[243] Osho, *The Last Testament, Vol. 4,* pp. 6-7, 168-169, 198; Osho, *From Death to Deathlessness*, pp. 14, 215.

[244] Osho, *From Misery to Enlightenment,* pp. 208-209.

philosophical but denounces philosophy as useless, an outspoken, a care-free rebel who is against all codified religions and human traditions, undoubtedly the most controversial of all the contemporary gurus – this is Osho Rajneesh, a man of celebration, dance and enjoyment. He is different from the other three gurus investigated in this book in many respects – while the other gurus are all God-centred and faithful to Hindu religious tradition, Osho denies God's existence and is utterly against any religion tradition as he claims non-adherent to any codified religion of the world. Again, unlike the other three gurus Sri Sathya Sai Baba, Paramhansa Yogananda and Sri Sri Ravishankar, he does not base his teachings on any of the written Scripture nor does he care to follow any philosophical school. Another significant difference is his emphasis on enjoyment and celebration including the fulfilment of carnal desire, and his peculiar method of attacking, mocking and speaking ruthless words against persons, institutions or organizations, or an outrageous verbal attack on religious traditions and the founders of religions which is done most probably to provoke the thinking of people and get media attention.

He looks at Jesus from the perspective of a life-oriented, human-centred philosophy, interpreting him with utter humanness without the help of any supernatural force or divine intervention. In a way, this is the beauty of Osho's interpretation of Jesus Christ. As there is no place for God in his teaching, there is no room for the well-known Indian recognition of Jesus Christ as one of the *avatāras* in Osho's religious and philosophical narration. Similar is the case with Jesus as God or the Son of God and his identity as one of the members of the divine holy Trinity. Anything that looks supernatural including the virgin birth, miracles, etc. is simply denied or reinterpreted as symbolic and non-historical. By doing so, Osho wants to see Jesus as standing minus God, a real and bare human, thereby making Jesus totally different from the Jesus of the Bible and the Jesus of Christianity. His emphasis on Jesus' humanity is quite commendable in the light of an over emphasizing of his divinity which is prevalent among many conservative Christians. His perception of Jesus as a man of celebration and a rebel, though looks contradictory, gives us a glimpse of a multi-faceted Jesus which cannot be exhausted due to its richness, and such an attempt definitely enhances the image of Jesus Christ and adds to its diversity.

Again, Osho's insistence on direct mystical knowledge of Jesus Christ rather than academic-intellectual knowledge of him through a written scripture and theology is laudable. As this is a common point raised by all the gurus investigated in this book, it may be one of the viable Indian approaches to Jesus. Cross as the symbol of the destruction of the ego, resurrection as a representation of a new life as suggested in Osho's interpretation is also another positive contribution to an overall Christological consideration. However, a complete cessation of individual soul, a discontinuity with a new consciousness that emerged, is foreign to the Semitic religious worldview. Presumably, it is borrowed from the Buddhist *no-soul* theory. Osho, by saying that Jesus cessed as individual when he assumed Christhood at the cross, tries to inject his own idea into a completely different religious setting. It is not only arrogant to do so but also methodologically inappropriate as it looks more of an imposition rather than a contextual interpretation of the event, because any authentic interpretation should strike a balance between the contextual realities of the interpreter and the interpreted.

Ohso's conception of Christ as a universal principle which is not the monopoly of Jesus son of Mary but equivalent to *buddhahood* is quite common among the Indian interpreters. The presence of that 'Christ' in Hindu religious tradition and its availability to all people belonging to various religions has been highlighted by a number of Hindu scholars and Indian theologians like Raimundo Pannikar and S.J. Samartha. Such a conception of a universal 'Christ' or '*buddha*' – Christ-consciousness or Buddha-consciousness or Kṛṣṇa-consciousness, which according to Osho, are all the same, can serve as a meeting point for various religions, enhancing inter-religious relations. But problem comes when Osho maintains that Jesus attained Christhood at the cross in the last minute of his life, while he accepts Buddha as attaining *buddhahood* at the prime of his life. By doing so, he degrades the very thing which he tries to promote.

The Hindus and other interpreters of Jesus are unanimous in claiming that Christianity does not represent the real Jesus and that in the hands of Christian interpreters, because of their Western imperialistic and cultural superiority complex, the real Jesus is often covered up and distorted. Osho also follows the same line of thought. This may be true to a great extent. However, his complete denial of the Christian version of Jesus Christ is presumptuous, because it is not scientifically, spiritually and religiously probable that the version of 'other witnesses' to Jesus is more authentic than that of the adherents, the Christian community, who had been so ardent in trying to keep the authentic version of Jesus' story, though we do not rule out the possibility of some flaws here and there. Methodologically it is inappropriate to assume that the followers of Jesus will be less dedicated to him than the non-followers, the witness to the event is less reliable than those who are hearing the story of the witness, the primary source is less dependable than the secondary source. So, it is methodologically wrong to presume that Christianity totally misses the real Jesus.

The greatest weakness in Osho's interpretation lies in his overall approach to Jesus. He claims that he is not interpreting Jesus as such, rather, Jesus speaks through him and he is simply mirroring what happens when he listens to Jesus. However, in a close examination this claim seems to contain no water. On the contrary, Osho imprisons Jesus within the four wall of his ideology and makes him say what he wants to say. By and large, though there are several innovative ideas that enrich our understanding of Jesus in Osho's work, we have the impression that in interpreting Jesus, he only narrates his own spiritual experiences using Jesus as a vehicle. His interpretation does not go beyond himself. We see less of Jesus but more of Osho throughout his commentary.

Chapter 7

Sri Sri Ravishankar's Interpretation of Jesus Christ

It may not be an exaggeration to state that Sri Sri Ravishankar[1] is the leading living Hindu guru today. According to the official website, The Art of Living Foundation (AOL), founded by Sri Sri in 1982,[2] operates globally in 152 countries. There are a number of other organizations initiated by him which are active in the nook and corner of India helping people in need. The International headquarters of Sri Sri located at the outskirts of Bangalore city is flooded with all kinds of peoples from all walks of life and from various countries of the world. Guruji (as he has been commonly known by his devotees) has been honoured with more than ten Honorary Doctorate degrees by some of the leading Universities of India and abroad; he has been given some forty Awards/Honours by various International organizations and governments. His vision of a violence-free, stress-free world and his emphasis on harmony of religions earned him a worldwide recognition.

---

[1] Sometimes his name is written as Sri Sri Ravi Shankar, but we will write as 'Sri Sri Ravishankar' unless it is a direct quotation or the name of a book where the author writes 'Sri Sri Ravi Shankar'. Sri Sri Ravishankar is often called as 'Sri Sri' or 'Guruji', we also use these terms in this thesis.

[2] According to the Official Website of Sri Sri Ravishankar *http://srisriravishankar.org/service-organizations/art-of-living* (28.11.2012), the Art of Living (AOL) was founded in the year 1981, but some other authorities maintain that AOL was founded in 1982. This seeming contradiction may be explained as follows – In 1981 Sri Sri established Ved Vignan Mahavidhyapeeth where the Art of Living courses were taught. Even though the Art of Living Foundation was born in 1982, there was already the Art of Living course going on in 1981. Cf. Namrita Gautier and Francois Gautier, *The Art of Healing: Pranayama – The Breath of Life,* (New Delhi: HarperCollins Publishers, India, 2010), p. 9.

Ravishankar, like many contemporary gurus, clings faithfully to Advaita Vedānta of Śaṅkara which becomes the foundation of his religious and philosophical teachings. He is also true to his Hindu religious tradition which for him is broad enough to accept 'other' ways. His emphasis on religious harmony is also the product of his Hindu commitment on the theology of religious pluralism. It is from this perspective that he looks at Jesus Christ and has no reservation in accepting him as a valid path to God. Unlike the other three gurus studied, Sri Sri does not talk much about Jesus Christ, and produce comparatively less literature on him. But this does not indicate that he has less regard for Jesus and his teaching, nor does it nullify or lessen the importance of his interpretation.

This Chapter begins with a brief sketch of the life of Ravishankar, followed by highlights on his religious and philosophical teachings. The third section deals with his interpretation of Jesus Christ.

1. A Brief Life Sketch of Ravishankar

Ravishankar was born on 13th May, the traditional date for *Adi Śaṅkara Jayantī*, 1956 in Papanasam, a village in Tamil Nadu.[3] He was given a name on the eleventh day of his birth, which was considered as *Ramanuja Jayantī*. His father Venkataratnam, who was well versed in Sanskrit and Hindu literature, was a dedicated social worker; and his mother Vishalakshi was a devout Hindu Brahmin woman, immersed in tradition, busy in puja and visiting temples.[4] Sri Sri showed religious interest at a very early age, "for he was often found sitting in peaceful meditation,"[5] and it is said that he learnt Sanskrit and could recite part of Bhagavad Gītā at the age of four. When he reached the age of nine he protested the practice of untouchability in her maternal grandmother's village[6]. According to his sister, Sri Sri was a very different person right from childhood; he was very brilliant, "when he was in eighth standard, students from tenth standard would come to him for advice. In his company, everyone felt good… He was very artistic. He would write poem, write and direct play."[7] Ramanjit Garewal maintains that at the age of four Sri Sri could recite the entire

[3] It may be interesting to note that Sri Sri Ravishankar was born on the *Adi Sankara Jayanti* and was given name on the birthday of Ramanuja and the place where he was born 'Papanasam' means 'the removal of all sins'.

[4] M.L. Ahuja, *Gurus: Ancient, Medieval and Modern*, (New Delhi: Rupa & Co., 2009), pp. 225-226.

[5] Rajiv Mehrotra, *The Mind of the Guru*, (New Delhi: Hay House Publishers (India) Pvt. Ltd., 2010), p. 170.

[6] Francois Gautier, *The Guru of Joy: Sri Sri Ravi Shankar & The Art of Living*, (New Delhi: Hay House Publishers (India) Pvt. Ltd., 2011), p. 39. (First published in 2002).

[7] *India Today*, November 12, 2001, p. 64.

Bhagavad Gita and by the age of nine, he had mastered Ṛg Veda.[8] As a young boy he would often tell his friends, "People all over the world are waiting for me."[9] He studied science and graduated at the age of seventeen from St. Stephen's College, Bangalore. They used to say, "By age seventeen, He had completed His education in both Vedic literature and modern science."[10] After graduation he had a choice to make: a bank job or a job with God: he chose the latter.

He joined Maharishi Mahesh Yogi of 'Transcendental Meditation' and worked with him for some time. Though very young, Maharishi recognized his ability and he was sent to various places in India and abroad to give talks on Vedas and science.[11] He had a successful time with Maharishi but in 1980 he parted company.[12] The main reason as to why Sri Sri left Maharishi according to Gautier was that the Transcendental Meditation movement tried to close down all the schools in South India and move the students to Delhi which was disapproved by Sri Sri.[13] However, Ravishankar explains, "There was no ill feeling. (But) I was not very comfortable with his claims of people flying... I was more interested in rural development. So, I went into villages and help people to integrate their lives and get stress out. I helped children study both ancient and modern science."[14]

It was in the year 1982 in Shimoga where a course conducted by him was going on, something phenomenal happened in the life of Ravishankar. He decided to go silent for ten days. He narrates, "An instinct comes that you want silence and so you follow it... On the bank of the Tunga river in Bhadravati in Karnataka."[15] It was during this ten days silence that the *Sudarshan Kriya,* claimed as a powerful breathing technique that can eliminate stress and energize the body physically and emotionally, was revealed to him. Guruji says, "It came like a poem, an inspiration. I learnt it and I started teaching it."[16]

Ravishankar founded several organizations for the welfare of the people. The most important and famous one is The Art of Living Foundation founded

---

[8] Ramanjit Garewal in the Introduction of the book – *Precious Gems of Wisdom – His Holiness Poojya Sri Sri Ravi Shankar*, compiled by Karishma Bajaj, (Mumbai: Magna Publishing Co. Ltd., 2008), p. v.

[9] In the Appendix of the book, Sri Sri Ravishankar, *Bang on the Door: A Collection of Talks*, Second Revised Edition, (Bangalore: Sri Sri Publication Trust, 2008), also Namrita Gautier and Francois Gautier, The Art of Healing, p. 7.

[10] *Ibid.*

[11] Gautier, *The Guru of Joy*, p. 57.

[12] *Ibid.*, p. 58.

[13] See *Ibid.*, pp. 63-64.

[14] *Reader Digest*, February 2007, p. 96.

[15] *Ibid.*

[16] *Ibid.*

in 1982 (but the Art of Living courses were conducted earlier as well). The Art of Living (AOL) is "an international, non-profit, educational and humanitarian organization. Its educational and self-development programs offer powerful tools to eliminate stress and foster a sense of well-being."[17] It is claimed that AOL reached an estimated 300 million people worldwide.[18] Apart from AOL, Sri Sri initiated several service organizations – aiming at the development of the rural poor, giving education, empowering women, etc. Some of the organizations that Sri Sri initiated include - International Association for Human Values (IAHV), a non-profit international organization founded in 1997. The purpose of IAHV is to foster a deeper understanding of the values that unite the global human community, and to encourage the practice of human values in everyday life. Another organization is Ved Vignan Maha Vidya Peeth (VVM). Under this organization various service projects such as rural development programmes, women's empowerment projects and educational initiatives, Vedic research, medical research and social research are carried out in India. In the year 1999, 'the Sri Sri Ravi Shankar Vidya Mandir' (SSRVM) Trust' was founded which is a charitable spiritual and educational public institution to impart a value-based education in a stress-free and child-friendly environment. The Trust supports several educational institutions, from rural schools to urban universities. Apart from these, for the development of rural areas 'the Sri Sri Rural Development Trust' was founded in 2001, with a vision to provide permanent and alternative sources of income to the rural population in India. The Trust initiates empowerment of rural women, vocational training programs for women and youth, self development workshops, free medical camps, and the Youth Leadership Training Program. Sri Sri and his organization also started various educational institutes like Agricultural Institute, Schools and Colleges, and for Management studies and Ayuvedic research, etc.[19]

Ravishankar also was involved in several social services like what they called 'Inclusive development' (or 5H – health, hygiene, homes, human values and harmony in diversity), peace initiatives, disaster relief, promoting literacy, women empowerment, prisoner rehabilitation, etc.[20]

Ravishankar, like many contemporary gurus, is associated with miracles, though it is not the primary feature of his teaching or ministry. Miracles like changing stone into diamond or silver or gold, healing of sick from cancer, heart problems, mental illness, etc. are reported to have taken place in his

---

[17] In the Official website of Sri Sri *http://srisriravishankar.org/biography* (28.11.2012).

[18] In the official website of Sri Sri *http://srisriravishankar.org/service-organizations/art-of-living* (28.11.2012).

[19] See Official website of Sri Sri, *http://srisriravishankar.org/*

[20] For details see Sri Sri Ravishankar, *Belongingness to Silence,* (Bangalore: Vyakti Vikas Kendra, India Publications, 2006), pp. 45-50.

ministry.[21] But the greatest miracle of all associated with Guruji, according to Francois Gautier, is changing the lives and natures of his disciples in a near-impossible way.[22]

2. Philosophical and Religious Teachings of Ravishankar: An Overview

Michael Fischman, an American instructor of AOL consciously or unconsciously summarizes the main purpose of Ravishankar and his AOL when he says in the introductory speech of one of the AOL courses: "We all want happiness, love, and peace. We fail to realize this because we are stressed. The breathing techniques that we learn here will help to release stress."[23] This is in consonance with the vision of Ravishankar inscribed in his Official Website: 'Violence-free, stress-free world.' His teaching covers a wide range of subjects that includes commentaries on the scriptures; discourses on love, wisdom, meditation, environmental and human rights issues, happiness, terrorism, dance and laughter, silence, other religious traditions, aphorism, guru, spirituality, etc. Books published by the Sri Sri Publications Trust that bear the name of Ravishankar as the author, are all collections of his numerous discourses on various subjects and they are not systematically or thematically arranged. His teaching is not put in a systematic order and the task of a research is to systematize and organize his religious and philosophical teachings by collecting and arranging from the numerous lectures and discourses published in a number of books.

An attempt is made here to systematize and summarize his philosophical and religious teachings as follows:-

2.1. God, Human Being and Creation

It is difficult to ascertain as to how far Sri Sri was influenced by his former guru Maharishi Mahesh Yogi but we may take it for granted that he would have

---

[21] For further study on this subject cf. Francois Gautier, *The Guru of Joy*, where Chapter 10 of this book talks about miracles associated with Sri Sri Ravishankar. Cf. for miracles Sri Sri Ravis Shankar, *An Intimate Note to the Seeker Vol. 4*, p. 80; Sri Sri Ravi Shankar, *An Intimate Note to the Sincere Seeker, Vol. 5*, compiled by Anne Elixhauser & Bill Hayden, (Bangalore: Vyakti Vikas Kendra, 2002), pp. 31, 68, 77, 84, 97. Cf. also Sri Sri Ravi Shankar, *An Intimate Note to the Seeker, Vol. 6,* compiled by Bill Hayden and Anne Elixhauser, (Bangalore: Vyakti Vikas Kendra, 2002), pp. 25, 27, 65; Sri Sri Ravi Shankar, *An Intimate Note to the Seeker, Vol. 1,* compiled by David L. Burge, (Santa Barbara: Art of Living Foundation, 2002; first published in 1997), p. 61. Also Sri Sri Ravi Shankar, *An Intimate Note to the Seeker, Vol. 2*, compiled by David L. Burge, (Santa Barbara: Art of Living Foundation, 2000), p. 66. Cf. also Namrita and Gautier, *The Art of Healing, op.cit.* In this book, the authors reported the testimonies of the devotees who received miraculous healing from different types of sickness, physical and mental.

[22] Gautier, *The Guru of Joy*, p. 159.

[23] *Ibid.*, p. 21.

been shaped to a great extent by the teachings and practices of Mahesh Yogi as he spent a number of his formative years with him. When asked: "What was Maharishi's influence on you", Sri Sri replies, "Love and a commitment to make a better society, an ideal society."[24] His pro-life philosophy, his understanding of life as having two aspects - matter and spirit, his 'this-worldly' orientedness, his concern for blending Vedas and modern science and the likes were all apparently inherited from his master Maharishi. Gautier, an ardent disciple of Sri Sri, says that the seed of a beautiful blend of Veda and science "sprouted in him when he came in contact with His Holiness Maharishi Mahesh Yogi."[25]

It is claimed that the Transcendental Meditation, Mahesh Yogi's primary yoga technique has a wide range of benefits, including reduction of stress and anxiety, improvement of health and brain function, enrichment of mental functioning, enhancement of personal relationships, an increase in job productivity and job satisfaction, and an increase of self-actualization.[26] Though the steps and actual technique vary between Sri Sri's *Sudarshan Kriya* and Transcendental Meditation, the primary goal of these two is almost the same, so it is apparent that Maharishi had a lasting impact upon the life of Ravishankar. We may even postulate that Sri Sri's organization – the 'Art of Living' and its whole activities is also an adaptation from Maharishi's book *The Science of Being and the Art of Living*.[27]

Maharishi is definitely the follower of non-dual philosophy of Śaṅkara but with substantial modification. He believes in a *nirguṇa* God, a God beyond qualities which he calls 'Creative Intelligence'. Unlike most of the Advaitin, he does not ascribe creation as *māyā*. He accepts Jñāna Yoga and Bhakti Yoga as paths of liberation but prefers the path called 'Transcendental Meditation' as it is, according to him, the easiest path to liberation.[28] In this sense, Sri Sri seems to be more faithful to Śaṅkara's Advaita Vedānta.

---

[24] Sri Sri in a personal interview by Rajiv Mehrotra, in Rajiv Mehrotra, *The Mind of the Guru: Conversations with Spiritual Masters*, (New Delhi: Hey House India, 2003), p. 174.

[25] Gautier, *The Guru of Joy*, p. 57.

[26] An Official website of Transcendental Meditation (TM), http://www.tm.org/tm-is-different (18.01.2013), and http://www.tm.org/maharishi (18.01.2013).

[27] Mahesh Yogi, *The Science of Being and the Art of Living*, (New Delhi: Allied Publishers, 1963). This book is one of the most important works of Maharishi. It is the summation of the practical wisdom of Vedic Ṛṣis and modern science. It deals with the practical philosophy of life – the purpose of life, individual and cosmic life, the 'Art of Living' – how human beings shall live full values of life, and paths to God realization and so on.

[28] Vishal Mangalwadi, *World of Gurus: A Critical Look at the Philosophies of India's Influential Gurus and Mystics*, Revised Edition, (Chicago: Cornerstone Press, 1992, first Published in 1987), pp. 74-77; also Yogi, *The Science of Being and the Art of Living, op.cit.*

Sri Sri follows and praises Advaita Vedānta system as: "Einstein's theory of relativity correlates with the *Advaita* (non-dual) philosophy."[29] He maintains the essential oneness of God, human and the rest of the creation. Sri Sri admits that God is not easy to explain in human terms and categories. God is beyond all concepts. It is an experience. "God is the eternal 'I don't know.'"[30] In the midst of the unknowable-ness, the good part is "You can be God. You can live in God." Though you cannot know God, "You can experience God. Whether you know it or not, experience it or not, you are That."[31] No doubt that with these words Sri Sri reflects Upaniṣadic explication of Brahman as *neti neti* and *tat tvam asi*. He explains the indwelling God, the *tat tvam asi* God as follows:

> God is the junction of presence and present. Whenever every cell, every atom of the mind and body get totally immersed in the presence and present, you experience something ecstatic, something beyond this world. An experience of eternity comes. This is "Me! Me" dissolves... There is something. And what is that something? You don't know? That is presence. A presence where only knower remains, is God.[32]

According to Guruji, God is Omnipresent which means He is everywhere, in the rich or in the sinner as much as He is in the wonderful. "There is Divinity everywhere...The bird singing outside in that small, little body is Divine!"[33] In a personal interview he states:

> God is permeating like air everywhere...nothing can exist outside of it. So, Brahman is in every cell, in every cell of everything in the universe. So, there is no one thing that is devoid of God... We say mother, father, the guru and the guest are all form of God. ... There is that concept that God lives in everyone, in everybody... We say God is existence, consciousness and love. Whenever you find existence, consciousness and love, that is the manifestation of God.[34]

---

[29] Sri Sri Ravi Shankar, *An Intimate Note to the Sincere Seeker, Vol. 7*, compiled by Bill Hayden &Anne Elixhauser, (Bangalore: Vyakti Vikas Kendra, 2003), p. 71.

[30] Sri Sri Ravishankar, *God Loves Fun*, (Bangalore: Sri Sri Publications Trust, 2008), p. 41.

[31] *Ibid.*

[32] *Ibid.*, p. 53.

[33] Sri Sri Ravishankar, *Living the Mystery of Life*, (Bangalore: Sri Sri Publications Trust, 2012), p. 132.

[34] A personal Interview with him on 27.11. 2012 at his āśram, Bangalore, where the author of this book met him and had extensive interaction with him.The script of Author's Interview with Sri Sri is put in Appendix.

As we are not separate from God, it is wrong to say "God is speaking to me" or "I have a message from God," because, this is just our consciousness split into two where one part of our own consciousness becomes God, another part becomes our mind. That is not God. God is the totality. Everything is in God. There is nothing that can be outside of God. Whether good or evil, both exist in God.[35] Having stressed the *nirguṇa* aspect of God as a true *advaitin*, Ravishankar, in the mean time, projects God as *saguṇa*, who possesses six attributes and God in this aspect is called *Bhagawan*. The Six attributes of God are - God as the *Presence* whom we can approach in prayer; God as the *True Fame* – the entire creation tells his story, the fame which lasted not for few years but goes beyond time and space; God as *Wealth* – material comfort, health, success, courage, friendliness, skill, dignity and the memory of our Source; God as *Dharma* – righteousness, the path, the goal, the totality of life; God as *Wisdom*; and God as *Renunciation*.[36]

Primarily, God for Sri Sri is characterless, ineffable eternal Consciousness, but he also acknowledges God with personality who is the object of worship. This is to make concession for the beginners to worship God as a *person* as the first step and then move on to the higher level of spirituality where God is recognized in its true reality, as pure consciousness, the *nirguṇa* Brahman.

Ravishankar explains God in relation to human being beautifully as follows:

> God is never an object of isolation but the very core of your being. The difference between Self (human) and God is just like the wave and the ocean. Can there be a wave without the ocean?...So you are made up of God!...When you want to see God as something, as an object, then it is not everywhere. Then you are not God. This wanting to see God as separate from you is also an illusion. God is not an object of senses, but the feeling of feelings, the presence of presence, the sound of silence, the light of life, the essence of the world and the taste of bliss… God is never an object of isolation. God is the sum totality. When you dissolve, God remains. When you are there, there is no God. Either you can be there, or God can be there, not both. So when you meditate, you become one with God. You are God. That is why it is said, *Tat tvam asi*, meaning, 'Thou art that.'[37]

---

[35] Ravishankar, *God Loves Fun*, p. 41.

[36] Cf. Sri Sri Ravishankar, *Punarnava: New Again*, (Bangalore: Sri Sri Publications Trust, 2009), pp. 35-49.

[37] In an official website of AOL: http:// srisriravishankar.org/node/50, (4.7.2011).

As a non-dualist, Sri Sri has high regard for human being. He said that when a river meets the ocean, the river no longer maintains separate identity, it becomes the ocean. Likewise the moment a devotee meets God, he or she becomes God.[38] Thus, Sri Sri's concept of God, human and creation as essentially non-dual and the relationship between them as a non-dual relationship perfectly reflect Śaṅkara's Advaita Vedānta.

2.2. Love is God

An interesting feature of Sri Sri Ravishankar's concept of God is that for him God and Love are synonymous, that is why he emphasized so much on love in all his lectures and discourses. Responding to a question: "Who is God", Sri Sri says, "Love is God and everything is love. The whole creation is filled with love." Moving away from the general conception of love as 'feeling or emotion' he says, "… get into that God consciousness, the highest consciousness. That is love."[39] Sri Sri is reluctant to say God is love, but rather he says, "God is not love, love is God."[40]Again, "Love is what you are made up of. The consciousness in you is love. Love is not just emotion. It is the very state of your being. It is the pulse in you. You may call it God. You may call it pure consciousness. You may call it the supreme or unseen power… When you become love you dissolve, you go beyond."[41] In his Commentary on *Bhakti Sūtra* of Nārada, he says, "Life spring from love – the origin is love,"[42] indicating that the source of existence is Love itself. The place he assigns to love is interesting:

> Love is present in the entire creation… Because of love the planets are moving in their orbits, the sun is shining, and the stars are there. There is love in every atom, and that is why the electron is moving around the charged particle. The charge of attraction, the charge in this entire creation is a power, is love.[43]

---

[38] Ravi Shankar, *An Intimate Note to the Seeker, Vol. 6*, p.18.

[39] Ravishankar, *Living the Mystery of Life*, p. 139. For detail study of his concept of love, see Sri Sri Ravishankar, *Love is not an Emotion-It is Your Very Existence*, (Bangalore: Sri Sri Publications Trust, 2012).

[40] Ravishankar, *Love is not an Emotion*, p. 45.

[41] Sri Sri Ravishankar, *Bang on the Door: A collection of Talks*, Second Revised Edition, (Bangalore: Sri Sri Publication Trust, 2008), pp. 93-94, see Sri Sri Ravi Shankar, *An Intimate Note to the Sincere Seeker, Vol. 3*, compiled by David L. Burge, (Santa Barbara: Art of Living Foundation, 2000, first published in 1998), p. 43.

[42] Sri Sri Ravishankar, *Nārada Bhakti Sūtra*, (Bangalore: Sri Sri Publications Trust, 2003), p. 1.

[43] Sri Sri Ravishankar, *Wisdom for the New Millennium*, (Mumbai: Jaico Publishing House, 2005), p. 74.

2.3. Ways of Spiritual Elevation

Ravishankar teaches several processes or practices by which one can elevate his/her spiritual life. *Firstly*, it is by *Seva* (service) which is strongly emphasized by him. He maintains, "Our first and foremost commitment in the world is to do *seva* or service."[44] The realization that we are here in this world to do *seva* dissolves the "I" and when the "I" dissolves, worries dissolves.[45] Nevertheless, the motive of service should be right. He says, "Most of the work in the society is done out of ego... Real service is when you feel that you have not done enough."[46] Again, "*Seva* is not something you do out of convenience or for pleasure. The ultimate purpose of life is to be of service... when you make service your sole purpose in life, it eliminates fear, brings focus in your mind and purposefulness,"[47] it will reward you immediately, the reward is for sure and is always more than your doing.[48] His emphasis on *seva* led him run several social service centers for the benefit of the needy as highlighted before.

Secondly, having stressed the importance of joy and because of which he earned the appellation 'Guru of Joy', Sri Sri also emphasizes the importance of singing, dancing and laughter for the improvement of the quality of life and growing in the spiritual life. He even exaggerates its essentiality by proclaiming thus:

> God will dance in our life when the day dawns in laughter and love. The true prayer is laughing in the morning. Don't just be laughing outside but from deep inside. Laughter comes from the center of our Being, from the core of our heart... True laughter is true prayer... There is nothing in life that is more worthy than your laughter.[49]

He advises his disciples to see life as a game to play joyfully. "You are God, you know it. I am God, I know it. So let us play."[50] This will result in oneness. God is inviting us every day to sit with Him, "I am doing everything. You come and sit with me. Whatever needs to be done, I will get it done through

[44] Sri Sri Ravishankar, *Celebrating Silence*, Second Edition, (Bangalore: Sri Sri Publication Trust, 2008), p. 108.

[45] Sri Sri Ravishankar, *Celebrating Silence*, Second Edition, (Bangalore: Sri Sri Publication Trust, 2008), p. 108.

[46] Gautier, *The Guru of Joy*, pp. 214, 217.

[47] Sri Sri Ravi Shankar, *An Intimate Note to the Seeker, Vol. 4:* July 30, 1998 – July 28, 1999, compiled by Anne Elixhauser & Bill Hayden, (Bangalore: Vyakti Vikas Kendra, 1999), p. 37.

[48] Ravi Shankar, *An Intimate Note to the Seeker, Vol. 2*, p. 84.

[49] Ravishankar, *God Loves Fun*, p. 33.

[50] *Ibid.*, p. 61.

you. You simply stop existing.[51] Here Sri Sri suggests that our ego, our pride, the 'Me-*ness*' should be put to death in order to have oneness with God.

Thirdly, the apparent opposite to what is suggested above as another important practice to be cultivated is *Silence* which is another watchword of Guruji. It is no wonder that he emphasized so much on silence because it is silence, we may say, that made Ravishankar as he is now – as pointed out earlier, it was during his ten days silence in 1982 that the *Sudarshan Kriya* was born. Sri Sri believes that communication is possible, sometime more effectively, in silence. He says, "You should have belongingness to silence. Silence is the mother of all creativity. Silence is the mother of invention. Silence is the basis of love."[52] For him silence is the key to reach God in us: "The moment you relax, and go deep into silence, you perceive the Self, right there."[53] Thus, he advices his listeners to observe silence at least once in a while –"Take some time off – three-four days, and go deep into silence. This is essential," because this will make you grow in your spirituality very fast.[54] In deep silence there is the absence of feeling somebody, some things, some objects, only one feels God. Here, duality ends, oneness is attained. Celebration such as singing, dancing, which are integral to Sri Sri's programme and silence look contradictory, but, he says that they are not. "Spirituality is a harmonious blend of outer silence and inner celebration; and also inner silence and outer celebration!"[55]

2.4. Enlightenment

Though Sri Sri emphasizes stress-free, violence-free life on the earth, this is not the end of his religious and philosophical teaching, but just a mean to the end. Like all the Masters, his religious teaching points to the state where humans receive salvation or enlightenment, though this subject is not frequently discussed by him. For Sri Sri enlightenment is the realization that all is one – "When we see that there is no other, it is all me, that is enlightenment". The problem with us is we exist as having separate identity, "when you stop existing, you become everybody, you become noting, empty"[56] and that is enlightenment.

---

[51] *Ibid.*

[52] Ravishankar, *Belongingness to Silence*, pp.1-2.

[53] *Ibid.*, pp. 28-29.

[54] *Ibid.*, p. 40.

[55] Ravishankar, *An Intimate Note to the Sincere Seeker, Vol. 5*, p. 20.

[56] Ravishankar, *Living the Mystery of Life*, p. 163.

2.5. The Place of Other Religions

According to him religions of the world are essentially the same, teaching the same spiritual truth and leading us to the same goal or God. Insofar as moral and spiritual values are concerned all religious traditions talk the same thing. Symbols, practices, rituals and customs vary from one tradition to another. "Unfortunately", says Ravishankar, "the so-called spiritual journey has divided human beings and torn apart the whole society."[57] This is because we focus on the skin of banana, the outer visible aspect of religion and throw away the banana, the inner spiritual reality of each religion.[58] He has a strong view of the interconnectedness of all religions at the deeper spiritual level. When we meditate deep enough, we see what is present in the *akashic* records - in the subtle atmosphere we will see that connection between all the religions of the world does exists.[59]

His positive attitude towards other religions is well attested from his speeches, discourses and writings; his organization, *The Art of Living* even published the collection of scriptures of major world religions under the title: *Timeless Wisdom: The Book of All Religions*.[60] The main Hall of his *āśram* at Bangalore, which is called Vishalakshi Mantap, contains symbols and images of all major religions of the world to show that none of these is discriminated.[61] Sri Sri concludes:

> It is not necessary to see one tradition as better than another. All the religions of the world belong to all the world's people. The Divine has brought forth knowledge in different parts of the world at different times. Each of us belongs to the Divine and can claim all that the Divine has given as our own.[62]

Christianity is a bridge between Eastern and Western traditions, the bridge between Hinduism and Judaism, the two oldest living religions. Sri Sri draws many similarities between Hinduism and Christianity. The use of orange robe, bells for worship, altars and icons, rosary and *japamala*, incense, sacred thread, ash, holy water, leaves, candles and lamps, religious processions, meditation and fasting, monasteries and *gurukulas*, praying for the departed souls, etc. are

---

[57] Sri Sri Ravishankar, *Bang on the Door,* (Bangalore: Sri Sri Publication Trust, 2008), p. 10.

[58] *Ibid.*

[59] Sri Sri Ravishankar, *Hinduism and Christianity*, 2nd Edition, (Bangalore: Vyakti Vikas Kendra India, 1999), p. 2.

[60] In this book scriptures from Hinduism, Buddhism, Jainism, Christianity, Judaism, Islam, Sikhism, Zoroastrianism, Taoism and Confucianism are collected. See Timeless Wisdom: The Book of all Religions, (Bangalore: Sri Sri Publication Trust, 2008).

[61] He stated this in a personal interview with him at his āśram, Bangalore on 27.10.2012.

[62] Gautier, *The Guru of Joy*, p. 203.

some of the common practices Sri Sri has listed along with so many common beliefs in Hinduism and Christianity.[63]

2.6. Belongingness to Others

One of the most striking features of Sri Sri's teaching is the emphasis on 'belongingness' that we, irrespective of gender, caste, race, nationality and religion, belong together. We should keep aside the narrowness of our religious and ethnical convictions because we belong to each other. An enlightened and matured person would claim the whole world as his/her wealth. The ability to say that 'the whole entirety belongs to me and I belong to everybody' is enlightenment.[64] Sri Sri emphasizes that all religions belong to us. "What I would tell you is you own everything, all the ten religions in the world belong to you."[65] In divine creation, there is no separateness. It is oneness, whole human race is one. "The search for this unity, the uniting factor, is the real spiritual journey."[66] Consequently, he advises: "Have belongingness to the Universe... to Divinity... to everybody."[67]

2.7. Sudarshan Kriya

Sudarshan Kriya, the yoga technique developed by Ravishankar consists of cycles of rhythmic breathing patterns of long, medium and short durations. It is claimed that *Sudarshan Kriya* cleanses the body, mind and spirit from within thereby bringing the rejuvenation of mind and body, enhancing better atmosphere for meditation to climb the ladder of spirituality.[68] As it is meant to be taught by the experts in the Course conducted by the AOL organization only, the details of *Sudarshan Kriya* are not made available in the form of book or other means to people who are not enrolled for the course. Our sources of knowledge come from the testimonies of those who had done *Sudarshan Kriya* in the AOL course. The following steps are involved in the practice of *Sudarshan Kriya*:[69]

---

[63] For details cf. Ravishankar, *Hinduism and Christianity.*

[64] Ravishankar, *Wisdom for the New Millennium*, p. 33.

[65] Sri Sri Ravishankar, "Jesus Embodiment of Love", a lecture delivered at California, USA on 8th Aug. 1996, in Audio CD produced by Sri Sri Publication Trust, Bangalore, 2011.

[66] Ravishankar, *Bang on the Door*, p. 10.

[67] Ravishankar, *Belongingness to Silence*, pp. 5-6.

[68] Official website of Art of Living Organisation - http://www.artofliving.org/in-en/what-is-sudarshan-kriya (16.01.2013). *Cf.* for the difference between Yoga and Sudarshan Kriya *http://www.artofliving.org/in-en/sudarshan-kriya-faq* (16.01.2013); *http://www.artofliving.org/in-en/sudarshankriya-origin* (16.01.2013) for the origin of Sudarshan Kriya; and *http://www.artofliving.org/in-en/sri-sri-sudarshan-kriya* (16.01.2013) for Sri Sri Ravishankar on Sudarshan Kriya.

[69] These steps are adopted from Sam Thomas who himself attended AOL Basic Course, cf. "Art of Living in the Teaching of Sri Sri Ravi Shankar: An Appraisal", (An unpublished B.D.

Sudarshan Kriya is done in the AOL Basic Course after practicing *Prāṇāyāma*, *Ujjāyi*, and *Bhastrikā*. In *Prāṇāyāma* one takes arms from down to up incrementally which helps muscles in the neck and shoulders to relax, relieving pressure built-up in them due to stress. *Ujjāyi* breathing technique concentrates attention in the spinal cord which controls breathing in normal circumstances also. *Bhastrikā* is a process of breathing out forcefully by which the respiratory tract gets purified and expanded. These steps help the body and mind and prepare one to do *Sudarshan Kriya*. *Sudarshan Kriya* involves the following steps:

- Sitting in a *Vajrāsana* or *Sukhāsana* position that straightens the spinal cord
- Closing of eyes in order to prevent one from external disturbances
- Rhythmic inhalations and exhalations of long, medium and short duration. The *long duration* breath involves twenty time inhalations and exhalations. The *medium duration* breath is done forty times and the *short duration* breath is also done for forty times.
- Repeat the process of *long*, *medium* and *short* cycles of breath two more times.
- To close with five *long* cycle of breath and relax.

With this the '*Short Sudarshan Kriya*' is completed. The *Long Sudarshan Kriya* has more sets of cycles of breath. The *Short Sudarshan Kriya* is normally practiced in the presence of the AOL teacher and it takes 30-45 minutes. It is recommended to be practiced in an empty stomach after bath and it is advised not to take bath right after it. It is patently clear that *Sudarshan Kriya* points primarily to the stress-free-happy life here on the earth as the principal goal and the liberation of the bonded soul, which is the primary concern of Hinduism, is not the focal point here or rather it is neglected.

Ravishankar's philosophy is never deviated from Advaita Vedānta, his concept of God as the indwelling God; human being in his/her true nature as God - all reflect Śaṅkar's Advaita Vedānta. However, he seems to be more concerned for the life here and now – a stress free, violence-free, productive and happy life. His *Sudarshan Kriya* is also primarily sailing towards this. This emphasis brings the importance of celebration, singing, dancing and laughter which all have their productive effects on the stressful and violence-prone individuals. Otherworldly motif appears to be secondary in his thought. His

---

Thesis submitted to Bishop's College, Kolkata, 2006), pp. 53-54, and also Sumana Kamath of Vyakti Vikas Kendra, Mangalore Information Centre, as he explained to the Times of India, Bangalore, in http://articles.timesofindia.indiatimes.com/2003-09-09/bangalore/27189063_1_sudarshan-kriya-sudarshan-kriya-spinal-cord (16.01.2013). Cf. http://pranajournal.com/art-of-living/sudarshan-kriya/ (18.01.2013).

lectures and discourses are more of 'wisdom sayings' that deals with day to day life of a human, but less a scriptural discourse.[70] He is a model of religious tolerance who does not shy away from using Bible alongside Buddhist teachings and other religious texts to elaborate his philosophical proposition. Respect and acceptance of other religions is the hallmark of Sri Sri religious teaching because he considers that all religions lead us to spiritual upliftment, they teach oneness and there is a striking similarity.[71] He teaches us that we should own religious resources of others as others own ours. His positive attitude towards human as 'potentially Divine' encourages Sri Sri to take up tremendous social services for those who are in need, because, according to him, we are one, we belong together.

3. Ravishankar's Interpretation of Jesus Christ: *Jesus, the Embodiment of Love*

Unlike the other three gurus we have discussed, Ravishankar does not produce huge literatures on Jesus Christ and this leaves us with a limited source to construct his Christology. One of the most important sources is his lecture on 'Jesus the Embodiment of Love' which is available in the form of Audio CD[72] and also part of which forms a Chapter of his book *Wisdom for the New Millennium.*[73] A part from this, a recent publication - *Living the Mystery of Life*[74] contains a chapter on 'Jesus and Christianity', which also helps us in our investigation. Few other books also contain his references to Jesus.[75] The writer of this book Sri Sri at his Bangalore *āśram* on the 27th October, 2012 and had personal interview with him. By using these sources I venture to advance Ravishankar's interpretation of Jesus Christ.

3.1. The Background of his Interpretation

As underlined before, Ravishankar has three basic commitments in relation to religion and spirituality – commitment to Advaita Vedānta school of thought, commitment to traditional Hinduism and commitment to the validity of all religions as the expression of One and the same God. It is natural that Sri Sri

---

[70] It may be mentioned here that Sri Sri published few commentaries on religious texts, cf. *Patanjali Yoga Sutras: A Commentary by H.H. Sri Sri Ravi Shankar, Vol. 1*, (Bangalore: Sri Sri Publications Trust, 2010), *Shiva Sūtras: A Commentary by His Holiness Sri Sri Ravi Shankar,* (Bangalore: Sri Sri Publications Trust, 2010), Sri Sri Ravishankar, *Nārada Bhakti Sūtra: The Aphorism of Love*, (Bangalore: Sri Sri Publications Trust, 2003).

[71] Ravishankar, *Hinduism and Christianity*, p. 1.

[72] Ravishankar, "Jesus Embodiment of Love".

[73] Ref. Ravishankar, *Wisdom for the New Millennium.*

[74] Sri Sri Ravishankar, *Living the Mystery of Life*, (Bangalore: Sri Sri Publication Trust, 2012).

[75] Sri Sri Ravishankar, *Hinduism and Christianity,* op.cit. and Gautier, *The Guru of Joy.*

would have been influenced by these factors in his interpretations of Jesus Christ as no interpreter is free from subjectivity.

Sri Sri states that the true knowledge of Jesus is gained only with the heart by people who have the Spirit, the Life Force (*prāṇa*). You cannot understand what Jesus said if you are not living with the Life Force; concepts will be there at the head, but heart can be understood by the heart only. Mind cannot understand Jesus, only heart can feel the presence of Jesus. The Jews who crucified him were not bad people, they were ignorant. As they were not born out of the spirit though they have read all the scriptures and books, they could not understand Jesus. To know Jesus one has to be born twice, born of the Spirit, *Prāṇa*, the Life Force.[76] Sri Sri asserts that vision of Jesus is possible, "When you go deep in meditation, there are other realities. There is the world of light… When you go deep in meditation mind is still, there are no thoughts, there is no eye, then the knowledge become very spontaneous… In that level in meditation, you are in touch with the world of light. Jesus is definitely part of that light."[77] So, he acknowledges intuitive, mystical and experiential knowledge of Jesus as more authentic than the knowledge gained from the reading of scriptures and theological books.

3.2. Jesus as One of the Prophets

Ravishankar is reluctant to give any special status to Jesus Christ; his philosophy of religion allows him not to do so. As all are conceived as one, higher and lower concepts have no room in him. So, Jesus is also understood as one of the prophets. He is unique in his own way but not in comparison with others. Sri Sri puts Jesus in the same category with Lord Kṛṣṇa and Lord Rāmā and declines to comments who is higher and who is lower just as it is not possible to say which is higher between banana and apple.[78] Jesus is the son of God just as we all are. He is also God in so far as he is Love,[79] the embodiment of love. For that matter we are also God because all is God. Hinduism testifies that father, mother, guru, guest – all are God. In this sense Jesus is also God.[80] The uniqueness of Jesus lies, according to Sri Sri, not on his body but on he being the manifestation of love. "That is the uniqueness of Jesus, not as a body but as love, as consciousness, he is in your heart, in everywhere. In that sense he

---

[76] Ravishankar, "Jesus Embodiment of Love".

[77] This is the answer he gave when I asked him, "Have you ever have vision of or communion with Jesus", indicating faintly that he knew Jesus not only from the scripture but by experiencing personally in mystical union. Personal interview with him at his āśram, Bangalore on 27.10.2012.

[78] *Ibid.*

[79] *Ibid.*

[80] *Ibid.*

all permeates."[81] Ravishankar, therefore, is not interested in interpreting Jesus as the Son of God, a member of the Trinity, an incarnate God or God himself as most Christians believe him to be. Those are not the categories in which he sees Jesus.

3.3. Jesus the Embodiment of Love

Ravishankar exalted Jesus as the embodiment of love. "Jesus and love are synonymous. If you say love, you need not say Jesus."[82] Love makes people courageous. That is why Jesus was courageous. He completely overthrows the common concepts of people such as the strong shall inherit the earth; for Jesus it is the meek that will inherit the earth, for love makes people meek. "Love is the strongest force in this universe and yet, it makes you meek, it makes you weak."[83] When Jesus says, "It was better Judas had not been born at all", he did not say those words out of anger but of love. He could feel the pain and suffering Judas would go through. "His love for him was so great that saying, 'I wish he was not born' shows the height of love he had for him."[84] Jesus' love for the people is seen in his identification with his disciple as 'friend'. He says, "See, I call you friend, I treat you like my friend, not as servant." It is the best way to share love. Because of love Jesus identified himself as 'friend' and not as king or lord or one who is in authority. He is opening his arm and says, "Come, you are my friend... Give me a seat in your heart. See me in everyone you see around you. Love everyone as much as I love you, or as much as you love me. Share that with everyone around."[85]

Sri Sri emphasizes the importance of loving Jesus who is living today. He says, "When you are truly in love with Jesus, you will see Jesus in every name, in every form, in every nook and corner of the planet and beyond."[86] He cautions people not to limit Jesus to a certain time in history and place. He advices his audience to go to the values that Jesus truly represents so that they will know that Jesus "is not the past, he is here now. And he will be in future, also forever and ever and ever."[87]

3.4. The Kingdom of God is within You

The disciples fought for a place in the right and left hands of Jesus because they did not know that in the Kingdom of God there is not right or left. "Once

---

[81] *Ibid.*

[82] Ravishankar, *Wisdom for the New Millennium*, p. 113.

[83] Ravishankar, *Wisdom for the New Millennium*, p. 113.

[84] *Ibid.*, p. 115.

[85] *Ibid.*, p. 118.

[86] *Ibid.*, p. 122.

[87] *Ibid.*, p. 123.

you go within, there is not right or left! There is no front or back."[88] Jesus did all he could to make the disciples get into the soul, the spirit, the source of life, the Self. In order to do this we need to break through the limited concepts of relating ourselves with something or somebody or identities and recognize the Divinity within us. That is to realize that we are much more than just a human. "You are part of the Divine and you will inherit the kingdom, which is right here, right within you."[89] Jesus may have lived two thousand years ago, but Christ consciousness being eternal was in existence even before, because, the Divine consciousness is beyond time and space.[90] This is suggestive of the possibility and importance of realizing the living Jesus, or what we may call 'Christ consciousness'.

3.5. Jesus is *Not* the Only Way!

Hindu spiritual leaders who try to interpret Jesus positively have always struggled with the exclusive claim of Jesus: "the only begotten Son of God" and "I am the only way. No one come to the Father except through me." Ravishankar is no exception. He explains - When Jesus said that he is the only Son of our Father, he meant 'our Father', the Father of everybody. Jesus' intention was to say "I am the son of the only Father." He explicates this problem as follows –

> This has been wrongly understood. If Jesus is the only son of the Father, who are the others then? Is the whole mankind the sons of Satan? Then you would call him Jesus' Father, not 'Our' Father. From the original Hebrew when the words were translated, a lot was lost on the way. Often Jesus has said, 'Let us pray to Our Father in heaven'. Again he says 'Our Father', and he means the Father of all the living beings in the world.[91]

It is clear from this quotation that Sri Sri is not well-versed in Christian scripture, but what he wanted to convey is clear, that Jesus is not the 'only' Son of God. However, Sri Sri gives compensation to Jesus when he says, "Of course, he is worthy calling 'the only son' because he embodies what the Father is, totally. Though everyone is still the son of the same Father, or daughter of the same Father, it is, in a way, justified to call Jesus the only son."[92]

Ravishankar, while defending the validity of 'other saviours' in accordance with his theology of religion and at the same time trying to be

[88] *Ibid.*, p. 114.

[89] *Ibid.*, p. 115.

[90] Ravishankar, *Hinduism and Christianity*, p. 18.

[91] *Ibid.* Cf. Sri Ravishankar, *Living the Mystery of Life,* p. 131.

[92] Ravishankar, *Wisdom for the New Millennium*, p. 118.

true to Jesus, fosters an interesting interpretation of Jesus' words – "All those who came before me are robbers and thieves." He says that Jesus meant to indicate that those who came before him – possibly other 'saviours' like Kṛṣṇa or Rāmā, etc.

> are robbing your mind of the present moment… You are dreaming of somebody in the future or glorifying someone in the past! The Divine is in the resent… Your mind has been stolen by the past or the future. I am here to bring it to now, the present moment. I am the only way. If you cannot see the Divinity in me when I am right in front of you, do you think you are going to see the Divinity in the future or in the past? Forget about it. I am the gate. Look at me, see what I manifest and that is what you are…[93]

Elsewhere Sri Sri also says - Jesus said 'they are robbers' because they have stolen your mind. You are always thinking about the past, longing for some great person in the past. So he said, "NOW! NOW! You see greatness right NOW, in front of you. See it and surrender."[94]

When Jesus says, "I am the only way," he does not mean that you cannot attain the Kingdom of God unless you believe in Jesus. Kṛṣṇa and Buddha also made the same exclusive statement. God is one eternal and omnipotent; we cannot limit the scope and mercy of God that he makes only one way. "I am the only way" means that the abstract cannot be approached directly, but only through persons like the teachers, the enlightened ones. Another reason for saying this is to draw the attention of the people. Still another meaning of this statement is that the teacher comes to be a bridge so that you can move from what is known to what is unknown.[95] It was his way of saying, "I am the only goal for you. What are you looking for here and there? Come to me… When I am here in front of you, you are thinking about Moses and Isaac…No, drop all this, surrender to me. When you surrender here, right now, that is how you reach my father."[96] So, Jesus' words should not be taken literally because there could be contradictions and problems. For instance, Jesus is described as the only begotten Son of God, at the same time he instructs us to pray, "Our heavenly Father." Is there one son or many sons? These things need to be pondered upon.[97]

---

[93] *Ibid.*, p. 119.

[94] Ravishankar, *Living the Mystery of Life*, p. 128.

[95] Gautier, *The Guru of Joy,* pp. 201-203. Cf. Ravishankar, *Living the Mystery of Life,* p. 128.

[96] Ravishankar, *Living the Mystery of Life,* pp. 127-128.

[97] Gautier, *The Guru of Joy*, p. 203.

Therefore, Jesus is the 'only way' for those who are listening to him. If one is not able to see Divinity through Jesus, there is less hope for him/her to see through 'other saviours' also, because "Jesus leads you to your own Being, your own Self, your own Divinity, that is deep within you."[98] So, the validity of 'other saviours' is not rule out, oneness – *advaita* is held high to show the fact of the existence of such saviours other than Jesus in this world. Sri Sri treads this path because his Hindu commitment *does not* allow having only one unique Saviour for the whole humanity, and his *advaitic* experience *does allow* him to hold all the divergent spiritual experiences as the expression of the One Ultimate Reality.

3.6. The Cross of Jesus

Jesus Christ is acknowledged by Christians as one who suffered and died on the cross for the sin of humankind. But Sri Sri does not endorse this view, because according to him, Jesus never said - "I am suffering for your sin". This statement is "just a way people used to awaken other people," a tactic to wake the sleeping people, another way of saying "Look, doomsday is coming, come on, wake up. Hell is going to open." In those days, this type of waking up call is needed because of the context. But today, we do not need to induce fear; we can use the tactic of love.[99] For Sri Sri, whether Jesus died on the cross or not is not important. "It does not matter to me whether he died on the cross or he did not die or he went to Kashmir (after crucifixion)… It does not matter. What is most important is the teaching, the message of love and universal brotherhood (*sic*)."[100] So, the significance of Jesus Christ is not what 'he did' on the cross – his death and resurrection, but his message of love. It was Jesus, who brought the idea of piety and love among the Jews who "only perceived God as one who is punishing, an angry God, a chief dictator,"[101] and the message of love that Jesus introduced to the Jewish thought is innovative and it is that which is the most significant.

3.7. Transcending Mind

Jesus said, "I have come to put man against man, father against son, daughter against mother." Quoting this verse, Ravishankar says that very few people have really understood what it means. According to him, this particular verse indicates that some people whom we consider as friends are making us to have faith in the material things thereby weakening our faith in the spiritual thing. So, they are not our friend! When Jesus said, "I have come to put fire, not peace,"

[98] Ravishankar, *Wisdom for the New Millennium*, p. 120.

[99] *Ibid.*, pp. 124-125.

[100] Personal Interview with Sri Sri Ravishankar.

[101] *Ibid.*

it shows that he knew the depth of slumber. When we talk something nice, peaceful, everybody will go to sleep and when there is something sensational, people wake up and listen. These rather harsh words of Jesus should not be taken to indicate that Jesus did not show love, but it is his method to wake you up. This is how human mind operates. Ravishankar, thus, concludes saying, Jesus made all efforts so that people may cross the mind and get into the soul, the spirit, the source of life, the Self. Jesus wanted us to recognize that we are not limited human being, small and helpless. Divinity is within you.[102]

3.8. Jesus at the Doorsteps

Jesus said, "I am not yet one with my Father", but at the same time he also said, "I and my Father are one". There is no contradiction here. In reality Jesus was already at home, if he is not, nobody will follow him. But when he said that he is not yet one with his Father, he meant to say that he is at the doorstep, waiting for the others to come, waiting in the rain, in the snow, in the storm, in the sun – a perfect demonstration of perfect love.[103]

3.9. Jesus Lived in India

Ravishankar appears to believe in the popular notion that Jesus at the age of around fourteen came to India and lived here till he reached the age of thirty when he returned to Palestine to finish his mission. During his stay, he visited many places, preaching and teaching to the Indian people side by side learning from them. "Christianity has so many similarities to Indian traditions, that is a good indication that Jesus spent a lot of time in India."[104] He maintains, "If you look at many of the teachings of Jesus you find that all are from the Upaniṣadic lore."[105] Sri Sri observes that by a direct knowledge from the consciousness, through deep meditation, which is a more reliable knowledge than any other, we can see that Jesus lived in India and went back to Palestine wearing an orange robe – the typical attire for a spiritual leader in India.[106] However, as this is a contentious issue, Sri Sri, in attempting to evade controversy, softens his stand on this issue by saying that the authenticity of Jesus lived in India is not yet proven, though "there is a lot of thing to believe that Jesus spent twelve years in India," so, he leaves this controversy to scholars and historians.[107]

Unlike Paramhansa Yogananda and Osho Rajneesh, who attempted to interpret Jesus' teaching by a systematic commentary to the written scripture

---

[102] Ravishankar, *Wisdom for the New Millennium*, p. 115.

[103] *Ibid.*, p. 116.

[104] *Ibid.*, p. 127.

[105] Ravishankar, *Hinduism and Christianity*, p. 18.

[106] *Ibid.*, pp. 2-3.

[107] Personal Interview with Sri Sri Ravishankar.

either from the Bible or apocryphal writing, Ravishankar does not give serious effort to look at the Bible or interpret it systematically in order to bring out the meanings of Jesus. His speeches reveal that he has fairly good knowledge of the Gospels, he even admits that he used to read the Bible,[108] but he does not care to look at the context of those verses. In his interpretation, he picks the verses randomly that suit his purpose and gives his own meanings. His pre-supposed idea, which is in tune with general Hindu conviction, that there are plural ways to reach the one God, and his commitment to *advaitic* notion of oneness of existence, appear to be the guiding principle in his interpretation of Christ. He takes some events in the life of Jesus and some of his utterances and presses down between Advaita Vedānta and the Hindu worldview to produce a new meaning of Jesus. Looking at Jesus from *advaitic* or Hindu perspective cannot be condemned, but to ignore most of the important events in the life of Jesus such as the incarnation, the death and resurrection, as Sri Sri does, may commit the danger of misunderstanding the person and work of Jesus Christ. In all the process of his interpretation, Sri Sri neither goes beyond the general Hindu view of Jesus as one of the saviours nor moves even an inch away from his *advaitic* world view and Hindu commitment.

However, our study reveals few innovative ideas in his interpretations, such as:

- Jesus as the manifestation and embodiment of Love where Love is understood by him as another name of God. By saying that Jesus and Love are synonymous, Sri Sri, consciously or unconsciously admits Jesus as God.
- The possibility and importance of realizing the living Jesus, the Christ Consciousness is implicit in his teaching.
- Contact with Christ, an ecstatic union with him, communion with the living Jesus is possible when one is deep in meditation, deep down at the level when the mind is still without any thought. The authentic and direct knowledge of Jesus Christ is possible at this stage as the knowledge gained through deep meditation is more reliable than knowledge acquired through logical understanding.

Concluding Remarks

Ravishankar is not only one of the most popular contemporary gurus in the world, but also the only living gurus we have selected for our investigation. Though he did not consider himself as God so as to demand worship from his devotees as did Sri Sathya Sai Baba, his followers regard him no less than a God. His academic knowledge of science and post-modern mentality coupled

[108] *Ibid.*

with his spiritual experiences make him relevant for the stressed-prone post-modern youths, and no wonder that he attracts a large crowd of youths from the nook and corner of the world. His theology of religion, which may be put as '*pluralism*' (though he goes beyond the general notion of *pluralism* as a mere 'acceptance of other religions as valid path as one's own), his commitment to the world peace and the harmony of religion, his dedication to the service of the poor and the downtrodden make him popular all over the world. His teaching does not confine to the so called 'religion and spiritual' arena, but touches all aspects of human life and its environment. As a matter of fact, he seems to be more inclined towards achieving a stress-free, violence-free happy life here on earth than the attainment of *mokṣa* in the next life. Among the four gurus studied, he may be most faithful to Śaṅkara's Advaita Vedānta that compels him to accentuate oneness of human beings, essential similarity of the core of all religions, and makes him emphasize owning each other, considering others as belonging to us.

There is hardly any doubt that Ravishankar has high regards for Jesus and his message. However, his interpretation is unsystematic because there is hardly any proper biblical hermeneutic with a systematic approach and coherence. In fact, he denies or shuns away from some of the crucial Christological issues such as incarnation, death and resurrection as significant for human salvation. He seems to have put his Hindu doctrines into Jesus Christ, and analyzed the content of Jesus' teaching selectively from advaitic worldview which of course is the way most of the Indian interpreters do. He selects few verses from the Gospels and gives his own meanings to them. There is always a danger of making hermeneutical mistake in picking verses from the Bible randomly and selectively out of the context without taking the whole message into consideration. That is where Sri Sri is found to be wanting. In this sense, Sri Sri needs to work more on the Bible in order to have the fuller understanding of Jesus Christ and his message as the Bible is one of the main sources, if not the sole authority, of knowing Jesus Christ and any attempt to interpret Christ cannot afford to avoid systematic inclusive treatment of the Bible.

Again, Ravishankar is neither serious in his dealing with the Bible nor in his interpretation of Jesus Christ. It is apparent that his knowledge of Christian history and theology is also very limited. He reads Bible and speaks of Jesus mainly for the purpose of inter-faith meetings and relations. His interpretation of Jesus is not enough to bring to light the wholistic understanding of Jesus and his mission.

However, in spite of several flaws in his treatment of Jesus and his message, Sri Sri's understanding of Jesus as the embodiment of love, the one whose essential identity is love, is definitely innovative and encouraging. His assertion that a living Jesus can be known with more accuracy by means of personal experience in a mystical communion at the deeper level of meditation than from the written scripture appears to be in line with the other select gurus' argument. This is significant in the context of Christian churches' emphasis on the written Word of God as the sole or primary authority for the knowledge of Jesus and his message.

Ravishankar claims that he owns Jesus Christ as much as Christians own him; he insists that we should own other religious resources to enrich our own spirituality as all are one. He sees the universal significance of Jesus as the embodiment of love; he treats his message as significant as other great Masters, thereby opening up a new horizon in inter-religious relations in a pluralistic country like India where Jesus as Love could be one of the uniting strings. Sri Sri's contribution towards harmony of religion is seen in the way he regards Jesus Christ as a unique person, as unique for all of us as Lord Kṛṣṇa or Lord Rāmā. The next Chapter will throw more light on how his understanding of Jesus could contribute for achieving cordial inter-religious relations in India.

Chapter 8

The Unveiled Christ of the Indian Gurus
A Critical Consideration

Now let's us try to conclude our discussion on the Indian gurus' interpretation of Jesus Christ by recollecting what has already been said and recapitulating some of the important issues emerged from select Indian gurus' interpretations with some critical notes.

Contemporary guru movement with its wholistic-therapeutical element and theological liberalism attracts a large number of people from various religious traditions. One's religious affiliation and religious community attachment becomes less significant in the company of a guru where the guru requires no conversion as long as a devotee is faithful to him/her and adhered to his/her teachings. So, the *āśram* of any internationally known guru is more or less like 'a parliament of religions' where people of various religions flock together, maintaining unity in diversity. Considering the diverse religious background of the devotees, these gurus not only maintain harmony of religions but also wisely teach the essential oneness of religious experience.

Thus, Ravishankar emphasizes 'belongingness' to one another where one feels that all religions of the world, the whole entirety belong to him or her. Stressing on the vitality of belongingness, he even goes to the extent of saying that the ability to say that 'the whole entirety belongs to me and I belong to everybody' is enlightenment. For Sathya Sai Baba all of us are the children of God and we should think in term of 'We' not 'I'. Considering others as belonging to us, we must strive to achieve 'brotherhood/sisterhood of human'. 'All are one; be alike to everyone' is his slogan. For Osho the basic problem lies with religion itself – the codified religion with its structure, dogmas, doctrine and tradition bar the followers from having cordial relationship. A 'religionless' spirituality, where a devotee feels the whole universe as his/her family, having communion not only with fellow humans but even with trees and animals, is a solution to inter-religious conflict. Yogananda is no less a devout to harmony of religions. One of his primary missions was to establish the unity among all the true religions of the world. He even built a 'Church of All Religions' where people belonging to every religion are welcomed. According to him, an enlightened person can no longer think exclusively for himself/herself.

Having committed to harmony of religions, they turn to Jesus Christ and interpret him.

1. Why Look to Jesus?

The Indian gurus' interest in Jesus apparently sprouted from various factors, ranging from genuine appreciation and deep attachment to partial commitment imposed on them by situational compulsion due to their Western devotees who are predominantly Christians or are deeply influenced by Christian worldview. Their interpretation of Christ is also due to the above reasons on one hand, and on the other hand their dissatisfaction with the way Jesus has been presented in popular Christian theology which, according to them, distorts the real Jesus Christ. They attempted to unveil the real and original Jesus, devoid of any Western cultural and philosophical elements by using Indian spiritual and philosophical resources which for them is a necessity in order to understand the real Jesus who was an Orient in need of Oriental methodological tools to unravel truth concerning him. By and large these gurus looked at Jesus from advaitic worldview coupled with their own distinctive philosophical stand and religious practices. The claim of superiority of Indian spiritual resources over against Greco-Roman and Jewish philosophical and religious assets for the interpretation of Jesus and his message seems to be unreasonable. However, it is not an unwelcomed practice to use Indian resources in interpreting Jesus Christ because even popular Christology bred in the Western soil did the same thing with Greco-Roman and European philosophical stuff as Panikkar says, "… the Christology that has reached us today is the result of 'Christian' faith in dialogue with Judaism and the Greco-Roman world, later with the mentality of the new European peoples, and finally with Islamic culture."[1] The attempt to let Jesus and his message engage in dialogue with Indian spiritual treasures, therefore, is of no offence.

2. Their Perspectives

The hermeneutical principle adopted by these gurus in reading Jesus and his message, and the perspective from which they looked at him were through and through Indian without considering the contextual realities of his Palestinian

---

[1] Raimon Panikkar, *The Fullness of Man: A Christophany,* (New York/New Delhi: Orbis/ ISPCK, 2006), p. 4.

world and the biblical linguistic milieu. As Jesus is considered to have spent half or even more than half of his earthly life, and most of his theological and religious formative years in India, these gurus thought that Indian context is more important than Palestinian one. However, this story lacks sufficient proof and many scholars belonging to both Christian and people of other faiths decline to believe in this theory. Moreover, it is difficult to substantiate the total negligence of Palestinian context and the linguistic background of Jesus in their interpretations. Among the Indian gurus investigated, Yogananda, Osho and Ravishankar are more or less depended on biblical accounts of Jesus. They worked out their interpretations basing on the written scripture, but reading it intuitively rather than rationally, pressing down between *advaitic* worldview and their distinctive philosophical stand without systematic contextual and linguistic analysis of the text. Sathya Sai Baba, on the other hand, did not care to see the biblical correctness of his discourses on Jesus. Many professing Christians who are faithful to or at least in respect of the Bible may be disturbed, but his disciples have no problem with it on account that Baba is Omniscient God who knows Jesus in and out and is able to tell things which are not recorded or are wrongly recorded in the Bible.

These gurus are selective in the way they chose texts and events to interpret – selecting those which seem to go well with their theological and philosophical commitment and leaving others which are less connected with their ideas. There is always danger of making hermeneutical mistake by choosing few passages and work on them, because, such practice often produces fractional picture. Thus, it can be said that select Indian gurus' interpretations of Jesus Christ produce an incomplete picture of Jesus.

3. Methodological Error

The greatest methodological error committed by these gurus in the process of their interpretations is that they seem to have put Jesus inside their theological and philosophical box, imprisoning him in their system rather than reading him in the light of Indian religious resources or interpreting him in relation to Indian sources. In other words, instead of giving us an Indian reading of Jesus Christ, they conditioned him to suit their philosophical and religious position by making Jesus said and done what they wanted to say and do. By doing so, they made the same mistake which Christian theologians were alleged to have made through the ages. The result is, we see in their interpretations not a 'real' or an 'original' Jesus, but a 'Hinduised Jesus' or 'Indianised Jesus', the exact parallel of Jesus of the Western Christology – a Westernised Jesus – which is denounced by these gurus as a distortion of a real Jesus.

4. Relations with other Indian Interpretations

It is difficult to ascertain as to how far these gurus were affected by other Indian interpreters of Jesus Christ. During the spiritual and theologio-philosophical formative years of Yogananda, Raja Rammohun Roy, K.C. Sen and Swami Vivekananda had already advanced their interpretations of Jesus Christ and these 'Christological formulations' had been widely spread among the learned Bengalis in Calcutta (Kolkata) and surrounding areas. It cannot be ruled out that such interpretations impacted Yogananda, especially when we consider the similarities in the content of some of their interpretations. For example, the separation of Jesus and Christ as we see in Sen and Swami Vivekananda is quite similar to Yogananda's dichotomy of Jesus, a human person and Christ, the universal consciousness. It may not be too wrong to conclude that either Yogananda or his Bengali guru Sri Yukteswar of Serampore had been influenced by these Bengali forerunners. It may be assumed that the other gurus investigated are less influenced by other Indian interpretations.

There are a number of similarities between the select Indian gurus' interpretation of Jesus Christ and other Indian interpretations. The Oriental Christ of the gurus is similar with the 'Oriental Christ' of P.C. Mozoomdar and Swami Akhilananda and Sen's 'Asiatic Christ'. Some of the prominent similarities include Jesus as avatāra; the idea that Jesus, a true human being, attaining Christhood, a state of consciousness attainable for all of us as well; emphasis on Jesus' moral and ethical teachings rather than the work of Jesus Christ as having salvific power; taking the death and resurrection of Jesus Christ as a symbolic act; the denial of Jesus' uniqueness as the only path to God and acceptance of him as 'one among the many'. They all agree that Christian theology does not represent the real and true Jesus. Their methodological framework is almost the same where emphasis is laid on the use of Indian philosophical and religious resources as a tool for a correct interpretation of Jesus Christ.

However, in the midst of such similarities and commonalities, there are a number of innovative ideas emerging from the Indian gurus' interpretations of Jesus Christ. The understanding of Jesus as 'Love' as we see in Ravishankar, Sathya Sai Baba and Osho is one of the inventive ideas emerged from gurus' interpretations. The emphasis on 'mystical communion with Christ'; the possibility of meeting the risen Jesus in flesh and blood as he is active in the world, as he is still retaining his human form as suggested by Yogananda; Sathya Sai Baba's notion of Jesus as *amsāvatār* (fractional *avatāra*) and *Karana-Janma* – a master born with a purpose which negates a full-fledged *avatār*-ship to Jesus – are all innovative. Sai Baba's comparison of Jesus' three progressive identities – 'Messenger of God', 'Son of God' and 'Oneness with God' with three schools of Vedānta - Dvaita, Viśiṣṭādvaita and Advaita Vedānta respectively is also inventive and interesting. Again, Osho's interpretation contains a number of pioneering and original ideas like Jesus as a rebel, a man of celebration, an enlightened master, and a much emphasis laid on Jesus' humanness, etc. These gurus also suggest that Jesus' core teaching and the teachings of Indian religions are by and large similar.

The Indian gurus' interpretations of Jesus Christ, though retained much of the contents of the earlier Indian interpretations, had gone far ahead in a number of areas. They seemed to have been drawn comparatively closer to Jesus Christ than most of the earlier interpreters. They have produced much more literature on Jesus Christ and talked more extensively on him than most of the Hindu reformers and Neo-Vedāntins. The main focus of their interpretations is on the direct mystical communion with Christ in order to change individual spiritual life aiming at 'individual pietism', a resemblance of which we see in a pietistic movement of the German Lutheran Churches during the 17th and 18th centuries, but, it does not end there; there are rooms for larger societal interest in the Jesus they projected. In other words, the Jesus of the Indian gurus concerns primarily individual spiritual upliftment, and attempts to give inner peace and tranquility and finally enlightenment to those who attained him in spiritual-ecstatic union. At the same time the relevance of Jesus for peace, equality and justice in the society and created order at large is not neglected either.

5. Their Weaknesses

No interpretation, whatever sophisticated and academically sound or spiritually helpful it might be, is perfect and faultless; so also is the Indian gurus' interpretation of Jesus Christ. The Indian gurus have their own presuppositions and pre-formulated ideas from which perspectives they looked at Jesus Christ. Their assertion that the true meaning of Jesus can be drawn, not from the existing Christian traditions but from Indian spiritual resources is an exclusive claim that may invite criticism from Christians because it is not only arrogant to have such claim but also is the very denial of pluralistic theological stand these gurus have adopted. The possibility of using Indian religious resources in unveiling the true and original Jesus may not be questioned, but denouncing all other methodological frameworks and hermeneutical principles that had been used by Christian theologians and biblical scholars to interpret Jesus Christ is presumptuous and unacceptable. V. P. Thomas' argument holds some water when he says, "We cannot understand the Christ of the N.T. without a proper understanding of the Jewish and Greek backgrounds."[2] Their interpretations look like putting of their philosophical stuffs into Jesus Christ rather than

[2] V. P. Thomas, "Towards an Indian Christology," *Indian Journal of Theology, Vol. 14,* No. 1, 1963, p. 5.

interpreting him in relation to Indian religious resources. Indian Christians may not be able to take such attempts positively, and it could hinder inter-faith relations rather than promoting it.

There are a number of elements in their interpretations of Jesus which are objectionable to Indian Christians. Sathya Sai Baba rendered Jesus as inferior to him; while accepting himself to be a full-flagged *avatāra*, a *purnāvatār* like Lord Kṛṣṇa, he regards Jesus as *amsāvatār* or fractional *avatāra* or *Karana-Janma* – a master born with a purpose, who reached the highest spiritual realization towards the end of his life. These are not only inconsistent with the biblical account which is considered as the main source of Jesus' life and ministry, but also impossible to provide the authentication of the claim. This way of irresponsible and unreasonable interpretation of Jesus Christ will only hurt the feelings of Christians and others who have high regards for Jesus, and bring about inter-religious conflict. He also gives a number of stories concerning Jesus which are not found in the Bible or are contradictory with the biblical narratives. Moreover, Sai Baba contradicts himself several times in the facts and figures he produces concerning Jesus Christ that make us skeptical of the authenticity of his readings. Another derogatory comment Sathya Sai Baba made on Jesus is the progressive identity of Jesus where Jesus a normal human being considered himself at first as a 'Messenger of God' and after serious contemplation he realized that he is the 'Son of God' and finally towards the end of his life as spiritual growth progressed Jesus attained oneness with God. This looks like trying to fit Jesus incongruently into the Vedantic school of thought where we have dualism (*dvaita*), qualified non-dualism (*visistadvaita*) and non-dualism (*advaita*). Sathya Sai Baba says that these three schools are not to be taken as separate and in conflict, but they are the various stages in human's spiritual journey. We start with dualism, come to the stage of qualified non-dualism and finally reach the highest stage, the absolute non-dualism. The whole idea where Jesus Christ is made progressing from dualism and then finally reaching a state of non-dualism is foreign to the Palestinian religious worldview to which Jesus belonged.

Osho objected a number of important Christian beliefs concerning Jesus Christ, such as, the incarnation, the virgin birth, Jesus' miracles, Jesus as Son of God, etc. Like Yogananda, Osho also said that at the cross Jesus, the human body was killed, not Christ, the consciousness, and that Jesus got enlightenment at the cross, just before he died. These are some of the elements which go against the biblical account of Jesus and the Christological formulations of the Church. It is presuming to say that Indian gurus are nearer to the truth of Jesus Christ than the tradition of the Church or the biblical witness. We also should not forget that Osho after the 'Silence period', i.e. from the last part of 1984 denounced all positive comments he had made on Jesus saying that they were just a methodological tools to draw the attention of the people, and reduced Jesus to be a neurotic, a mental case, a fascist just like Adolf Hitler.

Ravishankar leaves out a number of Christological issues like incarnation, cross and resurrection in his interpretation. His inadequate knowledge of the Bible and of Christian fundamental doctrines is quite evident together with his lukewarm response to the total reality of Jesus Christ. Yogananda's selectiveness in dealing with the Gospels is questionable; his absolute separation of Jesus Christ into Jesus, the man and Christ, the consciousness is also objectionable in the light of biblical witness and Indian Christian adherence to Chalcedonian Formula; his overemphasis on Christ Consciousness and the total negation of the role of Jesus, the historical person is also repulsive. Again, projecting Jesus as endorsing the doctrine of transmigration of soul is also a one sided view. Few biblical passages are quoted in support of this; but the case is that there are multitudes of other biblical verses that speak otherwise. In the light of this, some of these gurus' arguments concerning Jesus' endorsement of the doctrine of 'reincarnation' is weak and could not stand among the much stronger counter witnesses.

Indian Christians may expect more respectful treatment of their Bible from these gurus and more seriousness in dealing with some of the most fundamental Christological issues like incarnation, trinity, Jesus' death and resurrection, otherwise they may find it difficult to celebrate all the contents of gurus' interpretations and dance to the beat of their rhythms. Unless these problems are addressed Indian Christians may not be encouraged to participate in meaningful dialogue with these gurus in seeking mutual understanding.

Indian gurus categorically denied Jesus' uniqueness as the only Saviour. The exclusive interpretation of Jesus Christ as the *only* incarnation of God and the *only* way to the Father, is considered as standing on the way of inter-religious relations whereas the alternative explanation advanced by these gurus that puts Jesus as standing alongside other 'Masters', but without diminishing his vitality as a Saviour, is deemed as enhancing inter-faith relations. Exclusive claim and statement, the-only-way-type of attitude are always connected with one's faith affirmation and experience. Jesus Christ is unique and he is the only Saviour insofar as Christians are concerned, and it cannot be otherwise. Hindus or Muslims, etc. may have the parallel claim which is also true insofar as they are concerned. However, that does not make any difference in Christian understanding of Jesus Christ as the only way. It is possible to have harmony between different faiths and ideologies while holding fast to our own religious beliefs. To think that only when we give up some of our religious claims and practices, that we will come to the point of mutual understanding and harmony, is negation of inter-religious relations itself because so long as religion is religion, there must be unique claims, practices and experiences. Religious discord is there not because Christians maintain that Jesus is the only way, or Muslims assert that Muhammad is the last prophet which all should listen to, or Hindus believe that *Sanatana Dharma* is the only valid religion, but because of selfish and vested interest of the people. Thus, Indian gurus' denial of Christians' claim of Jesus Christ as the *only way* to the Father is unacceptable because of the fact that each religion, even gurus themselves, has its own claim of uniqueness. These gurus will never accept if they are asked to give up some of their unique claims and practices. The denial of such claim is not necessary for cordial inter-faith relations. Thus, the contemporary gurus' interpretation of Jesus Christ when they explain away the professed uniqueness of Jesus Christ, rather than fostering inter-faith relation will retard the progress of inter-faith discussions and dialogue.

Most of the modern Indian gurus uncritically accepted oneness of religion – that at the inner spiritual level, beyond the visible and measurable level, at the deepest spiritual level religions are one and the same as the same truth resides in them. This is easy to say for those who follow Advaita Vedānta as ultimate reality is conceived as non-dual. But for those, even within Hindu religious tradition and others like Christian, Muslims, etc. who have totally different metaphysical worldview, oneness of religion, and as a matter of fact, oneness of reality is inconceivable and unacceptable. For them, religions need not be one in order to have cordial inter-faith relations or at least harmony of religions.

The above non-exhaustive list of problems seen in the Indian gurus' interpretations of Jesus Christ could evoke inter-religious conflict or at least stand on the way of religious harmony rather than fostering inter-faith relations. On the other hand, although there are several weaknesses in the select Indian gurus' interpretations of Jesus Christ, as no interpretation or Christological formulation is perfect, there are a number of laudable innovative ideas emerged which are not seen in other Indian interpretations or popular Christian Christology. Their interpretations add yet another dimension to our knowledge of the multidimensional and multifaceted veracity of Jesus Christ in Indian pluralistic context, thereby helping us to enrich our knowledge and experience of the inexhaustibility of Jesus, the Christ in India. If Christ is universal, cannot be otherwise, if Jesus Christ is risen and active now in our world, therefore, he is beyond Christianity and Christendom. He is as much 'Jesus of India' as 'Jesus of Nazareth'. As a matter of fact, it is not possible to limit him within the four walls of Christian religion and Christian religious experiences, because there are a number of people who have experienced and have personal relationship, even communion with the risen Christ among people who are NOT called by the name 'Christian'. It is, therefore, futile or rather foolishness to limit the work of Jesus within Judo-Christian tradition alone as it would betray the inexhaustibility and multifaceted reality of Jesus himself. Jesus is a global, or rather, universal phenomenon! His work transcends human-made religious barrier. His significance permeates the entire universe. His love and grace know no boundary. He is celebrated not only in Christian churches but in Hindu *ashrams*! He is preached not only by Christians but by people of other faiths and ideologies. He is adored and loved not only by Christians but by people of all religions. The *Unveiled Christ* of the Indian gurus will continue to lead people from untruth to truth, from darkness to light, and from death to immortality.

Appendix

Personal Interview with Sri Sri Ravishankar at his Ashram, Bangalore on 27 October, 2012

I met Sri Sri Ravishankar at his Bangalore Ashram on the 27th October, 2012 (Saturday), around 11:30 AM for personal Interview. The interview session was recorded by means of Digital Voice Recorder and Cell Phone and the following is the script of the interview. Some portions which seem to be less important for my research purpose are not included here in order to make the Script shorter. **RD** – stands for the myself, Rodinmawia Ralte, **Sri Sri** for Sri Sri Ravishankar.

(I introduced myself stating the reason I was there, my theological journey, my previous research and the present one. I thanked him for giving me his time, then proceed on to the interview)

RD: *What is Jesus Christ to you? Do you consider Jesus as one of the great teachers or more than that?*
Sri Sri: Here we consider Jesus as one of the prophets; Jesus is one of the prophets. Many saints and many prophets are the prophets of God; Hinduism always recognizes, …embraces many things and Jesus has spoken truth.

RD: *If you compare Jesus with Lord Kṛṣṇa or Lord Rāmā, do you put him below or above them?*
Sri Sri: No, we don't put someone above or, below we say "everybody is unique". And he is one of the unique saints like Kṛṣṇa or Lord Rāmā. And, you know, one thing is we don't say (*sic*) hierarchy in Hinduism, it is just like a ball, which is the first point which is the second point in a ball, nothing like

that. Now if you ask me between banana and apple which is higher and which is lower, what I would say, no, banana is banana, apple is apple.

RD: *So, you mean that Jesus is as unique as Lord Rama?*
Sri Sri: Yes, and Lord Kṛṣṇa, in his own way. And, you see, there are lots of similarities between Jesus and Lord Kṛṣṇa. Both are born in the middle of the night. Lord Kṛṣṇa says, "I am here to redeem you of your sins, come unto, come back to me I will redeem you of all your sins". Exactly what Jesus had said "I have come to redeem you of your sins." There are several verses, if you see, in Gītā and if you read Bible, you see, there is a striking similarity.

RD: *As Christians we say that Jesus is the Son of God or Jesus is God Himself. From your statement that Jesus is saint and Christian claim that Jesus is not only saint but God Himself...*
Sri Sri: You know Jesus always said "you pray to our Father in the Heaven". 'Our' means he is the father of all of us. In India also we say, 'God, my father', 'My father' means everybody is his sons. The main difference comes when you say Jesus is the **only** son of God or we say that God is the father of the entire creation, the whole universe. We all belong to him. That is the difference.

RD: *Do you consider Jesus as God?*
Sri Sri: God, if it is Love, yes. According to Hinduism, God is permeating like air everywhere. It's like Brahman, Brahman means nothing can exist outside of it. So, Brahman is in every cell, in every cell of everything in the universe. So, there is no one thing that is devoid of God. You understand?

RD: *Yes, I understand. In that sense he (Jesus) is God, just like 'myself' also is God.*
Sri Sri: Yes. We say mother, father, the guru and the guest are all form of God – the four main pillars... See God in the mother, in the father, in the teacher and in the guest. I also remember one Catholic Nun who told me – "If you don't see Jesus in the first person you meet in the morning, you are not going to see him." There is that concept that God lives in everyone, in everybody… We say God is existence, consciousness and love. Whenever you find existence, consciousness and love, that is the manifestation of God. Jesus definitely is the manifestation of Love.

RD: *That means Jesus is not that unique as Christians projected him as the Son of God or one person of the Trinity?*
Sri Sri: He is very unique in that, no doubt he is unique; but as I say we don't put one above the other. That is the uniqueness of Jesus not as a body but as

love, as consciousness, he is in your heart, in everywhere. In that sense he all permeates.

***RD:** The death of Jesus on the cross and his resurrection from the death is central to Christianity. Do you believe that Jesus died on the cross and resurrected on the third day from the tomb? Is there any significance in these events?*

Sri Sri: You know, what is more significant is what he said – "Unless you become like a child you cannot reach heaven." The simple words of Jesus – love thy neighbour, love and compassion for all. These are more important. Whether he died on the cross or he went to Kashmir or in the twelfth year of his life, he spent in Mailapur in Chennai, there are so many theories. I leave that controversy to historians. It does not matter. What is most important is the teaching, the message of love and universal brotherhood.

***RD:** You do not believe that he died on the cross?*

Sri Sri: That's what I am saying. It does not matter to me whether he died on the cross or he did not die or he went to Kashmir (after crucifixion). There is a book *Jesus Lived in India* and they had given a lot of evidences about it, so I leave that to scholars to go into, I don't have time to go into all the literature had said. One thing I know that there is a lot of thing to believe that Jesus spent twelve years in India. He studied quite a lot of Vedānta, Upanishad principle in Mylapur. That's why he sent the doubting Thomas to India, doubting Thomas, because he always doubts. Whenever someone doubt, you say, "you can always see for yourself" and he said "you go to India, to see for yourself." Then Thomas came to India and he died in Chennai, you know about that. And then there is a Mar Thomas in Kerala, the sect of Christians who are followers of St. Thomas. So, I feel there is lot of connections in the ancient time between them and Jesus had a very hard time in telling people in the Middle East that God is love because there Jews only perceived God as one who is punishing, angry God, chief dictator but it is Jesus who brought the concept of piety, the love... In that sense it is very significant.

***RD:** Do you read Bible?*

Sri Sri: I have read it

***RD:** During you College days in the Christian College?*

Sri Sri: No. Not in the College, afterword. I have personal interest as I believe in knowing a little bit of others. I am not a scholar; I have read a little bit.

***RD:** Guruji, some of the Hindu Gurus I have studied claim that they have personal communion with Jesus...*

Sri Sri: You mean Paramhansa Yogananda?

***RD:** Yes, yes, he is also one of them. Even Osho Rajneesh claimed to have such a direct knowledge, he says, "My knowledge of Jesus is not from the Bible or Christian theology, but it is directly from Jesus himself. I am an enlightened person, any enlightened person knows another enlightened person". Paramhansa Yogananda is different in the sense that he claims to have personal communion with Jesus, a sort of vision.*
Sri Sri: (interrupting the question): Yeah, yeah, vision.

***RD:** Do you believe that? Is it possible to have a vision of Jesus?*
Sri Sri: Visions are possible because this is not the only reality that we are living. When you go in deep meditation, there are other realities. There is the world of light… when you go deep in meditation mind is still, there are no thoughts, there is no eye, then the knowledge become very spontaneous. Spontaneous knowledge is there.

***RD:** Do you have any contact with Jesus in spiritual level or something like that?*
Sri Sri: As I say you know when you go deep in that level in meditation, then you are in touch with the world of light. Jesus is definitely part of that light.

***RD:** O.K. So you don't have problem in preaching about Jesus to your devotees and asking them to, also sometimes, pray to him?*
Sri Sri: Yeah, we have Jesus picture… in our hall, all religious symbols are there. We have Cross… Buddhism, Jainism, Islam, Parsees; we put symbols of all the religious. I have no, we have no problem in it. We never say, "Only this is it', we say, "One truth, one reality, many ways to one truth". This is the beauty of Hinduism. It is never rigid and says, "This is the only way, if you don't do this, you will go to hell"… One truth, one truth perceived and adored in many ways."

***RD:** In regards to the problems of inter-religious relationship in India, what is your suggestion for the problem of Inter-religious conflicts?*
Sri Sri: You know India has been the most tolerant in the whole world. There has never been religious persecution. The Parsees were persecuted, Jews were persecuted elsewhere in the world; Christians were persecuted greatly. But they all came to India, they preached, they lived their lives very happily. And the kings of this land and public have supported them in the past. If you go to Goa, if you go to Gujarat, if you go to Kerala, you will find them. Muslims were also welcomed though their traditions were totally opposite to Hinduism in many ways, but even they were all welcomed here. So, India has a very

broad mind set, embracing everybody as part of the family. The difficulty comes when someone says, "No, you are all wrong, you are all bad, you are all Satanic, only I am right." Then one fundamentalism in somewhere, one fanaticism in somewhere, then it will have repercussion in other religion... There are groups of people (who say), "Only my religion will take you to heaven, everybody will go to hell, then the other person will also start... This is happening out of ignorance. There are good things in every religion and today modern human beings should know a little bit of every religion and honour each other's diversity. See, Jesus was only one, today there are seventy two sects of Christianity, each one claim that they are the right. Only one prophet Muhammad, there are... It was happening in Pakistan, they are fighting among themselves. In Hinduism there are innumerable sects, you can even count, you know... when people start honouring each other, learning a little bit about each other, deepen your own religion, deepen your roots but broaden your vision, but like what you are doing, you know, inter-religious dialogue, honouring each other, communicating with each other. Where there is appeared to be too much difference... but there are many things that are common. If we focus on the commonality, we can rid our world of terrorism. Today terrorism has sprung unfortunately out of religion. And the reason is, let's say, "my religion is the supreme and only this will bring salvation, you all have no right. This is the tone of terrorism. If that has to change, every child has to know a little bit of Buddhism, a little bit of Hinduism, a little bit of Christianity, Islam. Then their minds will become broad, they don't have ill-feeling towards anyone. This is my conclusion. What do you think?

RD: *I think it is a very wise advice. Thank You.*
Sri Sri: Thank you.
(After the interview session, we stood together for photograph. We have a brief chatting, where he asked me the following question:-)

Sri Sri: How do you think about Hinduism?
RD: *For me it is a great religion. One thing that surprised me about Hinduism is its strength. Hinduism survives nearly a thousand years of foreign domination and comes out stronger and stronger. Christian missionary enterprise for nearly two thousand years could not produce great impact on Hinduism. You see, since 1981 census, the percentage of Christianity has gone down slowly and slowly. So, I feel that there is inner strength in Hinduism.*

Bibliography

A. Bibliographical Note

A brief Bibliographical Note is considered to be necessary in view of the diversity of sources used in this book, and it may be confusing for the reader unless a brief explanation is made. The Bibliography is, as usual, broadly divided into two – **Primary Sources** and **Secondary Sources** which are further classified into Personal Interviews, Books, Edited books, Journals, Magazine, News Papers, Internet Sources and Unpublished Materials. The Primary Sources are divided into three sections – Books, Internet Sources and Audio CD. Again, books in the Primary Sources are divided into two categories. In the first category I put books written by the four gurus investigated namely, Paramhansa Yogananda, Sri Sathya Sai Baba, Osho Rajneesh and Sri Sri Ravishankar. The second category comprises of books authored by individuals whose theological and philosophical writings are discussed as *separate sub-headings*, for example Raja Rammohun Roy, K.C. Sen, Swami Vivekananda, Mahatma Gandhi, S. Radhakrishnan, Swami Sivananda, etc. Though other primary sources are extensively used in our research, I put them under 'Secondary Sources' as their theological and philosophical writings do not form separate sub-heading of the chapters. For example, theologians and scholars like Raimundo Panikkar, S.J. Samartha, K.P. Aleaz, Paul F. Knitter, Israel Selvanayagom, etc. are put in the Secondary Sources though while discussing their contributions and referring to their works I used their own writings.

There are books published in volumes like *Complete Work of Swami Vivekananda* (8 volumes), *The Collected Works of Mahatma Gandhi* (98 volumes), *Sathya Sai Speaks* (42 Volumes), etc. When the publisher, the place and the year of publication are the same and when all the volumes published are used, I do not put each volume separately. However, in the case where these volumes are published in different year and by different publisher, or when I did not use all the volumes published, I put each volume used separately. Again, some books are downloaded in a Portable Document Format *(pdf)* from the official website of the respective organization or some other website, though they can be considered as part of the Internet Source, I do not put them under the Internet Sources category as these books are downloaded from the official website, etc. in the form of book, I treat them like the published books but indicate that they were downloaded from the website and also give the site address. I also used On-line Library in the case of Osho Rajneesh. The Osho Commune International runs an On-line Library where they put most of his books, a number of which are referred to in this book. In the On-line Library, each Chapter starts with page number 1, so it is indicated in the footnotes. In the Bibliography I put the On-line Library books under the published book category but indicate that they are taken from the On-line Library by giving the site address. It is to be noted also that only sources which are used or referred to are put in the Bibliography.

B. Bibliography

I. Primary Sources

1. Personal Interview

Personal Interview with Sri Sri Ravishankar at his Ashram, Bangalore on 27 October, 2012. (The script of this interview is put in the appendix)

2. Books

(a) Paramhansa Yogananda

God Alone: The Life and Letters of a Saint Sri Gyanamata, Dakshineswar: Yogoda Satsanga Society of India, 2007, first published in 1984.

Paramhansa Yogananda In Memoriam: Personal Accounts of the Master's Final Days, Dakshineswar: Yogoda Satsanga Society of India, 2012, first published in 1958.

Sayings of Paramhansa Yogananda, Dakshineswar, Kolkata: Yogoda Satsanga Society of India, 2008, first published in 1980.

Yogananda, Paramhansa, *The Second Coming of Christ: The Resurrection of the Christ Within You – A Revelatory Commentary on the Original Teachings of Jesus, Vol. I & II,* Los Angeles: Self-Realization Fellowship, 2004.

________, *Autobiography of a Yogi*, New Delhi: Ananda Sangha Publications, 2010; first published in 1946.

________, *Man's Eternal Quest: Collected Talks and Essays on Realizing God in Daily Life*, Dakshineswar: Yogoda Satsanga Society of India, 2008, first published in 1975.

________, *How to be Happy All the Time*, Gurgaon: Ananda Sangha Publications, 2010.

________, *Divine Romance: Collected Talks and Essays on Realizing God in Daily Life, Volume II,* Dakshineswar, Kolkata: Yogoda Satsanga Society of India, 2008.

________, *To be Victorious in Life*, Dakshineswar, Kolkata: Yogoda Satsanga Society of India, 2011, first published in 2002.

________, *Journey to Self-Realization: Collected Talks and Essays on Realizing God in Daily Life, Volume III,* Dakshineswar, Kolkata: Yogoda Satsanga Society of India, 2004.

________, *Whispers from Eternity*, Dakshineswar, Kolkata: Yogoda Satsanga Society of India, 2008, first published in 1959.

________, *Metaphysical Meditations*, Dakshineswar, Kolkata: Yogoda Satsanga Society of India, 2007, first published in 1964.

________, *Living Fearlessly: Bringing Out Your Inner Soul Strength*, Dakshineswar, Kolkata: Yogoda Satsanga Society of India, 2011, first published in 1903.

________, *Spiritual Diary: An Inspirational Thought for Each Day of the Year*, Dakshineswar, Kolkata: Yogoda Satsanga Society of India, 2010, first published in 1982.

________, *Why God Permits Evil and How to Rise Above It*, Dakshineswar, Kolkata: Yogoda Satsanga Society of India, 2010, first published in 2002.

________, *Scientific Healing Affirmations*, Dakshineswar, Kolkata: Yogoda Satsanga Society of India, 2008.

________, *Where there is Light: Insights and Inspiration for Meeting Life's Challenges*, Dakshineswar, Kolkata: Yogoda Satsanga Society of India, 2008.

________, *The Science of Religion*, Dakshineswar, Kolkata: Yogoda Satsanga Society of India, 2008, first published in USA, 1953.

________, *How You Can Talk With God*, Dakshineswar, Kolkata: Yogoda Satsanga Society of India, 2005, first published in 1957.

________, *The Yoga of Jesus: Understanding the Hidden Teaching of the Gospel*, Los Angeles: Self-Realization Fellowship, 2009.

________, *Yogoda Lessons in Self-Realization, S.5-L-129*, Dakshineswar: Yogoda Satsanga Society of India, n.d.

________, *Christian Yoga: Super Advanced Course Number One Lesson 1 to 12*, Los Angeles: Yogoda Satsanga Society, 2007.

Undreamed-of Possibilities: An Introduction to Yogoda Satsanga Society of India, published by Yogoda Satsanga Society of India/Self-Realization Fellowship.

(b) Sathya Sai Baba

Baba, Sri Sathya Sai, *"Be Like Jesus": The Good News of Jesus*, compiled by Debra and William Miller, Prasanthi Nilayam: Sri Sathya Sai Sadhana Trust, Publications Division, 2009.

________, *Summer Showers in Brindavan 1974, Part – I: Discourses by Bhagavan Sri Sathya Sai Baba on Brahman*, Prasnathi Nilayam: Sri Sathya Sai Books and Publications Trust, 2004.

His Story as Told by Himself: A Compilation from the Divine Discourses of Bhagawan Sri Sathya Sai Baba, Prasanthi Nilayam: Sri Sathya Sai Sadhana Trust, Publications Division, 2011, first published in 2005.

Miracles of Divine Love, Vol. 1, Prasanthi Nilayam: Sri Sathya Sai Sadhana Trust, Publication Division, 2011.

Prasanthi Nilayam Information Booklet, compiled by Public Relations Office, Prasanthi Nilayam: Sri Sathya Sadhana Trust, Publications Division, 2003.

Voice of the Avatar: Extracts from the Divine Discourse of Bhagavan Sri Sathya Sai Baba, Part I, compiled by D. Hejmadi, Prasanthi Nilayam: Sri Sathya Sai Books and Publications, 1980.

Sathya Sai Speaks, Vol. 1: Discourses of Bhagavan Sri Sathya Sai Baba, Downloaded in a *pdf* format from the official website of Sri Sathya Sai Sadhana Trust, Publications Division - *http://www.sssbpt.info/english/sss.htm*, 10.8.2012.

Sathya Sai Speaks, Vol. 2: Discourses of Bhagavan Sri Sathya Sai Baba, Downloaded in a *pdf* format from the official website of Sri Sathya Sai Sadhana Trust, Publications Division - *http://www.sssbpt.info/english/sss.htm*, 10.8.2012.

Sathya Sai Speaks, Vol. 3: Discourses of Bhagavan Sri Sathya Sai Baba, Downloaded in a *pdf* format from the official website of Sri Sathya Sai Sadhana Trust, Publications Division - *http://www.sssbpt.info/english/sss.htm*, 10.8.2012.

Sathya Sai Speaks, Vol. 4: Discourses of Bhagavan Sri Sathya Sai Baba, Downloaded in a *pdf* format from the official website of Sri Sathya Sai Sadhana Trust, Publications Division - *http://www.sssbpt.info/english/sss.htm*, 10.8.2012.

Sathya Sai Speaks, Vol. 5: Discourses of Bhagavan Sri Sathya Sai Baba, Downloaded in a *pdf* format from the official website of Sri Sathya Sai Sadhana Trust, Publications Division - *http://www.sssbpt.info/english/sss.htm*, 10.8.2012.

Sathya Sai Speaks, Vol. 7: Discourses of Bhagavan Sri Sathya Sai Baba, Downloaded in a *pdf* format from the official website of Sri Sathya Sai

Sadhana Trust, Publications Division - *http://www.sssbpt.info/english/sss.htm*, 10.8.2012.

Sathya Sai Speaks, Vol. 8: Discourses of Bhagavan Sri Sathya Sai Baba, Downloaded in a *pdf* format from the official website of Sri Sathya Sai Sadhana Trust, Publications Division - *http://www.sssbpt. info/english/sss.htm*, 10.8.2012.

Sathya Sai Speaks, Vol. 9*: Discourse of Bhagavan Sri Sathya Sai Baba*, compiled by N. Kasturi, Delhi: Bhagavan Sri Sathya Seva Samithi, n.d.

Sathya Sai Speaks, Vol. 9: Discourses of Bhagavan Sri Sathya Sai Baba, Downloaded in a *pdf* format from the official website of Sri Sathya Sai Sadhana Trust, Publications Division - *http://www.sssbpt.info/english/sss.htm*, 10.8.2012.

Sathya Sai Speaks, Vol. 10: Discourses of Bhagavan Sri Sathya Sai Baba, Downloaded in a *pdf* format from the official website of Sri Sathya Sai Sadhana Trust, Publications Division - *http://www.sssbpt.info/english/sss.htm*, 10.8.2012.

Sathya Sai Speaks, Vol. 11: Discourses of Bhagavan Sri Sathya Sai Baba, Downloaded in a *pdf* format from the official website of Sri Sathya Sai Sadhana Trust, Publications Division - *http://www.sssbpt. info/english/sss.htm*, 10.8.2012.

Sathya Sai Speaks, Vol. 12: Discourses of Bhagavan Sri Sathya Sai Baba, Downloaded in a *pdf* format from the official website of Sri Sathya Sai Sadhana Trust, Publications Division - *http://www.sssbpt. info/english/sss.htm*, 10.8.2012.

Sathya Sai Speaks, Vol. 13: Discourses of Bhagavan Sri Sathya Sai Baba, Downloaded in a *pdf* format from the official website of Sri Sathya Sai Sadhana Trust, Publications Division - *http://www.sssbpt. info/english/sss.htm*, 10.8.2012.

Sathya Sai Speaks, Vol. 14: Discourses of Bhagavan Sri Sathya Sai Baba, Downloaded in a *pdf* format from the official website of Sri Sathya Sai Sadhana Trust, Publications Division - *http://www.sssbpt.info/english/sss.htm*, 10.8.2012.

Sathya Sai Speaks, Vol. 15: Discourses of Bhagavan Sri Sathya Sai Baba, Downloaded in a *pdf* format from the official website of Sri Sathya Sai Sadhana Trust, Publications Division - *http://www.sssbpt. info/english/sss.htm*, 10.8.2012.

Sathya Sai Speaks, Vol. 17: Discourses of Bhagavan Sri Sathya Sai Baba, Downloaded in a *pdf* format from the official website of Sri Sathya Sai Sadhana Trust, Publications Division - *http://www.sssbpt. info/english/sss.htm*, 10.8.2012.

Sathya Sai Speaks, Vol. 18: Discourses of Bhagavan Sri Sathya Sai Baba, Downloaded in a *pdf* format from the official website of Sri Sathya Sai Sadhana Trust, Publications Division - *http://www.sssbpt. info/english/ sss.htm,* 10.8.2012.

Sathya Sai Speaks, Vol. 19: Discourses of Bhagavan Sri Sathya Sai Baba, Downloaded in a *pdf* format from the official website of Sri Sathya Sai Sadhana Trust, Publications Division - *http://www.sssbpt. info/english/ sss.htm*, 10.8.2012.

Sathya Sai Speaks, Vol. 20: Discourses of Bhagavan Sri Sathya Sai Baba, Downloaded in a *pdf* format from the official website of Sri Sathya Sai Sadhana Trust, Publications Division - *http://www.sssbpt.info/english/ sss.htm*, 10.8.2012.

Sathya Sai Speaks, Vol. 21: Discourses of Bhagavan Sri Sathya Sai Baba, Downloaded in a *pdf* format from the official website of Sri Sathya Sai Sadhana Trust, Publications Division - *http://www.sssbpt.info/english/ sss.htm*, 10.8.2012.

Sathya Sai Speaks, Vol. 23: Discourses of Bhagavan Sri Sathya Sai Baba, Downloaded in a *pdf* format from the official website of Sri Sathya Sai Sadhana Trust, Publications Division - *http://www.sssbpt.info/english/ sss.htm*, 10.8.2012.

Sathya Sai Speaks, Vol. 24: Discourses of Bhagavan Sri Sathya Sai Baba, Downloaded in a *pdf* format from the official website of Sri Sathya Sai Sadhana Trust, Publications Division - *http://www.sssbpt.info/english/ sss.htm*, 10.8.2012.

Sathya Sai Speaks, Vol. 25: Discourses of Bhagavan Sri Sathya Sai Baba, Downloaded in a *pdf* format from the official website of Sri Sathya Sai Sadhana Trust, Publications Division - *http://www.sssbpt. info/english/ sss.htm*, 10.8.2012.

Sathya Sai Speaks, Vol. 26: Discourses of Bhagavan Sri Sathya Sai Baba, Downloaded in a *pdf* format from the official website of Sri Sathya Sai Sadhana Trust, Publications Division - *http://www.sssbpt. info/english/ sss.htm*, 10.8.2012.

Sathya Sai Speaks, Vol. 27: Discourses of Bhagavan Sri Sathya Sai Baba, Downloaded in a *pdf* format from the official website of Sri Sathya Sai Sadhana Trust, Publications Division - *http://www.sssbpt. info/english/ sss.htm*, 10.8.2012.

Sathya Sai Speaks, Vol. 28: Discourses of Bhagavan Sri Sathya Sai Baba, Downloaded in a *pdf* format from the official website of Sri Sathya Sai Sadhana Trust, Publications Division - *http://www.sssbpt. info/english/ sss.htm*, 10.8.2012.

Sathya Sai Speaks, Vol. 29: *Discourses of Bhagavan Sri Sathya Sai Baba,* Downloaded in a *pdf* format from the official website of Sri Sathya Sai Sadhana Trust, Publications Division - *http://www.sssbpt. info/english/ sss.htm*,10.8.2012.

Sathya Sai Speaks, Vol. 31: Discourse of Bhagavan Sri Sathya Sai Baba, Delivered during 1998, Prasanthi Nilayam: Sathya Sai Books and Publications Trust, n.d.

Sathya Sai Speaks, Vol. 32 (Part 2): Discourses of Bhagavan Sri Sathya Sai Baba, Delivered from July 1999- December 1999, Prasanthi Nilayam: Sri Sathya Sai Books & Publications Trust, 2001.

Sathya Sai Speaks, Vol. 33, Discourses of Bhagawan Sri Sathya Sai Baba, Delivered during 2000, Prasanthi Nilayam: Sri Sathya Sai Books and Publications Trust, n.d.

Sathya Sai Speaks, Vol. 34: Discourses of Bhagavan Sri Sathya Sai Baba, Delivered during 2001, Prasanthi Nilayam: Sathya Sai Books and Publications Trust, n.d.

Sathya Sai Speaks, Vol. 35: Discourses of Bhagavan Sri Sathya Sai Baba, Delivered during 2002, Prasanthi Nilayam, Sri Sathya Sai Books and Publications Trust, 2003.

Sathya Sai Speaks, Vol. 36: Discourses of Bhagavan Sri Sathya Sai Baba, Downloaded in a *pdf* format from the official website of Sri Sathya Sai Sadhana Trust, Publications Division - *http://www.sssbpt.info/english/ sss.htm*, 10.8.2012.

Sathya Sai Speaks, Vol. 37: Discourses of Bhagavan Sri Sathya Sai Baba, Delivered during 2004, Prasanthi Nilayam: Sri Sathya Sai Books and Publications Trust, n.d.

Sathya Sai Speaks, Vol. 38: Discourses of Bhagavan Sri Sathya Sai Baba, Delivered during 2005, Prasanthi Nilayam: Sri Sathya Sai Books and Publications Trust, n.d.

Sathya Sai Speaks, Vol. 39: Discourses of Bhagavan Sri Sathya Sai Baba, during 2006, Prasanthi Nilayam: Sri Sathya Sai Books and Publications Trust, n.d.

Sathya Sai Speaks, Vol. 40: Discourses of Bhagavan Sri Sathya Sai Baba, Delivered during 2007, Prasanthi Nilayam: Sri Sathya Sai Books and ublications Trust, 2008.

Sathya Sai Speaks, Vol. 41: Discourses of Bhagavan Sri Sathya Sai Baba, Delivered during 2008, Prasanthi Nilayam: Sri Sathya Sai Sadhana Trust, Publications Division, 2009.

Sathya Sai Speaks, Vol. 42: Discourses of Bhagavan Sri Sathya Sai Baba, Delivered during 2009, Prasanthi Nilayam: Sri Sathya Sai Sadhana Trust, Publications Division, 2010.

(c) Osho Rajneesh

It is divided into three categories – Printed Books, On-line Library and Books downloaded from the Websites.

(i) *Printed Books*

Osho, *Autobiography of a Spiritually Incorrect Mystic*, New York: Osho International Foundation, 2000.

________, *Glimpses of a Golden Childhood: The Rebellious Childhood of a Great Enlightened One*, Pune: Osho Media International, 2010.

________, *The Orange Book: The Meditation Techniques of Bhagavan Shree Rajneesh*, Pune: Rajneesh Foundation, 1980.

________, *Be Still and Know*, Pune: Osho Media International, 2010, first published in 1979.

________, *The Mustard Seed – The Revolutionary Teachings of Jesus: Commentaries on the Gnostic Gospel of Thomas,* Mumbai: Osho Media International, 2009, first published in 1975.

________, *From Sex to Superconsciousness*, Pune: Osho Media International, 2011, first published in 1973.

________, *The perfect Way*, Pune: Osho Media International, 2008, first published in 1975.

________, *Come Follow to You: Reflections on Jesus of Nazareth, Vol. 1,* Pune: Tao Publishing Pvt. Ltd., 2003, first published in 1976 as *Come Follow Me, Volume 1.*

________, *Come Follow to You: Reflections on Jesus of Nazareth, Vol. 2,* Pune: Tao Publishing Pvt. Ltd., 2003, first published in 1977 as *Come Follow Me, Volume 2.*

________, *I Say Unto You: Talks on the Sayings of Jesus, Vol. 1,* New Delhi: Diamond Pocket Books, Pvt. Ltd., 1996.

________, *Meditation: The Art of Ecstasy*, Pune: Osho Media International, 2009, first published in 1973.

Rajneesh, Bhagawan Shree, *The Great Pilgrimage from Here to Here*, Cologne: The Rebel Publishing House, 1988.

(ii) *On-line Library*

Osho, *The Last Testament, Vol. 1*, retrieved from Osho Internationals official website online - Library, *http://www.osho.com/library/online-library-blessed-moment-followers-9c6fd47a-413.aspx*

________, *From Unconsciousness to Consciousness*, retrieved from Osho Internationals official website online Library, *http://www.osho.com/library/online-library-brainwashing-mahavira-points-b58e703c-4d4.aspxp*

________, *I Celebrate Myself: God is No Where, Life is Now Here*, retrieved from Osho Internationals official website online Library, *http://www.osho.com/library/online-library-celebrate-nietzsche-cleans-9b073fa4-46a.aspx*

________, *Socrates Poisoned Again After 25th Century*, retrieved from Osho Internationals official website online Library, *http://www.osho. com/library/online-library-foundation-zorba-the-buddha-man-72e3a20b-1ac.aspx*

________, *The Rebellious Spirit*, retrieved from Osho Internationals official website online Library, *http://www.osho.com/library/online-library-revolution-centeredness-first-44ba8ff4-42a.aspx*

________, *Christianity: The Deadliest Poison and Zen: The Antidote to All Poisons,* retrieved from Osho Internationals official website online Library, *http://www.osho.com/library/online-library-tozan-yakusan-finger-48bf6651-269.aspx*

________, *The Zen Manifesto: Freedom from Oneself*, retrieved from Osho Internationals official website online Library, *http://www.osho.com/library/online-library-ego-self-mirrors-80a24f5d-6d5.aspx*

________, *Dance your Way to God*, retrieved from Osho Internationals official website online Library, *http://www.osho.com/library/online-library-revolution-centeredness-first-44ba8ff4-42a.aspx*

________, *From the False to the Truth*, retrieved from Osho Internationals official website online Library, *http://www.osho.com/library/online-library-enquiry-eve-eternal-60a0b539-500.aspx*

________, *Yoga: The Science of Living*, retrieved from Osho Internationals official website online Library, *http://www.osho.com/library/online-library-love-indivisible-fasting-38173b16-34e.aspx*

________, *Showering Without Clouds*, retrieved from Osho Internationals official website online Library, *http://www.osho.com/library/online-library-love-passion-attachment-5de53298-b88.aspx*

________, *From Bondage to Freedom*, retrieved from Osho Internationals official website online Library, *http://www.osho.com/library/the-books.aspx*

(iii) *Downloaded from Websites*

Osho, *From Misery to Enlightenment*, downloaded in a *pdf* format from *http://www.messagefrommasters.com/Ebooks/Osho_Discourse_Series.htm,* 09.04.2013.

________, *From Personality to Individuality*, downloaded in a *pdf* format from *http://www.messagefrommasters.com/Ebooks/Osho_Discourse_Series.htm,* 09.04.2013.

________, *The Rebel*, downloaded in a *pdf* format from *http://www.messagefrommasters.com/Ebooks/Osho_Discourse_Series.htm,* 09.04.2013.

________, *This, This, A Thousand Times This: The Very Essence of Zen*", downloaded in a *pdf* format from *http://www.oshorajneesh.com/osho-zen-books.htm*, 09.04.2013.

________, *From Death to Deathlessness*, downloaded in a *pdf* format from *http://www.messagefrommasters.com/Ebooks/Osho_Discourse_Series.htm,* 09.04.2013.

________, *The Path of the Mystics*, downloaded in a *pdf* format from *http://www.oshorajneesh.com/osho-world-tour-discourses.htm*, 09.04.2013.

________, *Come, Come Yet Again Come*, downloaded in a *pdf* format from *http://www.oshorajneesh.com/osho-discourses.htm*, 09.04.2013.

________, *A Rose is a Rose is a Rose,* downloaded in a *pdf* format from *http://www.messagefrommasters.com/Ebooks/Osho_Darshan_Diaries.htm,* 09.04.2013.

________, *Beyond Psychology*, downloaded in a *pdf* format from *http://www.oshorajneesh.com/osho-world-tour-discourses.htm*, 09.04.2013.

________, *Satyam Shivam Sundaram*, downloaded in a *pdf* format from *http://www.messagefrommasters.com/Ebooks/Osho_Discourse_Series.htm,* 09.04.2013.

________, *Zorba the Buddha*, downloaded in a *pdf* format from *http://www.messagefrommasters.com/Ebooks/Osho_Darshan_Diaries.htm,* 09.04.2013.

________, *Unio Mystica, Vol. 1*, downloaded in a *pdf* format from *http://www.oshorajneesh.com/osho-books-on-sufi.htm*, 10.04.2013.

________, *Until You Die*, downloaded in a *pdf* format from *http://www.oshorajneesh.com/osho-books-on-sufi.htm*, 10.04.2013.

________, *Dance Your Way to God*, downloaded in a *pdf* format from *http://www.messagefrommasters.com/Ebooks/Osho_Darshan_Diaries.htm,* 09.04.2013.

________, *The Path of Mystic*, downloaded in a *pdf* format from *http://www.oshorajneesh.com/osho-world-tour-discourses.htm*, 09.04.2013.

________, *Blessed are the Ignorant*, downloaded in a *pdf* format from *http://www.messagefrommasters.com/Ebooks/Osho_Darshan_Diaries.htm,* 09.04.2013.

________, *My Way the Way of the White Clouds*, downloaded in a *pdf* format from *http://www.messagefrommasters.com/Ebooks/Osho_Discourse_Series.htm,* 09.04.2013.

________, *From Darkness to Light*, downloaded in a *pdf* format from *http://www.messagefrommasters.com/Ebooks/Osho_Discourse_Series.htm,* 09.04.2013.

________, *The Madman's Guide to Enlightenment*, downloaded in a *pdf* format from *http://www.messagefrommasters.com/Ebooks/Osho_Darshan_Diaries.htm*, 09.04.2013.

________, *Vigyan Bhairav Tantra, Vol 2*, downloaded in a *pdf* format from *http://www.messagefrommasters.com/Ebooks/Osho_Books_on_Tantra_&_Mantra.htm,* 09.04.2013.

________, *I Say Unto You: Talks on the Sayings of Jesus, Vol. 2,* downloaded in a *pdf* format from *http://www. oshorajneesh.com/osho-books-on-jesus-christ.htm*, 8.03.2013.

________, *Sufis: The People of the Path, Vol. 2*, downloaded in a *pdf* format from *http://www.oshorajneesh.com/osho-books-on-sufi.htm*, 10.04.2013.

________, *Come Follow to You: Reflection on Jesus of Nazareth, Vol. 3,* downloaded in a *pdf* format from *http://www.oshorajneesh.com/osho-books-on-jesus-christ.htm*, 8.03.2013.

________, *Come Follow to You: Reflections on Jesus of Nazareth, Vol. 4*, downloaded in a *pdf* format from *http://www.oshorajneesh.com/osho-books-on-jesus-christ.htm*, 8.03.2013.

________, *Yoga: The Alpha and the Omega, Vol. 2*, downloaded in a *pdf* format from *http://www.oshorajneesh.com/osho-yoga-books.htm*, 10.04.2013.

________, *Yoga: The Alpha and the Omega, Vol. 3*, downloaded in a *pdf* format from *http://www.oshorajneesh.com/osho-yoga-books.htm*, 10.04.2013.

________, *Yoga: The Alpha and the Omega, Vol. 10*, downloaded in a *pdf* format from *http://www.oshorajneesh.com/osho-yoga-books.htm*, 10.04.2013.

________, *God's Got a Thing About You*, downloaded in a *pdf* format from *http://www.oshorajneesh.com/osho-darshan-diaries.htm*, 07.05.2013.

_______, *The Wisdom of the Sands, Vol. 2,* downloaded in a *pdf* format from *http://www.oshorajneesh.com/osho-books-on-sufi.htm*, 10.04.2013.

_______, *Yoga: The Alpha and the Omega, Vol. 6*, downloaded in a *pdf* format from *http://www.oshorajneesh.com/osho-yoga-books.htm*, 10.04.2013.

_______, *Tantra: The Supreme Understanding*, downloaded in a *pdf* format from *http://www.messagefrommasters.com/Ebooks/Osho_Books_on_Tantra_&_Mantra.htm* 09.04.2013.

_______, *The Beloved, Vol. 1: Talks on the Baul Mystics* downloaded in a *pdf* format from *http://www.oshorajneesh.com/osho-books-on-indian-mystics.htm*, 08.05.2013.

_______, *The Path of Love: Talks on Songs of Kabir*, downloaded in a *pdf* format from *http://www.oshorajneesh. com/osho-books-on-indian-mystics.htm*, 08.05.2013.

_______, *The Last Testament, Vol. 3*, downloaded in a *pdf* format from *http://www. oshorajneesh.com/osho-personal-glimpses.htm*, 09.04.2013.

_______, *The Last Testament, Vol. 4*, downloaded in a *pdf* format from *http://www.oshorajneesh.com/osho-personal-glimpses.htm*, 09.04.2013.

_______, *The Last Testament, Vol. 5*, downloaded in a *pdf* format from *http://www.oshorajneesh.com/osho-personal-glimpses.htm*, 09.04.2013.

_______, *Last Testament, Vol. 6*, downloaded in a *pdf* format from *http://www.oshorajneesh.com/osho-personal-glimpses.htm*, 09.04.2013.

(d) Sri Sri Ravishankar

Bajaj, Karishma, (Comp.), *Precious Gems of Wisdom – His Holiness Poojya Sri Sri Ravi Shankar*, Mumbai: Magna Publishing Co. Ltd., 2008.

Patanjali Yoga Sutras: A Commentary by H.H. Sri Sri Ravi Shankar, Vol. 1, Bangalore: Sri Sri Publications Trust, 2010.

Ravishankar, Sri Sri, *Bang on the Door: A Collection of Talks*, Second Revised Edition, Bangalore: Sri Sri Publication Trust, 2008.

________, *An Intimate Note to the Seeker, Vol. 1*, compiled by David L. Burge, Santa Barbara: Art of Living Foundation, 2002; first published in 1997.

________, Sri Sri, *An Intimate Note to the Seeker, Vol. 2*, compiled by David L. Burge, Santa Barbara: Art of Living Foundation, 2000.

________, *An Intimate Note to the Sincere Seeker, Vol. 3,* compiled by David L. Burge, Santa Barbara: Art of Living Foundation, 2000, first published in 1998.

________, *An Intimate Note to the Seeker Vol. 4: July 30, 1998 – July 28, 1999*, compiled by Anne Elixhauser & Bill Hayden, Bangalore: Vyakti Vikas Kendra, 1999.

________, *An Intimate Note to the Sincere Seeker, Vol. 5*, compiled by Anne Elixhauser & Bill Hayden, Bangalore: Vyakti Vikas Kendra, 2002.

________, *An Intimate Note to the Seeker Vol. 6*, compiled by Bill Hayden and Anne Elixhauser, Bangalore: Vyakti Vikas Kendra, 2002.

________, *An Intimate Note to the Sincere Seeker, Vol. 7,* compiled by Bill Hayden &Anne Elixhauser, Bangalore: Vyakti Vikas Kendra, 2003.

________, *Belongingness to Silence*, Bangalore: Vyakti Vikas Kendra, India Publications, 2006.

________, *Celebrating Silence*, Second Edition, Bangalore: Sri Sri Publication Trust, 2008.

________, *God Loves Fun*, Bangalore: Sri Sri Publications Trust, 2008.

________, *Hinduism and Christianity*, Second Edition, Bangalore: Vyakti Vikas Kendra India, 1999.

________, *Living the Mystery of Life*, Bangalore: Sri Sri Publications Trust, 2012.

________, *Love is not an Emotion-It is Your Very Existence*, Bangalore: Sri Sri Publications Trust, 2012.

________, *Nārada Bhakti Sūtra: The Aphorism of Love*, Bangalore: Sri Sri Publications Trust, 2003.

________, *Punarnava: New Again*, Bangalore: Sri Sri Publications Trust, 2009.

________, *Wisdom for the New Millennium*, Mumbai: Jaico Publishing House, 2005.

Shiva Sutras: A Commentary by His Holiness Sri Sri Ravi Shankar, Bangalore: Sri Sri Publications Trust, 2010.

Timeless Wisdom: The Book of all Religions, Bangalore: Sri Sri Publication Trust, 2008.

(e) Others

Akhilananda, Swami, *Hindu View of Christ*, Boston: Branden Press Publishers, 1949.

Chidananda, Sri Swami, "Christ's Divine Life" in Swami Shivananda, *Life and Message of Jesus Christ*, Shivanandanagar: The Divine Life Trust Society, 1996, first published in 1959.

________, "Thy Kingdom Come" in Swami Shivananda, *Life and Message of Jesus Christ*, Shivanandanagar: The Divine Life Trust Society, 1996, first published in 1959.

Gandhi, M.K., *My Experiments with Truth: An Autobiography*, Ahmedabad: Jaico Publishing House, 2010.

Keshub Chander Sen, edited and compiled by David C. Scott, Madras: CLS Press, 1978.

Krishnananda, Swami, "A Sacramental Life" in Swami Shivananda, *Life and Message of Jesus Christ*, Shivanandanagar: The Divine Life Trust Society, 1996, first published in 1959.

________, "The Christ to the Spiritual Aspirant", in Swami Shivananda, *Life and Message of Jesus Christ*, Shivanandanagar: The Divine Life Trust Society, 1996, first published in 1959.

________, *Spiritual Import of Religious Festivals*, Third Edition, Shivanandanagar: The Divine Life Society, 2006.

Miracles of Sivananda, Third Edition, Shivanandanagar: A Divine Life Society Publication, 1992.

Prabhupada, A.C. Bhaktivedanta Swami, *The Science of Self Realization*, Los Angeles: Bhaktivedanta Book Trust International, 1972-2004: Internet Version.

Radhakrishnan, S., *East and West in Religion*, London: George Allen & Unwin Ltd., 1933.

________, *Eastern Religions and Western Thought*, London: Oxford University Press, 1940.

________, *Recovery of Faith*, Delhi: Orient Paperbacks, 1967.

________, *The Bhagavad Gita*, New Delhi: HarperCollins Publishers, 2010.

________, *The Heart of Hindustan*, Madras: G.A. Natesan & Co., 1936.

________, *The Hindu View of Life*, London: George Allen & Unwin Ltd., 1931.

________, "Reply to Critics" in *The Philosophy of Sarvepalli Radhakrishnan*, edited by Paul Arthur Schilpp, Delhi: Motilal Banarsidass Publishers, 1992, pp. 789-842.

________, "The Religion of the Spirit and the World's Need: Fragments of a Confession" in *The Philosophy of Sarvepalli Radhakrishnan*, edited by Paul Arthur Schilpp, Delhi: Motilal Banarsidass Publishers, 1992, pp. 5-82.

Roy, Raja Rammohun, "An Appeal to the Christian Public in Defence of 'The Precepts of Jesus'", in *The English Works of Raja Rammohun Roy*, in *The English Works of Raja Rammohun Roy*, edited by Kalidas Nag and Debajyoti Burman, Calcutta: Sadharan Brahmo Samaj, 1995.

________, "Final Appeal to the Christian Public in Defence of 'The Precepts of Jesus'", in *The English Works of Raja Rammohun Roy*, edited by Kalidas Nag and Debajyoti Burman, Calcutta: Sadharan Brahmo Samaj, 1995.

________, "Second Appeal to the Christian Public in Defence of 'The Precepts of Jesus'", in *The English Works of Raja Rammohun Roy*, edited by Kalidas Nag and Debajyoti Burman, Calcutta: Sadharan Brahmo Samaj, 1995.

________, "The Precepts of Jesus: The Guide to peace and Happiness; Extracted from the Books of the New Testament, Ascribed to the Four Evangelists", *The English Works of Raja Rammohun Roy*, edited by Kalidas Nag and Debajyoti Burman, Calcutta: Sadharan Brahmo Samaj, 1995.

Shivananda, Swami, *Life and Message of Jesus Christ*, Shivanandanagar: The Divine Life Trust Society, 1996, first published in 1959.

________, *Practice of Karma Yoga*, Shivanandanagar: A Divine Life Society Publication, 1995.

The Collected Works of Mahatma Gandhi, Vol. 8, New Delhi: Publications Division, Ministry of Information & Broadcasting, Government of India, 1999, (Revised and CD-ROM Version).

The Collected Works of Mahatma Gandhi, Vol. 15, New Delhi: Publications Division, Ministry of Information & Broadcasting, Government of India, 1999, (Revised and CD-ROM Version).

The Collected Works of Mahatma Gandhi, Vol. 17, New Delhi: Publications Division, Ministry of Information & Broadcasting, Government of India, 1999, (Revised and CD-ROM Version).

The Collected Works of Mahatma Gandhi, Vol. 18, New Delhi: Publications Division, Ministry of Information & Broadcasting, Government of India, 1999, (Revised and CD-ROM Version).

The Collected Works of Mahatma Gandhi, Vol. 20, New Delhi: Publications Division, Ministry of Information & Broadcasting, Government of India, 1999, (Revised and CD-ROM Version).

The Collected Works of Mahatma Gandhi, Vol. 22, New Delhi: Publications Division, Ministry of Information & Broadcasting, Government of India, 1999, (Revised and CD-ROM Version).

The Collected Works of Mahatma Gandhi, Vol. 23, New Delhi: Publications Division, Ministry of Information & Broadcasting, Government of India, 1999, (Revised and CD-ROM Version).

The Collected Works of Mahatma Gandhi, Vol. 24, New Delhi: Publications Division, Ministry of Information & Broadcasting, Government of India, 1999, (Revised and CD-ROM Version).

The Collected Works of Mahatma Gandhi, Vol. 26, New Delhi: Publications Division, Ministry of Information & Broadcasting, Government of India, 1999, (Revised and CD-ROM Version).

The Collected Works of Mahatma Gandhi, Vol. 29, New Delhi: Publications Division, Ministry of Information & Broadcasting, Government of India, 1999, (Revised and CD-ROM Version).

The Collected Works of Mahatma Gandhi, Vol. 31, New Delhi: Publications Division, Ministry of Information & Broadcasting, Government of India, 1999, (Revised and CD-ROM Version).

The Collected Works of Mahatma Gandhi, Vol. 33, New Delhi: Publications Division, Ministry of Information & Broadcasting, Government of India, 1999, (Revised and CD-ROM Version).

The Collected Works of Mahatma Gandhi, Vol. 34, New Delhi: Publications Division, Ministry of Information & Broadcasting, Government of India, 1999, (Revised and CD-ROM Version).

The Collected Works of Mahatma Gandhi, Vol. 36, New Delhi: Publications Division, Ministry of Information & Broadcasting, Government of India, 1999, (Revised and CD-ROM Version).

The Collected Works of Mahatma Gandhi, Vol. 39, New Delhi: Publications Division, Ministry of Information & Broadcasting, Government of India, 1999, (Revised and CD-ROM Version).

The Collected Works of Mahatma Gandhi, Vol. 40, New Delhi: Publications Division, Ministry of Information & Broadcasting, Government of India, 1999, (Revised and CD-ROM Version).

The Collected Works of Mahatma Gandhi, Vol. 41, New Delhi: Publications Division, Ministry of Information & Broadcasting, Government of India, 1999, (Revised and CD-ROM Version).

The Collected Works of Mahatma Gandhi, Vol. 44, New Delhi: Publications Division, Ministry of Information & Broadcasting, Government of India, 1999, (Revised and CD-ROM Version).

The Collected Works of Mahatma Gandhi, Vol. 45, New Delhi: Publications Division, Ministry of Information & Broadcasting, Government of India, 1999, (Revised and CD-ROM Version).

The Collected Works of Mahatma Gandhi, Vol. 48, New Delhi: Publications Division, Ministry of Information & Broadcasting, Government of India, 1999, (Revised and CD-ROM Version).

The Collected Works of Mahatma Gandhi, Vol. 50, New Delhi: Publications Division, Ministry of Information & Broadcasting, Government of India, 1999, (Revised and CD-ROM Version).

The Collected Works of Mahatma Gandhi, Vol. 52, New Delhi: Publications Division, Ministry of Information & Broadcasting, Government of India, 1999, (Revised and CD-ROM Version).

The Collected Works of Mahatma Gandhi, Vol. 54, New Delhi: Publications Division, Ministry of Information & Broadcasting, Government of India, 1999, (Revised and CD-ROM Version).

The Collected Works of Mahatma Gandhi, Vol. 61, New Delhi: Publications Division, Ministry of Information & Broadcasting, Government of India, 1999, (Revised and CD-ROM Version).

The Collected Works of Mahatma Gandhi, Vol. 63, New Delhi: Publications Division, Ministry of Information & Broadcasting, Government of India, 1999, (Revised and CD-ROM Version).

The Collected Works of Mahatma Gandhi, Vol. 64, New Delhi: Publications Division, Ministry of Information & Broadcasting, Government of India, 1999, (Revised and CD-ROM Version).

The Collected Works of Mahatma Gandhi, Vol. 68, New Delhi: Publications Division, Ministry of Information & Broadcasting, Government of India, 1999, (Revised and CD-ROM Version).

The Collected Works of Mahatma Gandhi, Vol. 70, New Delhi: Publications Division, Ministry of Information & Broadcasting, Government of India, 1999, (Revised and CD-ROM Version).

The Collected Works of Mahatma Gandhi, Vol. 71, New Delhi: Publications Division, Ministry of Information & Broadcasting, Government of India, 1999, (Revised and CD-ROM Version).

The Collected Works of Mahatma Gandhi, Vol. 74, New Delhi: Publications Division, Ministry of Information & Broadcasting, Government of India, 1999, (Revised and CD-ROM Version).

The Collected Works of Mahatma Gandhi, Vol. 81, New Delhi: Publications Division, Ministry of Information & Broadcasting, Government of India, 1999, (Revised and CD-ROM Version).

Vivekananda, Swami, *Chicago Address*, Kolkata: Advaita Ashrama, 2010.

________, *The Complete Works of Swami Vivekananda* 1-8 volumes, Mayavati Memorial Edition, Calcutta: Advaita Ashrama, 1994.

3. Internet Sources

"Life of Paramhansa Yogananda", in the Official website of Self Realization Fellowship at *http://www.yogananda-srf.org/tmp/py_notitle.aspx?id=44#.UZc7gUpPXi4,* 18.05.2013.

Chidananda, Sri Swami, "Essence of Christianity", in the Facebook account created by Divine Life Society Mumbai Circle at *http://www.facebook.com/note.php?note_id=171079982929051*, 23.07.2012.

Krishnananda, Swami, "Characteristics of the Teachings of Jesus" a Chapter from a book - *World* Christmas celebrations at Amritapuri 2009, in *http://www.amritapuri.org/7414/09christmas.aum,* 14.07.2012.

The Official website of Sri Sri Ravishankar *http://srisriravishankar.org/biography*, 28.11.2012.

The official website of Sri Sri Ravishankar *http://srisriravishankar.org/service-organizations/art-of-living,* 28.11.2012.

The official website of Sri Sri Ravishankar *http://srisriravishankar.org/*.

The Official Website of Sri Sri Ravishankar *http://srisriravishankar.org/service-organizations/art-of-living*, 28.11.2012.

The official website of AOL: *http:// srisriravishankar.org/node/50*, 4.7.2011.

4. Audio CD

Ravishankar, Sri Sri, "Jesus Embodiment of Love", a lecturer delivered at California, USA on 8th Aug. 1996, in Audio CD produced by Sri Sri Publication Trust, Bangalore, 2011.

II. Secondary Sources

1. Personal Interview

Gangadhar Sastri in a personal interview at Prasanthi Nilayam, Puttaparthi on 29th October, 2012.

Swami Smaranananda, the General Secretary of Yogoda Satsanga Society of India, Yogoda Satsanga Skha Math, Ranchi, India on 20th July, 2013.

2. Books

Abhedananda, Swami, *Journey to Kashmir and Tibet*, Calcutta: Ramakrishna Vedanta Math, 1987.

Ahuja, M.L., *Gurus: Ancient, Medieval and Modern*, New Delhi: Rupa & Co, 2009.

Aleaz, K.P., *Jesus in Neo-Vedanta: A Meeting of Hinduism and Christianity*, Delhi: Kant Publications, 1995.

________, *An Indian Jesus from Sankara's Thought*, Calcutta: Punthi Pustak, 1997.

________, *Theology of Religions: Birmingham Papers and other Essay*, Calcutta: Moumita Publishers & Distributors, 1998.

________, *Dialogical Theologies: Hartford Papers and Other Essays*, Kolkata: Punti Pustak, 2004.

Apte, Vaman Shivram, *The Student's Sanskrit-English Dictionary*, Delhi: Motilal Banarsidass, 2000.

Baago, Kaj, *Pioneers of Indigenous Christianity*, Madras: CLS, 1969.

Bakshi, S.R., *Raja Rammohan Roy: Pathmaker of India*, New Delhi: Om Publications, 2001.

Bartsch, Hans Werner (ed,), *Kerygma and Myth* by Rudolph Bultmann and Five Critics, New York: Harper & Row, 1948.

Bhagavad Gītā with the Commentary of Śri Śaṅkarācharya, translated by A. Mahadeva Shastri, Mysore: Government Oriental Library, 1901.

Brent, Peter, *Godmen of India*, Middlesex: Penguin Books, 1972.

Broke, Tal, *Avatar of Night: The Hidden Side of Sai Baba*, New Delhi: Tarang Paperbacks, 1982.

Bultmann, Rudolph, *New Testament & Mythology and Other Basic Writings*, Philadelphia: Fortress Press, 1984.

Carpenter, J. Estlin, *The Historical Jesus and the Theological Christ*, Boston: American Unitarian Association, 1912.

Chakkaraia, V., *Jesus the Avatar*, Madras: Christian Literature Society for India, 1926.

Charpentier, Marie-Therese, *Indian Female Gurus in Contemporary Hinduism: A Study of Central Aspects and Expressions of their Religious Leadership*, Biskopsgatan, Abo, Finland: Abo Akademi University Press, 2010.

Chattopadhyaya, Sudakar, *Ethnic Elements in Ancient Hinduism*, Calcutta: The Principal Sanskrit College, 1979.

Cheriyan, C.V., *History of Christianity in Kerala*, Kottayam: Kerala Historical Society, 1973.

Cole, W. Owen, *The Guru in Sikhism*, London: Darton, Longman & Todd, 1982.

Courtois, Luc J., *The Promise Fulfilled*, Bangalore: Message Publications, 2008.

D'Costa, Cavin, *Christianity and World Religions: Disputed Questions in the Theology of Religions*, West Sussex: Wiley-Backwell, 2009.

Dasgupta, B.N., *The Life & Times of Raja Rammohun Roy,* New Delhi: Ambika Publication, 1980.

Dasgupta, Sailendra Bejoy, *Paramhansa Swami Yogananda: Life-portrait and Reminiscences*, translated into English by Yoga Niketan Team, Michigan: Yoga Niketan, 2006.

Datta, D.M., *The Six Ways of Knowing*, Calcutta: University of Calcutta, 1997, first published in 1932.

Farquhar, J.N., *The Modern Religious Movement in India*, New York: Macmillan Co., 1915.

________, *The Crown of Hinduism*, London: Oxford University Press, 1920.

Forescue, Adrian, *The Lesser Eastern Churches*, London: Catholic truth Society, 1913.

Fredriksen, Paula, *From Jesus to Christ*, Yale: Yale University Press, 2000.

Gandhi and Communal Problems, Compiled & Published by Centre for Study of Society and Secularism, Mumbai: Centre for Study of Society and Secularism, 1994.

Gautier, Francois, *The Guru of Joy: Sri Sri Ravi Shankar & The Art of Living*, New Delhi: Hay House Publishers (India) Pvt. Ltd., 2011, (First published in 2002).

Gautier, Namrita and Francois Gautier, *The Art of Healing: Pranayama – The Breath of Life*, New Delhi: HarperCollins Publishers, India, 2010.

Geisler, Norman, *Baker Encyclopedia of Christian Apologetics*, Grand Rapids: Baker Books, 1999.

Ghosh, Sri Sananda Lal, *"Mejda": The Family and the Early Life of Sri Paramhansa Yogananda*, Dakshineswar: Yogoda Satsanga Society of India, 2012, first published in 1980.

Giri, Swami Sri Yukteswar, *The Holy Science*, Dakshineswar, Kolkata: Yogoda Satanga Society of India, 2007, first published in 1949.

Gokak, V.K., *Bhagavan Sri Sathya Sai Baba: The Man and the Avatar – An Interpretation*, New Delhi: Abhinav Publications, 1989.

Goswami, Satsvarupa Dasa, *Srila Prabhupada Lilamrta: A Biography of His Divine Grace A.C. Bhaktivedanta Swami Prabhupada*, Los Angeles: Bhaktivedanta Book Trust, 1980.

________, *Prabhupada: He Built a House in Which the Whole World Can Live*, Los Angeles: Bhaktivedanta Book Trust, 1983.

Guidelines on Dialogue, Geneva: World Council of Churches, 1982, first published in 1979.

Gyan, Satish Chandran, *Sivananda and his Ashram*, Madras: Christian Literature Society, 1980.

Hazra, R. C., *Studies in the Puranic Records on Hindu Rites and Customs,* Dacca The University of Dacca, 1940.

Hick, John, *God and the Universe of Faiths: Essays in the Philosophy of Religion*, London: Macmillan, 1973.

Hone, William, *Apocryphal New Testament*, London: Ludgate Hill, 1820.

Jacobs, Alan, *When Jesus Lived in India: The Quest for the Aquarian Gospel: The Mystery of the Missing Year,* Mumbai: Yogi Impression, 2010.

Joshi, Vasant, *The Luminous Rabel: Life Story of a Maverick Mystic*, New Delhi: Wisdom Tree, 2010.

Kahler, Martin, *The So-Called Historical Jesus and the Historic Biblical Christ*, translated by Carl E. Braaten, Philadelphia: Fortress Press, 1964.

Kalapati, Joshua, *Dr. Radhakrishnan and Christianity: An Introduction to Hindu-Christian Apologetics*, Delhi: ISPCK, 2002.

Kant, Immanuel, *Critique of Pure Reason*, translated by Paul Guyer and Allen W. Wood, Cambridge: Cambridge University Press, 1998.

Kasturi, N., *Sathyam Sivam Sudaram, Vol – 1 (Life Story of Bhagavan Sri Sathya Sai Baba 1926-1961*), Prasnathi Nilayam: Sri Sathya Sai Sadhana Trust, 2009, first published in 1990.

________, *Sathyam Sivam Sudaram, Vol – 2 (Life Story of Bhagavan Sri Sathya Sai Baba 1962-1968*), Prasnathi Nilayam: Sri Sathya Sai Sadhana Trust, 2009, Third Edition.

________, *Sathyam Sivam Sudaram, Vol – 3 (Life Story of Bhagavan Sri Sathya Sai Baba 1969-1972)*, Prasnathi Nilayam: Sri Sathya Sai Sadhana Trust, 2008, Revised and Enlarged.

________, *Sathyam Sivam Sudaram, Vol – 4 (Life Story of Bhagavan Sri Sathya Sai Baba 1973-1979)*, Prasnathi Nilayam: Sathya Sai Books and Publication Trust, 2003.

Kersten, Holger, *Jesus Lived in India: His Unknown Life Before and After the Crucifixion*, New Delhi: Penguin Books India Pvt. Ltd., 2001.

Kheirabadi, Masoud, *Sri Satya Sai Baba*, Philladelphia: Chelsea House Publishers, 2005.

Kierkegaard, Soren, *Concluding Unscientific Postscript to Philosophical*, edited and translated by Howard V. Hong and Edna H. Hong, Princeton: Princeton University Press, 1992.

Kriyananda, Swami, *Revelations of Christ Proclaimed by Paramhansa Yogananda*, Gurgaon: Ananda Sangha Publications, 2007.

________, *Paramhansa Yogananda: A Biography with Personal Reflections and Reminiscences,* Gurgaon: Ananda Sangha Publications, 2011.

Kumar, Kailash & Jorgen Hovgaard, *Sai Baba: The Source of Light, Love and Bliss*, New Delhi: Sterling Paperbacks, 1995.

MacGregor, Geddes, *Reincarnation in Christianity: A New Vision of the Role of Rebirth in Christian Thought*, Wheaton, Illinois: The Theosophical Publishing House, 1978.

Mahajan, V.D., *The Nationalist Movement in India,* New Delhi: Sterling Publishers Pvt. Ltd., 1979.

Mangalwadi, Vishal, *The World of Gurus: Critical Look at the Philosophies of India's Influential Gurus and Mystics*, Revised Edition, Chicago: Conerstone Press, 1992.

Manson, Peggy & Ron Laing, *Sathya Sai Baba: The Embodiment of Love*, London: Sawbridge, 1982.

Mathew, P.V., *Acta Indica: (The Acts of St. Thomas in India)*, Ernakulam: P.V. Mathew, 1986.

Mazzoleni, Don Mario, *A Catholic Priest Meets Sai Baba*, translated by Christian Moevs, Prasanthi Nilyam: Sri Sathya Sai Books & Publications Trust, 2008.

Mehrotra, Rajiv, *The Mind of the Guru: Conversations with Spiritual Masters*, New Delhi: Hey House India, 2010.

Mehta, Uday, *Modern Godmen in India: A Sociological Appraisal*, Bombay: Popular Prakashan, 1993.

Mueller, Friedrich M., *Last Essays*, New York: AMS Press, Inc., 1973, first published in 1901.

Mullan, Bob, *Life as Laughter: Following Bhagavan Shree Rajneesh*, London: Routledge & Kegan Paul plc, 1983.

Mundadan, A.M., *History of Christianity in India, Vol. 1*, Bangalore: Theological Publications in India, 1984.

Murphet, Howard, *Sai Baba: Man of Miracles*, Delhi: Macmillan, 1975.

________, *Sai Baba: Invitation to Glory*, Delhi: Macmillan India Limited., 1982.

Murthy, B.N. Narasimha, *Sathyam Sivam Sudaram, Vol – 5 (Life Story of Bhagavan Sri Sathya Sai Baba 1980-1985)*, Prasnathi Nilayam: Sathya Sai Books and Publication Trust, 2005.

________, *Sathyam Sivam Sudaram, Vol – 6 (Life Story of Bhagavan Sri Sathya Sai Baba 1986-1993)*, Prasnathi Nilayam: Sathya Sai Books and Publication Trust, 2007.

________, *Sathyam Sivam Sudaram, Vol – 7 (Life Story of Bhagavan Sri Sathya Sai Baba 1980-1985)*, Prasnathi Nilayam: Sri Sathya Sai Sadgana Trust, Publication Division, 2010.

Nag, Kalidas, *Tolstoy and Gandhi*, Patna: Pustak Bhandar, 1950.

Nanda, Meera, *The God Market: How Globalization is Making India More Hindu*, Noida: Random House Publishers India, 2009.

Narayan, Sreejith, *Sai, Thy Kingdom Come: A Deliberation on the Possibility of Sri Sathya Sai Baba's "Return"*, New York: Premjith Narayan, 2012.

Neill, Stephen, *A History of Christianity in India: The Beginnings to A.D. 1707*, London: Cambridge University Press, 1984.

Notovitch, Nicholas, The *Unknown Life of Jesus Christ*, translated from French by Alexina Loranger, Fourth Edition, Chicago: Indo-American Book Agency, 1916.

Panikkar, Raimundo, *The Fullness of Man: A Christophany*, New York/New Delhi: Orbis/ ISPCK, 2006.

________, *The Unknown Christ of Hinduism. Towards an Ecumenical Christophany*, Revised and Enlarged Edition London: Darton, Longman & Todd, 1981.

Parekh, Manilal C., *Brahmarshi Keshub Chunder Sen*, Rajkot: Oriental Christ House, 1926.

________, *A Hindu Portrait of Jesus Christ*, Rajkot: Sri Bhagavata Dharma Mission, 1958.

Philip, T.V., *Krishna Mohan Banerjea. Christian Apologist*, Madras/Bangalore: CLS/CISRS, 1982.

Phipps, Peter, *Sathya Sai Baba and Jesus Christ: A Gospel for the Golden Age*, Third Edition, Auckland: Sathya Sai Publications of New Zealand, 1996, first published in 1994.

________, *Greater than You Know: Sathya Sai Baba, Jesus Christ and Christianity*, Auckland: Sathya Sai Publications of New Zealand, 1997.

Pieris, Aloysius, *An Asian Theology of Liberation*, Maryknoll: Orbis Books, 1988.

Pillai, A.S. Appasamy, *The Use of Yoga in Prayer*, Madras: CLS, 1926.

Pistis Sophia, translated into English by G.R.S. Mead, Leeds: Celephais Press, 2007, first published in 1896.

Prophet, Elizabeth Clare, *The Lost Years of Jesus: Documentary Evidence of Jesus' 17-Year Journey to the East*, Gardiner: Summit University Press, 1984.

_________, *Reincarnation: The Missing Link in Christianity*, Montana: Summit University Press, 1997.

Pryse, James M., *Reincarnation in the New Testament*, New York: Theolophical Society Publishing Department, 1904.

Purnaiya, Nagamani, *Divine Leelas of Bhagwan Sathya Sai Baba*, Puttaparthi: Sri Sathya Sai Towers Pvt. Ltd., 1998.

Ram Chandra Prasad, *Rajneesh: The Mystic of Feeling*, Revised Edition, Delhi: Motilal Banarsidass, 1978.

Samartha, S.J., *The Hindu Response to the Unbound Christ*, Madras: CLS, 1974.

Sarma, D.S., *Studies in the Renaissance of Hinduism in the Nineteenth and Twentieth Centuries*, Benares: Benares Hindu University, 1944.

Sarma, P.P.S., *Bhagawan Baba's Glory of Unity*, Prasanthi Nilayam: Sri Sathya Sai Sadhana Trust, Publications Division, 2010.

Schmidt, Peter, *Krishna Meets Jesus: A.C. Bhaktivedanta Swami Srila Prabhupiida's Interpretations and Conclusions about Christianity,* Germany: Books on Demand GmbH, 2002.

Singh, Khushwant, *Gods and Godmen of India*, New Delhi: HarperCollins Publishers & India Today Group, 2003.

Singh, Kirpal, *Godmen*, Delhi: Ruhani Satsang, 1967.

Thomas, M.M., *The Acknowledged Christ of the Indian Renaissance*, Madras: CLS, 1970.

Uban, Sujan Singh, *The Gurus of India*, New Delhi: Sterling Publishers Pvt. Ltd., 1978.

Vermani, R.C., *Colonialism and Nationalism in India*, New Delhi: Gitanjali Publishing Home, 2000.

Vining, Marvin, *Jesus the Wicket Priest: How Christianity was Born of an Essene Schism*, Vermount: Bear & Company, 2008.

Voorst, Robert E. Van, *Jesus Outside the New Testament: An Introduction to the Ancient Evidence,* Grand Rapids: William B. Eerdmans Publishing Company, 2000.

Waardenburg, Jacques, *Classical Approaches to the Study of Religion: Aims, Methods and Theories Research,* The Hague: Mouton & Co., 1973.

Walker III, Ethan, *The Mystic Christ: The Light of Non-Duality and the Path of Love According to the Life and Teachings of Jesus,* Redmond, Oregon: Devi Press, 2003.

Weeraperuma, Susunaga, *Divine Messengers of Our Time*, Delhi: Sri Satguru Publications, 1998.

Woodroffe, Sir John, *Shakti and Shakta,* Madras: Ganesh and Co, 1951.

Yogi, Mahesh, *The Science of Being and the Art of Living*, New Delhi: Allied Publishers, 1963.

3. Edited Books

Amitabh, Swami Prem, "Shree Rajaneesh Ashram Poona: A Provocative Community", in *Osho Rajneesh & His Disciples: Some Western Perceptions*, edited by Harry Aveling, Delhi: Motilal Banarsiadss, 1999, pp. 93-128.

Bassuk, Daniel E., "Six Modern Indian Avatars and the Ways they Understand their Divinity" in *Dialogue & Alliance*, Vol. 1 no 2, summer 1987, pp. 73-92.

Berger, Peter L., "The Desecularization of the World: A Global Overview", in *The De-secularization of the World: Resurgent Religion and World Politics*, edited by Peter L. Berger, Washington, D.C./Grand Rapids: Ethics and Public Policy Center/ William B. Eerdmans Publishing Company, 1999, pp. 1-18.

Borg, Marcus J., "The Spirit-Filled Experience of Jesus", in James D. G. Dunn, *The Historical Jesus in Recent Research*, Winona Lake: Eisenbrauns, 2005, pp. 302-314.

Carter, Lewis F., "The 'New Renunciates' of Bhagavan Shree Rajneesh: Observations and Identification of Problems of Interpreting New Religious Movements", in *Osho Rajneesh and His Disciples: Some Western Perceptions*, edited by Harry Aveling, Delhi: Motilal Banarsidass Publishers, 1999, pp. 175-218.

Chaubey, B.B., "The Nature of Guruship According to the Hindu Scriptures" in *The Nature of Guruship,* edited by Clarence O. McMullen, Delhi: ISPCK, 1976, pp. 9-25.

Crawford, Cromwell, "Raja Ram Mohan Roy's Attitude toward Christians and Christianity", in *Neo-Hindu Views of Christianity*, edited by Arvind Sharma, Leiden: Brill Academic Publishers, 1988, pp. 16-65.

Lal, Ratan, "Sri Sathya Sai Baba", in *Gurus, Godmen and Good People*, edited by Khushwant Singh, Bombay: Orient Longman Ltd., 1975, pp.

Lsatkin, Carl A., "Seeing Red: A Social-Psychological Analysis of the Rajneeshpurum Conflict" in *Osho Rajneesh and His Disciples: Some Western Perceptions*, edited by Harry Aveling, Delhi: Motilal Banarsidass Publishers, 1999, pp. 337-362.

Lsatkin, Carl A., et.al. "Who Lives in Utopia?: A Brief Report on the Rajneeshpuram Research Project" in *Osho Rajneesh and His Disciples: Some Western Perceptions*, edited by Harry Aveling, Delhi: Motilal Banarsidass Publishers, 1999, pp. 359-407.

Mahadevan, T.M.P, "The Religio-Philosophic Culture of India" in *The Cultural Heritage of India*, Suniti Kumar Chatterji, etc. (eds.), Calcutta: Ramakrishna Mission Institute of Culture, 1982, pp. 163-181.

Marchetto, Monia, "The Function of the Guru in Tantric Traditions", in *Guru the Spiritual Master in Eastern and Western Traditions: Authority and Charisma*, edited by Antonio Rigopoulos, Venice: Venetion Academy of Indian Studies, & New Delhi: D.K. Printworld (P) Ltd., 2007, pp. 227-233.

McMullen, Charence O., "The Nature of Guruship: A Sociological Perspective", in *The Nature of Guruship,* edited by Clarence O. McMullen, Delhi: ISPCK, 1976, pp. 163-170.

Nambiaparambil, Albert, "Religions in Dialogue: Indian Experience Today", *Meeting of Religions: New Orientations and Perspectives*, edited by Thomas A. Aykara, Bangalore: Dharmaram Publications, 1978, pp. 76-88.

Nirmal, Arvind P., “Theological Implications of the Term ‘Indigenous’” in *Dialogue in Community: Essay in Honour of S.J. Samartha*, edited by C.D. Jathanna, Mangalore: The Karnataka Theological Research Institute, 1982, pp. 169-177.

Panikkar, Raimundo, “The Jordan, the Tibera, and the Ganges: Three Kairological Moments of Christic Self-Consciousness” in *The Myth of Christian Uniqueness: Towards a Pluralistic Theology of Religions*, edited by John Hick and Paul F. Knitter, New York: Orbis Books, 1995, first published in 1987, pp. 89-116.

Patrick, John, *Origen's Commentary on the Gospel of Matthew, Book XIII,* in Ante-Nicene Father, Vol. 9, edited by Philip Schaff, Edinburgh: T&T Clark, 1897.

Prem, Ma Ananda, “Bhagavan Shree Rajneesh: The Modern Buddha” in *Gurus, Godmen and Good People*, edited by Khushwant Singh, New Delhi: Orient Longman Ltd., 1975, pp. 7-14.

Sharpe, Eric J. “Neo-Hindu Images of Christianity” in *Neo-Hindu Views of Christianity*, edited by Arvind Sharma, Leiden: Brill Academic Publishers, 1988, pp. 1-15.

Singh, Khushwant, “Gurus, Godmen and Good People”, in *Gurus, Godmen and Good People*, edited by Khushwant Singh, New Delhi: Orient Longman Ltd., 1975, pp. vii-xv.

Wallis, Roy, “Religion as Fun? The Rajneesh Movement” in *Osho Rajneesh & His Disciples: Some Western Perceptions*, edited by Harry Aveling, Delhi: Motilal Banarsiadss, 1999, pp. 129-162.

4. Journals, Magazines and Newspapers

D'Souza, Mervyn C., “Krishna and Arjuna: A Model of Guru - *Sisya* Relationship”, in *Journal of Dharma*, Vol. XI, No. 1, January-March, 1986, pp. 9-16.

Devdas, Nalini, “The Christ of the Ramakrishna Movement”, in *Religion and Society*, Vol. 11, No. 3, 1964, pp. 13-28.

Duraisingh, Christopher. “Indian Hyphenated Christians and Theological Reflection Part II: An Alternate Modes of Theologizing now Prevalent in India” in *Religion and Society*, Vol. XXVII, No. 2, June 1980, pp. 81-101.

Fallon, P. “A Critical Evaluation of Hindu Interpretation of Christ” in *Indian Journal of Theology*, Vol. 18, No.1, January-March, 1969, pp. 81-87.

Gupta, Ravi M., “‘He is our master’: Jesus in the Thought of Swami Prabhupada”, in *Journal of Hindu-Christian Studies*, Vol. 23, Article 7, 2010, pp. 15-19.

Joseph, Simon J., "Jesus in India?" *Journal of the American Academy of Religion,* Volume 80, Issue 1, pp. 161-199.

Malkovsky, Bradley, "Some Recent Developments in Hindu Understandings of Jesus" in *Journal of Hindu-Christian Studies*, Vol. 23, Article 5, 2010, pp. 3-8.

Mlecko, Joel D., "The Guru in Hindu Tradition" in *Numen*, Vol. 29, No. 1 J1, 1982.

Pape, W. Roy, "Keshup Chunder Sen's Doctrine of Christ and the Trinity: A Rehabilitation" in *Indian Journal of Theology*, Vol. 25, No. 2, April-June 1976, pp. 55-71.

Paradkar, Balwant A.M. "Hindu Interpretation of Christ from Vivekananda to Radhakrishnan" in *Indian Journal of Theology*, Vol. 18, No. 1, January-March, 1969, pp. 65-80.

Prasannabhai, C.M.I., "Sadguru" in *Vidyajyoti: Journal of Theological Reflection*, Vol. XL, No. 7, August, 1976, pp. 315-319.

Ralte, Rodinmawia, "'Jesus of India': The Unveiled Christ of the Contemporary Hindu Gurus", *Bangalore Theological Forum*, Vol. XLV, No. 1, June 2013, pp. 163-180.

Russell, J., "The Guru in Hinduism", in *The Pilgrim: The Quarterly Bulletin of the Christian Society for the Study of Hinduism,* Vol. V. No. 3, October, 1945.

Samartha, S.J., "S. Radhakrishnan: Jesus Christ – One among the Many" in *Religion and Society*, Vol. 11, No. 3, 1964, pp. 38-52.

Santram, Philip J., "Christ of the Brahmo Samaj Movement", in *Religion and Society*, Vol.11, No. 3, 1964, pp. 7-12.

Thomas, Daniel, "What Jesus Meant to Gandhi", in *Religion and Society*, Vol. ii, No. 3, 1964, pp. 29-37.

Vandana, "The Guru - *Sisya* Relationship in the Indian Tradition", in *Third Millennium*, Vol. III, No. 2, 2000; April-June, pp. 60-68.

Reader Digest, February 2007.

5. Electronic Sources

'The Findings' in *http://www.npi-news.dk/page152.htm*, 2.01.2013.

"Interfaith Organization Worldwide" in *https://sites.google.com/site/interfaithdialoguebasicseu/a-new-church/interfaith-organizations-worldwide*, 23.10. 2012.

"May the Christ take birth in your heart" Christmas Celebrtation at Amritapuri, 2008, in *http://www.amritapuri. org /2472/christbirth.aum*, 14.07.2012.

"Osho Rajneesh" *The Famous People website*, 2013, in *http://www.thefamouspeople. com/profiles/osho-rajneesh-23.php*, 13.02.2013.

"Understanding Kṛṣṇa and Christ" in *http://theharekrishnamovement.wordpress.com /2012/04/08/ understanding -krsna-and-christ-2/#more-3139*, 24.07.2012.

Christmas celebrations in Amritapuri 2006, in *http://archives.amritapuri.org/news/2006/612xmas.php*, 14.07.2012.

http://askbaba.helloyou.ch/discourses/d1974/d19740600-18.html, 27.07.2011.

http://barrypittard.wordpress.com/2010/04/11/ typical-testimony-of-sathya-sai-babas-sex-abuse-of-young-males/, 30.12.2012.

http://en.wikipedia.org/wiki/Patanjali_Yogpeeth, 20.07.2012.

http://exposedsaibaba.blogspot.in/2009/05/murder-deception-debauchery-and-deciet.html, 2.01.2013.

http://ibnlive.in.com/news/what-makes-indians-keep-the-faith/32015-3.html, 21.07.2007.

http://saibaba-invigilator.blogspot.in/2007/06/my-story-by-diana-scott-later-mrs.html, 30.12.2012.

http://www.saibaba.ws/ miracles2/abookonhim.htm, 27.07.2011.

http://www.saibaba.ws/ miracles2/abookonhim.htm, 27.07.2011.

http://www.saibaba.ws/miracles.htm, 12.10.2012.

http://www.saibabacontroversy.com/abs.html, 30.12.2012.

http://www.saibabacontroversy.com/Summary.html, 2.01.2013.

http://www.saibaba-x.org.uk/30/Haraldsson.html, 4.01.2013.

http://www.saibaba-x.org.uk/6/saisex1.htm, 30.12.2012.

http://www.saiguru.net/english/ (30.12.2012); *http://77.170.120.22/ex-baba/engels/articles/ allegations.html*, 30.12.2012.

Video record of Interview with him, in *http://www.youtube.com/watch?v=AIWqJ8tJ8JU*, 27.07.2012.

Yogananda, Paramhansa, "Contacting God in Meditation" in

http://www.anandaclaritymagazine.com/2003/09/yogananda-meditation-god-peace/ 24.07.2011.

Glossary of Sanskrit Terms

Ācārya – religious teacher

Ādi – original

Aham Brahmāsmi – I am the Brahman

Ahiṃsā – negatively it means abstinence from violence either by thought, word, or deed. In a positive sense, it implies compassion and cosmic love

Amsāvatār – fractional incarnation, partial incarnation

Andhakar – darkness

Āśram – hermitage

Āśrama – life stage, there are four *Āśramas* in Hinduism

Ātma/Ātman – Supreme Soul, Brahman

Aum – a mantra and mystical sacred sound

Avatāra – Incarnation of God

Avidyā – ignorance

Bande Mātaram – 'I bow to thee, mother'

Bhagawān – God

Bhakta – devotee, religious person, one who practices *bhakti*

Bhakti – loving devotion

Bhastrikā – a kind of breathing technique where breathing is forcible and through the nose, with equal time for inhalation and exhalation

Bhasya – commentary

Brahmacharya – the first stage in life, student stage

Chaitanya - Pure Consciousness, the Cosmic Intelligence

Darśana – vision, it is rendered as philosophy

Dehi – the soul

Dharma - that which upholds or sustains the positive order of things; the eternal law of the cosmos. It can also means religion, duties, rights, laws, conduct, virtues and right way of living

Dhyāna – meditation

Dṛta – seer

Dvaita – dualism

Ekam sad viprā bahudhā vadanti – truth is one, sages call it by many names

Gṛhasthya – the second stage in life, a stage of householder

Guhā – cave, mountain cave, hiding place, a secret place; the heart

Guru – spiritual teacher and guide

Gurukula – a type of school residential in nature, with pupils living near the guru, often within the same house

Hiranyagarbha – source of the creation of the Universe or the manifested cosmos, it is called 'golden egg' in Ṛg Veda

Īśvara – Lord, denoting personal God or God in relation to created order

Jada – matter, inert, lifeless

Japamala – a set of prayer beads 108 in number

Jayantī – birthday

Jivanmukta – one who is liberated while living in a human body

Jñāna – knowledge

Karana-Janma – a master born with a purpose

Karma – action, activities

Karma-Saṃsāra – doctrine of transmigration of soul from one body to another; doctrine of rebirth

Karsevak – one who offers services for free to a religious cause

Karuṇā – compassion, tender

Kirtan – praise; eulogy or corporate/ community singing in praise of God

Kutaṣtha – Changeless, immutable, dweller in the height, a name of Brahman

Langar – free kitchen for the people, this practice is common among Sikhs and Sufis

Līlā – pastime, sport or play

Mahant – a religious superior like a chief priest of a temple or a head of a monastery

Mahaṛṣis - Great Sages

Mantra - a sacred utterance, numinous sound, or a syllable, word, phonemes, or group of words believed by some to have spiritual power

Māyā – (loosely) illusion; it is also understood as 'supernatural power of God'

Mokṣa – liberation, freedom, salvation

Neo-Vedāntins – Followers of Advaita Vedānta with slight modification especially emphasizing on the social aspect of it.

Nirguṇa – beyond quality or supra-personal

Nirvāṇa – 'blown out' – It refers to the imperturbable stillness of mind after the fires of desire, aversion, and delusion have been finally extinguished or blown out; Liberation

Pañcabhūtas - five basic elements such as earth, water, fire, air and ether that constitute the entire universe

Paramhansa – 'supreme swan', *sannyāsin* of the highest order

Pāshandinas – atheists, irreligious people

Prakṛti – 'nature'; matter; the primordial element with which material world is made

Pramāṇa – source of valid knowledge

Prāṇa – breath, the life force

Prāṇāyāma – regulation of breath through certain techniques and exercises

Prasavā – birth through normal conception

Pratika – image or symbol of God

Pratyakṣā – that which is present before the eyes, perceptible, cognizable by any of the sense organs

Praveśa – birth not through a normal human conception but through divine intervention, like incarnation

Prema – love

Premāvatāra – *i*ncarnation of Divine Love

Pūjā – prayer ritual, a form of worship

Punarjanma – reincarnation, rebirth

Pundit – a learned person in religion and philosophy

Purnāvatara – full-fledged incarnation

Purohita – priest of the Vedic religion

Puruṣārtha – human end, human goal

Raja yoga – royal yoga, a form of yoga intended to achieve control over the mind and emotions

Rāmjanmabhūmi – the birth place of Rāmā

Ṛṣis – Sages

Saccidananda – the combination of *sat* (being), *cit* (coinsciousness) and *ānanda* (bliss)

Satya – truth

Ṣaḍ darśanā – six schools of Hindu philosophy

Sadguru/satguru – true guru, a title given to those who are truly enlightened masters

Sādhanā – spiritual discipline practiced with intended goal

Sādhu – holy man, sage, ascetic

Saguṇa – with qualities, with characters

Śākta – worshipper of the Mother Goddess; it is also used in Vedic time to refer to a teacher

Samādhi – the final stage of Yoga; it is also used to denote the state of final enlightenment

Sampradāya – tradition, religious system

Sanātana – eternal, having no beginning

Sangāthan – organization, unity

Sannyāsin – one who is in the *sannyāsa* order/stage - the life stage of the renouncer. It also refers in general to those who renounce the world and worldly pleasures and dedicate fully in the pursuance of spirituality

Sannyāsya – the last and final stage in life where a person completely gives up/ renounces the world

Sant – Saint

Śānthi – peace

Sarsanghachalak – RSS chief

Sarva dharma samabhav - equal respect to all religions – *sarva* (all), *dharma* (religion), and *Samabhav* (benevolent, kind, equability)

Śāstras – scripture

Satori – seeing into one's true nature or essence, it is generally translated as 'enlightenment'

Satsang – a spiritual discourse or sacred gathering; it can be translated literally as the company of a guru

Sāyujya – oneness with the Lord/God; merging into the effulgence of the Lord

Seva – selfless service rendered for the sake of others

Siddhi – supernatural power

Śiṣya – disciple

Smṛti – secondary Hindu religious texts which includes *sūtras*, *dharma śāstras*, epics – Mahābhārata with *Bhagavad Gītā* and Rāmāyaṇa, *purāṇas*, etc.

Śṛuti – primary scriptures of the Hindus that includes the four Vedas with their respective Brahmānas and Upaniṣads

Sthitadheeh Muni – a sage who is steady in happiness and sorrow, heat and cold, unaffected by praise and criticism

Śuddhi – purification, re-conversion

Sukhāsana – a yoga posture where the practitioner sits at ease by crossing legs

Śūnyatā – emptiness, voidness, openness, hollowness

Svastika – literally means 'it is good', it is connected with the worship of Śiva

Swāmi – technically a yogi who has been initiated into the religious monastic order; it also means lord or master.

Tapasyā – penance, deep meditation

Tat tvam asi – you are that

Tathya – truth, reality

Tīrthaṃkara – 'ford maker'; a saviour who has succeeded in crossing over the ocean of births and re-births and has made a path for others to follow

Titikṣa – endurance, patience, resignation, forbearance

Trikalajana - one who knows the past, present and future

Turīya – the experience of pure consciousness, the fourth state of consciousness beyond waking consciousness, dreaming, and dreamless sleep

Ujjāyi – a type of breathing in which the lungs are fully expanded and the chest is puffed out

Upādhyāya – one type of guru who taught part of the Vedas, during the period of *Dharma Śāstras*

Upanayana – one of the sacraments of the Hindus, it is initiation ritual by which initiates are invested with a sacred thread

Vaiṣṇava – a member of Viṣnavism, a devotee of Lord Viṣnu

Vajrāsana – a yoga posture where the practitioner sits on the heels with the calves beneath the thighs

Vanaprasthya – the third stage in life where a person leaves his/her home to live in a forest as a hermit showing that one gradually withdraws from the world

Viśiṣṭādvaita – qualified non-dualism

Yajña – ritual sacrifice

Yogi/yogin – the practitioner of yoga; one who is a master of yoga

Index

A

Abba 135
Abhedananda, Swami 24
Abraham 189
Abrahamic covenant 115
Absolute Spirit 87, 102
Ācārya 1, 4, 6, 8, 10, 129, 160-161, 180
Adinatha 168-169
Advaita 126, 129-130, 153, 209, 222, 232
Advaitic framework 47, 56-57
Aeroplane route 86, 114
Agricultural Institute 206
Aham Brahmāsmi 17
Ahiṃsā 62, 131
Ahuja, M.L. 159
Akashic 214
Akhilananda, Swami 24-25, 42, 48-53, 59, 97, 230
Aleaz, K.P. 92
Allah 127
Altars 214
Amen 106
America 48, 73, 76, 90
Amitabh, Swami Prem 176
Amma 67-68
Amritanandamayi, Mata 17, 19, 67, 71
Amritapuri 67
Amsavatāras 121
Ānanda 33
Anarchist 157
Andhakar 5
Andhra Pradesh 118
Antelope 162
Āpastamba 8
Apostles 23, 29, 111, 143
Arabian kings 141
Arjuna 9, 86
Art of Living Foundation 203, 205
Ascetic-guru 6, 10
Asiatic 14, 37, 41, 59, 97, 230
Āśram 6, 18, 67, 94, 113, 117, 125, 143, 153, 161-163, 180, 214, 217, 227
Āśrama Dharma 6
Astral World 83, 92, 102
Atharva Veda 6
Atheistic philosophies 13
Ātma 67, 70, 127
Ātman 63, 127-128, 133, 171
Atomic Illumination 63
Atonement 28-29, 56, 58, 143, 196
Aum 106
Aurobindo, Sri 121, 139, 172
Authentic individuality 157
Autobiography 35, 73, 75-76, 94, 102
Avatār of Night 123
Avatāra 4, 9, 14, 32, 43-44, 47, 49, 55, 61, 65, 67, 70-71, 77, 80, 97, 101, 110, 112-115, 119, 121-122, 124, 134, 139-140, 142, 200, 230, 232
Avatārship 97, 121
Avidya 5
Ayurveda 19
Ayuvedic research 206

B

Ba-Ba 145, 154
Baba, Sri Sathya Sai 3, 12, 14, 17-19, 61, 117-155, 158, 200, 224, 227, 229-230, 232
Babaji, Mahāvatar 74-76, 78, 93
Babulal 158
Bailey, David 123
Bailey, Faye 123

Balarama 121
Bangalore 203, 205, 214, 217
Baptist missionaries 26, 93
Beatitudes 64, 108-109
Belongingness 91, 135, 153, 155, 213, 215, 227
Bengali 74, 230
Berger, Peter L. 11
Bhadravati 205
Bhagavad Gītā 1, 9, 15, 41, 62, 73, 78, 90-91, 93, 96, 108, 114, 204-205
Bhagavan 14, 17-18, 44, 90, 97, 113, 124, 126-128, 131-132, 135, 138, 143, 147-148, 150, 153, 157, 161, 163, 180
Bhāgavata Purāṇa 10, 121
Bhagavatta 161
Bhagawāns 1
Bhagwatta 173
Bhakta 47, 51
Bhakti 18-19, 30, 51, 88, 114, 129-130, 150, 153, 208, 211
Bhakti Sūtra 211
Bhakti yoga 19, 51, 208
Bharat 152
Bharatiya Vidhya Bhavan Auditorium 160
Bhastrikā 216
Bhasya 1
Bible 36-37, 41, 58, 73, 78, 90-91, 93-96, 101, 113-114, 116, 135-136, 138, 140-141, 148, 150-154, 181, 200, 217, 224-225, 229, 232-233
Big Muddy Ranch 162
Blessed One 161, 163
Blessed Spirit 81
Bliss 13, 40, 63-64, 66, 79-80, 82, 106, 122, 128, 149, 189, 210
Blissful Kingdom of Heaven 64
Bliss-God 89
Bombay 160-161
Book of Revelation 93, 135
Bose, Subhas Chandra 160
Boston 76
Brahma 79
Brahmacharya 6, 62, 75
Brahman 1, 6-7, 17, 32-34, 45, 59, 64, 79, 99, 106, 114, 128, 197, 209-210
Brahmanism 12, 14, 16, 18, 21, 175
Brahmin 14, 34, 122, 204
Brāhmo Samāj 26
Brent, Peter 15
Bṛhannāradiya-puraṇa 9
Bṛhaspati 9
British 25
British administration 25
Brook, Tal 123
Brotherhood of Man 133-134
Buddha 37, 43-47, 50, 55, 57, 97-99, 121, 125, 136, 138, 157, 163-165, 167-169, 171, 175-176, 181-187, 189-190, 193-194, 198, 201, 221
Buddhahood 170, 173, 194, 201
Buddhas 45, 99
Buddhism 2, 23, 101, 157, 163-164, 168
Bukkapatnam 120
Bultmann, Rudolf 99

C

Caitanya Vaiṣṇava 70
Calcutta University 75
Carey, William 93
Carter, Lewis F. 162
Caste 14, 16-19, 21, 81, 119, 132, 175, 215
Catalepsy 183
Catalytic 182
Catastrophe 183
Catharsis 174, 183
Cause of matter and intelligence 79
Celebration 67, 113, 126, 141, 153, 175, 177, 179, 185-188, 200, 213, 216, 231
Chaitanya 38, 87, 100, 103, 108, 111
Chalcedonian Creed 99
Chalcedonian Formula 233
Chāndogya Upaniṣad 6-8
Charpentier, Marie –Therese 18
Chatterjee and Datta xv
Chaubey, B. B. 3
Children of God 109, 133, 227
Chit 33, 128
Christ Center 85, 87
Christ Consciousness 64-65, 84, 87, 91, 95-100, 103-108, 111-112, 114, 116, 181-183, 189-190, 201, 220, 224, 233
Christ of faith 99, 116
Christ Will 44, 68, 101, 232
Christendom 91, 234
Christhood 45, 189, 201, 230
Christian 12-13, 16, 20, 23-35, 37, 39-40, 42, 46, 48-50, 53-55, 57-60, 62-63, 66-68, 70-72, 78, 80, 83, 86, 89-91, 93-94, 96-97,

99, 101, 104-105, 110, 113-116, 136-138, 141-142, 144-145, 150, 154-155, 166, 174, 176, 179, 181-185, 187, 190, 192, 196, 200-201, 219-220, 222, 225-226, 228-235
Christian era 23, 137
Christian missionary 12, 16, 25, 54, 58
Christian missions 12
Christian mystics 114, 183
Christian theologians 48, 116, 229, 231
Christian tradition 29, 231
Christian worldview 71, 228
Christian-Hindu relations 73
Christianity 12-13, 21, 29-30, 33, 37, 39-41, 45-46, 49, 54, 56, 58-59, 64, 70, 90, 92-93, 96, 104, 110, 116, 125, 145, 168, 175, 182, 184-185, 195-196, 200-201, 214-215, 217, 223, 234
Christification 32
Christified 180, 192
Christmas 58, 62, 67, 113, 125-126, 137, 141-142, 152
Christmas Day 118, 137
Christmas Discourse 139-140, 143-145
Christmas Eve 113
Christ-ness 71
Christogenesis 192
Christological formulations 115-116, 230, 232
Christological title 31, 65
Christology 31-35, 93, 99, 116, 137, 145, 217, 228-229, 234
Christs 45, 99
Church 13, 30, 37, 87, 90-91, 110-111, 114, 143, 152, 159, 228, 232
Church of All Religion 90, 228
Church of New Dispensation 30
Civilization 168, 177
Commentary 67, 78, 95-96, 111, 181, 198, 202, 211, 223
Commonwealth 66
Communion 33, 36, 76, 87-88, 93-96, 103-104, 111-115, 224-225, 228, 230-231, 234
Con Man 157
Congress 36, 76
Consciousness 53, 57, 64-69, 71, 74, 79-80, 82, 87-89, 91-92, 95-100, 102-109, 111-112, 114, 116, 122, 128-129, 133, 140, 147, 170-171, 174, 176-177, 182, 187-190, 193-194, 196, 200, 209-211, 218, 220, 223-224, 230, 232-233
Contemporary guruism 11, 16, 18, 20
Contemporary gurus 11-12, 16-20, 47, 68, 73, 134, 157, 180, 184, 190, 196, 200, 204, 206, 224, 234
Contextual Critiquing xiv
Contingent truths 99
Conversion 183, 227
Cosmic Consciousness 79, 82, 87-88, 95, 104-108, 122
Cosmic energy 84, 86, 101
Cosmic Flame 81
Cosmic illusion 51, 82
Cosmic Intelligence 45, 87, 98-99, 106
Cosmic Magician 107
Cosmic Mother 106
Cosmic Ruler 106
Cosmic Vibration 98, 106
Courtois, Luc J. 136, 142
Creative Intelligence 208
Creator 31, 33, 79-80, 102, 196
Creed 10, 36, 54-55, 58, 99, 134, 167
Crescent and the star 125
Critique of Pure Reason 99
Cross 28-29, 33-34, 38-39, 43, 46-48, 51-53, 56-61, 64-65, 69-70, 72, 101-102, 125, 133, 136, 143-145, 183, 185, 190-194, 199-201, 222-223, 232-233
Crossianity 185
Crucifixion 33, 39, 46-47, 56, 66, 69-70, 95, 102, 143-144, 148-149, 152, 154, 192-193, 199, 222

D

D'Souza, Mervyn C. 4
Danish 24, 99
Darkness 2-6, 52, 57, 64-65, 129, 235
Darśanā 126, 180
Date of Christmas 152
Day of judgment 104
Death 6, 11, 19, 27-29, 38-39, 41, 46, 51-53, 56-59, 63, 65, 69-70, 72, 77, 79, 81, 108, 111, 119, 122, 136, 142-145, 148, 151, 159, 168-169, 183, 187-188, 213, 222, 224-225, 230, 233, 235
Deathless Yogi 74, 93
Dehi 147
Deity 8, 10, 28, 31
Devil 52, 107, 179

Devotee 9, 18-21, 38, 40, 45, 60, 67, 69-70, 84-85, 87, 102, 104, 107-109, 113, 117-118, 120, 122, 124, 126, 130, 135, 137-138, 141, 143, 150, 155, 161, 203, 211, 224, 227-228
Dharma 2, 6, 8-9, 16, 18, 41, 93, 97, 125, 131, 153, 210, 234
Dharma Śāstras 8-9, 18
Dhyāna 10, 174
Direct experience of Truth 78
Discourse 15, 118, 122-123, 125, 128, 134-135, 137, 139-141, 143-145, 157-158, 161, 163, 166, 168, 171, 177, 180, 198, 207, 211, 214, 217, 229
Divine 3-4, 9, 14-15, 25, 29, 31, 34, 42, 45, 47, 50, 54-59, 69, 74, 76, 81-82, 87-88, 97, 103, 105, 108-109, 112, 115-116, 121, 126-128, 133, 136-137, 140-141, 146-148, 170, 179, 183, 186, 191, 200, 209, 214-215, 217, 220-221
Divine Deliverer 64
Divine humanity 29, 31, 34
Divine incarnations 49, 138
Divine Kingdom 63
Divine Life 17, 61, 63-65, 71, 77, 132
Divine Life Society 61, 63, 65, 71, 77
Divine Love 77, 139
Divine Messenger 62, 138
Divine Mother 80, 121, 135
Divine Oneness 82
Divine Persons 138
Divine Reality 108
Divine Saviours 138
Divine Teacher 28, 38
Divinity 5, 30-34, 38, 41, 45, 52, 55, 58-59, 63, 78, 80, 89, 128, 131-132, 138, 140, 145-148, 150-151, 153, 188, 192, 200, 209, 215, 220-223
Divinity incarnate 63
Doctrine 4, 21, 26-28, 32-35, 37, 39, 41, 46, 53-54, 57, 59, 63, 71, 81, 91-92, 104, 107, 110-111, 113-114, 141, 145, 147, 153-154, 166, 184, 196-197, 225, 227, 233
Downtrodden 185, 225
Draṣta 120
Drunkards 185
Duraisingh, Christopher 93
Durkheim, Emil 11
Dvaita 17, 42, 127, 129-130, 140, 153, 230, 232
Dynamic Meditation 19, 161, 174

E

East 54, 89, 97, 100, 141, 163
Easter 52
Eastern 54, 67, 73, 142, 164, 180, 214
Eastern spirituality 73, 164
Easwaramma 119
Ecstasy 95, 104, 115, 159, 189
Education 14, 18, 25, 93, 117, 121, 123-124, 153, 158-160, 205-206
Egypt 28, 34
Einstein 209
Eli, Eli, lamasabachthani 192
Elias 110
Elijah 63, 110-111
Eliseus 110
Elisha 110-111
Embodiment of Love 139, 190, 217-219, 224-226
English 24, 30
Enlightenment 4, 13, 56, 159-161, 168, 170-173, 178-179, 184, 192-194, 198, 213, 215, 227, 231-232
Enreligionization 91
Epics 9, 18
Epistemology xv
Epistles 104
Essenes 193
Eternal 27-28, 31-32, 34, 43, 46, 52, 55, 57, 60, 64, 79-80, 83-84, 104, 108, 116, 127, 171, 189, 192, 209-210, 220-221
Eternal Bliss 80
Eternal Kingdom 108
Eternal Light 64
Eternal Word 55
Ethics 94, 106
Europe 37
Ever-present Presence 64
Exclusivism 54
Existence 14, 57, 76, 81, 83, 117, 128, 146, 169-171, 173, 177-179, 190, 193-194, 200, 209, 211, 220, 222, 224
Existentialism 13
Experience 5, 7, 13, 21, 25, 36, 42, 46-47, 52, 56, 59-60, 66, 71, 74, 77-79, 82-83, 87-88, 92-95, 99, 108-109, 111-115, 126, 146, 160-161, 177-179, 181-184, 192-193, 198, 202, 209, 222, 225, 227, 233-234

F

Fascism 177
Fasting 44, 187-188, 214
Father 2, 8-9, 10, 16, 28, 30, 31-35, 41, 44, 46, 50-51, 59, 62, 66-67, 69, 75, 78, 81, 84, 88, 91, 95, 102, 105-107, 119, 121, 135-136, 140, 142, 144-145, 149, 152, 192, 194, 196-197, 204, 209, 218, 221-223, 233-234
Father in heaven 50, 66, 91, 220
Fatherhood of God 126, 133-134, 146
Father's kingdom 32, 107
Filial incarnation 31
First-Begotten Son 31
Fischman, Michael 207
Fisherman 185
Five pillars 130-131
Flesh and blood 52, 94, 102-104, 112, 115, 148, 230
Francis, St. 103
French 24
Freud, Sigmund 11, 169
Friend of India 27
Fulfillment 4, 21

G

Gadarwada 159
Gamblers 185
Gandhi, Mahatma 24-26, 35-41, 59
Ganges 34
Gauranga, Shri 44
Gautier, Francois 205, 207-208
Geddes MacGregor 111
German Lutheran Churches 231
Ghosh, Mukunda Lal 74
Globalization 14-15, 21
God incarnate 38, 46, 64, 80
God is dead 169
God of Jesus 109
God of Moses 109
God of wrath 109
God's lila 82
God-consciousness 66, 108
Godhead 10, 52, 55, 64, 69
Godliness 161, 169-170, 173-174, 179
Godman 9, 31, 119
Godmen 15, 154
God-realization 51, 65, 100, 108
God-realized masters 107
Good Friday 58
Good News of Jesus 137
Gorakhpur 74
Gospel 23, 26, 28, 36, 41, 44-45, 53-55, 58, 61-62, 73, 78, 92, 95-96, 104-105, 111, 116, 154, 194, 224-225, 233
Gospel of Christ 73
Gospel of John 28, 44-45
Gotak,V. K. 126
Great Sages 1, 100, 138
Great Teachers 35, 37-38, 138
Greece 28, 34
Greek philosophers 104
Gṛhasthya 6
Gupta, Ravi M. 69-70
Gurdjieff 157, 164
Guru 1-21, 23, 47, 53, 61-78, 89, 91-94, 96-97, 101-102, 104-105, 107, 112-115, 118, 124, 134, 136, 138, 157, 160, 164, 180, 184, 190, 194, 196, 199-200, 203-204, 206-207, 209, 212, 218, 224-235
Guru movement 12, 14, 19-20, 227
Guru Nanak 12, 136, 138
Guru of Joy 212
Guruism 2, 5-6, 10-16, 18, 20-21, 71
Gurukulas 214
Guru-worship 11, 18

H

Hades 107-108
Hail Almighty 64
Hazra, R. C. 9
Heaven 31-32, 46, 50, 60, 63-64, 66-69, 71, 83, 87, 91, 102-104, 107-108, 142, 144, 146-147, 149, 163, 167, 194, 220
Heavenly Father 75, 78, 95, 107, 221
Hebrew language 37
Heidegger 13
Hell 68, 107, 163, 167, 198, 222
Hermeneutical principle 59, 228, 231
Heterosexuality 15
Hill View Stadium 126
Himalaya 103
Himalayan region 76, 152
Himalayan Yogi 74, 76
Hindu 2-5, 11-14, 16-18, 21, 23-60, 63, 68, 71, 73, 80-81, 90-91, 94, 97, 99-101, 104, 106-108, 111, 113, 115-117, 119, 123, 125-126, 135, 142, 147, 151-153, 157, 159,

174-176, 183-184, 197, 200-201, 203-204, 220, 222, 224-225, 231, 234-235
Hindu Dharma 2, 16, 18, 41
Hindu interpreters 30, 58-60, 68, 97, 152, 184
Hindu reformers 12, 24-26, 34, 42, 59, 231
Hindu Renaissance 12
Hindu Śāstras 5, 123, 126, 135
Hindu Scriptures 5, 106
Hinduised Jesus 114-115, 229
Hinduism 1-21, 23, 25-26, 33, 53, 59, 70, 92-93, 101, 104-106, 110, 116, 153, 168, 171, 182, 214-218
Hindustan Times-CNN-IBN 14
Historical Jesus 41, 55, 99
Hitler, Adolf 199, 233
Holiest Symbol 61
Holy Science 93
Holy Scripture 61
Homo novus 176
Homosexuality 15, 171
Hospital 117, 136
Hugging saint 67, 71
Humanhood 185
Humanism 12
Humanity 18, 27, 29-34, 37, 44, 51, 56, 59, 65-66, 69, 76, 89, 97, 119, 132, 135-136, 139-140, 146, 155, 168-169, 172-177, 185-186, 188, 191, 200, 222

I

I AM 122, 196-197
I Am sayings 111
I am the Brahman 17, 197
I and my Father are one 51, 67, 81, 105, 140, 197, 223
Iconoclast 157
Ignorance 2-5, 51-52, 112, 129, 139, 145, 168
Image of God 80, 91, 105
Immortality 6, 46, 52-53, 57, 64-65, 102, 128, 235
Incarnation 4, 9, 18, 27-28, 31, 34, 37, 43-45, 48-53, 55, 59, 63, 65, 67-68, 77, 81, 97, 101, 110, 114, 121, 124, 135-136, 138-139, 143, 152-153, 196, 224-225, 232-233
Incarnation of Divine Love 77
Incarnational theology 30, 32
Inculturation 91
India 12, 14-16, 21, 23-24, 27-29, 33-35, 41-43, 58-60, 72-73, 77, 79, 86-88, 90, 92-94, 99-100, 105, 112-114, 117, 124, 135, 142, 145-146, 152, 155, 157, 162, 193, 197, 203, 205-206, 223, 226, 229, 234
India Independence 35
Indian Ambassador 90
Indian Christian Theology 34
Indian Christians 40, 72, 232-233
Indian culture 2
Indian delegate 76
Indian gurus 13, 23, 61-72, 101, 118, 227-235
Indian National Army 160
Indian philosophy 94
Indian renaissance 26
Indianised Jesus 229
Individual Freedom 157, 165, 178-180
Individuality 157, 170
Infinite 31, 45, 55, 81-82, 86, 89, 99, 103, 148, 187
Interculturation 91
International Association for Human Values 206
International Congress of Religious Liberals 76
Interpretations 24, 26, 29, 42, 47-48, 60-61, 68, 72-74, 105, 111, 115, 136, 152, 154, 158, 218, 224, 227, 229-234
Inter-religious harmony 73
Inter-religious relations 34, 42, 60, 68, 71, 90, 92, 155, 201, 226, 233
Intuition 89
Iran 152
Isa 135, 142, 152, 154
Isaac 221
ISKCON 19, 68
Islam 110, 125
Islamic Unitarianism 26
Īśwara 106, 135, 154
Itihasas 8

J

J. Russell 16
Jada 128
Jail Diary 36
Jain 158-159
Jain, Saraswati 158
Jainism 2, 157, 168, 175
James, William 163
Jan Gonda 3

Janakananda, Rajarsi 77, 90
Japamala 214
Jaspers 13
Javadva 98
Jehovah 32
Jesus' Baptism 111, 152, 194
Jesus Christ 20, 23-234
Jesus of history 99, 116
Jesus of Nazareth 34, 37, 43, 45-46, 49, 99, 116, 234
Jesus' second coming 104, 145-146
Jewish 62, 114-115, 222, 228, 231
Jīva 171
Jivanmukta 47, 66
Jñāna 6, 19, 51, 129-130, 150, 153, 208
Jñāna yoga 19, 153, 208
Jñāna Yogi 51
John the Baptist 110-111, 193
Jones, Stanley 41
Joseph 142, 152, 189, 193
Joshi, Vasant 161, 163
Judaism 110, 214, 228
Judas 152, 219

K

Kahler, Martin 99
Kalpasūtras 8
Kamalapuram 120
Kant, Immanuel 99
Kārana-janma 137, 139, 230, 232
Karma yoga 19, 51
Karma Yogi 51
Karma-Saṃsāra 81-82, 107, 110-111
Karnataka 205
Karuṇā 139
Kashmir 142, 145-146, 199, 222
Kaṭha Upaniṣad 7
Kaula School 4
Kheirabadi, Masoud 120
Khumbh Mela 76
Kierkegaard, Soren 99
Kindnes 66, 70, 88
Kingdom of God 46, 50, 52, 64, 71, 91, 108, 110, 147, 184, 190, 219, 221
Kingdom of Heaven 46, 63-64, 66-68, 71, 87, 142, 147
Kingdom within 71
Kolkata 145, 230
Koran 47
Koregaon Park 161
Krishnamurti 157
Krishnananda 65-66
Kṛṣṇa 9, 43-44, 55, 61-62, 69-71, 73, 76, 78, 80, 83, 86-87, 89-92, 97-98, 107, 113, 121, 127, 134, 139-140, 218, 221, 226
Kṛṣṇa Consciousness 68, 87, 91, 98, 100, 111
Kṛṣṭa 69
Kshtriya 119
Kuchwada 158
Kulārnava Tantra 3, 10
Kutashtha Center 87
Kutaṣtha Chaitanya 87, 100, 103, 108, 111

L

Lamb 145, 154
Last supper 51, 148, 152, 154
Latkin, Carl A. 162
Law 28, 39, 63, 65, 69-70, 82, 97, 108, 115, 167, 191
Lazarus 50
Lessing, Gotthold 99
Lewis, M. W. 90
Liberation 1, 5, 10, 65, 88, 104, 129-130, 135, 140, 208, 216
Life Force 88, 170, 218
Logos 31, 34, 99-100, 106, 116
Lord 1-2, 9, 31, 45, 61-64, 66, 70, 73, 76, 78, 80, 83, 89-90, 92, 96-99, 113-114, 134, 139, 218-219, 226, 232
Lord of Love 64
Lord's Prayer 111
Love 2-3, 15, 17-18, 30, 33-34, 37, 49-51, 55, 57, 61-66, 68, 70, 72-73, 77-78, 80, 83, 86, 88, 91, 94, 97, 103, 109, 113, 115, 119, 122, 125, 130-135, 137, 139, 141, 145-146, 148-153, 155, 158, 160, 171, 176-177, 179, 185-187, 190-192, 195-196, 198, 207-209, 212-213, 217-219, 222-226, 230, 235
Love is God 131-132, 150, 211

M

Madhva 129
Madhya Pradesh 158
Maha Mudra 84, 86
Maha Mudra Technique 84, 86
Mahābhārata 9
Mahadevan, T. M. P. xv
Mahant 4
Maharṣis 1

Mahasaya, Lahiri 74-75, 78, 83, 86, 89, 92, 114
Mahavira 136, 167, 187
Maitreyi 8
Malaysia 145
Man of celebration 186, 188, 200, 231
Man of Galilee 62
Mangalwadi, Vishal 12-13
Man-God 31
Manifestation 33, 43-45, 49-50, 52, 55, 127-128, 131, 190, 209, 218, 224
Mantra 4, 10-11, 174
Manu 8
Manu Smrti 8
Marshman, Joshua 93
Marx, Karl 11
Mary 64, 97, 116, 141, 151, 189, 193, 196, 201
Master 9-10, 30, 65, 69-71, 74, 77, 94, 113, 139-140, 142, 151, 160, 162, 169, 178, 182, 198, 208, 230-232
Mata, Sri Daya 19
Materialism 13, 76
Māyā 44, 79, 82, 101-102, 106-107, 109, 120, 208
Mazzoleni, Don Mario 136
McMullen, Charence O. 13
McMullen, Clarence O. 2
Meditation 17, 19, 50-51, 70-71, 83-88, 98, 112-113, 115, 124, 140, 160-162, 169, 172-174, 179, 181, 192, 204-205, 207-208, 214-215, 218, 223-225
Meditativeness 173
Mehta, Uday 164
Melbourne 68
Message of Jesus Christ 24, 35, 40, 48, 95-96, 105
Messenger of God 140-141, 230, 232
Messenger of mercy 64
Messiah 28, 41, 197, 199
Metaphysics 42, 94, 106
Methodological framework 158, 165, 167, 198, 230-231
Mind 11-12, 14, 19, 31, 36, 40, 48, 52, 68, 74, 80, 82, 87-89, 92, 96, 102, 127, 129, 131, 147, 164, 169-174, 179, 182-183, 188-190, 193, 209-210, 212, 215-216, 218, 221-224
Mini-satori 193
Miracles 17, 19-20, 27, 29, 41, 50-51, 53, 66, 74, 77-78, 95, 101, 118-120, 122, 134, 143, 152, 154, 194, 199-200, 206, 232
Mishra thathwa 147
Mission 12, 29, 48, 50, 53, 66, 69, 73, 78, 83, 89, 90-91, 111, 114, 116, 121, 136, 139, 144-146, 153, 165, 223, 225, 228
Mlecko, Joel D. 5
Modern Review 41
Modernization 11
Mohammedanism 168
Mohan, Rajneesh Chandra 158
Mokṣa 1, 131
Monasteries 142, 171, 214
Monk 48, 122, 158
Morality 27, 119, 186, 191
Mortality 52, 64
Mortuary Director 77
Mosaic Law 115
Moses 46, 109, 221
Mosque 126, 159, 168
Mother Mary 141, 151
Mother of God 64
Mozoomdar, Pratap Chander 24, 230
Muhammad 36, 136, 138, 182, 234
Mullan, Bob 161
Muller, Max 101
Mumbai 161, 163
Mundaka 1, 6
Mundaka Upaniṣad 1, 6
Muslim 16, 119, 121, 126, 176, 183, 233-234
Muzumdar, Ram Gopal 74
My India 73, 90
Mysterious Being 5
Mystic Christ 66
Mysticism 30, 157, 164
Mystique 13-14, 134

N

Nachitekas 8
Nanda, Meera 11, 14-15, 18
Nārada 211
Narayan, Sreejith 135
Nation Survey 14
Nationalism 177
Nationality 109, 215
Navaratri 133
Necessary truths 99
Neo-Hinduism 25, 48
Neo-sannyāsins 161, 175-176

Neo-Vedāntins 23-60, 231
Neti neti 209
New Dispensation 30, 33
New humanity 168, 177
New Testament 63, 111, 113, 116
Nietzsche, Friedrich 11, 157, 169, 172
Nirguṇa 127, 208, 210
Nirvāṇa 184, 190
Non-orthodox 29
Non-violence 35, 36, 52, 130, 148, 153
No-soul 171, 201

O

Occidental 90
Old Testament 28, 107, 116
Om 98, 106, 125
Omnipotence 66
Oneness 6, 25, 27-28, 42, 51, 53, 59, 66-67, 79, 81-82, 87-88, 90-91, 94, 98, 102, 105, 107, 109, 112, 126-127, 134-135, 140, 142, 146, 153, 156, 176-177, 181, 190, 209, 212-213, 215, 217, 222, 224-225, 227, 230, 232, 234
Oneness of religion 234
Only begotten son 38, 98, 106-107, 196-197, 220-221
Ontological truth 167
Oppressed 185
Orient 97, 228
Oriental 43, 49-50, 53, 89, 96-97, 100, 105, 115, 228, 230
Orientedness 208
Orient-ness 97
Origen 111
Orthodox Christian 24, 27-29, 37, 49, 53, 55-56, 59, 113
Osho 12, 19, 61, 157-202, 223, 227, 229-232
Osho Commune International 161
Osho movement 162
Ouspensky, P. D. 164

P

Palestine 23, 223
Palestinian Jewish 115
Pañcabhūtas 130, 154
Panikkar, Raimundo 92, 201, 228
Papanasam 204
Paradkar, Balwant 53
Paramhansa, Yogananda 12, 17, 19, 48, 73-116, 200, 223, 240
Parekh, Manilal 32
Parliament of religions 153, 227
Patanjali yoga 84
Patanjali Yogpeeth 19
Paul, St. 52-53, 86, 149
Person of Jesus Christ 48, 96, 101, 116
Personality 5, 10, 25, 43, 51-52, 54, 63-65, 69, 93, 170, 173, 210
Peter 11, 15, 147, 150-151
Phenomenal level 165-167
Philosophical study xiv
Philosophy 13, 17, 24-25, 35-36, 41-42, 47, 54, 73-74, 92-94, 134, 150, 153, 157, 160, 180, 182, 200, 208-209, 216, 218
Philosophy of religion 36, 41, 54, 74, 94, 218
Pluralism 58, 135, 204, 225
Poor 15, 18, 81, 108, 136, 149, 185, 199, 206, 225
Portuguese 24
Positive attitude 24, 41, 63, 67-68, 71-72, 117, 126, 135, 155, 214, 217
Potentially Divine 45, 217
Prabhavananda, Swami 24
Prabhupāda, Śrīla 68
Pramānas 89
Prāṇa 218
Pranabananda, Swami 74
Prāṇāyāma 88, 216
Pranic 86
Prasannabhai 2
Prasanthi Nilayam 117-118, 125-126, 141, 153
Prasavā 119
Prashad, Ram Chandra 164
Pratika 44
Praveśa 119
Prayer 9, 14, 32-34, 50, 75, 79, 102, 106, 111, 113-114, 192, 210, 212
Preceptor 1-2, 6, 9-10, 15
Precepts of Jesus 26-27, 29
Prema 130-131
Premāvatār 77
Presence 53, 64, 120, 128, 159, 169-170, 173, 182-183, 201, 209-210, 216, 218
Prince of purity 64
Prince of purity and peace 64
Prophets 28, 107, 218-219
Prostitutes 185
Pūjā 10, 204

Pūjāris 15
Punditb 4
Pune 161-163
Purāṇas 8-10, 18
Pure consciousness 170, 210-211
Puritarianism 15
Purnavatāra 121, 139
Purohita 4
Purohita-guru 6, 10
Puttaparthi 117-118, 121, 158

R

Radhakrishnan, S. 13, 24-25, 42, 48, 54-59, 115
Raipur 160
Raja Yogi 51
Rajneesh 12, 14, 17-18, 157-202, 223, 240
Rajneesh Dhyana Yoga 174
Rajneesh International Meditation University 162
Rajneeshpuram 162
Raju, Pedda Venkama 119
Raju, Sathyanarayana 118
Rāmā 9, 43, 55, 134, 218, 221, 226
Ramakrishna 24, 44, 47-48, 53, 121, 139
Ramakrishna movement 24, 47-48
Ramakrishna Order 24, 48, 53
Ramakrishnananda, Swami 48
Raman, Maharishi 157
Ramanjit Garewal 204
Ramanuja 129
Ramanuja Jayantī 204
Rāmāyana 9
Ramdev, Baba 17, 19
Ranchi 75
Ranganathananda, Swami 24
Rashtriya Swayamsevak Sangh 160
Rationalism 13, 27
Ravishankar, Sri Sri 2, 17, 19, 61, 134, 200, 203-227, 229, 230, 233
Reality 5, 10, 42, 47, 57-59, 62, 67, 79, 82, 95, 108, 111, 115, 120, 127-128, 153, 159, 169, 180, 182, 185, 210, 214, 222-223, 233-234
Realization 6, 11, 17, 20, 35, 45-46, 49-51, 53-54, 58, 63, 71, 73, 96, 99, 105, 109, 111-112, 115, 129, 132, 173, 212-213, 232
Rebel 5, 37, 157, 165, 186, 200, 231
Redeemer 28, 106, 139, 143
Redemption 39, 56, 63, 69, 76
Reformer 12, 24-26, 34-35, 42, 59, 116, 231
Reincarnation 63, 81, 108, 110-111, 233
Religion 2, 10-18, 20, 26-27, 29-30, 35-36, 40-43, 46-48, 50, 54-55, 60, 64, 70-71, 74, 87, 89-92, 94, 110, 117, 119, 121, 124-126, 132-133, 135, 153, 155, 159, 163, 165, 168-169, 175-180, 183-185, 195-197, 200-201, 203, 214-215, 217-218, 220, 225-228, 231, 233-235
Religion of the spirit 30, 54
Religionless 168, 177, 227
Religious toleration 176
Renunciation 50, 66, 108, 175, 177, 187-188, 210
Resurrection 27, 29, 31, 33-34, 41, 43, 48, 50-53, 57-58, 60, 64-65, 69-70, 72, 95, 102-103, 107-108, 112, 143-146, 152, 154, 184, 191-194, 200, 222, 224-225, 230, 233
Ṛg Veda 6
Rich Man's Guru 157
Rishikesh 65
Rolls-Royce Guru 157
Roman Catholic Priest 136
Roman emperor 37
Rome 34, 147
Rosary 214
Rowe, Harry T. 77
Roy Pape 34
Roy, Raj Rammohun 24-29, 59, 230
Ṛṣis 1
Russia 152

S

Saccidānanda 33-34
Sad darśan 126, 153
Sadguru 17
Sādhanā 119
Sādhu 70
Sages 1, 77, 100, 123, 134, 138-139
Saguṇa 15, 127, 210
Saguṇa Brahman 106
Sai Baba of Shirdi 119, 121
Śākta 6
Śakti 121
Salvation 3, 6, 14, 27-28, 39, 41, 46-48, 55, 59-60, 66, 76, 114-116, 140, 197, 213, 225, 241
Samādhi 88, 192-193
Samartha, S.J. 29, 53, 201
Saṃkhya Philosophy 93

Saṃsāra 133
Sanātana Dharma 93, 97, 234
Śaṅkara 1, 17-18, 42, 76, 79-80, 106, 114, 121, 126-129, 135, 139, 153, 157, 204, 208, 211, 225
Śaṅkara Jayantī 204
Śaṅkarites 114
Sannyāsin 15, 47, 75, 77, 161-162, 167-168, 175, 179-180, 197-199
Sannyāsya 6
Sanskrit 2-3, 69, 135, 160, 174, 180, 204
Sanskrit College 160
Sant 1, 4, 67
Śānthi 131
Santram, Philip J. 30
Saraswati, Swami Daynanda 12, 17, 158
Sartre 13
Sarva dharma samabhav 41
Sarva dharma symbol 125, 153
Sat 33, 106, 128
Satan 91, 107, 179, 220
Sathya Sai Baba 3, 12, 14, 17-19, 61, 117-155, 158, 200, 224, 227, 229-230, 232
Sathya Sai Organization 125, 133
Sathya Sai Speaks 137
Sathyam 122
Satori 193
Satprakashnanda, Swami 24
Satya 15, 35, 62, 120-121
Saviour 12, 28, 35, 37, 58, 60, 62, 97, 106-107, 116, 138-139, 142, 196, 199, 220-222, 224, 233
Sāyujya 140
Science 73, 86, 93, 96, 114-115, 127, 157, 164, 172, 205, 208
Scientific advancement 11, 13
Scott, David C. 30
Second Coming of Christ 104-105, 112, 136
Seers 77, 134
Self 1, 14-15, 46, 53, 56-58, 64, 70, 80, 92, 102, 128, 139-141, 171, 174, 183, 206, 210, 213, 220, 222-223
Self-Appointed Bhagavan 157
Self-Realization 73, 87-88, 109
Self-Realization Fellowship 73, 76, 83, 87-88, 90, 92, 113-114
Semitic religions 110
Sen, Keshub Chunder 24, 29
Serampore 26, 75, 93, 230
Serampore College 75, 93
Sermon 40, 61, 73
Sermon on the Mount 27, 39-41, 64, 111
Service 7, 9, 14, 18, 66, 90, 117, 123, 130, 132-133, 135, 137, 142-143, 145, 148-149, 153, 155, 206, 212, 217, 225
Seva 130, 132, 212
Sex 157, 160, 164, 171-172, 179, 196
Sex Guru 157, 160
Sexuality 171-172
Shashi 159
Shastri, Gangadhar 124-125
Sheaf of flames 125
Sheela, Ma Anand 162
Shimoga 205
Shivam 122, 183
Shuddha thathwa 147
Siddh 10
Sikhism 2, 18
Silence 7, 48, 89-90, 159, 162-163, 167, 175, 178-179, 189, 193, 198, 205, 207, 210, 213
Silence period 180, 198, 232
Singh, Khushwant 1
Singh, Kirpal 3
Sinlessness 38
Śiṣya 4-5
Śiva 4, 10, 79
Sleepless saint 74
Smaranananda, Swami 86, 111-112
Son of God 27-28, 31, 34, 37-38, 41, 62-63, 65-67, 98-99, 102, 107, 109, 116, 140-142, 152, 188, 196-197, 199-200, 218-221, 230, 232
Son of Man 28, 65-67, 98, 102, 135, 188
Son of Peace 37
Sonhood 197
Sonship 31, 34, 56, 59
South India 205
Spirit 7, 30-31, 46, 52, 54-55, 57, 59, 62-66, 80-82, 87, 91, 95, 98, 102-103, 106-108, 111, 122, 127, 133, 135-136, 139, 143, 146-148, 151, 188, 194, 208, 215, 218, 220, 223
Spiritual freedom 56, 157
Spiritual terrorist 157
Spirituality 5-6, 14-15, 20, 49-50, 60, 62, 73, 89, 103, 130, 164, 168-170, 176-177, 207, 210, 213, 215, 217, 226-227
SRF Lesson 83-84

Sri Sri Ravi Shankar Vidya Mandir 206
Sri Sri Rural Development Trust 206
Śṛuti 6
Śrutivādin 116
Sthitadheeh Muni 62
Stress free 203, 206-207, 213, 216, 225
Study of Developing Societies 14
Sudarshan Kriya 17, 19, 205, 208, 213, 215-216
Suffering 33, 56-57, 59, 62, 69-71, 82, 102, 139, 143-144, 149, 219, 222
Sufi 174
Sunday 145, 152
Sundharam 122
Śūnyatā 194
Superconsciousness 89, 160, 171-172
Superman 172
Suprapersonal 87
Supreme Being 67
Supreme Brahman 32
Supreme Cause 79
Supreme Deity 28
Supreme Reality 62
Supreme Treasure 63
Suudhra 122
Śvetaketu 8
Śvetāśvatara Upaniṣad 7
Swami Order 75-76, 79, 114
Swamis 1
Swaraj 35

T

Tantra Śāstras 10
Tantrika 1, 3, 9-10
Tapasyā 63
Tat 106
Tat tvam asi 209-210
Tathya 9
Teacher-guru 10
Teachers 1, 11, 25, 30, 35-38, 42, 48, 138, 221
Teachers of Divinity 138
Temple 87, 90-91, 103, 110, 127, 136, 143, 152, 154, 159, 168, 191, 204
Ten Commandments 113
The Chaotic 174
The only way 59, 80, 107, 142, 181, 196, 220-221, 233-234
The Quarterly 123
Theism 25, 59
Theory of relativity 209
Thomas 23, 103
Thomas, M.M. 25, 34, 42-43
Thomas, V. P. 231
Tibet 142, 152, 174, 193
Tiger Swami 74
Tirthamkara 47
Titikṣa 64
Tradition 1-21, 23-25, 29, 41, 54, 60, 63, 73, 88, 91, 111, 115, 117, 123, 129, 135, 145-147, 153-154, 157, 164-165, 174-175, 179, 186, 191, 200-201, 204, 207, 214, 217, 223, 227, 231-232, 234
Traditional Christian 37, 39, 196
Transcendent consciousness 106
Transcendental Intelligence 106
Transfiguration 45, 50
Transmigration of soul 63, 110, 147, 197, 233
Trikalajana 49
True Fame 210
Truth 5, 7, 9, 13, 25, 32-33, 35-36, 39-40, 53-54, 56-57, 59, 62, 64-66, 69, 71, 78, 90-92, 94, 99, 107, 109-110, 114, 119, 122, 124-127, 131, 133-135, 137, 139, 143, 145-146, 148, 151, 153, 166-167, 178, 183, 196, 198-199, 214, 228, 232, 234-235
Tunga 205
Turīya 190

U

Uban, Sujan Singh 83
Uddālaka 8
Ujjāyi 216
Ultimate Reality 222, 234
Unawakened human 164
Unborn 31, 57
Unchangeableness 82
Uniqueness of Jesus 142-143, 196, 218, 234
Unitarian belief 28
Uni-Trinitarianism 32, 35
Universal Christ 34-35, 55, 98-100, 104, 111
Universal Spirit 57, 98
Universe 44, 66, 79, 82, 100, 127-128, 130, 170, 177, 209, 215, 219, 227, 235
University of Jabalpur 160
Unreal 64-65, 82, 159
Unveiled Christ 235
Upādhyāya 8
Upanayana 4
Upaniṣadic period 7, 11

Upaniṣads 1, 6-11
Uravakonda 120-121
USA 73, 75-76, 90, 114, 162-163
Utter Pradesh 74

V

Vaasana thathwa 147
Vaishya 122
Vaiṣṇava 69-70
Vaiṣṇava sampradāya 68
Vajrāsana 216
Vanaprasthya 6
Vandana 5
Varāha Purāṇa 9
Varna 14
Vatican 184
Ved Vignan Maha Vidya Peeth 206
Vedānta 7, 15, 17, 24-26, 42-43, 53, 59, 105-106, 126-129, 135, 140, 146, 148, 150-151, 153-154, 204, 208-209, 211, 216-217, 224-225, 230, 234
Vedānta philosophy 17, 25
Vedāntic frameworks 58
Vedas 6, 8, 11, 16, 20, 32, 64, 126, 205, 208
Vedic corpus 20
Vedic literature 5, 205
Vedic period 2
Venkataratnam 204
Vibratory force 106
Violence-free 203, 207, 213, 216, 225
Virgin Mary 97
Vishalakshi 204
Vishalakshi Mantap 214
Viśiṣṭādvaita 7, 127, 129-130
Visiting Card 143
Viṣṇu 79
Viṣṇu purāṇas 8
Vivekananda, Swami 23-25, 42-49, 53-54, 58-59, 99, 101, 115-116, 230

W

Ward, William 93
Wealth 4, 14, 21, 63, 108, 118, 149, 210, 215
Weber, Max 11
West 12-13, 21, 40, 48, 54, 58, 73, 76, 89-90, 94, 96-97, 114
Western audiences 47, 49, 71
Western Christians 13, 37, 42, 89
Western Christology 229
Western colonizers 24
Western interpretation 24
Western missionaries 24
Western scientific education 25
Westerners 12, 15, 21
Wheel 125, 130
Wholistic-therapeutical 227
Wisdom 2, 56, 79-80, 95, 101, 105, 127, 148, 150, 207, 210, 214, 217
Witness 1, 12, 21, 62, 64, 77, 79, 111, 114, 116, 118, 136, 138, 152, 173, 175, 201, 232-233
Woodroffe, John 10
Word 2-8, 10, 15, 30-31, 38, 44, 49, 55, 64, 68-69, 73, 82, 88, 92, 95, 104, 106, 109, 111, 116, 131, 135-136, 139, 146-147, 150-151, 154, 163-164, 167, 174, 181, 185, 188, 190-192, 197-200, 209, 219-221, 223, 229, 231
Word of God 36, 53, 55, 73, 226
Work of Jesus Christ 36, 96, 143, 224, 230
World 12, 15, 20-21, 32-33, 36-41, 43-45, 48-51, 53-54, 57, 59, 62-68, 70, 73, 76-77, 80, 82-83, 86, 90-92, 96-97, 101-103, 108, 113-115, 117-118, 122-123, 127-128, 134, 138-139, 142, 146, 149-150, 153-154, 163, 168, 175-177, 187-189, 197, 199-200, 203, 205, 207, 209-210, 212, 214-215, 218, 220, 222, 224-225, 227-230, 234

Y

Yajña 39
Yājnayavalkya 8
Yama 8
Yoga 15, 17 19, 33, 50-51, 65, 153, 174, 208, 215, 223
Yoga Sūtras 15
Yoga-gurus 17
Yogananda xii-xiv, xvi-xvii, 12, 17, 19, 61, 73-116
Yogi, Maharishi Mahesh 12, 17-19, 70-71, 205, 207-208
Yogin 65
Yogoda Lessons 100
Yogoda Satsanga Brahmacharya Vidyalaya 75
Yogoda Satsanga Society of India 87-88, 92, 113-114
Youth Leadership Training Program 206
Yoyti Mudra 84

Yukteswa, Swami Sri 75-78, 89, 92-94, 102, 107, 114, 230

Z

Zen act 195
Zen manifesto 171
Zen Masters 157, 164
Zorba the Buddha 175-176, 186
Zorba the Greek 176, 186-187
Zoroaster 37, 125, 136, 138
Zoroastrianism 110, 125